In Hope of Liberty

In Hope of Liberty

Culture, Community, and Protest

Among Northern Free Blacks,

1700–1860

James Oliver Horton

Lois E. Horton

OXFORD UNIVERSITY PRESS

New York   Oxford

Oxford University Press

Oxford   New York
Athens Auckland Bangkok Bogotá Bombay
Buenos Aires Calcutta Cape Town Dar es Salaam
Delhi Florence Hong Kong Istanbul Karachi
Kuala Lumpur Madras Madrid Melbourne
Mexico City Nairobi Paris Singapore
Taipei Tokyo Toronto Warsaw

and associated companies in
Berlin Ibadan

First published in 1997 by Oxford University Press, Inc.
198 Madison Avenue, New York, New York 10016

First issued as an Oxford University Press paperback, 1998

Oxford is a registered trademark of Oxford University Press

Library of Congress Cataloging-in-Publication Data
Horton, James Oliver.
In hope of liberty : culture, community,
and protest among northern free Blacks, 1700–1860 /
James Oliver Horton, Lois E. Horton.
p. cm. Includes index.
ISBN-13 978-2-19-504732-5; 978-0-19-512465-1 (pbk.)
ISBN 0-19-504732-X; ISBN 0-19-512465-0 (pbk.)
1. Afro-Americans—History—To 1863.
2. Free Afro-Americans—History.
I. Horton, Lois E.   II. Title.
E185.H644 1966 973'.0496073—dc20 95–46427

7 9 8

Printed in the United States of America
on acid-free paper

Acknowledgments

Researching and writing this book has been time consuming, frustrating, occasionally intimidating, and constantly challenging and rewarding. It began as a simple survey of northern black community life in the antebellum years of the nineteenth century, an extension of our earlier book on Boston's free black community. Though we started with a straightforward design, the complex and more expansive questions that arose during the years of our research transformed the project into a much longer perspective on African-American life, race, and the American culture that unfolded by the time of the Civil War. The many types of research, variety of sources, and search for often obscure information that this undertaking demanded was daunting and sometimes overwhelming. It could not have been accomplished without the assistance of a great many colleagues who shared their work with us and the guidance of the many professional librarians and archivists who helped us negotiate our way through manuscript collections. Librarians, historians and archivists in research institutions too numerous to mention individually provided us with advice on sources and special collections, pointed us to local authorities, and helped make our research travel productive. Historical societies in large cities and small towns offered their materials and research support. We are greatly indebted to the dedicated women and men who staff these research centers for their time, their expertise, and their encouragement.

A legion of friends, colleagues, and family members cheered us at critical moments, and offered advice and comments. Christine Berry, Michael James Horton, and Nancy L. Smith read portions of the manuscript and made valuable suggestions. Ira Berlin, Stanley Engerman, David Blight, Shane White, Vernon Burton, Marie Tyler-McGraw, and Idus A. Newby read the manuscript closely at various stages and helped us shape our thoughts and argument. The interpretations of broad issues in this book owe much to their work and to their perceptive questions and observations. We have profited greatly from Roger Kennedy's encouragement, intellectual support, and wealth of historical reflections. W. Jeffery Bolster and his studies expanded our appreciation for the importance of black seafaring and the role of sailors as information carriers. Reginald Butler, Patrick Rael, and Shannon Barker read various chapters and contributed to our conceptualization of the cultural interaction between black and white Americans during the Jacksonian period. Manuela Thurner was a diligent researcher and a perceptive reader and critic. Anthony Tucker provided invaluable assistance with the analysis of computerized data. John Vlach generously provided us with archival data from the Parting Ways Project at Plymouth, Massachusetts. Jennifer Williams, Melissa McLoud, Cynthia Stout, Jeanne Houck, Amy Bowles, Michele Gates-Moresi, and Anna Speicher provided important research and editorial assistance.

We gratefully acknowledge funding provided to this project through grants from the National Endowment for the Humanities, the Scholarly Studies Program of the Smithsonian Institution, the National Museum of American History of the Smithsonian Institution, and Lionel Pincus. George Washington University and George Mason University provided faculty research grants and were generous in granting necessary leave time for our writing.

We also wish to acknowledge our indebtedness to the great body of scholarship in African-American History on which this study rests, work produced over the last generation by scholars such as John Hope Franklin, Benjamin Quarles, Leon Litwack, Herbert Gutman, Gary Nash, Lawrence Levine, John Blassingame, Jacqueline Jones, and Ira Berlin. Our editor, Nancy Lane, displayed unimaginable patience and faith over the life of this project, especially during its last decade. To a special group of friends, Raymond Arsenault, Mitchell Snay, Frederick Hoxie, and (many dinners later) Stephen J. Whitfield, we give thanks for their encouragement, enthusiasm, criticism, insistence on high intellectual standards, and a quarter of a century of friendship.

Contents

Introduction

The story of African Americans is deeply embedded in the history of America. It simultaneously provides an alternative viewpoint and experience, and a commentary on the nation's social, political, and economic development. It both illustrates and contradicts the promise of America—the principles embodied in the nation's founding documents. Africans were among the first nonindigenous peoples to settle in British North America. Their cultures, with characteristic beliefs, values, languages, music, and aesthetic styles, blended from the beginning with Native American and European cultures to create a distinctive American culture. During the same time, African-American culture evolved as a unique variation on the American theme, blending a greater admixture of African cultures than other American variations and shaping black communities with common approaches to the joys and pains of daily life. In the eight generations between 1700 and 1860, African-American culture became more American and American culture became more African. Typically, African Americans stressed cooperative organization centered on extended and expanded families and households, the importance of self-determination and personal dignity, mutual aid, and shared responsibility for the progress of the race.[1]

Although a few Africans came to America as free people, and some African Americans gained their freedom early in our country's history, the vast majority were brought as slaves, and most of their descendants remained in slavery for hundreds of years. The slave labor system was an integral part of the economy in nearly all the colonies and into the early national period in some northern states; it was the foundation of the economy in the South until the Civil War. Slavery was the basis of much of the nation's wealth and the source of untold suffering for tens of millions of people. For African Americans and sympathetic whites, slavery and the racism that justified it gave the lie to America's rhetoric of liberty and equality. The elimination of slavery was among the primary aims of virtually all black community organizations, including churches, schools, fraternal organizations and mutual aid societies. Black people's claim to freedom as their right was based on philosophy and faith and on their status as Americans. As African Americans gained freedom in the North, they organized their communities and acted in the hope that their efforts would win freedom for slaves and bring full citizenship for all black people, the hope of finally achieving liberty, what some called the "manhood rights" of the race.

The title of this book is derived from *The Hope of Liberty*, a book of poems written by a North Carolina slave named George Moses Horton. Born about 1797 and originally held by William Horton, George was transferred in 1814 to William's son, James Oliver Horton, who moved to Chatham County eight miles from the small college town of Chapel Hill. On Sundays, George traveled the short distance from the Horton plantation to the University of North Carolina to sell fruit, and by 1820 he was selling love poems for a quarter, fifty cents, and occasionally seventy-five cents, to male students eager to impress their female friends. George claimed to have influenced "the tip top belles" in Virginia, South Carolina, and Georgia. George Moses Horton became something of a celebrity at the school, was befriended by the university president, invited by the students to deliver a Fourth of July lecture during the same festivities that featured commencement speaker President James Buchanan. His owner agreed to allow Horton to buy his time to write the poems intended to produce the money to buy his freedom. George Moses Horton's personal hope of liberty—his talent for poetry—brought him to the attention of free blacks in the North, and in the late summer of 1828, New York's *Freedom's Journal*, their voice across the North, campaigned to secure his freedom. Black abolitionist David Walker, Boston agent for *Freedom's Journal* was a prominent participant in this effort. They raised the money to purchase Horton's freedom, but apparently the sum was insufficient to convince his owner to part with him.[2] Refusing to be discouraged, Horton then published *The Hope of Liberty* in 1829 under the auspices of the American Colonization Society, hoping to raise enough money to induce James Oliver Horton to change his mind. Additionally, Horton promised that with freedom he would emigrate to the society's West African colony of Liberia. None of these strategies worked, however, and Horton remained a slave, albeit a slave of extraordinary status. His poetry was printed in the *Lancaster Gazette* in Massachusetts and in William Lloyd Garrison's *Liberator*, and even after reaction to the Nat Turner slave rebellion in Virginia hardened southern proslavery attitudes, his poetry continued to appear in the North. The quest for his freedom became a celebrated cause among abolitionists, and his name evoked the link between free blacks in the North and the cause of slaves in the South. Despite these efforts, Horton found liberty only through the war that ended slavery.[3]

One of the authors of this work, James Oliver Horton, has a special identification with the story of George Moses Horton, beyond bearing the name of Horton's owner. His grandfather, James Robert Horton, and great-grandfather, John Horton, were born and grew up in eastern North Carolina near the place where George Moses was held in slavery. Although we cannot say with certainty, given the ambiguities in the historical record, the family oral history and available evidence tend to confirm our belief that George Moses Horton's daughter, Rhody Snipes, was the person that the author's grandfather called Aunt Rhody, his great-aunt. If this is so, it is likely that George Moses Horton's younger brother was James Oliver Horton's great-great grandfather.

George Moses Horton wrote throughout the first half of the nineteenth century, composing romantic poems, religious verse, and antislavery poems of protest. In "On Liberty and Slavery," he wrote:

> Alas! and am I born for this.
>   To wear this slavish chain?
> Deprived of all created bliss,
>   Through hardship, toil and pain!
>
> How long have I in bondage lain,
>   And languished to be free!
> Alas! and must I still complain—
>   Deprived of liberty.

Free black people shared Horton's hope of liberty for themselves, for the slaves, and ultimately for the nation. Many believed and several wrote that America would never be fully free until all of its people were free. The voice of black America between the Revolution and the Civil War was the voice of America's conscience. Often ignored but never stilled, it was a voice calling on America to recognize all those who had helped create the nation and to be faithful to that nation's professions.

This book tells the story of black northerners, in bondage before the Revolution, as they made the transition from slavery to freedom at the turn of the nineteenth century and as they organized to sustain themselves, built communities, and protested the racial injustice they faced. We use the term "community" to include both institutions (social, political, economic, and religious) and sentiments based on shared experience and a sense of common destiny that bound community members together. Black communities were networks of family, friends, and coworkers cemented by bonds of obligation and shared disadvantage and were both based in and transcended geography. These networks provided mutual support and created the foundation for political action.[4] As free black people African Americans were never isolated, they were never passive, and they were never a monolithic group. They were highly diverse in background, experience, and opinion, linked to one another across regions by communications that helped them join their communities in a common struggle. As an integral part of American society, they affected and were affected by political, social, and economic changes in the country. In local, state, and national meetings their lively debate expressed the variety of opinion and open disagreements involved in devising strategies for survival, progress, and protest. Their tactics aimed at gaining liberty and equality changed over generations, shifting sometimes according to their distance from African roots, local and national experiences, and their assessment of the chances for success. Though after the mid-eighteenth century the vast majority of blacks had been born in America, Africa retained its importance as the ancestral home. Even in the most optimistic times, black people were ambivalent about America, and by the nineteenth century, most black Americans had a dual identity, recognizing their American and their African heritage.

Most historical interpretations of black society during this period have focused on contentions among blacks over whether to pursue political strategies emphasizing one or the other of their identities, assuming them to be mutually exclusive. The dichotomy is often posed as integration versus black nationalism, where the implication is that integration means replacing an African identity with an American identity. This assumption overlooks the African heritage carried by all Americans. Indeed, to be American and to be integrated into American society was to share in a heritage that was partly African. Generally choices between integration and separation, or even emigration, were not irrevocable positions, nor were they always mutually exclusive. People had strong feelings and there were sometimes long-standing animosities, but lines were often quite fluid as opinions changed with shifting options. Black protesters and reformers generally preached racial uplift. Some historians have taken this as an indication of their desire to assimilate into the white middle class, but racial elevation had value to blacks irrespective of white society. American values were not bounded by color, and the desire for liberty and equality was strongest among those to whom they were denied.

In this book we seek to explore these issues that illustrate the complexity of African-American society and illuminate the aspirations of generations of a people struggling for liberty. At one level this is a social history about the formation and function of northern black communities. We try to understand the significance of gender, class, and color in relationships within free black society and the impact of region on black community life. Finally, we try to understand the meaning of community as a foundation for the activism of African Americans who sought liberty for themselves, freedom for the slaves, and the liberation of America from its degraded status as a slaveholding society. In the late 1850s, black editor Thomas Hamilton objected to free blacks' leaving America and migrating to Africa. "Our work in the United States would remain to be done," he argued. "Our work here is to purify the [nation], and purify Christianity from the foul blot which here rests upon them." For many blacks during this period their responsibility and their opportunity were intertwined. They fought to secure their freedom and to redeem their nation, living and working together in hope of liberty.[5]

In Hope of Liberty

1

Slavery and Slave Trading
in the Colonial North

One afternoon, while Money Vose was selling his baskets at the market, he disappeared—taken by white men. He never returned home. Sold and resold, he finally left his native West Africa aboard a slave ship bound for a "new world." It was the late-eighteenth century, the exact date and his exact age are not known, but he was not much older than the new nation taking shape and calling itself the United States.

Fortunately for Money, the slave ship on which he arrived did not enter an American port immediately but lay offshore somewhere along the eastern coast, probably off New England. It was then, guided only by the light of the moon, that he and a companion plunged into the sea in a desperate bid for freedom. After a long swim they reached shore, exhausted and frustrated by underwater vegetation, which slowed their progress and made their escape even more perilous. They collapsed almost at the point of their landfall, sleeping under some bushes until daybreak when they awoke to find a white face framed in a broad-brimmed hat staring down at them. "Hallo boys! You are from that ship at anchor?" the man asked, indicating the vessel from which they had escaped only a few hours before. What was to be said at this moment? They indicated the affirmative, trusting to luck and to the gods whom they hoped watched over them even in this foreign place.[1]

Their trust was well placed; this stranger became an ally, providing them with food, clothes, shelter, and temporary safety. Aboard the slave ship the boys were missed, but most assumed that they had drowned, not an unusual occurrence since many Africans lost their lives attempting to escape in this way. No search was mounted, and they were written off as a business loss by the captain and his merchant employer. Under these conditions the fugitives were free to enter the society of the Africans in this place, many of whom seemed American in their manner and even in their appearance. Money was luckier than most Africans attempting escape—he spoke enough English to pass as a free black man.

Wherever Money came ashore on the northern East Coast, he was likely to have found a small but growing free black community. Africans had never been as large a proportion of the population in the northern British American colonies as in the southern. Northern markets started offering Africans for sale in the mid-seventeenth century. They were held as slaves in the households of the urban elite, by merchants and traders in the port cities and smaller inland towns, and by large estate owners and middling farmers throughout the northern colonies. The spectacle of finely dressed white gentlemen, often accompanied by their equally well-attired ladies, browsing among angry and confused Africans was a common sight in colonial ports along the North Atlantic coast. The Yankee trader was not likely to be a large slaveholder; his great fortunes were founded on providing finished goods to be bartered for slaves.

The English were latecomers to the African slave trade, two centuries behind the Portuguese and the Spanish. Portuguese traders began transporting slaves from Africa to Spanish and Portuguese colonies in America early in the sixteenth century. The Dutch, well established in the trade by the seventeenth century, brought the first Africans to the Jamestown colony in British North America in 1619. Yet, by the turn of the eighteenth century, British traders dominated the enterprise. In 1672 the Crown had granted the Royal African Company an import monopoly facilitating the sale of corporate stock and bolstering public confidence in the company. The profits were so great and the geography so vast that it proved impossible to defend the monopoly from interlopers, and before the mid-eighteenth century the company ceased its slave-trading operation.

American shippers became important participants in the slave trade during the eighteenth century, particularly after the 1730s. With their English counterparts they supplied the increasing needs of the labor-hungry British American colonies. The number of Africans brought to British North America rose from 1,600 between 1626 and 1650, to over 50,000 between 1721 and 1740, and to over 100,000 during the peak period between 1741 and 1760. While the number of Africans imported decreased slightly to just over 91,000 between 1781 and 1810, the total number reached almost 380,000 for this entire period. Charleston was the major port of entry for slaves bound for the colonies of the lower South. In the North, Philadelphia, Boston, New York, and Newport, Rhode Island supplied their respective regions. The Faneuils and the Waldos of Boston, the Browns of Rhode Island, the Livingstons and the Schuylers of New York, and the Morrises of Pennsylvania were but a few of those northern traders who participated in and profited from the sale of human cargo.[2]

Shipbuilders in Massachusetts, Rhode Island, New Hampshire, and Connecticut supplied the vessels, while northern businessmen financed the voyages and owned the ships used in the trade. Yankee captains were prominent among those who commanded the slavers that delivered Africans to seventeenth- and eighteenth-century America. Northern firms built financial empires writing insurance policies that protected slave traders against the loss of their cargo. In Connecticut the DeWolf family's Bristol Insurance Company was one of the earliest of such American ventures to compete with British concerns. By the Revolution other firms in Boston, Newport, and New York underwrote the slave trade.[3] The economic significance of the slave trade grew in the northern urban centers of New England and the middle colonies. There, slaveholding was less economically important than slave trading.

This situation contrasted sharply with that in the southern colonies where the large tobacco plantations of the Chesapeake region and the rice plantations of the low country of South Carolina presented a very different economic and social structure. Although there were some important southern slave merchants, the slaveholding planter was the dominant figure of the region. By the early eighteenth century, slavery had evolved in Virginia from an ambiguous form of indefinite indenture to a permanent, inherited status. The growth of slavery was different in South Carolina, where the institution emerged almost full blown by the 1660s. Whites who settled there came largely from the British West Indian colony of Barbados where Africans turned a fine profit for their masters in the sugar cane fields. There was never a doubt that slave labor could also be profitable in South Carolina, where initially slaves were set to herding livestock and felling the timber to be shipped to Barbados.[4] Large plantations became a major feature of the colonial tidewater South. There, Africans imported in large numbers were able to preserve much of their African cultures and created the most African-like society in British North America. African cultural impact was most substantial on the large plantations of South Carolina with its majority black population until 1750. It was generally less significant in New England, where most slaveholders owned fewer than two slaves and the African population was small. But even there African influence could be substantial where their concentration tended to exaggerate the effect of their smaller numbers. Generally, however, the impact of African culture and the number of blacks tended to dwindle as the distance from the South increased.[5]

Pennsylvania, bordering the South, had a significant black population early in the colonial period. By the second quarter of the eighteenth century, almost one of every three inhabitants of the Quaker colony was of African descent, with the number of blacks rising from five thousand in 1721 to eleven thousand by mid-century. Beginning with the 150 Africans imported in 1684 to help clear the land for the establishment of the colony, slaveholding among Pennsylvanians became increasingly common.

Their uneasy accommodation with slavery, however, created continual changes in the institution. In 1682 Governor William Penn proposed limiting slavery in his colony, relying instead on indentured labor, and treating Pennsylvania slaves as indentured servants to be freed after fourteen years of service. Once free, many blacks received land, the customary freedom dues. As in other colonies, though, perpetual slavery in Pennsylvania was encouraged by acute labor shortages. Within three years Penn reversed himself and supported slave-trading ventures originating in the colony's capital city of Philadelphia.

In fact, the trade had begun before Penn's change of heart. In 1684 English slave traders landed 150 Africans at the Philadelphia port, setting the stage for the measures Penn approved the next year. The need for labor was great and slaves sold rapidly, but the gradual establishment of slavery in Pennsylvania encountered continual opposition. In 1688 Germantown's Dutch-speaking Quakers, descended from persecuted Mennonites, formally registered their opposition, arguing that the existence of slavery contradicted the experiment in religious freedom established in Pennsylvania. Their petition was passed through a succession of meetings to the Philadelphia Yearly Meeting where no action was taken. Antislavery sentiment continued to be expressed in some Quaker meetings throughout the century, until finally tentative steps were taken in 1696. In response to the imprecations of Cadwalader Morgan and William Southeby urging the prohibition of slavery and slave trading, the Philadelphia Meeting agreed "not to encourage" slave importation.[6]

Africans in Pennsylvania continued to occupy an ambiguous status. Before 1700 they were often referred to as servants and sometimes served limited terms, although almost always longer than white indentured servants. The Pennsylvania legislature brought greater clarity in 1700 with "an act for better regulation of servants in this province and territories." This law acknowledged life service for black slaves and made provisions for a special "court" to be established for dealing with "Negro problems." Thereafter, there was little ambiguity in the status of black slaves.[7]

Within a single generation the black population in Philadelphia grew large enough to arouse the fears of white residents when they heard reports of slave unrest in neighboring New Jersey or of a black conspiracy to incinerate New York City in 1712. The popularity of slavery ebbed and flowed for the next three generations, depending in part on its profitability relative to white bond labor. Quakers were divided over the issue of slavery's morality; some from the West Indies were prominent among early slave traders in Pennsylvania. Despite fears and questions, slavery became increasingly central to the colony's labor system. By the middle of the eighteenth century, Pennsylvania's black population had grown to several thousand, providing Philadelphia merchants with great slave trading profits and ensuring Pennsylvania farmers a ready source of labor. Other blacks worked in iron manufacturing in several smaller towns. By 1767 nearly 1,400 African-American slaves provided Philadelphia's households with a reliable supply of servants and gave artisans both skilled and unskilled assistance.[8]

At this time Quakers in Pennsylvania and New England began to register more serious opposition to slavery. In response to a crisis of conscience accompanying their political position in Pennsylvania during the Seven Years' War, first the London Yearly Meeting and then the Philadelphia Yearly Meeting expressed concern about the institution. By 1758 members of the Philadelphia Yearly Meeting who bought or sold slaves were barred from full participation. Slaveholding drastically declined among the leaders of the Philadelphia Meeting, and some members convinced of slavery's immorality helped to support their former slaves.[9]

The Dutch West India Company brought the first slaves to New York in company ships in 1626. When the English seized New Netherlands in 1664, they took over an already-established system of African bondage, and the Africans, 300 slave and 75 free, accounted for more than one-fifth of the colony's population. Under Dutch rule, almost all blacks experienced forms of slavery and servitude which, although restrictive, allowed them considerable latitude. The most flexible bondage employed by the Dutch was called "half freedom," generally a compromise between slavery and servitude. Under this system slaves paid a yearly tax and performed periodic labor for their owners, generally the Dutch West India Company. In return, slaves were allowed to live independently, supporting themselves and their families and enjoying many of the rights of free persons. This arrangement was not perpetual but might continue for several years beyond the customary seven-year period of indenture for white servants. In 1644, for example, the Council of New Netherlands freed a number of slaves who had served half free for almost twenty years. Thus, despite its modifications, Africans could easily serve a lifetime under this less-restrictive slave system.[10]

Slaves generally favored half freedom because it provided a measure of independence and allowed them to establish families in individual households. They pressed the Dutch West India Company to pass this status to their children and protested when the company refused. Resourceful slaves then turned to other efforts to improve their status within the Dutch colony. Many adopted Christianity and baptized their children, hoping to improve their chances for freedom.

The advent of British rule in 1664 introduced a more rigid form of slavery as the Royal African Company displaced the Dutch West India Company's control over New York's slave trade, and the British regularized and finally codified the formerly ad hoc system with the Slave Regulating Act of 1702. In 1712 a restrictive law made it difficult for slaveholders to manumit their slaves, ensuring that the free black population remained small. Despite the yellow fever epidemic of 1702, the African population of the colony tripled over the next generation, reaching 6,000 by 1725, almost all of them slaves. New York's black population continued this dramatic rise throughout the eighteenth century, and on the eve of the Revolution, it numbered over 19,000, more than ten percent of the colony's population.[11]

As in other northern colonies, slaveholding never dominated New York's economy, but it was an important part of the labor system. At the beginning of the eighteenth century, more than four out of every ten white New York City residents were slaveholders.[12] Although the percentage of slaveholders in the population declined over the century, the actual number of slaves increased and the presence of the institution in the city remained obvious. One English visitor to New York City in 1774 was distressed by its visibility there. "It rather hurts the European eye," he remarked, "to see so many negro slaves upon the streets." In the counties outside of New York City, slaves constituted from one-fifth to more than one-third of the population. The great estates of the Hudson River Valley and those on Long Island employed large slave forces and came to resemble the plantation South. There, slaveholding remained important into the nineteenth century, but even in urban New York a significant proportion of the white population held, hired, or traded slaves well beyond the Revolution. By one recent estimate, slightly more than twenty percent of New York City households held slaves as late as the end of the eighteenth century.[13]

The English carved New Jersey from the land just west of the lower Hudson River. King James II granted Sir George Calvert and Lord Berkeley proprietorship of the region in 1664, and New Jersey too looked to the importation of Africans for labor. Its proprietors awarded parcels of land to new settlers, with larger awards for those who imported servants and slaves. With Perth Amboy and later Cape May as major supply depots, slavery was firmly rooted in the northern and southeastern parts of the colony by the end of the century, and most New Jersey households employed slave labor.

Despite the Crown's continued strong support for slavery as a practical and profitable labor system, Quaker ambivalence slowed the pace of its growth in West Jersey. Thus the largest slave concentrations were in the eastern and northern regions, where many Dutch slaveholders remained. As the black population grew to 2,500 by 1725 and doubled in the next generation, Africans became agricultural workers, domestic servants, skilled craftsmen, iron workers, municipal maintenance workers, and a major part of the harbor labor force in the colony's port cities.

As slavery evolved in New Jersey, a series of regulations distinguished that institution from other forms of servitude. They asserted greater control over slave movements and gatherings, imposed more severe punishments for crimes committed by slaves, and finally, in 1713, provided for perpetual service, a condition never imposed on the colony's white servants. Slave restrictions were irregularly enforced but were more rigidly applied whenever colonial authority felt threatened by the growing number of slaves. The 1712 slave conspiracy and rebellion in neighboring New York City prompted horrific penalties for perceived slave rebelliousness in northern New Jersey. The Monmouth Court of Sessions sentenced one black man convicted of murder to be hanged. Before the execution, the court instructed, "Thy hand shall be cut off and burned before thine eyes." After his death his body was to be burned, presumably as an object lesson for other slaves.[14]

Normally, however, the relatively small numbers of blacks in the colony encouraged milder treatment. European travelers gave surprising accounts of extensive interaction between New Jersey's free and unfree population, depicted an unexpected ease in master-slave relationships, and even suggested that slaves enjoyed equal treatment with white servants. Although such descriptions may have been exaggerated, recent studies confirm that small numbers had a moderating effect on their treatment.[15]

West Indian slavery had a direct effect on New Jersey by the 1720s as slaveholders and their slaves emigrated from British Barbados and settled in northern New Jersey. Like the large estate owners of New York, these slaveholders attempted to style their holdings and lives on the manner of the plantation gentry of the West Indian sugar islands. In Monmouth and Bergen counties these slaveholders became powerful in the politics of the northern sections of the colony, while farther south the slave traders of Perth Amboy and Middlesex County held sway. Their financial and political influence ensured that New Jersey slavery continued well into the nineteenth century, though evolving and adapting to local conditions. The few large estates aside, most holdings remained small.[16]

In New England the climate and soil were less favorable for large-scale agriculture, and slaveholdings and the slave population remained small throughout the colonial period. One scholar dates the origin of African slavery in New England from 1624, when Samuel Maverick became the first slaveholder with two Africans bound to his service. The slave population grew slowly, depending largely on a trickle of West Indian slaves imported mainly from Barbados. By the last quarter of the seventeenth century, Connecticut officials reported only "three or four" slave arrivals in that colony each year. The pattern continued during the opening decades of the next century with reports of a few dozen per year in all of New England.[17]

Although early Quaker antislavery was centered in the Delaware Valley, Quaker opposition to the slave trade was also influential in New York and New England. In addition to Quakers, there were influential early Puritans who objected to the importation of slaves on both theological and practical grounds. The centrality of the collective life of the congregation in Puritan society led to an emphasis on equality and unity. A theology including the equal rights of believers and a philosophy that saw diversity as a potential threat to unity may have limited the growth of slavery and the slave trade.[18]

By 1700 there were about one thousand African Americans in all of New England, with roughly half of those in Massachusetts. New England regulations reflected the moral debates and conferred a peculiar status on black servants. The Massachusetts Body of Liberties of 1641 justified slavery only for those who sold themselves or who were taken captive in "just wars." In 1637 a tortured interpretation of this principle had allowed several hundred Indian men captured by colonists in wars with the Pequot tribe to be transported to the West Indies and traded for Africans who were then brought to New England as slaves. The captured Pequot women and children remained in Massachusetts as servants to the colonists. Despite its questionable justification, many viewed the plan as an inexpensive alternative to the use of English servants.[19]

Legal ambiguities were resolved in 1645 when the Massachusetts General Court ruled that slaves could be legally purchased from "legitimate" slave traders. One remaining issue was addressed in 1670 when slave offspring were declared to inherit the status of their mothers, allowing enslavement of children produced by free men and slave women, thereby safeguarding the property of slave masters. Other New England colonies followed Massachusetts' example and by the end of the seventeenth century slavery was a legal as well as an actual institution in the region. Theological and philosophical reservations gave way to economic pressure, ensuring an important but limited role for African slavery in New England.[20] Most New England slaves labored on small farms or as domestics, unskilled workers, or even skilled artisans in the cities. They also worked in the distilling industry, producing rum from sugar shipped from the West Indies, where other slaves cultivated that crop to profit other European masters. Ironically, slaves helped build the New England ships that brought sugar to North America, American finished goods and rum to Africa, and African slaves to New World bondage.[21]

Massachusetts, the major slaveholding colony in the confederation, had only a small number of slaves. By 1690 Boston with the largest black population in the region, included only 150 slaves. This number tripled within the next generation but was still fewer than 500 slaves. Individual holdings were small but relatively widespread. Almost twelve percent of Boston families held at least one slave by the end of the seventeenth century. Although small in number, slaves played an important role in New England's commercial and economic life during this period. Massachusetts' Governor John Winthrop expressed the feelings of many in colonial New England when he articulated his doubts that the colony could survive without "a stock of slaves sufficient to dow [sic] all our business."[22]

In New England as elsewhere in the colonies, slaves were regarded as legal chattel, human property to be bought, sold, rented out, mortgaged, or gambled away. Unlike their southern counterparts, northern courts recognized the right of slaves to hold and dispose of some forms of property. As Chief Justice Hutchinson explained, the laws of Massachusetts provided that property rights be protected, "notwithstanding that he [the property holder] is called a slave."[23] Slaves who worked during time not obligated to their masters were legally entitled to keep the wages from such work. This situation might be complicated by the fact that a slave-holder's permission was generally required in order that a slave could "hire out," but it did establish the recognition of some slave property rights.[24] The middle colonies imposed greater restrictions than in New England, where such ruling applied to all forms of property. New York and New Jersey restricted slaves from ownership of real property, but these limitations did not generally extend to personal property. Personal possessions passed to a slave through a master's will remained that slave's property even when the slave was acquired by a new master. Furthermore, slaves might sue to protect their property rights. Although such action was not common and may not have always been effective, and slaves had little property to protect, such protections distinguished legal interpretations of slavery in the eighteenth-century North from that in the South.[25] There was one area in New England, however, where the structure and significance of slavery was comparable to the plantation South. In the South County and Narragansett regions of Rhode Island, several planters grew tobacco on large estates. Forces of fifty or more slaves were employed, and the black population of the region was correspondingly large. More commonly, though, small New England slaveholdings meant small black populations.[26]

Colonial accounts seem to indicate that many African slaves were not imported directly from Africa but spent at least some time in British colonies in the West Indies or elsewhere south of British North America. In 1702 one newspaper reported the arrival of a Dutch privateer in New York harbor bringing a load of thirty slaves from the Spanish colonies. Years later a colonial official recalled the incident, referring to "prisoners" taken from the Spanish in war who were sold in New York as slaves because "of their color which is swarthy."[27] Some northern slaveholders were convinced that these seasoned blacks were more resistant to European diseases. Despite the similarity in climate between West Africa and the West Indies, many believed that seasoned slaves tended to survive the northern winters better than those brought directly from Africa. African-born slaves, sometimes called outlandish or saltwater Negroes, were thought to succumb to "fever" or "lung disease" more often than New World slaves. As one writer looking back to those early times observed, "the rigor of New England climate never put a sharp note in the mellow voices of these children of the sun." The impact of winter weather in the North was so severe that some masters refused to add new Africans to their holdings except during spring and summer. The records of New

England slaveholders make clear the risks that masters measured in ster-ling and Africans counted in lives.[28]

Until the middle of the eighteenth century, most northern slaves were transported from the West Indies; a few came from southern colonies, es-pecially South Carolina. After 1700 slaves imported from the Americas became increasingly suspect among colonial officials, slave importers, and their customers. Apparently, many American slave buyers were convinced that West Indian cargoes could not be relied on for high quality slaves. There was fear that the best were kept in the islands or sold to Latin America, leaving only "refuse," or worse, "rogue" Africans to be traded in the North American market.[29] Joseph Dudley, colonial governor of Massachusetts, complained that slaves imported from the West Indies were of poor quality, "Usually the worst Servants they have." This opin-ion was shared by most colonists who agreed with one Pennsylvanian's observation that such transferred slaves were "seldom pleasing to factors here, because tis Troublesome and hard to make ye Sale." Buyers were al-ways suspicious that "They [the slaves] are Criminalls or otherwise of Little worth who are So Transported."[30] Indeed, slave traders often used the less lucrative northern markets to "dump" slaves they could not sell elsewhere. One trader was informed that "your negro man is craizie [and] does little or noe work" and advised to "dispose of him to ye northward." Even New England traders dumped refuse slaves in New England when they could not be sold outside the region.[31]

New York slaveholders were early advocates of direct African trade. During the first fifteen years of the eighteenth century, two out of every five blacks brought to the colony came directly from Africa, and the pro-portion of direct imports increased throughout the century. Groups like the Angolans, Coromantines, and Paw Paws from West Africa and others from the East African island of Madagascar gave New York an ethnically diverse African population.[32] Slave trading was always a very small part of the colony's total overseas trade, but by 1750 it was becoming extremely profitable. Seventeen slave ships outfitted and owned by New Yorkers made twenty-one voyages to the west coast of Africa between 1715 and 1747. After this, traffic increased dramatically; at least 103 ships made more than 130 trips before the Revolution. Many of New York's largest merchants like Philip Livingston shifted their attention to the African trade. In the 1760s Livingston was joined by his sons in investing in at least four African slave-trading vessels.[33]

During the early years of the French and Indian War, English and American slave trading slowed, endangered by hostile French sea forces. After 1759 the British navy secured the sea routes again and slave trading resumed apace. The growing involvement of New York traders was en-couraged by the rise in slave prices resulting from the restricted wartime supply. As the number of trading voyages to West Africa rose, the num-ber of slaves brought from the West Indies declined. Increasingly after the late 1740s, blacks brought to North America came directly from Africa, and West Indian shipments of slaves became rare.

This direct importation of African slaves was also stimulated by the colonial duty structure. To discourage the importation of potentially disruptive slaves from other American colonies, some colonial assemblies imposed rates twice as high on imports from New World areas as on those brought directly from Africa. Rhode Island used its duties to channel its slave import trade toward Africa, and although New Jersey did not impose a duty on slave imports during most of the eighteenth century, its assembly debated several attempts to use duties for that purpose. The French and Indian War also stimulated interest in the direct African slave trade by threatening the supply of indentured servants. The hostilities not only disrupted the trans-Atlantic emigration of indentured servants, but those already in the colonies were often impressed into military service by the British. Two thousand Philadelphia servants were drafted by 1755 causing the colonial Assembly to warn the governor that such action was sure to adversely affect the system of indenture and lead to the importation of more African slaves since "the Property in them and their Service seems at present more secure."[34]

Philadelphia traders only imported about twenty slaves a year in the 1740s. After British maritime control was reestablished, their importation of slaves grew to over 500 during the colony's peak trading year of 1762. After the 1750s, Pennsylvania's direct African imports grew, and the proportion of West Indian blacks declined accordingly.[35] Trade duties also profoundly affected slave imports in Philadelphia, and African imports rose as duties fell. In 1729 under the pressure of local iron manufacturing labor needs, Pennsylvania lowered its duties, abolishing them altogether in 1731. Historian Gary Nash studied burial and mortality records for blacks in Philadelphia during this period and reaffirmed contemporary observations in 1730 that "we have negroes flocking in upon us since the duty on them is reduced."[36]

It is difficult to draw an accurate picture of slave imports because of the existence of smuggling to avoid duties and colonial restrictions. Estimates of the relationship between direct and indirect slave imports are almost certainly skewed by the fact that smuggling was most likely to involve West Indian slaves. Slave smuggling proved very lucrative for both legitimate and illegitimate traders, making it impossible to know exactly how many Africans were imported into any colony. Smuggling allowed American traders to circumvent colonial trade restrictions protecting British monopolies. It also enabled traders to avoid duties imposed on slave imports by individual colonies. New Jersey was a favored landing spot for slavers, in part, because between 1721 and 1769 the colony had no duty on incoming slave cargo. Slaves could be put ashore in Perth Amboy or Cape May and smuggled overland into New York or Pennsylvania.[37]

In Pennsylvania, slaves were most likely to be sold to Philadelphians and used in a wide variety of occupations. Although all Pennsylvania slaveholders were wealthier than the general population, there was a greater concentration of wealth in the hands of rural masters. The top tenth of Philadelphia taxpayers in 1767 held less than half of the city's slaves, while in rural Philadelphia County, the top tenth of the taxpayers held over three-quarters of the slaves. Thus, in Philadelphia, slaveholding was not an enterprise confined to the rich. The wealthy were greatly overrepresented among slaveholders, but slaveholding penetrated well into the middle strata of urban society. Philadelphia's artisans, shopkeepers, and especially those associated with maritime trades were likely to be small slaveholders.[38]

Similarly, in Boston, the wealthy were more likely to hold slaves, but middle-class artisans and businessmen were also involved in the practice. In New York City, there was a wide range of slaveholding. One recent study suggested that nearly three times as many New York slaveholders came from the bottom half of the city's list of taxpayers than in other cities. There, as elsewhere, women were prominently represented among slaveowners; human property was an important source of support for widows and unmarried elderly women.[39]

Slaves who served artisans were often skilled workers assisting their masters. Woodworkers, metalworkers, sailmakers, gold and silversmiths, bakers, and caterers all worked beside slaves whose skilled hands molded the materials and created many of the finished products that supported their masters and enhanced their reputations as craftsmen. Slave sale records reveal the skills possessed by colonial slaves. One twenty-eight-year-old black woman was advertised as being fit for "country or business use" because "she can card, spin, knit and milk." A male slave was said to be "by trade a Bricklayer and Plasterer." Another was a blacksmith and a third was a lime burner. Slave skills were as varied as the work to be performed in colonial society. The large number of slaves owned by mariners suggests that slaves were often taken to sea and performed labor for which the master was paid.[40]

In Philadelphia, in 1767, almost one-third of the slaveholders were merchants and retailers. By 1790 in New York City more than forty percent of slaveholding households were headed by men in these occupations. Their slaves not only maintained offices and storage facilities, loaded, unloaded and hauled goods; some exceptional slaves even provided more technical business services like accounting or sales. Other slaves were the teachers of their white masters. One advertisement, for example, sought a runaway slave who was a music tutor for the flute and the violin.[41]

During the last decades of the eighteenth century a small proportion of Philadelphia's slaveholders (7.5 percent in 1767) and New York City's slaveholders (7.2 percent in 1790) were professional men. More than ten percent of Philadelphia slaves and nine percent of New York City slaves were held by such professionals as doctors, lawyers, teachers, and ministers. There was an advantage to some slaves in having a highly skilled or professional master. Some acquired professional skills themselves and provided important services to their fellow blacks. Slaves in New England became an important part of the shipbuilding work force. They not only did the unskilled jobs but were well represented among the ship's carpenters, joiners, and caulkers. A few lucky ones used their skills to earn the money to secure their own freedom.[42]

James Derham, a bright, eager-to-learn young boy, was a slave owned by Dr. John Kearsly in pre-Revolutionary Philadelphia. He learned to read and write and so impressed the doctor that while still a youth he assisted in the medical practice. At first James learned to mix medical compounds, and after some informal instruction he administered them to the doctor's patients. When Dr. Kearsly died James was sold. He served a succession of masters until he became the property of Dr. George West, a surgeon with the British army. During the Revolution James performed medical service for the British under the direction of his master. After the war James was sold again, this time to a doctor in New Orleans who found him so remarkable that he allowed James to purchase his freedom by providing medical assistance to his master's practice. By the last decade of the eighteenth century, James Derham was a free man, practicing medicine in New Orleans and doing a brisk business. Apparently he and his wife lived comfortably on an income of at least three thousand dollars a year.[43]

A few slaves also became accomplished in the law or were preachers. Others worked in wood, metal, stone, or leather. Some made and stitched cloth or worked as butchers, bakers, or brewers. They were important to the colonial economy, but more significantly from the viewpoint of the slave, their skills could be passed on to their children. The labor needs of the colonial North demanded mainly strong backs, but a few African Americans were able to secure work that called for skilled hands and creative minds.[44] Slaveholders selected slaves capable of performing the tasks the master's work required, but there were other considerations as well. The demands of the severe northern climate also dictated the preferences expressed by northern masters. One Philadelphia slave dealer told his customers that Gambia Africans were stronger, more easily controlled, and more resistant to winter weather than others. Another touted his shipment of 170 Gold Coast Africans as particularly well suited to local work conditions. These dealers generally held the upper hand in their trade because in the North slave buyers were often unsophisticated in the national and cultural identification of Africans. These northerners were limited in their experience with blacks and lacked the eye for African diversity possessed by West Indian planters or even the planters of South Carolina.[45]

Yet many northern slaveholders were well aware of the characteristics they most needed in their slaves, even if they could not attach these traits to a particular national or ethnic African type. Since northern slave labor was not as likely as southern to demand continual heavy work, less premium was placed on obtaining adult male slaves. In fact, many masters preferred younger slaves because it was generally believed that they were more easily controlled and learned more quickly. Since northern slaves generally worked and lived with the master and his family, these were important considerations. As one New Yorker said, "For this market they must be young, the younger the better if not quite children." A Philadelphian agreed that slaveholders in his colony would purchase few slaves, "except boys and girls." In New England the demand was similar. Younger Africans, they believed, were more easily trained and posed less of a threat to masters and their families. Although young slave women were useful, especially as domestics, boys and young men were preferred. This preference for young males shaped the working and living conditions encountered by arriving Africans and had important consequences for black family and community life during the eighteenth century.[46]

Northern slaves, unlike slaves in the colonial South, lived primarily in the white community, often within white households. One historian studying New England slavery termed this institutional pattern "family slavery." Under this arrangement masters and their families ate, slept, and socialized in a common residence with their few, often no more than one or two, slaves. Even in households where slaves performed tasks that went beyond domestic service, such living arrangements were common. This was one important reason why northern masters were so concerned about the character of their slaves. Masters were keenly aware of the proximity of their slaves and their own vulnerability to slave rebelliousness.[47] Quasho, Pompey and his wife Phyllis, and Prince, the household cook, shared two rooms above the kitchen in the LaBaron home in Plymouth, Massachusetts. Dr. Lazarus LaBaron, twice a widower, supported his numerous children from his local medical practice and the work of his four slaves. Although Dr. LaBaron controlled his slaves as expected, they were sometimes allowed certain privileges not generally granted to slaves in the South. Phyllis, for example, was able to control her own money to the extent of investing in a business venture, the trade of a schooner. Plymouth was a busy commercial port in which a sharp trader could make a sizable return on an investment. Phyllis was successful and she used a portion of the profit to buy a set of "Guinea-gold beads" that she wore along with her distinctive "portentous turban," both of which set off her homespun checked petticoat and short gown.[48]

At times a northern master, living under the same roof as his slaves, might even give in to the will of a particularly tenacious slave, as did happen when Dr. LaBaron and Quasho locked horns over a proposed change in the slave's name. Already having Pompey as one of his slaves, the doctor decided that it might be appropriate to have a "Julius Caesar" in his household and so proposed that Quasho accept that name. The slave, however, informed his master that his name was Quasho Quando, that his mother had called him by that name in Africa, and that he did not intend to take another. The doctor attempted a number of punishments ranging from deprivation of food to whipping and then tried bribery, but he had no success in changing Quasho's mind. Finally the matter was dropped.[49]

Despite close contact with their slaves and their consequent vulnerability, northern slaveholders were not always restrained in their treatment of slaves. Silvia Dubois grew up as the slave of a New Jersey farmer and tavern keeper, and this spirited youngster with an abusive mistress suffered greatly over the years. On one occasion when Silvia had not held her tongue in a heated discussion, her mistress hit her in the head with a "fire-shovel" fracturing her skull. Another time her mistress kicked her in the stomach until the slave, still a young child, had to be protected by her master.

As Silvia grew to maturity she gained stature and strength, attaining five feet ten inches in height and weighing over two hundred pounds. Gradually it became more and more difficult for her mistress to punish her so severely, until finally the confrontation came. "It happened in the bar-room [of her master's tavern]"; as Silvia recalled, "there was some grand folks stopping there, and she wanted things to look pretty stylish and so she set me to scrubbing the bar-room." Her reluctance to perform this task provoked her mistress who scolded her. When Silvia spoke up in her own defense her mistress struck her. "Thinks I, it's a good time now to dress you out," challenged Silvia, "and damned if I won't do it." A struggle ensued during which Silvia remembered, "I stuck her a hell of a blow with my fist. I didn't knock her entirely through the panels of the door; but her landing against the door made a terrible smash, and I hurt her so badly that all were frightened out of their wits." Silvia was a bit concerned too. As she explained, "I didn't know myself but that I'd killed the old devil." Fortunately for all concerned, she had not.[50]

Whatever the relationship, the small number of slaves and the nature of the work they performed encouraged extended periods of direct contact between master and slave in work and even in social circumstances. This situation led to the relatively rapid acculturation of Africans enslaved in the North. Many, especially the young, learned English quickly. After only two years in the colonies one fourteen-year-old boy in Boston was described as speaking "very good English." For an adult it was likely to take longer. One twenty-five-year-old male servant was said to speak only "pretty good English," after being in America for more than three years.[51] Northern blacks were likely to develop a facility with the language beyond the minimal work-related words expected from southern slaves who encountered whites infrequently. Many had extensive vocabularies and were able to converse with whites on a variety of subjects. European missionaries working in the North noted this and reported fewer difficulties in conversing with slaves than did those who worked in the South. Northern slaves, then, were more easily taught by those dedicated to converting them to Christianity, a process that included teaching them to read the Bible.[52] Obviously Africans who had lived longest among Europeans were most conversant with European languages. Many blacks were also familiar with a trading language used in West Africa that combined elements of English and several African dialects. This West African Pidgin English (WAPE) developed as the number of British traders in West Africa increased during the seventeenth century. Examples of this combination of languages appear in the writings of European and American recorders of African speech, from Cotton Mather and the English writer G. L. Campbell to Benjamin Franklin. Some historians see WAPE as the foundation for what is now known as Black English.[53]

For new Africans brought to the colonies, English was often a difficult language to master. In the pages of colonial newspapers masters described the linguistic skills of slaves for sale or of those who ran away. For some slaves, such as two in Pennsylvania, a young woman named Betty who had been in America only a month in 1740 and spoke "very little English" or Scipio who ran away in 1749 and spoke "but indifferent English," their chances of making good their escapes were limited by their lack of fluency in English. Thirty-seven-year-old Norton Minors was more likely to be successful in his escape since he could speak "good English, [could] read and write; and [was] a very sensible fellow." Some Africans learned only minimal English as a form of private protest against the system that bound them, and still others declined to reveal the extent of their knowledge. It was believed that Esop knew very little English until he forged a pass that he used to escape from his master in Newark, New Jersey in 1755.[54]

Many slaves arrived in the colonies with virtually no English, but there were a few who spoke several languages. During the eighteenth century blacks in the region formerly controlled by the Dutch were often bilingual. One master from New Brunswick, New Jersey explained that his runaway man, Claus, spoke both "Dutch and good English." Toney, a Philadelphia fugitive, was apparently considered something of a "dandy." He was described as "a likely lusty" young man of twenty-four years who spoke English and "High Dutch." Toney's dress confirmed the image. When he left his master he was wearing a "striped Linsey Woolsy Jacket," a "Tow shirt," matching pants, and a felt hat. One mulatto runaway from Chester County, Pennsylvania was fluent in both English and "Swede." French and Spanish were often among the languages spoken by blacks imported from the West Indies. John, born in Dominica, ran away shortly after arriving in Philadelphia in the spring of 1745. At the time he spoke French well but could also speak a little English. Another fugitive spoke Spanish but no English and still another was fluent in all three languages.[55]

With such a great variety of languages, not to mention the many African languages and dialects spoken by the slaves coming from the West Indies, from other American colonies, or from Africa, it was no wonder that English became the common language for communication between whites and blacks and also among blacks. The practical aspects of communication needs among blacks encouraged their linguistic assimilation into European-American society, but they maintained many language characteristics which gave a distinctiveness to African-American speech in the colonial North. The English spoken by blacks in colonial New England, commented on by many whites, was in fact a combination of English words and African grammar. Thus what seemed to white colonials as "bad English" may have been simply "Africanized" English, no more unusual than the Americanized English increasingly spoken by British colonials in America. In 1692 a slave defended herself in Massachusetts' famed Salem witch trials, using a typical West African Pidgin–English construction. "He tell me he God," she reported, describing her vision, but insisted, "I no hurt them."[56] When Cotton Mather recalled that several blacks whom he heard spoke "brokenly, and blunderingly, and like idiots," his judgment was undoubtedly an inaccurate comment on the intelligence of the blacks in question. As historian and folklorist William D. Piersen observed, "The blacks were not speaking English like idiots, but like Africans; and they would have been able to communicate . . . with . . . the wide range of Afro-Americans in the English New World."[57]

British-American-born blacks were generally most limited in their communication skills, speaking English without the French or Spanish influences found in the West Indies. Their brand of English eventually imposed itself on the more varied language of entering blacks. There were individual cases of Africans who maintained African languages after being in America for a generation or more. Yet, by the end of the colonial period, this brand of Afro-English was becoming the common black language and was most often heard among African Americans in the North.[58]

As Africans learned to converse in English and seemed to adopt European-American ways, they seemed more familiar and less dangerous to the whites with whom they worked and lived. Some whites pressed for the education of slaves at least in reading and writing as an aid to their civilization, Christianization, "de-Africanization," and ultimately as a means for controlling them. Although advocates of education argued that basic education contributed to the ability of slaves to use the English language effectively, creating more reliable and obedient servants, this was always a controversial issue. As early as 1636, Dutch officials in New Amsterdam had educated black and white children in integrated schools. Integrated education remained the norm in the New Netherlands until the English took control of the colony. Under the British, however, life in New York became more racially divided. By the end of the seventeenth century, seating in the Anglican Trinity Church was racially restricted, and even the church cemetery was segregated. Not much education was offered to the colony's blacks; what little there was was provided by the Anglican church as part of its religious mission.

Even this minimal education was often opposed by masters who feared any "outside influence" over their slaves. The church was able to carry on their educational activities as a part of its evangelizing among blacks only because of the powerful Society for the Propagation of the Gospel in Foreign Parts that administered England's New World missionary program. The society opened a formal school for blacks in New York City in 1704, offering a strictly religious education as a means of preparing its students for baptism. Instruction, however, was hampered by the fact that slaves worked long and hard hours. It was difficult to teach tired students who were often discouraged by masters and who were only beginning to learn the language. Still, as a result of dedicated teachers like Ellis Neau, a young French-born evangelist, hundreds of New York blacks learned to read and write. Neau was especially effective as a teacher of slaves because it was known that as a former Huguenot he had been the victim of religious persecution and had even been chained in the slave galley of a French ship. He was trusted by blacks who respected him not only for his past suffering but also because he continued to suffer at the hands of those in the colony who believed it dangerous folly to attempt to educate African Americans.[59]

Clerical educators hoped their efforts would encourage mandatory religious education for all slaves. However, many whites resisted any education which might lead to the Christianization of slaves, believing at that time that baptism demanded emancipation. To allay these fears colonial officials took steps to ensure that education and consequent baptism would not alter the status of a slave, passing a law to that effect in 1706. Despite the difficulties they experienced, the number of black students continued to grow. By 1710 over two hundred were educated at Neau's school alone. A slave rebellion in New York City in 1712 confirmed the fears of many whites and black educational activities were temporarily halted, but such efforts ultimately continued throughout the colonial period.[60]

The clergy also promoted education for slaves and free blacks in New England. During the seventeenth century John Eliot, a Puritan minister, was active among Indians and African slaves teaching them to read the Bible and convincing many masters that the religious education of their slaves was their Christian duty. Eliot's work was carried on after his death by Cotton Mather who broadened the concept of slave education beyond the simple teaching of scriptures. "I will put Bibles and other good and proper books into their hands; will allow them time to read and assure myself that they do not misspend this time," he pledged. He then went on to assure masters that he would be watchful that no "wicked books" fell into the hands of their slaves. Slaves could not be taught critical thinking, for the dangers of such thought were far too great, but they could learn reading and writing without harmful effect.[61]

In 1717 Mather opened a night school for blacks and Indians for general religious instruction. Although Mather's school was short-lived, others were encouraged to follow his example. In the first half of the eighteenth century, several schools for blacks opened throughout New England, teaching reading and writing and providing religious instruction. Some of these were individual efforts, such as that of Nathaniel Pigott, who offered classes for blacks in the church. New England was ahead of most other regions in the North where there was little education for blacks except what they provided for themselves.[62] The Society for the Propagation of the Gospel was very active in the colonies. A vast network of instruction was established by a British minister, Dr. Thomas Bray, who dispatched missionary-teachers to bring education to servants and slaves. An evangelical Anglican group known as the Associates of Thomas Bray conducted schools for blacks, and a few black teachers were trained and provided with books so they might educate other blacks. Before the Revolution, Associate schools were opened in Newport, New York, Williamsburg, and many other cities.[63]

Like other groups concerned with black education and religious conversion, the Associates continually struggled to assure masters that their actions posed no danger to the institution of slavery. Specifically at issue was the question of whether such conversion and baptism demanded emancipation. This question was important because one powerful justification of slavery was the presumed "pagan" character of African society. It was difficult therefore to defend the continued enslavement of a baptized African. In order to win the support or at least the tolerance of masters, educators were forced to argue that religious education and subsequent conversion did not entitle Africans to freedom. This encouraged a shift in the justification offered for black slavery from the grounds of religion to those of race. Starting with the New York law of 1665, which provided that baptism did not affect the status of a slave, northern colonies gradually codified the irrelevance of religious standing to freedom.[64]

Slaveholders, however, remained convinced that literate slaves were harder to control, though in reality educated blacks were not necessarily more prone than illiterates to violent slave rebellion. At first some believed that several blacks from Elias Neau's New York school were deeply involved in a slave plot uncovered in 1712, but only two of the school's students were charged in the case. One was found innocent of any involvement, a determination unfortunately made after his execution. Gradually whites were satisfied that the school did not pose grave danger to the community. During the colonial period educated blacks were not likely to publicly advocate violence or to lead violent revolt. When Jupiter Hammon, of Huntington, Long Island, one of the colony's most educated slaves, urged his fellow blacks to learn to read and write, he made it clear, perhaps because as a slave he had to, that the only reason for such education was so that blacks might read the Bible.[65]

In Pennsylvania Quakers handled much of the work of educating slaves. Led by activists like Anthony Benezet and John Woolman, the Friends provided education for slaves and free blacks in Philadelphia and the surrounding region before the mid-eighteenth century. These schools began as individual undertakings when Quakers tutored small numbers of slaves and free blacks in their homes. Benezet was well known for his work as a teacher of blacks, and he labored a lifetime in the cause. In 1758 the Associates of Thomas Bray established a school in Philadelphia. Encouraged by Benezet and by Benjamin Franklin who was a member of the Associates, the Bray school prepared black children beyond the basics to a level that led a few whites like Benjamin Franklin to speculate on the possibility of intellectual equality between the races. In 1770, largely through Benezet's efforts and with the intention of preparing slaves for freedom, Philadelphia Quakers established the Friends African School for slaves and free blacks. Such formal education for blacks was rare, however.[66]

Masters were correct when they worried that education made slaves more difficult to control. The ability to read allowed for the acquisition of valuable knowledge that might aid in escape or be used to temper the master's control. Slaves used any kind of knowledge to their advantage. Thus it was often in the master's interest to keep slaves as isolated as possible. This was more difficult for northern masters because of the urban character of northern slavery. Clearly, northern slaves were exposed to many more people and more information than southern slaves, most of whom lived on rural plantations, more likely to be cut off from the outside world.

American born blacks even without formal education were likely to be harder to control than new arrivals. They generally knew more about their environment and were more likely to have established contacts among blacks and whites. American born blacks and others who were long-time residents in a locale were more likely to have friends and relatives to hide them or otherwise aid them in escaping. Masters were aware that blacks maintained an informal underground system that aided fugitives as early as the mid-eighteenth century. Runaway ads were filled with speculation by slaveholders about people who might harbor their fugitives and with warnings that such action would be severely punished. Masters were especially concerned that their slaves might escape aboard ships, for this would enhance their chance of success. Ships' captains were given special warning, as in one ad, "All masters of vessels, and others are forbid to conceal or transport said Negro [Caesar, a forty-year-old fugitive from Suffolk County, New York] at their peril".[67]

Controlling slaves was a constant concern for slaveholders. Some of the most interesting attempts at indirect control were white efforts to influence the political structure of slave societies. The slave practice of selecting a local "governor" or "king" was sometimes encouraged by whites who tried to use this structure covertly to control blacks. Negro Election

Days or Black Coronation Festivals were common in many places throughout North and South America and in the West Indies. They became popular in New England during the mid-eighteenth century. The festivals accompanying the elections featured parades, competitive games, and a feast that could last for up to a week. In Derby, Connecticut the competition included a "test of wind and muscle, the successful candidate being he who first climbed a steep and almost unscalable sand bank." There were also precision drills like the "fire and fall off" in which participants fired guns and then literally threw themselves from their horses—a hilarious example of black satire but undoubtedly also a chance to display superior horsemanship. One account interpreted the interest of blacks in the Negro elections as a fascination with the general colonial elections, especially the pomp and ceremony of the inauguration of elected officials. There was generally a fancy dress ball at which the new governor and his lady were honored.[68]

The governors' power was largely ceremonial, but they could and did exercise control over other slaves and even occasionally over free blacks. In the larger towns and cities a variety of officials were often elected to act as an informal governing body among blacks. In some colonies like Rhode Island, blacks maintained a parallel court system which was allowed to function so long as whites were convinced that it operated in their best interest. Where whites exercised control over this black hierarchy, it approximated the system used on large southern plantations where black overseers or slave drivers often acted as intermediaries, disciplining the slaves in the master's name and acting as a buffer between him and those bound to him.[69] Masters sometimes referred unruly slaves to black officials for discipline, and the punishment meted out was often severe enough to reassure whites that such a system was an extension of their own power. For blacks the festivals had a different significance. Historians have recently seen these celebrations as an arena in which African traditions blended with European. William Piersen suggested an intriguing explanation of the difference in titles given blacks "elected" to ceremonial office. He noted that in New England colonies, where colonists were allowed to elect the colonial governor, "elected" black officials were referred to as governors, while in royal colonies where royal governors were appointed by the Crown, black officials were called kings. This is an example of the symbolic relationship between black festivals and the political setting in which they took place.[70]

Masters, of course, did not generally view these festivals as important events for their slaves' cultural preservation. Rather, they saw them as part of their paternalistic control—harmless outlets for blacks—simply the primitive imitation of European election holiday celebrations. Masters' encouragement of slave participation even extended to their financing the elaborate festivities, renting taverns, providing food and drink, and allowing slaves the use of fine horses and carriages. Some provided money to

bribe black voters, ensuring that their choice would be elected to hon-
orific positions and suggesting the extent to which white egos got caught
up in the celebration, imposing a European style competition.[71]

Not all whites were comfortable with these festive occasions. Some
were concerned about the "demoralizing . . . effect" of the pride or "sham
dignity" displayed by elected kings and by the way blacks and even some
whites honored them. In Norwich, Connecticut one former dignitary was
buried in the public burial ground with a "very decent grave stone" that
read, "In Memory of Boston Trowtrow, Governor of the African Tribe in
this town, who died 1772, aged 66." Sam Hun'ton who succeeded him as
long-term governor was particularly troubling to some as they saw him

> riding through the streets on his master's horses, adorned with plaited gear,
> his aids on each side, *a la militaire*, himself puffing and swelling with pom-
> posity, sitting bolt upright, and moving with a slow, majestic pace, as if the
> universe was looking on. When he mounted or dismounted, his aids flew to
> his assistance, holding his bridle, putting his feet into the stirrup, and bowing
> to the ground before him. The Great Mogul, in a triumphal procession,
> never assumed an air of more perfect self-importance than the negro Gover-
> nor at such a time.[72]

Many wondered at the effect of all this "in a town so rigid in its code of
morals."[73] Respect and dignity were undoubtedly among the most important aspects of the festivals and elections for black participants. Not only
did they recall the African past and its systems of honor and deference,
but they also provided affirmation of individuals' status and reinforced
identification within the community. They were times of respite for a
generally degraded and oppressed class.

Most whites were consoled by their assumption that blacks were simply
following examples set by their masters. But no matter what whites
thought, these festive times were important to blacks who saw them as
"their days," time to themselves and above all for family gatherings. Family time was very precious to northern slaves in part because of the special
circumstances of their bondage that made for small widely scattered
slaveholdings. Blacks in rural areas often found themselves at considerable distance from mates, but even in the towns forming and maintaining
stable families was difficult. If one or both partners was a slave, distance
might be particularly problematic, since masters were not likely to allow
bondspeople general freedom of movement. From the master's point of
view, there was the question of the time that courtship would take from
the duties of a slave. The marriage of slaves belonging to different masters was acknowledged by whites to pose difficult problems for all concerned, and sometimes one master would agree to purchase his slave's
mate. This arrangement would, of course, greatly simplify matters for the
couple, but unfortunately this was not the general pattern.[74]

Even the accommodations the most benevolent owners made to their slave's wishes were likely to be limited. Yombo, an African brought from Guinea as a boy, was a skilled leather worker sold to Aaron Melick of Bedminster in Somerset County, New Jersey in 1786. Melick was a small slaveholder, and by 1800 held only Yombo and a slave family with four children. He was also lenient, reportedly giving his slaves a good deal of autonomy in their work and even paying to have the children educated. Melick occasionally permitted Yombo to visit his wife who was a slave in Elizabethtown, providing him with money and a horse and carriage for his journeys. Yet it was only after twenty-three years of service and his master's death that Yombo was sold to a tanner in Elizabethtown and was finally able to join his wife.[75]

In some cases, masters might agree among themselves that one or both slaves be given time off to visit. This was most easily arranged when slaves resided on neighboring farms or in adjacent towns and cities. Through the efforts of Judge Samuel Seawall, two Boston slaves received permission from their master to be together and to work for their mutual support one day a week. A similar arrangement allowed Prince Hall to spend Sundays with his wife, Delia. Hall, the son of an English father and a mulatto mother, had come to the Boston area from Barbados when he was a young man. Although Prince Hall was free, Delia was a domestic slave in the home of the Walker family on Beacon Street in Boston. They did not live together, but he visited her there between his trips as a steward on ships sailing out of New England.[76]

Urban slaves were likely to have a great deal more freedom of movement and therefore more opportunity for association. Testimony from the trial of two slaves, Mark and Phyllis, convicted and executed for poisoning their master John Codman, a merchant in Charlestown, Massachusetts in 1755 implicated six slaves in Charlestown and Boston in the conspiracy. According to the court records, the slaves were able to obtain poison from other slaves whose masters were druggists and who delivered the poison by crossing by ferry from North Boston. Mark was a blacksmith who could read and write, and a trusted slave. In the course of running errands he was also able to socialize with his friends, obtain alcohol, and drink it with them in a lane near the wharf. The testimony in this case gives another indication of urban slaves' relatively greater opportunity for association and its implications for maintaining families: Phebe, one of Codman's house slaves, seemed routinely able to have her husband Quaco, the slave of local restauranteur James Dalton, visit overnight at least on weekends. The sentences given in this murder case indicate the seriousness with which this incident was regarded. Phyllis was burned at the stake; after he was hanged Mark's chained body was hung on Charlestown Common where his skeleton remained for many years.[77]

Slaves were well aware of the relative advantages of city life. In his study of slavery in New York City, Shane White cites many newspaper advertisements for slave sales that attest to the slaves' disinclination or refusal to move to the countryside. Evidently some masters in the 1770s and 1780s were compelled to sell their slaves for such reasons as the slave's having "an aversion to living in the country" or "not being willing to go" when the master moved.[78]

In Puritan New England, especially, but also in Quaker Pennsylvania and throughout the Middle Atlantic colonies, there were efforts to encourage slave masters to respect the family ties of their slaves. Religious leaders were most vocal on this issue but political officials also took part. Records in New England indicate the extent to which slave marriages were formalized. Colonial marriage records included the names and dates of slave marriages, just as for whites, and marriage ceremonies were generally performed by ministers or magistrates. Such efforts often met strong resistance from masters who viewed slave marriages as sometimes troublesome arrangements not only because of the complications of visitations among the slave couples but also because of the dependent and unproductive children produced. Some masters openly discouraged their slave women from becoming pregnant, threatening them with punishment or sale. In 1733 a Connecticut master sold his teenage slave, "for no fault but because she [was] like to be a good breeder."[79] In New York another slaveholder put his cook up for sale "because she breeds too fast for her owners to put up with such inconvenience."[80]

Even when masters tolerated the birth of children to their slaves, slave family relations seldom proceeded smoothly. Children were generally owned by their mother's owner, and so the mother-child unit was that most likely to be maintained. But slave children remained vulnerable to sale or in some cases were "given away" to friends and relatives of masters.[81] Such vulnerability existed in even the best situations. Dick and Nance and their three children were purchased by Aaron Melick in New Jersey in 1798. They lived together, had two more children, attended church, and celebrated holidays with gatherings of other blacks from the surrounding area. During the militia training days festivities each year in early summer, they set up shop at the training grounds, selling food and drink and keeping the money earned for their own spending money.

When Melick died the family was broken up, although their disposition was relatively benevolent. The parents, Dick and Nance, remained with Ann, the youngest girl, on the farm with Melick's son and his family. The four oldest children, two boys and a girl, were all sold for indenture lasting until age twenty-eight for the boys and age twenty-five for the girl. Diana, Sam, and Ben, ranging in age from thirteen to eighteen, were all sold to people in the surrounding towns. Joe, age nine, went to Melick's brother-in-law in New Germantown. In each case the children were sold to masters known to the Melick family, none was sold into the South where they would have brought a higher price, and all were sold for terms rather than for life. On this last point, New Jersey law would have protected only Ann, the youngest, from being sold into slavery. Given the possibilities the fate of the Melick slave family could have been much worse. Still, the fact remains that their future was decided by the terms of their master's will. They were not able to live together until the children were old enough to leave their places of indenture. They had been their master's trusted slaves, given a fair degree of mobility and a great deal of autonomy in running the farm, yet they were separated and auctioned off with the hay, grain, and the rest of their master's property.[82]

Under slavery in the colonial North the maintenance of family stability was terribly difficult but not impossible. Many fathers maintained contact with their families, and often traveled great distances to do so. Sundays and holidays, customarily days on which visitation was permitted, took on special significance for many slave families. Primus Hall reported his excitement as the holiday season drew near, since it was during this time that he and his mother were joined by his father, Prince. Although Prince Hall made the trip of forty or more miles on foot, he never failed to find his way.[83] The family emerging among African Americans as they adapted to conditions in the North only approximated the traditional African family unit. Gone was the formal authority of the matrilineal family structure over the choice of one's marriage partner. The extended family structure was particularly difficult to maintain in the colonial North, and the traditional exercise of fraternal authority, protection, and prerogative was all but impossible. Yet slaves maneuvered as best they could within the limits of the restrictive slave system to assert some control over their personal lives.

There were some advantages to northern blacks that often centered around their small proportions in the regional population. Especially in New England where the black population was tiny, even slaves enjoyed some legal rights and protections unparalleled in the South. Trial records from colonial Massachusetts bear clear witness to the right of judicial process accorded slaves who were allowed jury trials, legal counsel and a measure of legal protection. This was true even in cases which, had they occurred in the South, might have resulted in summary execution. In 1689 a black servant, Robin, was accused of the murder of John Cheeny, a white resident of Cambridge, Massachusetts. Cheeny had received "a mortall wound on the head with a stick." Robin received a jury trial at which he was allowed to challenge jury members and to test their partialities. When one juror refused to appear at the trial of a black man, he was fined by the court. Robin was found guilty but the jury recognized extenuating circumstances that led the court to impose only a heavy fine accompanied by a jail sentence which was to last until the fine was paid.[84]

Even when it was believed that blacks were guilty of crime, the rule of innocent until proven guilty was sometimes applied. In March 1735, two blacks were tried in Suffolk County Court in Boston. One was accused of burglary, the other of arson. Both were acquitted "for want of legal evidence . . . tho tis thought by all they were guilty of the facts." Although it is difficult to say, as some scholars have, that "a profound commitment to the law and the judicial process overpowered antithetical racial views," it is certainly true that in New England, particularly, and in the northern colonies, more generally, blacks, slave and free, could look to the law for some basic protection so long as the white population did not feel threatened by the black presence.[85]

When such a threat was perceived, the situation might be entirely different. Massachusetts authorized the burning of a slave for arson in 1681. After New York City's 1712 slave conspiracy, which resulted in several fires and the deaths of nine whites, nineteen blacks and two Indians were executed with three black leaders being tortured to death. In nearby Bergen County, New Jersey a slave was burned alive in 1735 for attempted arson, and after the revelation of a "Negro plot" in Burlington County, New Jersey in 1734, one slave was hanged and others had their ears cut off. Apparently the punishment was less severe because the plot never materialized and no whites were harmed. A few years later in New York City another slave conspiracy resulted in the hanging of eighteen blacks and the public burning of fourteen others, while in Hackensack, New Jersey, two blacks were burned at the stake for setting seven barns afire.[86] The key predictor in the treatment of blacks and the tolerance displayed by colonial whites was the extent of the perceived African-American threat. As historians have shown in the South, when the number of blacks increased substantially or at a rapid rate, whites fearing for their lives, property, or perhaps only the resulting social instability, reacted strongly.[87]

Thus the relationship between masters and slaves in the northern colonies was complex. It was determined by the demographics of that region as well as the climate and soil conditions that dictated labor force needs. Although slave trading was the more important economic activity in the North, by the early eighteenth century, slaveholding was an integral part of the economic and social system. Compared with the South, small slaveholdings ensured a less visible black presence. These differences profoundly affected the rate at which Africans became African Americans, influenced their ability to function in the overwhelmingly European-American world, and posed special problems for stable family formation among northern slaves.

During the eighteenth century, slavery based on race was formalized throughout the colonies. Although limited-term servitude continued as the only form of white bondage, periods of economic prosperity and political stability in Britain during the late seventeenth century decreased the incentives for English workers to accept American indentures. Pennsylvania received a wave of German servants after 1700, but generally Americans considered white servitude an unreliable labor source and it grew increasingly rare, replaced by perpetual, hereditary African slavery.[88] The major characteristics of northern slavery—the small size of slave-holdings, the greater frequency and variety of interracial contacts, the slaves' facility with English, access to some education, the more urban character of slavery, and the relatively small number of black people in northern society—shaped the African-American communities that emerged after the Revolution.

2

Culture, Race, and Class in the Colonial North

During the more than eight generations of black life in the colonial North, African customs and traditions mingled with those of Europeans and Native American Indians to produce a new culture. Each group, whether African or European, retained aspects of their own heritage and contributed to and produced a variation on a common tradition—creating a multilayered American culture. African ways blended with but did not totally succumb to the pressures of European customs and Christian beliefs. European missionaries working among blacks in the eighteenth century complained that their work was greatly hampered by "the prejudices of the slaves themselves." These dedicated churchmen were particularly frustrated by the tenacity with which Africans clung to their Old World ways. "Those born in Guinea [were] strangely prepossessed in favor of superstition and Idolatry," declared one Anglican minister in 1748. Their ethnocentrism prevented these clergymen from appreciating or even being curious about African beliefs, many of them hundreds of years older than Christianity, though some did recognize a "false Religion to be combated with."[1]

With the increase in the number of slaves imported directly from Africa after the mid-eighteenth century, African ways became even more influential among northern blacks and had an even greater cultural impact. African traditions were expressed in many aspects of black life, but perhaps most vividly in ceremonies and festivals. It was thus important to slaves that Sundays and holidays be maintained as "their days." They often saw these days off as owed to them under the emerging system of mutually recognized rights and responsibilities between masters and slaves and turned these days of "freedom" to their own purposes. For New World blacks, holidays provided opportunities for remembering African homes and for the temporary reunion of families.[2]

In New Netherlands blacks played an integral part in the festivities commemorating the Dutch two-day observance of Easter called Paas. Baking Paas cakes was traditional for the holiday, and there were apparently lively competitions among African Americans, especially the slaves, who prepared these special treats and vied with one another for the honor of Paas cake-throwing champion. "There was great rivalry among the colored people as to which could throw the Paas-cakes the highest and still successfully catch them." African Americans in New York and New Jersey continued to celebrate Dutch holidays long after these areas passed to English control. Alexander Coventry of Hudson, New York reported that slaves in the region continued to commemorate Paas well into the late eighteenth century.[3]

Some whites believed their slaves were more committed to enjoyment and relaxation than to the religious significance of Paas. Recalling her childhood in early nineteenth-century Long Island, Marian Gouverneur wrote that Cuff, "a old fashioned festive negro," would often announce that he was unable to perform some work task because of "Paas Monday or Paas Tuesday and so on continuing as the case required through the week." The implication was that for Cuff, Paas was simply an excuse to escape work, an excuse he extended well beyond the normal celebration. Obviously, Paas and similar celebrations were highly prized as nonwork days, but many blacks also valued them for a deeper significance.[4]

Although many of these holidays were European in origin, blacks brought to them their own special African meaning and style. Pinkster (Whitsunday or Pentecost as it was also known), a religious celebration with a strong tradition in Holland and Germany, was observed in the early spring, especially in the Hudson Valley. In June 1786, Coventry noted in his diary the significant role blacks played in all aspects of this holiday. By the late eighteenth century, African Americans dominated the celebration which lasted more than a week.[5] In the early nineteenth century, "Old King Charley," reportedly a "Guinea man" of noble birth from Angola brought to America as a slave, was the major actor among the free blacks and slaves who participated in the Albany festival. He rode at the head of the parade astride one of the best horses in the region and later, dressed in an elaborate costume and wearing a bright yellow lace hat, he led the "Guinea dance." This "original Congo dance as danced in their native Africa," was accompanied by a variety of traditional West African musical instruments including drums, fiddles, and banjos. The songs were distinctly African, one carrying an "African refrain 'Hi-a-bomba-bomba-bomba.'"[6]

Similarly, James Fenimore Cooper described the strongly African character of the Pinkster festivities in mid-nineteenth-century New York City. "By this time," he wrote, nine-tenths of the blacks of the city, and of the whole country within thirty or forty miles, indeed, were collected in thousands in those fields (upon which the celebration was to occur) beating banjoes, singing African songs, drinking, and worst of all, laughing in a way that seemed to set their very hearts rattling with in their ribs. . . .

The sheer numbers of black people participating and the African music "produce[d] a marked difference between this festival and one of European origin."[7] In the 1870s one contemporary reported that the observance was "only kept by negroes; with them, especially on the west end of the island, it is still much of a holiday." Modern scholars agree that by the late nineteenth century Pinkster had been completely transformed from its Dutch roots to an African-American celebration.[8]

Like Pinkster, Negro Election Days mixed elements of other colonial festivals with uniquely African celebrations. Again, the dress, the music, the dance, even the languages of West Africa were included in these activities. One eyewitness at the elections reported that "all the various languages of Africa" combined with English to give the occasion an international quality.[9] His study of Pinkster celebrations and Election Day festivals convinced Sterling Stuckey that "African cultural influence in the North was widespread and continuous during the slave era." Furthermore, noting the similarities between these celebrations in the northern United States and those in the West Indies, Stuckey argued that "the evidence suggests that the parades of kings and governors were part of a larger cultural configuration," reinforcing his "claim that a Pan-African culture existed in the Americas."[10]

Folklorist Melvin Wade agreed that the Negro elections bore a strong resemblance to West African ceremonies. He pointed to the instrumentation used in the festival parade as well as the polytonal texture and the complex rhythms of the music employed. The omnipresent violin recalled the over thousand-year history of this instrument in West Africa with its basis in the virtuosity of the musicians who played string, wood, and percussion instruments in the medieval empire of Mali. The strutting and baton-twirling that fascinated those who viewed these parades were also rooted in African cultures. The music, the dance, the language, the food, and even the strutting, shaped a common cultural style, helping to form a singular African-American tradition from various African heritages.[11]

European observers concluded that these festivals were analogous to their own harvest celebrations, but evidence suggests that they meant much more to their African and African-American participants. Accounts of such gatherings from the colonial period to well after the Civil War include descriptions of a particular kind of dancing which came to be known as the ring shout. Such dancing was an integral part of the religious observance of the West African groups who constituted the majority of the slaves brought to North America. Robert Farris Thompson, assessing the impact of the West Africans' Bakongo culture, concluded:

Africans from Kongo and Angola shared fundamental beliefs and languages. When they met on the plantations and in the cities of the western hemisphere, they fostered their heritage. Kongo civilization and art were not obliterated in the New World: they resurfaced in the coming together, here and there, of numerous slaves from Kongo and Angola.[12]

In the spirituality of these West African peoples, the ring shout, dancing in a slowly moving counterclockwise circle with feet on the ground and the whole body rippling in rhythm with the music, was the physical expression of their beliefs. The circle or the circle quadrisected by a cross is a central symbolic expression of the cosmology of the Bakongo peoples. The end points of the horizontal axis represent dawn and dusk, the circle traces the transit of the sun, and the axis itself represents the division between the physical and the spirit world. The border between this world and the next is often represented by the ocean or a river. Moving in a circle is participating in the symbolic representation of the life process; crossing the barrier between worlds. Understood in its religious context, the ring shout is communion with other dancers in the circle, with God, and with the ancestors in the world of the spirit.[13]

Many African beliefs and practices indicate the permeability of the boundary between the spirit world and the physical world, in European terms between the sacred and the secular. African-American practices indicate the continuation of these beliefs, sometimes incorporated into Christianity. Baptismal ceremonies often performed in a river frequently included the use of a staff with a cross on top stuck into the water. In African perception such a staff would constitute a bridge between worlds. The Baptist preacher's explanation of total immersion as a symbolic death and rebirth would make perfect sense to the African who also saw the water as the symbolic border between the worlds.

Both Africans and Europeans had beliefs about spirits, and their shared belief in the ability of the spirit world to affect the events and people of the secular world brought blacks and whites together in one of the most celebrated and least understood episodes in the history of colonial New England—the Salem witch trials. Talk of "the devil in Massachusetts" had circulated in Essex County for decades and trials had occurred, but it was the events of late 1691 that gave this small village its historical notoriety. In Salem at that time a group of young girls met regularly to speculate about their future lives, loves, and fortunes. One of them devised a crystal to better see their prospects. The young girls' game led to inexplicable events. Some of the girls had bizarre experiences, and others started acting strangely. Reverend Samuel Parris, father of one of the girls, called for physician William Griggs, but the doctor could not explain what was happening to the girls except to say that he feared an "Evil Hand" was at work. In order to determine if the girls were bewitched, a village woman called on the supernatural skills of two West Indian slaves, Tituba and

John. The couple baked a special witch cake and fed it to a dog belonging to one of the girls, but the test was inconclusive.

Meanwhile the strange affliction spread to others in the village. In December of 1691 the malady struck seven or eight other girls between the ages of twelve and nineteen, then older women, some of them married. By February Tituba herself and two white women were accused of practicing witchcraft. They were jailed in Boston, but that did not stop the panic, and other accusations followed. Among the accused were several slaves including Candy and Mary Black from the Putnam household. Some, like Negro Betty, were among the accusers who claimed the ability to recognize witches.[14] Some people believed that Tituba could cast a spell over anyone she wished to control. Once possessed her victim might have strange visions and talk and act irrationally. Their suspicions were confirmed when Tituba confessed, described her powers, and even gave "eye witness testimony" to the form of the devil, "a thing all over hairy, all the face hairy, and a long nose." Before fears subsided, more than 140 suspected witches were jailed, and nineteen (all whites) were hanged.[15]

Witchcraft was well known in England and other parts of Europe, and blacks and whites in America shared a belief in supernatural powers, but European Americans recognized that Africans were especially familiar with the spirit world. Although both blacks and whites were involved as accused and accuser in the witch trials, their interpretations of the events were undoubtedly somewhat different. Much of ancient European beliefs in the powers of evil spirits had been submerged in Christianity and had become focused on the workings of the devil. Many African religions, however, retained a more complex relationship with the spirit world.

A whole system of specialized charms for power, healing, and foretelling the future was brought to America from a variety of African religions. Many Africans in America continued to communicate with their ancestors and to respect the power of spirits. When over 2,000 slaves gathered in colonial Philadelphia during the last days of the semiannual fairs to dance the whole afternoon on the graves of the burial grounds, it was a powerful expression of their shared faith. Clustered by ethnic group with each singing in their own language, dancing in circles as the sun dipped below the horizon and moved into the other world, these Africans maintained their connection with their God, their ancestors, and their homeland. As African Americans continued these practices, familiar rituals confirmed shared beliefs and forged the bonds of community.[16]

For North American blacks the holidays were accompanied by great feasts and provided opportunities for sharing community news and traditional tales. Recalling these gatherings, one ex-slave told of listening to elders reminisce about life in Africa. In other parts of the Americas similar celebrations were conducted in strikingly parallel ways. In the late eighteenth century an anonymous reporter recorded the merrymaking among Afro-Caribbean people during the John Canoe festivals in

Kingston, Jamaica. The dancing, the style of music, the types of instruments, the parading, and the storytelling he described would have been familiar to colonial New Englanders. Yet the Jamaican celebrations took on an even more distinctly African character than those in New England. The use of the drum as not only a musical instrument but also as a communication device announcing the beginning of a festival was, for example, one Africanism generally not observed in the northern colonies of British North America.[17]

In Cuba, Africans combined Spanish Christian festive traditions with "comparsas" or carnival organizing committees that injected African ritual into Spanish festivals. The Afro-Cuban comparsas functioned as quasi-labor associations and exercised more power than the African-American governors and their courts, but both are examples of African tradition taking root within the European New World society. In both cases the result was cultural interaction rather than cultural absorption. Especially striking evidence of this interpenetration occurred in Latin America, as Yoruba deities became transformed into Christian saints with parallel characteristics.[18]

Although these were black festivals, nonblacks were not excluded. David Cohen's research confirmed that Pinkster celebrations in Albany were "multi-ethnic (including Germans, Yankees, Scots, Irish, Welsh, and English), multi-regional (including French Canadians and Vermonters), multi-racial (including blacks, Indians, and whites), and multi-occupational (including jack tars and politicians)." Sometimes colonial elites amused themselves by joining their slaves in celebration, but their roles were generally superficial and very limited. White indentured servants, Indians, and lower class white workers, on the other hand, were likely to take part as the friends and associates of slaves and free blacks.[19]

European lower classes brought their own festival traditions to America. Squire days or Lord's days in Britain allowed peasants a period of release from their bleak daily existence. During these celebrations, generally in the spring or fall, there was drinking, eating, and general merrymaking including a ceremonial role reversal with the peasants acting as lords of the manor. In America similar celebrations included "General Election Day" in late spring, when white New Englanders elected colonial officials, and "Pope's Day" in November, an annual Boston "antipopery" (anti-Catholic) festival. There were also military celebrations like "Muster Day," when local militia entertained huge crowds of merrymakers with precision drills.[20]

Those who witnessed election days made clear the diversity of participants. As a poem written in 1760 described them,

> Of black and white, and every sort
> of high, low, rich and poor;
> Squaws, negroes, deputies in scores ...

Specific note was taken of the association between blacks, Indians, and whites bound together by poverty, described as "a motley crew Of Whites & Blacks & Indians too."[21]

As blacks struggled to cope with the system of slavery and racial restrictions, they found allies. Some were missionaries who provided important, often paternalistic, aid; others were poor whites or Indians who found interracial alliances practical, natural, and sometimes necessary. By the mid-eighteenth century, the union of the poor of all races became an increasingly powerful force in American politics and a source of growing concern to the colonial elites. The basis for such an alliance is suggested in *A Pinkster Ode* written about King Charles and his important role during the festival. The words carry special meaning for slaves who:

> Tho' torn from friends beyond the waves
> Tho' fate has doom'd us to be slaves,
> Yet on this day, let's taste and see
> How sweet a thing is Liberty.

They also might ring true to poor whites especially the lines:

> Tho' hard and humble be our lot,
> The rich man's spleen we envy not.[22]

Some authorities worried over disturbing signs that the lower classes, especially Indians and blacks, were not under control. Although New England religious officials attempted to closely regulate the personal moral behavior of everyone in the region, it often seemed impossible to enforce codes of behavior on those of the "dangerous classes." Throughout the colonial period conversions of Indians were hampered by their reluctance to give up their traditional ways, most notably the right to easy dissolution of marriages, which was practical under their system of matrilineal households, the virtual economic independence of women, and the availability of surrogate fathers among women's kinship networks.[23] Complaints about African Americans ignoring the rules of sexual conduct were plentiful in the eighteenth century. Slaves, perhaps continuing African practices of polygyny and premarital pregnancy, could not always be made to live by Christian notions of sexual propriety. Another requirement—the subordination of women to men—was also difficult for these non-Europeans to accept. To the European-American authorities, these problems indicated a dangerous lack of discipline and self-control.[24]

Their fears were exacerbated by racial stereotypes depicting nonwhites as governed by "baser passions." Conversely, such beliefs led some masters to expect, tolerate, even encourage "fornication" among their slaves. Boston minister Samuel Sewall reported that masters condoned the "immoral" practices of their slaves even to the point of paying the fines levied when such cases came to the attention of colonial courts.[25] One New England master was willing to do so even after his slave Arthur, "a young black man of inferior status and talents, (who) lacked the moral strength to resist temptation," was arrested for having "assaulted" a white woman and run-away to avoid punishment. The woman's husband was among those who pursued the slave, who was sheltered by a local Indian tribe with which he had lived and among whom he had hidden on other occasions. After he was captured, Arthur claimed that he had not assaulted the woman at all but that they had engaged in "Behavior . . . such, as we have Reason to be ashamed of, (but) I shall for her sake pass it over in Silence." Although Arthur had a history of running away and of numerous sexual exploits for which he was punished on several occasions, his master interceded on his behalf and claimed him from the authorities. It became clear, however, that Arthur would continue his "wickedness" when on a later occasion he stole his master's horse and a bottle of rum and got drunk. He proceeded to the home of his Indian mistress. Finding her unavailable, however, he then called on "the Widow Deborah Metcalfe, whom I," he testified, "in a most inhumane manner, ravished." At this point Arthur was beyond the protection of his master. He was tried, convicted, and executed, as much for his intractability as for this single act. Colonial authority was willing to accept his "rebellious Spirit," but was not willing to put up with his "continual disruption of the social order," a matter made even more alarming by Arthur's close alliance with the local Indians.[26]

Even though the Indian population had decreased dramatically, in many areas of the North before the introduction of significant numbers of African slaves, red-black relationships, sexual and otherwise, were common in the northern colonies. Such unions were dramatically affected by the demographics of early colonial society, at least partially created by the practices of the colonizers. The case of the Pequot War in seventeenth-century New England is instructive. After killing hundreds of Pequot women, children, and old men in a surprise predawn raid on their Mystic River village in 1637, the English spent months hunting those who had been absent at the time of the attack. Many of the Pequot men were captured and executed. The women and children were enslaved by the colonists or their Indian allies, and those men left alive were sold for shipment to the West Indies. Typically many of the conquered Indian men were shipped into slavery in the labor-hungry West Indies, while the conquered women and children were sold into domestic slavery.[27]

The exportation of mainland Indians to slavery in the West Indies, the extent of the enslavement of Indians in the colonies, and the incorporation of Native Americans into both the slave and the free black population are topics frequently overlooked in American history. J. Leitch Wright, Jr., studying American Indians in the Old South, noted the consequences of the labor shortage in the West Indies:

> From Columbus's time until well into the nineteenth century an insatiable demand for workers persisted. Africans, European indentured servants, con-

victs and political exiles, and aborigines from the American mainland all
helped fill this shortage. The Southern Indian slave trade was part of a worldwide phenomenon, and captives . . . had much in common with black Africans
and European convicts, political prisoners, and children kidnapped from the
streets of London, all of whom were sent to the islands.[28]

Indian males were more likely than females to be exported to slavery in
the West Indies, and the market for the importation of Africans to American slavery favored young males. During the seventeenth and early eighteenth centuries, the sexual imbalance favored women among many New
England Indian tribes and men among colonial blacks. Colonial records
are replete with accounts of Africans and Indians, born worlds apart,
brought together by history, circumstance, and personal choice.

Robin Eldridge was born in the African Congo. His father was an
African tribal chief and tobacco trader who had been kidnapped aboard an
American ship. Also taken were Robin's mother, his sister, two brothers,
and Robin himself. He was the youngest and least able to understand what
was happening to the family. Little is known of his family's fate. Probably
they were brought to Rhode Island, but did not remain together.[29] Robin
met and eventually married Hannah Prophat of the Narragansett Tribe in
Rhode Island. He and Hannah had very different backgrounds but they
had many things in common, not the least of which was that both their
fathers had been slaves. Hannah's father, a Narragansett Indian enslaved
in Rhode Island, had been emancipated through the efforts of Mary Fuller,
his wife and Hannah's mother. Both Robin, a slave at the time of their marriage, and Hannah knew all too well the obstacles that slavery placed in the
way of family life. Ironically, Robin served in the Revolutionary struggle
for the liberty of those who had enslaved his family. He won his own freedom in the process.[30] Service in the Revolution left Robin Eldridge free
but poor, providing him nothing tangible but worthless Continental script,
yet Robin was free to benefit from his own labor and to pass his earnings
on to his free-born children.

The extent of combined Indian and African heritage in the early American population is difficult to estimate. Generally whites treated such
interracial offspring as African Americans. In 1719 the governor of South
Carolina declared that all slaves "not entirely Indian" would be counted as
black. In New Jersey those of Indian and African descent were routinely
listed in official documents as "negro." Cyrus Bustill, a Philadelphia baker
born in 1732 in Burlington, New Jersey, married a Delaware Indian
woman. Their son, Cyrus Jr., who became a Quaker and a prominent antislavery leader was considered black.[31]

Often those of Indian and African descent kept a foot in each world
despite their official racial designation. Paul Cuffe of Massachusetts, the
son of an African father and an Indian mother, was referred to at various
times as Indian or black. Cuffe affirmed his dual ancestry. His signature

appears on petitions from "Indian men" and from others calling themselves "free Negroes and mulattoes." Various members of Cuffe's family, including his older brother John, lived with their Indian relatives.[32]

Some Indian-African relationships were formed when runaways, such as the slave Arthur, took refuge with Indian tribes. Although his presence among the tribe was sporadic, he did form a lasting relationship with them, taking an Indian lover and visiting her regularly.[33] Substantial numbers of other blacks remained with the Indians for years taking mates and producing children. These children were considered black or sometimes "mulatto" by white colonials, even though they might live as Indians for the major portion of their lives. One disadvantage from the perspective of colonial officials was that the offspring of unions of enslaved African-American men and free Indian women took the status of their free mother, and these unions threatened to create a substantial free black population. One authority reported that Indians were more likely to mix with Africans than with Europeans. This observation lends some support to the argument of one scholar that the intermixture of Africans and Indians was so common that during the seventeenth and eighteenth centuries it accounted for most of the free people of color.[34]

Colonial elites feared the consequences of interracial association and sought to discourage it by law. As early as 1705, New York officials tried to prevent black and Indian alliances with a law that prohibited slaves from traveling into the Indian region north of Saratoga. Later, treaties were struck with several Indian nations to prevent their sheltering of fugitives. Where enforced this provision sometimes amounted to forced separation of families, but generally these measures proved ineffective. Throughout the colonial period, whenever blacks and Indians came into contact, their mutual cooperation was always a possibility.[35]

Whites were uneasy about black-red alliances, but they were especially discomforted by relationships formed between blacks and whites. One of a series of laws passed in Pennsylvania in 1726 to control the black population demonstrated this concern about interracial association. The law provided that any free black person who married a white person could be sold into slavery. Partly to justify slavery, theories were advanced asserting the superiority of white civilization and the inherent intellectual and moral superiority of whites over nonwhites. Such beliefs convinced many European masters that God and nature gave them the right, some even argued the responsibility, to hold black people in bondage. Close equal relationships between blacks and whites contradicted these developing racial theories.[36]

Assumptions about racial superiority coexisted with another system of beliefs prevalent in colonial British society. Social hierarchy was a strong organizing principle in Britain and in the colonies. Although colonial elites could not generally aspire to British nobility, they did maintain elaborate social distinctions that placed "gentlemen" at the top of colonial society, followed by the yeoman or middling classes, with the "mean and vile" ranks filled by the "lower sort" at the bottom. They believed that the maintenance of a strictly delineated social ranking system was crucial to the stability of society and a shield against anarchy. Generally distrustful of poor whites, they argued that one's "social place" was determined by God who "hath Ordained different degrees and orders of men, some to be high and Honorable, some to be Low and Despicable."[37]

The privileged were known by reputation and demonstrated their station in their habits, dress, walk, and general demeanor. Titles such as "Gentleman" denoted one who did not support himself by his own labor. In New England and the middle colonies, no less than in the South, "Labor or working in order to live was thus traditionally considered to be servile, associated with dependency and a lowly status." Even Benjamin Franklin, who often spoke of the virtue of hard work, was content to retire in his early forties to the gentleman's life.[38]

The gentlemanly class was one bound together not only by commonality of elite status but by blood and marriage as well. Throughout the colonies, North and South, familiar surnames connoted kinship ties that defined the circle of privilege. The Lees of Virginia, the Shattucks and the Williamses of Massachusetts, the Shippens of Pennsylvania, these and other select family groups, regionally connected, socially and politically powerful, constituted the colonial hierarchy.[39]

Even the Quaker society of the middle colonies conformed to this picture of colonial hierarchial structure. Although they declared the equality of each person to find, worship, and be blessed by God and thus to experience eternal salvation, their egalitarianism did not extend to social relations. The Society of Friends was clear that "we design to level nothing but Sin," and that in so far as the structure of society was concerned, "these Natural Relations are rather better established," rather than diminished by the Quaker faith.[40]

As the colonies developed and their population grew, the social structure changed. During the eighteenth century the higher social ranks were not totally closed. A skilled worker with the proper values and attitude might ascend to the level of gentlemen once he had overcome the need for manual labor. The availability of land and the growth of new markets provided more opportunity for advancement to a broader range of people than existed in Europe. The growth of cities and the urban middling class blurred easily recognizable distinctions. Imitating the dress and manners of the upper class, this middle class seemed to introduce an element of unpredictability into the well-ordered social world. The wealthy were scandalized by the pretentiousness of those without proper background or breeding who sought by their dress to misrepresent themselves as members of the elite.

Still, wealth, background, and breeding determined political power in colonial cities of the Northeast—the top 10 percent of society controlled internal policy and 40 percent of the wealth. The bottom 50 percent had little impact on politics through formal channels and held less than 10 percent of the wealth. The lower level of this latter group was composed of white servants, apprentices, and unskilled laborers. These white workers crewed the ships and attended the docks of port cities like New York, Boston, and Philadelphia, and were sometimes reduced to working conditions that approximated those of free blacks or even slaves.[41]

Many colonial laborers, especially in New York and Philadelphia, were white indentured servants who purchased their passage to America by selling themselves into service for a fixed term, usually five to seven years. Estimates are that one-half to two-thirds of all Europeans migrating to colonial America after 1630 came as indentured servants. From a complete list of emigrants departing Britain for America between 1773 and 1776, historian Bernard Bailyn calculated that almost half (47.8 percent) were indentured servants. Although there were very important differences between slavery and indentured servitude, not the least of which was the length of bondage and the involuntary and hereditary nature of slavery, in day-to-day terms the statuses were similar.[42]

On arrival indentured servants often faced the auction block, and although it was technically their labor and not their person being sold, it was sometimes difficult to tell the difference. As one British officer in Philadelphia observed, "They sell the servants here as they do their horses, and advertise them as they do their beef and oatmeal." Although this spectator omitted the obvious comparison to the treatment of black slaves, in their own accounts indentured servants were quick to point out the similarities. As one wrote to a British newspaper, the indentured servant in America was sold "for a slave at public sale or [bartered] for country produce." Servants who could not be disposed of in port-city public markets were handed over to "soul drivers" who made regular circuits through the countryside in search of buyers for the indenture of those he drove before him like "sheep to the slaughter." One servant recalled the soul driver "exposing us for sale in all public fairs and markets as brute beasts."[43]

Theoretically, indentured servants were protected from an abusive master, but like slaves these servants were often isolated from those who might enforce protective laws even if they had been so inclined. In a system of greatly unequal power servants had few options and few defenders. The historical record convincingly shows that exploitation and cruelty were major problems for these poor whites. A comparison of household records shows similar living conditions, diet, and dress for poor people of all colors. The personal inventories of poor blacks and poor whites indicate that typical dress consisted of old shoes and yarn stockings, cable breeches and a woolen or homespun shirt. Occasionally fancier items could be acquired from masters or other affluent whites. Dick, a black runaway slave from Danbury, Connecticut, was said to have sported a red plush jacket with pewter buttons and split cuffs. Jack escaped from servitude decked out in a blue coat with white buttons, a white flannel jacket, and black manchester velvet breeches. These outfits were uncommon among slaves and servants and must have made their wearers quite conspicuous.[44]

The diet for poor people was dictated by the availability of local foods. Meat from domestic animals, especially pork, was common. In seafront communities clams and oysters were popular. Further inland, river and other fresh-water fish supplemented with locally grown vegetables or locally hunted game were common dietary items. Descriptions provided by white servants confirmed, as one did in 1775, that servants "are subject to the same laws as the Negroes and have the same coarse food and clothing." Shared diet and dress, like the often brutal treatment they were forced to tolerate at the hands of their "betters," created the shared perceptions and common interests that provided a basis for interracial cooperation among the colonial poor.[45]

Such interracial association was common in colonial society; popular festivals of all types seemed to encourage it. Colonial elites' uneasiness about all those at the lower end of society intensified their growing fears of such gatherings. Massachusetts authorities became increasingly concerned about the annual Pope Day displays on the fifth day of November, originating out of anti-Catholic spirit in Britain. In Boston the customary parading around with effigies (traditionally, grotesque representations of the pope, the devil, and the Catholic pretender to the English throne) was at first endorsed by council members as a means of "forming a Spirit of Loyalty in the Youth of the town," but the festivities sometimes turned violent. In 1752 Boston's celebration boiled over into a confrontation between groups from rival sections of the city, leaving several people injured and one dead. These excesses by the "lower sorts" prompted the Massachusetts General Court to pass measures restricting the activities of "men, children and negroes" in these celebrations. These regulations did not stop the violence however. Twelve years later a five-year-old child was killed during another Pope Day festival in the city.[46]

Not all celebrations were so violent. In 1765 Bostonians celebrated the birthday of the Prince of Wales. Like most festivities in the city, this was an interracial affair, but in this case city officials maintained greater control by ensuring that it included not only "white and black, bound and free" but also, as one report observed, "high and low, rich and poor, young and old." The city battery fired cannon, and in the evening young people lit bonfires. City fathers were gratified that control was maintained.[47]

Other occasions for diverse groups of common people to come together were provided by certain religious gatherings. The religious revival of the Great Awakening that swept the colonies after 1730 caught the spiritual imagination of massive numbers of the poor, both black and white. Slaves and free blacks, white wage laborers and indentured servants, Indians, and even women and children filled the congregations. Even more shocking to the colonial elites, such people shared the pulpit during these emotional services. One Boston observer reported "there are among the exhorters . . . young persons, sometimes lads, or rather boys; nay women and girls; yea, Negroes, have taken upon them to do the business of preachers." The established clergy objected to "private persons of no education and but low attainments in knowledge" preaching the gospel. More upsetting to slaveholders, the egalitarian ideology of the Great Awakening in the hands of ministers like Samuel Hopkins of Newport, Rhode Island became a weapon against slavery. Thus, colonial elites objected to the interracial character of the revivals, to their emotionalism, their use of lay clergy, and their stand against slavery. At stake was a loss of racial and class control; a potentially dangerous threat to the system of deference that ensured social order.[48]

This need to control society's lower ranks was particularly acute as it applied to bound people of whatever color. White servants, at least for their term of service, could marry only at the pleasure of their master and were forced to depend on his "good will" to ensure that families were not separated. Servants had little power; colonial America "was not democratic and certainly not egalitarian." One historian's description recalled the colonial aristocracy's servants as "men and women who were dirty and lazy, rough, ignorant, lewd and often criminal [who] thieved and wandered, had bastard children and corrupted society with loathsome diseases." Poor whites, it seemed, were as much a threat to order and stability as the other despised groups, Indians and blacks.[49] Historians verifying the similarity in circumstances have also documented the resulting tendency toward alliance between slaves, servants, and other poor whites. One historian, recounting the situation in colonial Virginia, stated, "It was common . . . for servants and slaves to run away together, steal hogs together, get drunk together . . . [and] not uncommon for them to make love together."[50]

Isaac Cromwell, a forty-year-old mulatto, escaped from slavery in northern Maryland. He was accompanied by Ann Greene, an English woman who was an indentured servant in the same area. They escaped to Philadelphia on two of Isaac's master's horses and were thought to be living together in the city as husband and wife. Peggy, a black slave who spoke with a Welsh accent, escaped from slavery with her Portuguese lover, an indentured servant. Meanwhile, Bill, a mulatto slave, ran away to join his mother whom he claimed was a white woman living in New England.[51]

Rhode Island passed an ordinance in 1708 requiring that a slave being entertained in the home of a free person be accompanied by his master. In New York City officials complained about lower class whites and free blacks who opened their homes as informal groggeries and places of illegal association. Those who gathered to drink and entertain themselves in interracial groups were seen as dangerous to good order, and the environment was considered "destructive to the morals of servants and slaves." In truth these were often the lairs of thieves and prostitutes, where stolen goods changed hands and sexual favors were bought and sold, "the principle bane and pest of the city," as one newspaper reported.[52]

John Romme, a white man, operated one interracial saloon in New York City. Reportedly Romme sold stolen goods and his major suppliers were several black thieves. Another notorious white underworld figure, John Hughson, was a shoemaker who ran an interracial bar as a front for his fencing operation. Hughson's associates were mainly black, slave and free. His pub, like Romme's, was a headquarters for interracial underworld business transactions. Its other major attraction was Margaret (Peggy) Sorubiero, "the Newfoundland Irish beauty," who entertained male patrons without regard to race or national origin. Hughson and Romme were business partners who plotted to gain control of crime in colonial New York City. They planned to use several black gangs like the Geneva Club and interracial gangs they would organize to control vice in each district of the city. Operated like fraternal organizations with secret oaths and rituals, this substantial underground organization was plotted at Hughson's and Romme's pubs. No doubt similar activities took place in the ten or more other underground establishments in New York City.[53]

Colonial authorities worried over these saloons as dens of vice that fostered interracial contact in an increasingly segregated society. But these places were much more than connection points for thieves and gamblers. Hughson's pub was well known among slaves for its regular Sunday dinners and became a favorite spot to congregate after church. Goose, mutton, and fresh baked bread were served, and rum, beer, cider and punch flowed as music and dancing provided a festive diversion. The exchanges of the colonial barter economy were conducted in a relaxed atmosphere as the relationships between those at the bottom of eighteenth-century society flourished within the deferential social framework of the colonial world. Slaves in these pubs were likely to complain about the injustice of slavery and of their masters, while whites often expressed resentment of those with money, many of them slaveholders, who seemed to profit most from the misfortune of the poor. Blacks and whites, servants and slaves, even a few off-duty British soldiers found Hughson's and pubs like it throughout the city places where those of similar circumstances could enjoy each other's company.[54]

Such relationships were not confined to slaves and indentured servants. Lemuel Haynes was born in 1753 in West Hartford, Connecticut, the son of an African father and a white New England-born mother. Until he was twenty-one years of age, Haynes was bond servant to Deacon David Rose of Granville, Massachusetts. After enlisting as a minuteman and serving the American cause in the Revolutionary army, he studied for the ministry. Haynes was eventually ordained as pastor to a white congregation in Connecticut, and in 1783 married Elizabeth Babbit, a young white school teacher. Knowing the general disapproval of such unions, Haynes consulted with a number of prominent white clergy before he married, receiving support from each for his plan. At the same time, the "better people" of Connecticut complained heartily about the "great familiarity between blacks and whites" at the lower end of the economic scale, familiarity epitomized by their eating together as equals. This is not to argue that interracial unions were generally accepted for middle-class blacks. Yet, when exceptions were made, they were likely to involve those in the middle class whom colonial elites saw as potential allies against the mob, and thus less dangerous.[55]

The problem of controlling the population in colonial America became more acute during the eighteenth century as colonial wealth and power became increasingly concentrated in the hands of the few. The greater economic disparity between society's top and bottom made social and economic mobility more difficult and discontent more likely. Although this trend was stronger in the southern colonies, the concentration of wealth occurred almost everywhere. The proportional growth in the elite share of the colonial wealth was apparent in the tax lists and in the increasingly ostentatious display by the wealthy in both the urban North and the plantation areas of the slaveholding South. As elites consolidated their hold on the colonial economy they also managed to control the politics of their regions through interlocking family connections.[56]

The economic and social structure of colonial society was reflected in the application of the law. Those of inferior rank found that social standing weighed heavily in settling legal disputes and that courts were likely to be swayed by the reputation and status of the trial participants. In 1767 the Superior Court in Massachusetts denied the petition of a "yeoman" of the colony, refusing to bring a judgment against a military officer who was also an appointee of the colonial governor, declaring that a "Gentleman by office" might "abate [such a] writ." Significantly, no "Gentleman" offender was ever whipped in colonial New York although this was a common sentence for those who committed even petty crimes.[57]

The growing gap between the rich and the poor led them to different political perceptions. By 1765 three times as many Philadelphians received poor relief as had before 1750, and more people were remaining poor longer. Those in different circumstances were likely to have different explanations for the problem. The more successful might agree with Benjamin Franklin that the misfortune of the growing numbers of urban poor was a result of their own failings. At the taverns, the cock fights, and the many sporting events where common people gathered, complaints about those in power who limited opportunities to get ahead were typical.[58]

Wherever interracial gathering places were found, authorities saw them as potential breeding grounds for mob insurrection. According to one historian, the town water pump in Providence, Rhode Island was one notorious gathering spot for slaves and white servants whose actions were of grave concern to authorities. These fears were not without foundation—

shared conditions and common perceptions of the problem did lead to alliances. Runaway ads in colonial newspapers confirm that blacks and whites frequently sought freedom together. When Charles escaped from slavery in 1740, he was accompanied by two white companions also making their break for freedom, one a "Scotch man" and the other an Englishman. One mulatto slave and his white comrade struck out from bondage and were believed to be heading for Britain where the mulatto was said to have an uncle who operated a London coffee house.[59]

Adventures of this kind were common, but they were not the only type of interracial action. Joint effort, sometimes in the form of violent protest, was frequent in colonial America. Working people, slaves and servants, were politically impotent, and riot was often their only means of affecting public policy. As historian Gary Nash observed, "the urban crowd was the watchdog of politics, always ready to chastise or drive from office those who violated the collective sense of propriety or equity." The potential for class alliance transcending color became strikingly clear when Nathaniel Bacon, a white frontier planter, led his populist interracial army against the Indians of western Virginia and against Virginia's colonial authority in 1676. Bacon was killed and his forces defeated, but among those who held out longest were eighty blacks and twenty whites.[60]

In April of 1712, a group of New York City black slaves joined by a few whites and Indians attempted to "revenge themselves for some hard usage ... from their masters" by burning several buildings. They also attacked those who responded to the alarm, killing nine and wounding six more. Repelled by the militia, the rebels sought sanctuary in the woods but were eventually captured. The city authorities' retribution was a stunning reflection of their fear. Several conspirators were tortured and hanged; others were burned at the stake, starved to death, or broken on the wheel. Two Indians were executed for their part in the conspiracy, and repressive laws were enacted against blacks and Indians.[61] The impact of the New York City conspiracy was far-reaching, intensifying fears in the surrounding colonies. A citizens' petition to the Pennsylvania Assembly demanded no further "importation of negroes and Indians" into the colony, as alliances between blacks and Indians were seen to endanger white Pennsylvanians. Duties were imposed on slaves imported into the colony in an effort to curtail the growth of the slave population.[62]

In Boston during the 1730s, unemployment combined with inflation to create hardships for laboring people. Local merchants were dismayed when many black and white "loose vain Persons," traveled to the countryside to escape the urban high prices by purchasing directly from the farmer. Finally in 1738 the "general murmurings against the government and the rich people" erupted into full-scale rioting. By the end of the decade violence by "young People, Servants and Negroes" had forced a change in market procedures and eased the economic crisis of the common consumer.[63]

Just as all the poor suffered from high food prices, so were people of all colors affected by the British practice of impressment, taking young men against their will to service aboard merchant and war seagoing vessels. The appearance of "press gangs" could spread terror in a community. The action of this summary draft was sometimes so swift and unexpected that workers were forced from half-completed tasks and husbands and sons taken from the family dinner table without warning. In Boston frustrations exploded into battles between "press gangs" and angry mobs in 1745 and 1747. When government troops attempted to suppress one mob by force, several thousand attacked the governor's house. The investigation of this impressment riot described the participants as a "riotous, tumultuous assembly of foreign seamen, servants, Negroes and other persons of mean and vile condition." Town officials acknowledged the unfair treatment of those pressed into service, but they condemned their violent response. A common danger brought a common response, and the impressment issue apparently cut across class lines, as several middling-class Bostonians were also part of the mob.[64]

Interracial mob action protesting impressment flared in New York, Casco Bay, Maine, and Norfolk, Virginia during the 1760s. In the summer of 1765 five hundred "seamen, boys and Negroes" rioted in response to five weeks of impressment in Newport, Rhode Island. As in Boston, elites condemned impressment but also expressed strong disapproval of mob action against it. Many like Benjamin Franklin and Tom Paine saw impressment as a gross injustice. John Adams understood the depth of feeling among the common people on this issue and predicted that it "accelerated revolution." In New York, with a broader franchise and a more extensive effort by the government to allow white working men a role in conventional politics, there were fewer mob actions on class issues. Yet interracial activities could lead to fears of conspiracies among "persons of mean and vile conditions," and colonial authorities often reacted swiftly and severely. A plot believed hatched in Hughson's pub in 1741 so aroused New Yorkers that thirteen blacks were burned at the stake, sixteen others were hanged, and more than seventy were banished from the British colonies. Significantly, four whites were also hanged and seven were banished for their part in the conspiracy.[65]

In the view of the authorities, one particularly undesirable effect of interracial associations was the possibility of black-white sexual union. Historians have noted the predisposition in European, particularly English, culture and language to view interracial sex as abnormal. Philip Morgan has argued that colonial authorities' tolerance of interracial sexual relationships differed according to the racial composition and the economic base of the society. In societies where the proportion of blacks was high and slavery was central to the local economy, the legal status of African Americans was often more fluid and interracial sexual relations between white men and black women were common and often coercive.

In British Jamaica, for example, with its large slave population and shortage of white women, black concubinage was widespread. One observer reported that "every unmarried adult [white] man, and of every class, has his black or his brown mistress, with whom he lives openly."[66]

In British North America, unlike the West Indies and Latin America, miscegenation was publicly condemned. According to Winthrop Jordan, colonial sentiment opposing interracial sexual relations was fully developed by the turn of the eighteenth century. Jordan attributed such opposition to a deep aversion to interracial sexual relationships, based, in large part, on the notion that they were against God's will and nature's law. European notions of the inferiority of black people were rooted in the belief that the African nature was expressed in the base physical, primitive instincts of uncivilized beings. Thus whites believed that the polarity of European and African skin colors reflected a juxtaposition of their natural proclivities. Whereas Europeans were believed to be people moved by intellect, Africans were seen as emotionally volatile people controlled by physical need. Many whites assumed that black men, driven by lust and passion and lacking civilized self-control, posed a significant threat to helpless white women. Thus, racial control was seen as a defense of white women in particular and white civilization in general.[67]

Disapproval combined with fears of interracial political alliances led colonial officials to discourage and generally outlaw interracial sexual unions. Still, colonial records bear ample testimony to the occurrence of sexual relations between blacks and whites, especially between masters and slave women. Several witnesses reported that children produced by interracial associations were in great evidence in all northern colonies. In New England some believed a relative shortage of white men in the late seventeenth century drove white women to seek generally informal unions with black men.[68]

New England was unusual among British colonies in the incidence of interracial marriages and liaisons involving black and mulatto men and white women. Its situation paralleled, but did not match, that in Great Britain itself where the gender imbalance among Africans, much greater than that among blacks in the West Indies, and their small numbers encouraged sexual unions between black men and English women. The marriage of Lemuel Haynes had many counterparts in British society, among them Olaudah Equiano, who had been captured in Africa while a child, served a time in America before obtaining his freedom, and immigrated to Britain where he became a celebrated abolitionist and married a British woman. Furthermore, many British women were not opposed to such relationships. English writer Samuel Johnson recounted stories of his servant Francis Barber, who "carried the empire of Cupid farther than most men" and was on occasion aggressively sought after by British women. Some English men explained this by claiming that it was the "lower class of women in England, [who were] remarkably fond of the blacks, for reasons too brutal to mention." Evidence suggests otherwise. In a telling expression of surprise, one Connecticut man visiting London reported observing one couple—"a well-dressed white girl, who was of ruddy complexion, and even handsome, walking arm in arm, and conversing very sociably, with a negro man, who was as well dressed as she, and so black that his skin had a kind of ebony scale." There were even rumors in proper British circles of a relationship between the duchess of Queensberry and her black servant, described by some as a lover the likes of Don Juan.[69]

Higher proportions of blacks combined with the availability of white women in British North America resulted in more restrictions on interracial relationships. In Virginia prohibitions against interracial marriage were the first race-based laws passed (1660), and even in the New England colonies authorities discouraged "race mixing." In some colonies like Massachusetts there were specific laws in 1705 prohibiting such interracial relationships. They provided that black men so involved be whipped, banished from the colony, and sold into slavery elsewhere, while white women were to be whipped and bound into service for a period. A white man involved with a black woman was to be lashed, fined, and held responsible for any children produced; a black woman was to be whipped and sold outside the colony.[70]

Neither regulation nor custom prevented social or sexual contact between blacks and whites in colonial America, however. In the South such association was so apparent that one Virginian remarked that, "the country swarms with mulatto bastards." In the northern colonies, though less common, mulattoes constituted from 20 percent to one-quarter of the black population in some locales. These percentages rose dramatically during the late eighteenth and into the nineteenth century. The numbers of mulattoes were significant even in the Middle Atlantic colonies where there was relative parity among white males and females in the general population.[71]

There were other important reasons for official colonial aversion to interracial sex. One was unwillingness to accept the offspring of such relationships as legitimate members of society. Throughout the eighteenth and nineteenth centuries, the presence of mulattoes in American society proved an embarrassment for many whites. They also symbolized the dangerous possibility of interracial alliance. Concerns about such alliances prompted the extension to certain whites of laws instituted especially to control black behavior. An act passed in Massachusetts to restrict the behavior of Indians and slaves in 1704 was used against white servants by mid-century and rewritten with no specific mention of race in 1761 as a general act to establish a "watch for the safety and better securing the good order of the Town of Boston." This act was meant to curb the activity of black and white "dissolute persons [who had] sometimes riotously met." Colonial gentry often lumped all blacks with poor whites using descriptive phrasing like "the unthinking multitude," "the rabble," or "the mean and vile classes." These pejorative terms were frequently used irrespective of race to connote the lowest positions in colonial society.[72]

Colonial America was forging a new and dynamic society by the eighteenth century. It was strongly rooted in the social hierarchial values and traditions of Europe but colored by the cultures of ancient North America and those of equally ancient Africa. It offered unprecedented opportunity to ordinary Europeans whose expectations were limited by their Old World experience. As Nash pointed out, the dream of colonial working people did not generally extend to lofty heights. "Their desire was not to reach the top but to get off the bottom." Theirs was a world that operated by the rules of social deference and tied the economic security of those at the lower end of society to the benevolence of their "betters." But this world was changing.[73]

Although by the second half of the eighteenth century the gap between rich and poor was growing, there remained far more economic equality in American society than in Europe. In a recent reinterpretation of the American Revolution, Gordon Wood argued that "social classes based on occupation or wealth did not set themselves against one another, for no classes in [the] modern sense yet existed." The most revolutionary aspect of the American Revolution, Wood argued, was a dramatic change in the social relationships within American society as social deference gave way to greater social equality. He saw the move toward revolutionary action as an attempt by the common people, fearful that British regulations would rob them of their political and economic liberty and their ability to hold on to their "hard-earned prosperity." To do less was to risk being reduced to the level of slavery or servitude. Some scholars have argued that the presence of those in the lowest ranks of society acted to unite those above in efforts at social control and containment. Wood, however, suggests that the servant classes provided a constant reminder to middling Americans of the dire consequences of allowing the loss of their independence. This analysis is an intriguing one that explicates the role and concerns of those at and above the middle ranks of colonial society. It provides no role for those at society's bottom, however, save that of frightening point of comparison.[74]

In the American setting this Old World organization by which the poor deferred to the rich did indeed become increasingly inappropriate as the ideals and the rhetoric of the Enlightenment and the theology of the Great Awakening gained currency. But the beliefs and ideals of the people subjected to slavery and indenture contributed much to the developing American philosophy of republicanism that animated protest activity in colonial American society. Servants, Indians, and slaves joined forces. Refusing to be powerless, they forced their masters to notice, respond, and even to fear them and the possibility of their retaliation for gross injustice.

Interracial ceremony and celebration, social interaction, and familial connection became the building blocks of their alliance. Arson, riot, and even armed insurrection became their political tools. Never quite free from racial divisions, yet often able to overcome these in favor of their shared circumstance, the "lower sort" in colonial America cannot be overlooked without consequently overlooking their contribution to liberty's struggle. The fierce individuality and democratic organization of Native American peoples, the communal organization and religion of the African peoples, and the determination of both to regain their lost freedom contributed more than the metaphors of slavery and freedom to the rhetoric and principles of the Revolution. Historian Edmund Morgan has analyzed this rhetoric as the idea of freedom from slavery that provided images which animated the struggle for independence; our analysis extends Morgan's by giving concrete reality to the experience of the loss of freedom as a motivating force for many unfree participants in the Revolutionary struggle.[75] As the century progressed, the poor of all colors and conditions became more likely to act on their developing ideals and more willing to express themselves through direct, often violent action. The problem of social order at home became as troubling to many colonial leaders as the injustices they felt at the hands of Britain.

Though racial divisions were clear, the rigid hierarchy of the colonial social structure that remained until the late eighteenth century, what Wood called the "vertical focus of American society," helped facilitate interracial cooperation along class lines. Interracial associations and kinship ties profoundly affected the social and political lives of colonial people. Increasingly after 1750, middling Americans and the colonial elite joined the "mob," protesting the tightening control of the colonial economy by the mother country and complaining that the rights of Englishmen were being systematically denied to colonists. Often the actions and concerns of the interracial "lower sort" appeared to complement those of the middling group, but the poor, the disenfranchised, the slaves, and servants had complaints of their own. In New England only 25 percent of adult white males had sufficient property to qualify as voters; in the southern colonies the figure was over 50 percent. Catholics, Jews, almost all blacks, Native Americans, and women were also excluded from full citizenship. Colonial elites who sought the redress of their grievances against the injustice of English economic and political policy generally remained unmoved by homegrown inequity.[76]

The end of the French and Indian War in 1763 brought a decline in trade and a postwar depression to colonial towns. Dock laborers and seamen were quick to feel the economic bite, and free blacks suffered alongside white laboring men. When mobs took to the streets in Boston, New York, Newport, and other colonial towns to protest against the Stamp Act and other such regulations, black sailors and laborers were among them.

In New York City the Queen's Head tavern at Broad and Pearl Streets became notorious as a center for such revolutionary activity. Operated by "Black Sam" Fraunces, a West Indian mulatto, the pub was the staging area for violence in opposition to the Stamp Act and later in 1774 for New York's counterpart of the Boston Tea Party.[77]

On October 2, 1750 the *Boston Gazette and Weekly Journal* carried an ad placed by William Brown of Framingham, Massachusetts describing his runaway slave named Crispus. The slave was described as a "well set" mulatto, twenty-seven years old, six feet two inches tall with short curled hair and "knees nearer together than common." Crispus Attucks, part African and part Nantucket Indian, was never captured. During the next twenty years he worked as a seaman on a whaling crew generally sailing out of Boston harbor and in a factory making rope in the city's North End.[78] Like other American seamen he knew the ever-present danger of British impressment. Attucks and his fellows also shared the economic pain of the limitations placed on American trade by England's navigation acts. It was to enforce these acts that British officials dispatched several regiments of redcoats to Massachusetts. By 1770 Boston streets bristled with the unwanted presence of these soldiers who symbolized the colonists' worst fears of royal oppression. Most disturbing for the city's working people, these soldiers often took part-time jobs during off-duty time to supplement their military incomes. They could afford to accept low wages and thus undercut American workers. For those forced to compete in the tight job market of the period, the added pressure of redcoat moonlighters was intolerable.

These tensions often resulted in harsh words and minor violence during the winter of 1770. Imbued with the spirit of protest that inspired many in Boston and elsewhere to action against what they saw as abuses of the Crown, Attucks took up the cause. He wrote to Governor Thomas Hutchinson, "Your [sic] are chargeable before God and man, with our blood." Attucks argued that in any action taken against Americans, British troops were only doing the bidding of higher authority. The governor himself must be held directly responsible for colonists' suffering. For his crimes against "the people in general," Attucks warned Hutchinson, "You will hear further from us hereafter."[79]

Thus, on the afternoon of the fifth of March when a British soldier entered the pub where Attucks and other seamen were gathered and inquired about local employment, already-heated tempers exploded. One sailor offered his outhouse for cleaning, and the insults and anger that followed boiled over into the streets. That evening Attucks led a group of twenty or thirty "saucy boys, negroes and mulattoes, Irish teagues and outlandish jack-tarrs" who wielded clubs and taunted the guard at the Custom House on King Street. Attucks took the lead in harassing the sentries, poking one with a stick and calling him a "lobster," a pejorative allusion to the red coat of the British uniform. The scene grew more tense as Attucks vowed to declaw the lobster, "the multitude shouting and huzzaing, threatening life, the bell ringing, the mob whistling and screaming like an Indian yell, the people from all quarters throwing every species of rubbish they could pick up in the street." "The way to get rid of these soldiers is to attack the main-guard"; Attucks asserted, "strike at the root: this is the nest."[80]

The general tension erupted into violence in a simultaneous confrontation between soldiers and civilians in another part of the city. There a soldier stabbed a "young lad" with his bayonet. Meanwhile, the situation at the Custom House escalated rapidly, and the guard was reinforced. Snowballs thrown by the mob became chunks of ice, and finally a few, including Attucks, attacked some of the troops with clubs. Apparently, the crowd assumed that the troops would retreat rather than fire on them, and indeed the captain of the guard had to give the order to fire at least twice before it was obeyed. Finally, the command came again, "Damn you, fire, be the consequence what it will"; the soldiers answered with a musket volley. Three colonials were killed and two others wounded. Among the dead was Crispus Attucks, shot twice, the first to die in what was becoming a revolutionary cause.[81]

At the trial held to consider the circumstances of that eventful evening, John Adams and Josiah Quincy acted as defense attorneys for the British soldiers. Adams condemned mob violence and asserted that Attucks was a ringleader of the mob action. It was Attucks who had "undertaken to be the hero of the night," Adams said, expressing neither surprise nor particular indignation that an interracial group would have been led by a black sailor. The interracial nature of such groups was not considered unusual in 1770. Black and white Americans were moved by the same words of liberty, and most knew it.[82]

Funeral services held for the fallen Americans, "attracted together the greatest concourse which had then ever assembled upon any one occasion in America." The patriots were borne to the Park Street "burying ground" followed by a "vast multitude of people, walking, six deep, and a long train of carriages belonging to the principal gentry of the town." No racial distinctions were made in honoring the dead who were buried in the same cemetery. Even colonial elites came to view these mobs as one necessary element in the evolving revolution. During the generation preceding independence the British government became the target of such mob hostility, as Americans of different economic levels allied against the perceived injustices of Crown rule.[83]

The Boston Massacre confirmed in the minds of Americans the danger British authority posed to their liberty. Sam Adams declared a standing army "always dangerous to the liberties of the people." Others vowed not to endure slavery at the hands of tyrants. African, Indian, and mixed-race people heard the rhetoric of freedom and noted the colonial leaders' use of the metaphor of slavery to describe what must be resisted at all costs. They noted with great interest that Americans declared to the world that "all men [were] created equal." Crispus Attucks was a proponent of freedom in word and deed, inspired by and inspiring other patriots of his generation.[84]

The age of the Revolution created a new nation and awakened forces that eventually changed relationships between Americans. Over the next two generations, the old structure of social and political deference gradually gave way to the ideals of social and political equality. As class gradually diminished, the crucial determinants of participation, race, and gender gained new importance in defining the limits of American democracy. The interracial alliances of the eighteenth century became more difficult to maintain, and race became the most important divider of Americans, even among those at the bottom of society.[85]

3

Revolution and the Abolition of Northern Slavery

It was clear to African Americans that the liberty most white Americans spoke of was intended only for whites, yet they did not accept this limitation willingly. Instead they reminded the patriots that they too sought liberty. In 1773 and 1774 a committee of slaves, organized to secure freedom for slaves in Massachusetts, sent a number of petitions to Governor Hutchinson and the general court. In straightforward language and with a certain irony they asserted, "We expect great things from men who have made such a noble stand against the designs of their fellow men to enslave them." Referring to themselves as Africans, the petitioners asked that slaves be allowed one day a week to work for themselves in order to accumulate enough money to purchase their freedom. Once free, the petitioners anticipated that blacks would return to Africa to enjoy their independence.[1]

When colonial authorities refused to act on these suggestions, other petitions were sent. One in June 1773 was sent "in behalf of all those who by divine permission are held in a state of slavery within the bowels of a free country." A year later there was another communication sent to the new colonial governor Thomas Gage from those held as slaves in "a free and christian country." This petition dated May 25, 1774 declared the natural rights of freedom and the love of liberty to be held by blacks "in common with all other men." Again the court made no response and in June came another petition. This time blacks asked not only for freedom but also for land in some unimproved and unsettled part of the colony on which they might farm, establish a community, and enjoy "the fruits of [their] labor."[2]

Throughout the 1770s Massachusetts' blacks continued to press for abolition, calling first on the British colonial government and then on the government in rebellion. Shortly before Americans fought at Bunker Hill, slaves in Massachusetts petitioned the Committee of Correspondence "to assist them in obtaining their freedom."[3] These were determined men who would not be discouraged by a continually unresponsive authority. Their determination fed rumors of violent conspiracies in the colony. Abigail Adams wrote of the excitement such rumors caused among her New England neighbors and explained to her husband John that "I wish most sincerely there was not a slave in the province." She also expressed her concern at the contradiction posed by the existence of slavery among a people who held to the ideal of freedom. "It always seemed a most iniquitous scheme to me," she wrote, "to fight ourselves for what we are daily robbing and plundering from those who have as good a right to freedom as we have."[4]

There were influential whites who believed that blacks should be included in the community of rights to be established by revolution. As early as 1765 James Otis suggested that blacks were part of the American citizenry. "The colonists," he said, "black and white, born here, are free born British subjects, and entitled to all the essential civil rights of such." Otis went so far as to argue that slavery must be ended, since "all men . . . white or black" were "by the law of nature free born."[5] Two years later Nathaniel Appleton, another New Englander, pointed to the inconsistency of white Americans struggling to secure freedom while denying that right to other human beings. Such inconsistency was often to be found in the lives of individual Americans. In 1773 Philadelphia physician Benjamin Rush published a strong statement opposing slavery, yet just three years later he himself purchased a slave, William Grubber. In 1777 Rush argued that Africans were the moral and intellectual equal of whites. It was slavery that brought on the deprivation which had been taken for racial inferiority, he maintained. Although Rush joined the Pennsylvania Abolition Society in 1784, he continued to hold Grubber as his slave for another ten years.[6]

The Quakers of Pennsylvania and western New Jersey, men like Anthony Benezet, John Woolman, Joshua Evans, and John Hunt, were among the first white Americans to urge the abolition of slavery. Before 1730 some crusading Quakers criticized slavery as incompatible with their faith. In 1758 the Yearly Meeting of Friends condemned the importation, trading, buying, or holding of slaves by their members and took steps to remove slaveholders from leadership positions within the church. In 1759 Benezet published a number of antislavery and antislave-trade pamphlets.[7] Individual state Quaker meetings often financed the support of freed slaves who could not support themselves as one means of encouraging manumission among their fellows. Starting in 1773 in New England and spreading to other regions in the North, Quaker meetings began disowning members who refused to emancipate their slaves. The antislavery Quakers gradually convinced the others, and finally by the last decade of the century Friends were no longer slave masters.[8]

Quakers spearheaded the formal organization of the opposition to slavery. In April 1775 less than a week before the clashes with the British at Lexington and Concord, a small group of ten men met at the Rising Sun Tavern in Philadelphia to form the Society for the Relief of Free Negroes Unlawfully Held in Bondage. The group called together by Anthony Benezet included Thomas Paine, and seven of the ten were Quakers. Of the group of twenty-four who met during the year before the society disbanded, seventeen were Quakers. When it was reconstituted in 1784, the "Society for Promoting the Abolition of Slavery, the Relief of Free Negroes Unlawfully Held in Bondage and for Improving the Condition of the African Race" had greatly expanded its purpose. Following the lead of the Philadelphians, antislavery organizations were established throughout the North and in the upper South. These groups attracted other progressive white reformers and became the backbone of the abolitionist movement of the Revolutionary and early national periods.[9]

Women committed to evangelical religion in both England and America gave impetus to the spread of antislavery sentiment. One such woman was the countess of Huntingdon in England, a staunch supporter of the Wesleys and the Methodism they founded. From the 1730s the countess contributed to the training of evangelical ministers, supported mission efforts and other aid to Indians and blacks, and counted among her friends Britain's best-known reformers and antislavery advocates, including Granville Sharp.

In Newport, Rhode Island, Sarah Osborn was the embodiment of evangelical principles, serving the poor and attempting to bring religious enlightenment and learning to people of all stations and conditions. She began supporting herself by teaching after her first husband died and began her own school when her second husband's business failed. By the 1760s her boarding school had as many as seventy male and female students. She also began to hold evening religious meetings in her home in the mid-1760s, starting with a women's group, expanding as "poor servants and white lads" were invited, and finally including over five hundred men, women, and children a week (over six evenings) by 1767. For many years an average of seventy blacks met at Osborn's home on Sunday evenings.[10]

The religious community of free blacks and slaves that formed under the sponsorship and protection of Sarah Osborn included African-born men later involved in the movement to Christianize Africa, Bristol Yamma, John Quamine, and Newport Gardner, and an African-born young woman, Obour Tanner, who was a friend of the Boston slave poet, Phillis Wheatley. Finally in the early 1770s, as Osborn's health failed, her work of religious and secular education was taken up by others under her influence, including Newport minister Ezra Stiles and the Reverend Samuel Hopkins, appointed pastor of Osborn's First Congregational Church.[11]

The organizational work of evangelical men and women helped publicize the antislavery cause. Not only did free education aid blacks in presenting their case for freedom, but the commitments and social ties connecting evangelicals helped build an international antislavery network. Hopkins took up the antislavery crusade, answering the arguments of slaveholders on both moral and practical grounds in his speaking and writing. In 1776 Hopkins published a pamphlet echoing the assertions of the earlier slave petitions and making a comprehensive case against slavery that he circulated to the members of the Second Continental Congress. Congratulating the members on their wartime prohibition of the slave trade, he asked that they also address the injustice of slavery itself. He contended that reconciling the inconsistency inherent in the "holding of so many hundreds of thousands of blacks in slavery, who have an equal right to freedom with ourselves, while we are maintaining this struggle for our own and our children's liberty" required the "total abolition of slavery."[12]

It was largely through the efforts of the circles of evangelical women that slave poet Phillis Wheatley gained international recognition and came to symbolize the common humanity and environmentalist arguments against slavery. Her mistress in Boston, Susanna Wheatley, encouraged her literary efforts and promoted the publication of her poetry through her connection to the evangelical networks. Susanna Wheatley frequently hosted ministers and reformers such as George Whitefield, when they were sent to America by the countess of Huntingdon. Through these connections she and Phillis were able to arrange for the publication of Phillis Wheatley's poems in London in 1773 and for her London trip to promote them. The links between Sarah Osborn in Rhode Island, the countess of Huntingdon in England, and the Wheatleys in Massachusetts were important components in the promotion of an evangelical religion concerned with the problems of the poor and the oppressed and the advocacy of the antislavery cause.[13]

The irony of a slaveholding people engaged in an armed struggle waged in the name of individual freedom was clear to many in England. Granville Sharp, England's most famous antislavery advocate and Phillis Wheatley's tour guide for a day in London, believed that slavery in America "weakens the claim [of] natural Rights of our American Brethren to Liberty." Samuel Johnson, less tolerant of American demands for freedom than Sharp, asked the pointed question, "How is it that we hear the loudest yelps [for] liberty among the drivers of negroes?" Other English critics quipped, "If there be an object truly ridiculous in nature, it is an American patriot, signing resolutions of independency with the one hand, and with the other brandishing a whip over his frightened slaves."[14]

Newspapers were filled with debate over the contradiction between slavery and the quest for the colonists' freedom, and slave petitions continued to point to the inconsistencies. Some Americans took individual actions to resolve the contradiction for themselves. Before leaving to join the Continental army, one Connecticut slaveholder freed his slaves saying, "I will not fight for liberty and leave a slave at home." During the war the Reverend Samuel Hopkins urged that slavery be abolished at all costs. He saw no possibility for America to gain its independence so long as Americans held slaves, as God would surely punish those who would not end "a sin of crimson die, which is most particularly pointed out by the public calamities which have come upon us."[15]

When revolutionary mobs donned the uniform of the Continental army, blacks stood with whites as they had in the streets of the pre-Revolutionary cities of the North. On that crisp April day in 1775, when British troops under Major Pitcairn marched through Lexington to the common, they were among the seventy or so minutemen. With these ill-trained American soldiers stood Peter Salem, the slave of the Belknaps of Framingham, freed in order that he might serve in the Massachusetts militia, Pompy of Braintree, Prince of Brookline, Cato Wood of Arlington, and others. Prince Estabrook, a slave in Lexington, was listed among those wounded in this first battle of the Revolution.

In all, more than 5,000 blacks, slave and free, served the cause of American liberty. In the northern colonies there was some reason for them to believe that this fight might win their liberty too. As several American leaders took a stand against slavery, their hopes rose that the lofty pronouncements of the great Revolutionary struggle might hold promise for blacks as well as whites.[16]

Even though blacks had been in the revolutionary mobs which initially clashed with the British, and though they stood as minutemen in the earliest fighting, their presence in the Continental army troubled many Americans. White southerners were especially uneasy about arming black soldiers to fight for the freedom of slaveholders. North Carolinians warned that arming slaves would invite violence against masters. Throughout the South there were similar warnings, and rumors circulated that the British were encouraging slave uprisings. These fears discouraged the recruitment of black soldiers in the southern states.[17]

In the North, where the black presence was less intimidating to whites and where blacks with local militia had already engaged the British, there were fewer objections to black soldiers. Even there, though, because of the national character of the Continental army, there were pressures to prohibit black enlistment. As one patriot put it, "Many northern blacks are excellent soldiers but southern troops would not brook an equality with whites."[18]

In July of 1775 General Washington ordered that no blacks be enlisted, although those already in service were allowed to remain. Coming just a few weeks after the celebrated heroism of the patriots at the Battle of Bunker Hill near Boston, this order must have been both mystifying and maddening to African Americans and their friends. The list of Massachusetts blacks who fought at Bunker Hill included Peter Salem, Salem Poor, whose official commendation called him "a brave and gallant soldier,"

Titus Coburn, Alexander Ames, Barzilai Lew, and Cato Howe.[19] After some debate over whether the ban on black enlistment should apply to both free blacks and slaves, it was decided that it should include all blacks. Many in the South, however, could not tolerate those blacks already in American uniform, and Edward Rutledge of South Carolina introduced a plan in Congress to discharge all black soldiers. The plan failed and African Americans remained on duty, but the order stood not to enlist them.

As summer gave way to the winter, Continental forces faced growing shortages of men and a chilling proclamation issued on November 7, 1775 by Lord Dunmore, royal governor of Virginia. The proclamation that Dunmore termed "the most disagreeable, but now absolutely necessary step" declared freedom for all indentured servants and slaves who would take up arms in the British cause. Dunmore hoped that this strategy would both increase his forces and profoundly affect the rebel will to continue the struggle. "My declaration," he reported, "has stirred up fears in [the rebels of Virginia] which cannot easily subside." Significantly, Dunmore's offer was a war measure, not an antislavery gesture. It was directed only at the servants and slaves of rebels; the slaves of masters who remained loyal to Britain were to be returned.[20]

Slaves responded to the British offer of freedom, and thousands walked off the plantation to seek the protection of the Crown. Although it is impossible to be certain how many sought freedom by going to the British, estimates range as high as 100,000. In 1778 Thomas Jefferson recorded the number of Virginia slaves who had run away to the British at 30,000. Historians placed South Carolina's runaways at 25,000 or more between 1775 and 1783, while in Georgia over 12,000 of the state's 15,000 slaves set out for freedom.[21]

Even where the British offer of freedom had not been heard, slaves took advantage of the disruption of war to escape from bondage. Facing the heavy loss of their slave property some Virginia slaveholders even resorted to the newspapers in attempts to address their slaves. At once slaveholders claimed no part in the continuation of the slave trade, threatened death to fugitives, and urged slaves to concentrate on the afterlife for their freedom. Even if it had reached large numbers of bondspeople, it is unlikely that this argument would have convinced them.[22] Some slaveholders believed that slave "insolence" was encouraged by the prospect of freedom offered by the British. The offer of freedom to both indentured servants and slaves raised again the specter of interracial alliances and conspiracies among the lower classes. The "malicious and imprudent speeches of some among the lower class whites," many thought, "induced [the slaves] to believe that their freedom depended on the success of the King's troops."[23]

Throughout the era there was ample evidence of slave conspiracies to aid the British, sometimes linking blacks and whites in common action.

Early in the war Boston was unsettled by the revelation that an Irishman had written to British officials on behalf of several slaves offering their military service to the Crown. Plans of attack by slaves alone or in concert with loyalist whites were uncovered in Elizabeth and Perth Amboy, New Jersey, Bucks County, Pennsylvania, Albany, New York, and scores of other communities.[24] One group of loyalists fought in New Jersey as an interracial band led by Tye, "a Negro who [bore] the title of colonel." The unit conducted frequent raids on the fortifications and large plantations of the area, sometimes freeing slaves and indentured servants. These guerrilla bands, called banditti, burned and looted plantations, stole horses, and attacked Continental forces in many regions. In South Carolina where the sheer size of the black population made any action against slavery potentially catastrophic, fugitive slaves, indentured servants, Cherokees, poor farmers, and "backcountry tories" joined banditti bands. Working with British forces and independently, these groups were commanded by men like "Captain" Jones, "Colored Power man," or the mulatto William Hunt who led an interracial band. Newspapers reported that "infamous banditti and horsethieves [including] a corps of Indians, with negro and white savages disguised like them" raided settlements and "stole" slaves throughout the region. For more than half a century after the Revolution, bands of black guerrillas calling themselves the King of England Soldiers continued to harass southern plantations, freeing slaves when possible.[25]

African Americans had good reason to associate British jurisdiction with freedom. With many blacks employed in seafaring and related occupations, they had an efficient transatlantic network of information. They were well aware of the celebrated case of *Somerset v. Stewart* in England. In 1769 a British customs officer named Charles Stewart had returned to England from the American colonies with his slave James Somerset. After living in England for two years, Somerset ran away from his master. When he was recaptured Stewart made arrangements to have him shipped to Jamaica to be sold. Abolitionist Granville Sharp instigated a court case that resulted in a 1772 ruling by William Murray, Lord Chief Justice Mansfield, that no slave could be forcibly taken from England. This carefully narrow decision was widely interpreted by people in England and America as implying that slavery was incompatible with the liberties guaranteed by English common law.[26]

The ruling in *Somerset v. Stewart* freed James Somerset and intimated freedom to any other slave brought to England. American newspapers carried erroneous reports that Mansfield's decision had freed all the slaves in England. Some slaves heard the news and attempted to make their way to England. Advertisements for runaways gave information about the slaves' motivation: it was anticipated that one Virginia slave would "board a vessel for Great Britain . . . from the knowledge he has of the late Determination of the Somerset Case." Another said a runaway couple was heading for Britain "where they imagine they will be free (a Notion now too prevalent among the Negroes . . .)." Interest in the case was rekindled in the colonies when a pamphlet containing the arguments was reprinted in Boston in 1774.[27]

This first important legal attack on slavery in British law gave added credibility to Dunmore's offer of freedom in 1775. By the end of the year three hundred blacks served in Lord Dunmore's "Ethiopian Regiment." At least eight hundred blacks wore the regimental uniform with its distinctive and expressive motto stitched on the shoulder, "Liberty to Slaves." The attraction to the British ranks for these blacks could hardly be mistaken. More than half of Dunmore's troops were black. They saw action in Virginia where they operated from the British fleet offshore, and hundreds died from battle wounds, typhus, and smallpox. By the late 1770s they moved to New York where they were divided between other British units. Many British commanders were reluctant to use black troops in combat roles, seeing them as fit only for the hard labor required in building fortifications or for jobs as cooks and servants. Dunmore argued strongly that blacks were good soldiers and the "most efficacious, expeditious, cheapest, and certain means of reducing the Country to a proper sense of their Duty." Dunmore espoused the popular belief that black men fought better than white men in warm weather and argued that in the warmer seasons blacks were far preferable to the Russian troops employed by the Crown.[28]

They also had psychological value—a victory by black troops would be both humiliating and infuriating to the Americans. "By employing them you cannot desire a means more effectual to distress your Foes," Dunmore assured his superiors. He also suggested that blacks receive a small payment as well as freedom in return for their service. Although the British treatment of black troops was not egalitarian, there were acts that demonstrated the respect that many English soldiers developed for their black fellow combatants. One American prisoner was shocked to see his British captors shaking hands with black soldiers and paying them personal tributes. For many Americans, such behavior confirmed their belief that England intended to instigate "race war" to subdue the colonies.[29] Dunmore's actions and suggestions were not universally approved in England. One London group, mainly merchants, sent a petition to the king expressing their displeasure at being associated with any attempt to promote any uprising of slaves against their "American brethren." Furthermore they made it clear they feared his actions might "encourage the most barbarous of mankind, to the most horrible crimes." Even to maintain control of the colonies many elite Englishmen could not condone encouraging black violence against the planter aristocracy.[30]

All and all more than one thousand blacks served the British cause, and many times that number sought refuge in the British lines. By the fall of 1783 when the British troops withdrew from the colonies, they took more than 14,000 blacks with them. Almost 4,000 blacks were evacuated from New York before November 25, when the British surrendered their last post to American forces. Many of those who had not served in the British armed forces remained slaves. For them, Jamaica or some other British West Indian colony replaced North America as the site of their bondage. Those who were granted freedom were given some choices. Phyllis Thomas "a free black woman" was granted passage to the West Indies or "elsewhere at her option." This opportunity was afforded other blacks freed by the Revolution, and in this way American slaves found their way to different parts of the world. By the 1790s some of these blacks were among the early settlers of the British West African colony of Sierra Leone. Others took up residence in parts of Europe, Latin America, Nova Scotia, or the British Isles.[31]

Many former slaves found success in England they would have been unlikely to achieve in America. One of these was Bill Richmond, the slave of the duke of Northumberland on Staten Island. When the duke was evacuated from New York his slave embarked with him for London. Once in England Richmond was sent to school and eventually became an accomplished boxer. By the turn of the nineteenth century, the "Black Terror," as Richmond was called, was middle-aged but still regularly defeating opponents. Finally in 1805 he lost to Tom Cribb, the bare-knuckle champion, in a hard-fought and brutal ninety-minute contest in Sussex. Upon his retirement from the ring, Richmond opened the successful Horse and Dolphin Inn. He also established a boxing academy at the Royal Tennis Court, where British notables like poet Lord Byron were regular patrons.[32]

Several hundred blacks settled in Canada, many in the colony of Birchtown or in Shelburne, both near Port Roseway in Nova Scotia. They made up as much as 10 percent of the new settlers in the Halifax area in the early 1780s. From September through November of 1783, almost all of the passengers on several ships sailing to Nova Scotia were black soldiers, slaves and indentured servants. Former slave Charles Dixon, his wife Dolly, and their five children were among those who left New York to be resettled in Port Roseway. The voyage in frigid weather took longer than a week. Life was hard in Canada and many did not fare well, but Charles was able to find work as a carpenter with the British army engineers and they survived.[33] In 1784 whites rioted in Birchtown, protesting black competition that they said devalued white labor. Many black homes were burned, and their occupants were driven from the town. Although there were some efforts to provide land for farming in Canada, most blacks could only find work as servants. One report in 1790 graphically described the living conditions of about one hundred black families in New Brunswick as "unimproved and destitute." In Canada, too, racial intolerance often grew as the black population increased and blacks seemed to pose a greater threat. Despite occasional hostilities, scattered settlements of blacks in eastern Canada remained. Many of the descendants of these black settlers found their way back to the United States during the nineteenth century.[34]

The British solicitation of black troops forced American leaders to reconsider their initial position. This reconsideration was also prompted by the disappointing response of white Americans to the patriotic call to the Continental army. These civilian soldiers were generally only willing to serve for a short enlistment, usually ninety days, in their home regions. Throughout the war the parochialism of many white Americans proved to be a major obstacle to raising and maintaining a reliable army. Congressional calls for troops could only be requests to the semiautonomous states which seemed unwilling to draft many of their citizens. Recruitment problems were exacerbated by the economic impact of the war. For many Americans patriotic service had to be weighed against the need to support a family during extremely difficult economic times.

The war was economically devastating for New England fishermen and for Atlantic port traders dependent on the British who monopolized American exports and imports during most of the colonial period. Northern farmers could still sell their foodstuff to the West, but farms required labor and constant attention. Farm production was also hampered by the scarcity of farm equipment formerly supplied by England. Urban workers experienced even more serious economic problems. British troops' occupation of the major seaport centers disrupted commercial activity, affecting business for the large merchants and creating great unemployment for common laborers. Shortages of food and other supplies produced dramatic inflation. Flour in Philadelphia, for example, rose to 113 percent above its prewar price, and the value of Continental currency declined until it was practically worthless by 1779. The population of urban areas declined during the war years because many working people could not afford to remain in the cities. New York City had lost about half its 1774 population by 1783, when the war ended. Some of these people joined the Continental army, but many more moved to rural areas to eke out a subsistence from the soil.[35]

Under these circumstances it was not easy for Congress to raise troops. Thus, the necessities of the war encouraged northern states to enlist blacks to fill out their troop quotas for the Continental army. In 1778 several New England states reversed earlier positions and allowed slaves to enlist. As early as 1776, New York permitted masters drafted into the state militia to substitute slaves in their place. Other states established similar rules. Connecticut provided that "any two men who provided an able bodied man to serve for three years or for the duration of the war were exempt from actual service." In 1777 Nathan Dibble and his son Eli both of Connecticut sent slave Jack Anthony to serve in their place. Anthony served until the end of the war at which time he was granted his freedom.[36]

London Hazard, the slave of Godfrey Hazard of South Kingston, Rhode Island, proved extremely useful to his master and his family. When Godfrey Hazard was drafted by the Rhode Island militia, London initially served one year as a private in his master's stead. He was stationed in Boston during this term, but before the war was over he served in many places, replacing several of his master's relatives who found the call of the military too difficult or inconvenient to answer personally. London was not paid for his service, although he did receive his freedom at the end of the war.[37] Likewise, slave William Wanton from Tiverton, Rhode Island who enlisted in 1777 served in the Rhode Island line for a number of whites in his town. He also received his freedom in return for military service. Surely, having a slave serve in the place of his master in the war for freedom carried an inescapable irony.[38]

Another irony of the war was that many of the slaves who fought for America's freedom were Africans who had lost their own freedom by being shipped to slavery in America. The French and Indian (or Seven Years') War fought in America and Europe had greatly affected the slave trade. From its beginning in the mid-1750s, the war interrupted the flow of white indentured servants from Europe and made shipments of slaves from the West Indies more difficult. More Africans were brought to the North American colonies to fill the need for labor, and many more were brought directly from West Africa. Henry Tabor, an African slave in his early thirties when the war began, belonged to a judge in Newport, Rhode Island. He was freed in exchange for fighting. Dan Mallory, another Revolutionary War soldier, was brought to Connecticut from Africa in 1755 when he was five years old. Caesar Shelton, known as Cezar Negro when he was Shelton's slave in Connecticut, had been born at sea while his mother was on her way from Africa. He gained his freedom by taking the place of his master's son in the war.[39]

One African's story seems especially fantastic. A slave called Prince had been born to a well-to-do African family. When he was about ten years old his parents decided to send him and his cousin to America to be educated. His older brother had returned to Africa with an American education about four years before. When their ship docked in Baltimore, the unscrupulous captain sold the two boys into slavery. They were bought by men from Portsmouth, New Hampshire, with Prince going to a man named Whipple. In the Revolution Prince served as bodyguard to his master General Whipple and then as an aide to General Washington. (In which capacity he is pictured in the familiar paintings of Washington crossing the Delaware.) Prince Whipple regained his freedom by being emancipated during the war. After the war, he settled in Portsmouth, married, had children, and died at the relatively early age of thirty-two years.[40]

Even southern colonies with large slaveholdings found it necessary to enroll black soldiers. During the early years of the war Virginia enlisted only free mulattoes in limited service positions but by 1780 also drafted blacks into military service. Only South Carolina and Georgia held out. In March 1779 the national government officially approved the use of black soldiers and suggested to South Carolina and Georgia that this could be a partial solution to manpower shortages. Alexander Hamilton argued that slaves would make good soldiers because they were accustomed to discipline. While he believed that their service required the reward of emancipation, he predicted that such an incentive would produce brave and effective fighters. Jefferson attacked Hamilton's proposal, asserting that blacks lacked the intelligence required of good fighting men. Jefferson believed that black troops appeared brave in battle only because they lacked the judgment with which to gauge the danger of a given situation and so acted out of ignorance not valor.[41]

Hamilton disputed claims of black intellectual inferiority arguing, "Their natural faculties are as good as ours. . . . The contempt we have been taught to entertain for blacks, makes us fancy many things that are founded neither in reason nor in experience." There were southerners who did want to enlist black troops. Washington favored it for military reasons, and Lieutenant Colonel John Laurens of South Carolina, armed with Hamilton's recommendation, argued for the plan in his home state. Blacks would serve in separate units commanded by white officers but receive no pay. Those who served well would be granted freedom and fifty dollars at the end of the war. Former masters would be compensated by the national government, receiving one thousand dollars for each able-bodied male under thirty years of age.[42] This plan was short-lived, disapproved by the South Carolina legislature in the fall of 1781. Laurens explained in a letter to Hamilton, "I was out-voted, having only reason on my side, and being opposed by a triple-headed monster, that shed the baneful influence of avarice, prejudice and pusillanimity, in all our assemblies." In Georgia too it was quickly dispensed with. "We shall be out-voted there," Washington wrote, "as we have been in this country [South Carolina]."[43]

Although he condemned his fellow southerners' lack of the "spirit of freedom," Washington was not surprised by their adamant opposition to enlisting black soldiers. Southern colonists with large, growing, and concentrated slave populations lived under the constant fear of slave uprisings. Arming blacks, even under the supervision of white officers, was almost unthinkable. In the North, on the other hand, Congress's suggestion encouraged the continuation of black recruitment. Slaves and free blacks served in integrated units in every state outside the lower South. They were more likely to serve in the Continental line than with limited service militia units, and thus were more likely to serve long enlistments of three years or more. White soldiers in the militia often served as few as three months. This high turnover in troops was in fact a major problem for the Americans. Although almost 400,000 men enlisted, there were only 35,000 on active duty at any one time. One historian speculated that "had even half of the enlisted men been available regularly, the Americans should easily have overwhelmed the British." Apparently the British never had more than 42,000 troops in America.[44]

The Continental forces in which most blacks served were involved in nearly all the major fighting. The service of African Americans was one answer to the need for long-term and geographically wide-ranging military participation. They shouldered both a disproportionate share of the wealth-producing labor for the new nation and a disproportionate burden for the acquisition of its freedom. Many black women served too—they accompanied their men to war and served the army as cooks and nurses. This however did not ensure African Americans' participation in the liberty their service helped secure. Black troops serving with white troops often troubled white officers, just as the interracial character of pre-Revolutionary mobs had worried colonial elites. One captain at Ticonderoga wrote to his wife of his displeasure at having blacks, old men, and boys under his command. Such a "nasty lousy appearance," he said, was "sufficient to make one sick of the service." A general in charge of a Massachusetts regiment declared that even though the black troops were generally physically fit and the army needed every able-bodied man, he was uncomfortable to see black and white troops mixed together.[45]

Even when blacks and whites served in the same military units, duty assignments sometimes separated them. Proportionately more blacks were placed in jobs that did not require them to carry arms. They were often used as laborers, servants, cooks, wagon drivers, or drummers. Barzilai Lew who was at the battle of Bunker Hill was a fifer, Primus Hall constructed fortifications near Riverton, Rhode Island, and Titus Coburn who was also at Bunker Hill later drove the quartermaster's wagon at West Point, New York. This placement of blacks provided for the performance of essential services while effectively distinguishing between black and white soldiers. Obed Coffin believed that blacks were assigned to certain jobs because whites did not want to allow blacks and whites to associate as equals, and so that the government might skimp on black pension allotments after the war. If there was a conscious attempt to separate blacks into noncombatant positions, it was not generally effective. James Cooper was a cook with the Virginia line at West Point, but he became a combat soldier when his unit confronted the British. As the necessities of war had forced the recruitment of blacks, the realities of battle determined their assignments.[46]

The First Rhode Island Battalion commanded by Colonel Christopher Greene was one of the combat units with a large black contingent. Greene was previously a Quaker, but broke his vow of pacifism to take part in the Revolution. He made his reputation in 1777 when he commanded a black unit in the valiant but unsuccessful defense of Fort Mercer. Congress, impressed with Greene's record, offered him the command of the Rhode Island unit in the summer of 1778. Greene found the First Rhode Island made up mostly of former slaves who had been promised emancipation in exchange for service. William Eustis, an army surgeon during the Revolution, described the unit: "In Rhode Island, where [blacks'] numbers were more considerable, they were formed, . . . into a regiment commanded by white officers." " . . . it is required, in justice to them," Eustis continued, "to add that they discharged their duties with zeal and fidelity." Eustis commended the unit for its brave defense of Red Bank, New Jersey and noted the devotion of the men to their officers. When Greene was wounded by the British, his troops reportedly formed a human wall around their fallen commander defending him from further attack.[47]

More than two hundred blacks served in the Rhode Island line. Many of these soldiers had been slaves on the large plantations of South Kingston. Men like Mingo Rodman served until the closing weeks of the war, and Rodman secured not only his freedom but also a small plot of land in payment of his service. African-born Richard Rhodes also served in the Rhode Island unit. Enslaved and brought to the colonies as a child, Richard was sold to the Nehemiah Rhodes family, one of the most prominent in the Rhode Island colony. When the war broke out Rhodes was offered freedom in exchange for his agreement to enlist in the local regiment, an offer which he eagerly accepted. He served five years from 1778 through the spring of 1783, taking part in the battles of Monmouth and Yorktown. When the war ended twenty-three-year-old Richard Rhodes became a mariner. One of the prices he paid for his independence was a severe wound to his arm that significantly limited his ability to support himself and his family. Still, he believed the cost worth his gain.[48]

Thousands of black men made such sacrifices at places like Saratoga, Ticonderoga, and Stony Point so that America might be "born free." Primus Coburn gave the better part of a leg at West Point and on discharge was awarded the "V" badge of honor. Prince Hazeltine received two badges of merit for his heroism at Worcester where he rescued several of his fellows from an explosion and fire that cost many lives. He was so badly injured in the process that for the rest of his life he was unable to work regularly. Years later several of those who served with Hazeltine in the Second Massachusetts Regiment testified to his bravery. Like other black soldiers Hazeltine's term of duty was longer than most whites'. In all he served for six years and was not discharged until the end of the war.[49] Black soldiers endured the snow and freezing temperatures alongside the white troops at Valley Forge. Cato Cuff was frostbitten so badly that he could never work outdoors in cold weather again. At the Battle of Champlain Samuel Coombs, though wounded himself, tended the wounds of other injured men. Prince Whipple and Oliver Cromwell were among those who manned the oars of the boat carrying George Washington across the Delaware River to the battle at Yorktown, and blacks like African-born Prince Bent of the Rhode Island regiment were serving with Washington when Cornwallis surrendered.[50]

Black soldiers suffered from the same economic problems as white soldiers during the war, but since blacks generally served longer and at a greater distance from home, their problems were magnified. Windsor (or Winsor) Fry enlisted in the Rhode Island regiment, served until the end of the war, and during that period was absent from his unit only once.

Between March and November 1780, Fry took an unauthorized leave to see to the economic needs of his family who were apparently in great distress.[51] Often commanders realized the special problems of their black soldiers and granted them furloughs when possible. Joseph Green, a mulatto private in the Massachusetts Second Regiment, asked for and received leave in January of 1782 for a happier reason—he returned home to get married. Immediately after the wedding Green with his bride, Sarah, rejoined the regiment where the new Mrs. Green served as a nurse. Sarah apparently remained with the unit until her husband's discharge at the end of the war.[52]

A few black recruits were lucky enough to be stationed near home. Thomas Hall served the first year of his enlistment in Philadelphia, only ten miles from Upper Darby where he had worked as a miller's apprentice before the war. When Hall did leave the city it was as a sailor aboard a "public armed vessel," *The Rising Sun*.[53] Some African Americans came from as far away as Santo Domingo as part of the French aid provided to America's revolution. Five hundred forty-five black Frenchmen came to serve at the battle of Savannah. Among them was young Henri Christophe who later fought against France for Haitian independence and eventually became king of Haiti. Some American blacks served with French forces for short periods of time. Primus Hall was one of those detached from his unit to join a corps of French "sappers."[54] One black unit from Boston who called themselves the "Bucks of America" was commanded by George Middleton. Although little historical record remains of their wartime exploits, they were later recognized with the award of a ceremonial banner by John Hancock, then governor of Massachusetts. Years after the war Middleton lived in Boston, a proud and respected member of the black community and one of the few blacks paid public respect by Boston whites.[55]

There was little resistance to black enlistment in the American navy because the tradition of blacks' being seamen was already firmly established by the mid-eighteenth century. In port towns like New Bedford, Boston, New London, Philadelphia, and New York black seamen were common sights. The manpower shortage on most American merchant and war vessels prompted the navy to depend on free blacks and slaves. These African Americans performed a wide variety of jobs, from cabin boys and cooks to skilled pilots and gunners. The South was more tolerant of blacks as sailors than as soldiers. The traditional role of blacks in the tightly controlled all-male world at sea was a major factor. Virginia and Maryland commonly used blacks to assist in navigating the region's bays and rivers because of their extensive knowledge of those waterways. Even in the lower South state of South Carolina blacks served in the navy during the war, as they had before it began.

James Forten of Philadelphia was one of the free blacks who enlisted in the navy during the war. Forten came from a family long established in

America. The family remembered that James' great-grandfather had been brought from Africa to the Delaware Valley as a slave before William Penn and his Quakers settled the area, probably by the Dutch. His grandfather had been able to purchase his own freedom. Thus, James had been born into a free black family, the son of sailmaker Thomas Forten, in 1766.[56] His father died when James was only seven years old. He continued attending the school for blacks taught by Quaker Anthony Benezet for a few more years before quitting to help support the family by working in a grocery store. James Forten joined the navy when he was fourteen and was assigned to the *Royal Louis* under the command of Stephen Decatur. On board ship, he was a powderboy and companion to the son of Captain Beasly. After one successful encounter with the British and a month at sea, the American ship was captured and the crew taken as prisoners of war. Although he was free, Forten was afraid of being sold into slavery in the West Indies—a realistic fear for a black captive. Captain Beasly recognized the danger that his son's friend was in and sent him to the prison ship *Old Jersey* with a letter urging that he be exchanged for a British prisoner of war. After seven months on the prison ship, Forten was returned to his family in Philadelphia.[57]

Free blacks who sailed under the American flag during the Revolution faced hazards not faced by their white shipmates. If their ship was captured by the British, they were treated as slaves unless they could produce "freedom papers" verifying their free status. Additionally, the British often retained possession of freedom papers as a captured document, leaving any free black who managed to escape or to be released without freedom papers vulnerable to enslavement by the French, British, or Americans. Several free blacks lost their freedom in just this way to British authorities in Jamaica who sent them to the sugar plantations.[58] While some blacks were fighting in the war in return for their freedom, others continued political and legal attacks against their enslavement. In 1779 New Hampshire blacks petitioned the court saying that they had been deprived of freedom illegally and were being held in bondage in violation of their birthright. In Massachusetts John and Paul Cuffe, two free blacks from Westport, protested their inability to vote by refusing to pay their land taxes between 1778 and 1780. After three years of controversy the brothers were jailed and forced to pay, but not before they had the opportunity to give orations on freedom in the court and in local town meetings. In 1780 the Cuffes were joined by six other blacks in a petition to the Massachusetts government requesting relief from land taxes so long as they were not allowed to vote. The petitioners made the revolutionary contention that they should not be subjected to taxation without representation.[59]

The petitioners were successful, and the 1780 Massachusetts state constitution limited voting only by sex, age, and property holding, removing restrictions against black and Indian men. Although black voting rights continued to be debated in Massachusetts well into the nineteenth century, blacks met fewer legal restrictions in the Bay State than elsewhere. The removal of voting restrictions in 1780, however, did not change the institution of slavery. During the Revolution only Vermont explicitly recognized the contradiction slavery posed in a free state and outlawed the institution. Its constitution of 1777 took the first stand, proclaiming:

> All men are born equally free and independent. . . . Therefore, no male person born in this country or brought from over the sea, ought to be holden by law to serve any person as a servant, slave or apprentice after he arrives to the age of twenty-one years, nor female in like manner after she arrives to the age of eighteen years, unless they are bound by their own consent after they arrive to such age, or bound by law for the payment of debts, damages, fines, costs or the like.[60]

State constitutions commonly incorporated the language of the Revolution. The inclusion of the words "all men are created free and equal" in the Massachusetts state constitution provided the basis for a court case attacking slavery. In 1781 Quok Walker, the slave of Nathaniel Jennison, sued Jennison on the grounds that Jennison had failed to make good on his promise of freedom to Walker. There had been other cases in the 1760s and 1770s in which slaves had successfully sued their masters on the bases of a contract established between master and slave. In 1694, for example, John Saffin had won his freedom in this way. Walker's counsel went farther, however, and argued that the words of the constitution established a kind of contract between the state and all of its inhabitants. "Can we expect to triumph over G. Britain," he asked, "to get free ourselves until we let those go free under us?" Chief Justice William Cushing sounded the death knell for slavery in the Bay State when he concluded that, "the idea of slavery is inconsistent with our own conduct and Constitution." Finally in 1783 the state supreme court recognized this inconsistency and outlawed slavery in Massachusetts.[61]

By the end of the war some masters had carried the principles of freedom into their personal lives and either freed their slaves or made provisions for their freedom in their wills. Most of the more than five thousand blacks who fought as patriots were freed after the Revolution. Many more, at least twenty thousand, found freedom by fighting for the British or fleeing to the British during the war. Some who remained with the patriots were freed through private agreements with their masters, many fighting in the place of the master or his son. Others were freed by law, as in New York where freedom was granted to any who served three years or until regularly discharged. In Rhode Island the commander of the black regiment required on principle that soldiers under his command be freed before being allowed to serve. Some served the Revolution but were not freed. Samuel Charlton, the slave of a New Jersey man named McDougal, enlisted in his master's place when he was in his mid-teens. As a reward McDougal gave him a silver dollar. After serving his enlistment as a teamster with the army, Charlton was returned to slavery. He received his freedom only when McDougal died, freeing all of his slaves in his will.[62]

Black and white abolitionists' intensified offensive against slavery resulted in the gradual advance of freedom state by state across the North. The actions of Vermont and Massachusetts brought immediate freedom to their slaves, but in New Hampshire the situation was unclear. In 1779 nineteen slaves, including Nero Brewster, Pharaoh Rogers, Seneca Hall, Cato Newmarch, and Caesar Gerrish, petitioned the legislature for freedom on the grounds "that the God of nature gave them life and freedom, upon the terms of most perfect equality with other men; That freedom is an inherent right of the human species." The legislature postponed action on the petition until "a more convenient opportunity," which never arrived.[63] Some claimed that slavery was outlawed by the New Hampshire Declaration of Rights in 1788 and was acknowledged by a change in the state tax law in 1789 that no longer included slaves as property to be taxed. Blacks continued to be held in bondage in New Hampshire—one hundred fifty in 1790, eight in 1800, and a few well into the nineteenth century. It was not until 1857 that slavery was explicitly prohibited and blacks provided with full rights as citizens of that state.[64]

Rhode Island moved to protect slave rights and preserve slave families during the Revolution with a measure in 1779 that prohibited the sale of Rhode Island slaves beyond state boundaries without the consent of the slave—an attempt to prevent masters from selling their slaves south in anticipation of state abolition. Led by Quaker activists like Moses Brown antislavery forces successfully pressed the passage of a law that freed slaves born after March 1, 1784 but required them to work for their former masters until adulthood. Powerful slaveholders gained a concession requiring local governments to assume the costs of the former slaves' education and support, but strong public objections forced the removal of this provision.[65]

Concerns about the necessity for providing public support for freed slaves led to restrictions on the movement of free blacks and on manumissions in many colonies. In 1722 the colonial assembly in Pennsylvania had discouraged masters from freeing elderly slaves in order to escape responsibility for their care, and in 1726 they required the master to post a bond against the possibility of a freed person's becoming destitute.[66]

The Connecticut assembly passed a series of acts between 1702 and 1777 attempting to assure that a freed slave would not become a public charge. After often unsuccessful efforts to require the master to care for a needy former slave, the law finally required selectmen to investigate proposed emancipations and empowered them to exempt former masters from any obligation if they determined the slaves to be well behaved and capable of self-support.[67] In January 1784 Connecticut passed gradual emancipation legislation very similar to that in Rhode Island, manumitting slaves born after March 1 of that year and requiring them to serve as indentured servants until they reached the age of twenty-five. Thus, within a few years of the Revolution, all New England states took steps to free their slaves. By the first decade of the nineteenth century, only a few hundred blacks remained in bondage, and the number was decreasing steadily.

Abolition was a more difficult process in the Middle Atlantic states, geographically closer to the South and with larger slave populations. Quakers were extremely influential in Pennsylvania, and they moved state officials to overcome proslavery interests. Intense antislavery pressure in Pennsylvania was largely responsible for the early action that made Pennsylvania the first state to pass a law providing for the gradual emancipation of slaves. The 1780 law freed all blacks born thereafter when they became twenty-eight years old. Some slaves gained immediate emancipation when their masters failed to register them as this law required. Others gained freedom as a result of being "born free behind British lines" in the occupations of Philadelphia in 1777 and 1783.[68]

Emancipation was delayed in New York and New Jersey, mainly because slavery was more important economically and slaveholding was more widespread in these states than in the rest of the North. Newspapers in both states carried heated debates between abolitionists and slavery's supporters over the question of the universal application of Revolutionary principles. The *New Jersey Gazette*, which supported the abolitionist cause in Pennsylvania, carried both antislavery and more moderate articles and letters on the question. The conservative voices of proslavery spoke from the pages of the *New Jersey Journal*. The debate centered on the question of the legitimacy of holding human beings as property and whether or not blacks desired or could benefit from freedom.[69]

The debate was just as contentious in New York. Quakers spearheaded the antislavery forces, but their efforts proved insufficient until they were joined by others concerned about the contradiction between American principle and practice in 1785. The result was the establishment of the New York Manumission Society, or "Society for Promoting the Manumission of Slaves and Protecting such of them as have been or may be liberated," whose membership included Alexander Hamilton, John Jay, and several other of the state's most influential Federalist politicians. The society dedicated itself to lobbying Congress and the state legislature for action opposing slavery and the slave trade and providing relief and education for free blacks. Senator Ephraim Paine introduced a plan for gradual abolition in the state legislature, while lawyer (and later vice president) Aaron Burr proposed a more radical plan for the immediate emancipation of all slaves. Neither was successful, as proslavery forces held out against the growing opposition by charging that abolition would be dangerous, economically catastrophic, and was being advocated by those not loyal to the new nation. On this last point the accusing finger was pointed at the pacifist Quakers who had refused to bear arms during the Revolution.[70]

Abolitionists did not win out in New York until the end of the eighteenth century, four years after John Jay, the Manumission Society's president, was elected governor. Even then they had to settle for a plan of gradual emancipation starting only in 1799. Thousands of blacks remained in bondage in New York well into the nineteenth century. Although there had been many more, as late as 1820 there were over five hundred slaves in New York City and one hundred ninety slaves in Brooklyn. New York State did not release its last slaves until 1827; even so it was more progressive on this issue than its sister state. New Jersey was the last northern state to abolish slavery, under a gradual plan adopted in 1804. Its last few slaves were not freed before the 13th Amendment to the United States Constitution in 1865 made all slavery unconstitutional. Although the abolition of slavery was a gradual process in the North, the post-Revolutionary period was the time of transition from slavery to freedom for the vast majority of northern blacks.[71]

After the Revolution slavery became increasingly isolated to the South. There was some tolerance of the manumission of individual slaves in the upper southern states of Virginia and Maryland. There antislavery groups were able to force a relaxation of the prohibitions on voluntary manumissions. Such concessions, however, marked the limit of what could be achieved in this region where tobacco crops depended on slave labor to be turned to profit. In the lower South, where slavery was so important economically and the black population was so large, slavery remained secure. There it was clear that independence from Great Britain for white Americans would not translate into liberation for the slaves. Historian Gary Nash observed that the laws for gradual abolition in the North notwithstanding, "most slaves got their release from bondage only by dying or running away, and their children were promised freedom only after long periods of indentured servitude."[72]

The American war for liberty was not intended to bring freedom to the millions of slaves who suffered under America's most important and profitable economic institution. Nor were Revolutionary leaders comfortable with black participation in the struggle. Only the necessities of the conflict persuaded the military to employ black troops, and only in those regions with small slave populations did masters risk arming slaves. Yet for many slaves and free blacks the rhetoric of independence bespoke the possibilities of black liberation from bondage and of black participation in America's great experiment.

The nature of slavery in the North tended to involve slaves more intimately in the life of the family and community of the slave masters. The developing culture of African Americans there was consequently more deeply and uniformly influenced by the dominant European-American culture. Northern slaves used their facility with the English language, their greater mobility, their familiarity with the legal system, and their understanding of the American self-image as effective weapons against bondage.

Revolutionary America committed itself to the lofty goals of human liberty and set itself up as the "Zion on a hill," bringing hope and illumination to humankind. Proclaiming these values before a skeptical world, America became vulnerable to the actions and protests of the slaves who tested the new country's commitment to its creed. The strident voice of black protest constantly urged and challenged the nation to fulfill the spirit of the Revolution. By the end of the war northern leaders and even the leaders of the upper South seemed willing to support some measure for the abolition of slavery in the new nation.

Historian J. R. Pole has contended, that "equality is normally the language of the underdog." Once freed of British rule it remained for America to determine the meaning of the liberty and equality the country had won. The initial encounters with British authority had been undertaken by lower class interracial mobs. Middle-class women had organized tangible support for the war, and lower-class women had served the armies directly as servants, cooks, and nurses. Slaves, indentured servants, free men and women had joined the Revolution. Yet after the Revolutionary era slavery remained entrenched in southern society, and property ownership, sex, and race provided barriers to participation in American citizenship.[73]

Historian Gary Nash has argued that the 1770s and 1780s was "the opportune time for abolishing slavery" in the United States, in that the sentiment against slavery was strong, the lower South was not powerful enough to break away from the nation on principle, the doctrine of black innate inferiority had not yet gained ascendancy, and the West provided land for either compensated emancipation or the colonization of free blacks. Some individuals in both the North and the South did follow their consciences prodded by Revolutionary principles and freed their slaves. Many slaves were freed by the gradual emancipation laws in the North, and in a relatively short time (relative to the existence of the institution of slavery) slavery was abolished in the free states. Yet economic fears and an eagerness for political compromise preserved slavery in part of the Union.[74]

The era of the Revolution established freedom as America's guiding principle. Yet, when it came to applying that principle to the people of the new nation there was equivocation. As historian David Grimsted concluded:

> When the war was over, most politicians, especially those with national ambitions, again chose silence. Washington could say nothing without forfeiting his position as focus of national unity, though he probably would have said nothing anyway. Jefferson stated that slavery was indefensible and became in fact its leading defender. John Adams and his son John Quincy Adams came

to the presidency in part because they never took a public position on slavery. James Madison's position was very close to Jefferson's, with the major exception of rejecting his friend's racist theorizing.[75]

The final irony of America's war for independence was that in sharpening the contradiction between slavery and freedom, the slaves' case for liberty was strengthened, but where slavery remained entrenched, stronger barricades against freedom were erected. Eventually this contradiction created an embattled slave system that circumscribed the liberty of all Americans. The freedom and promise of freedom won by African Americans in the North did facilitate the formation of more persistent independent black community institutions. It also left northern blacks and their allies (according to Grimsted, a few Quakers and evangelicals) with the responsibility for continuing the battle against the slave system, rescuing the slaves when possible, and, as Phillis Wheatley had said, convincing Americans "of the strange Absurdity of their Conduct whose Words and Actions are so diametrically opposite."[76]

4

A Life in Freedom:
The Evolution of Family
and Household

Twenty-year-old Cato Howe was a slave when he entered military service in the spring of 1775. He was released from bondage in return for three years service in the Continental army, but he was twenty-eight. His wife Althea was already thirty-six by the time he was mustered out. Wartime inflation meant prices were still high when Howe and his comrades returned from the war to the farms, and they hoped that good prices for their produce would bring them prosperity in their newly won freedom. But the postwar depression which began in 1784 kept farm prices low for the next five years, making life difficult for the illiterate ex-slave and his wife. Their troubles were exacerbated by the rheumatism that developed from Howe's war wounds and that often made it hard for him to work around the farm.[1]

The Howes lived in a small settlement that developed on mainly wooded land which had formerly included the common sheep's pasture land of Plymouth, Massachusetts. They settled there with three other black Revolutionary War veterans, Plato Turner, Quamony Quash, and Prince Goodwin and their families. The area was known by various names over the years, among them New Guinea and Parting Ways. The first available record of their settlement dates from 1779, when Plato Turner bought a house there at the crossroads on the border between Plymouth and Kingston. There is evidence though that at least one of the soldiers already had a home there, since on the same day that Turner acquired the house from Job Cushman, Cushman was acquitted of stealing five bushels of Indian corn from his neighbor across the street, a man identified only as

Quash. This neighbor was undoubtedly either Quash Quande (who also appears in official records as Quandry Quash, or Quandey Quashy), the slave father of the young Quamony Quash, or Quamony Quash himself.[2]

Following African custom, the four families built their houses in a cluster in the center of the tract. The basic component of their houses was the twelve-foot dimension common to African dwellings, rather than the sixteen-foot measure that was the Anglo-American standard. Mariner Plato Turner's work on ships carrying goods between Plymouth and the West Indies created another link with their ancestral past. Trade with the West Indies also allowed them to supplement their New England-grown produce with products from the Caribbean, including fruits originally grown in West Africa. Plato Turner kept some of this fruit in his root cellar in the red unglazed African-style West Indian pottery in which it was shipped.[3]

There is other evidence that suggests the residents of the small settlement maintained cultural memories of the African past over many years. Archeological research near the crossroads on the land of Quamony Quash has revealed a grave with many broken ceramic and glass vessels carefully placed in its center. The placement of these objects on the grave, including pieces of medicine bottles, toothpick holders, dishes, and a lamp base, recalls the Kongo custom of putting the last objects used by a person on the grave to safely "ground the spirit." An eighteen-inch West Indian tamarind jar was placed at each end of the grave. The late-eighteenth-century bottles on the grave suggest that this may have been the burial site of Quamony's father, Quandey Quash, formerly the slave of Lazarus LaBaron of Plymouth, freed in about 1786, and eighty years old when he died in 1806.[4]

An examination of the names of the residents of Parting Ways gives important clues to their cultural consciousness. African names and naming practices, European naming practices, and the Anglicization of African names and practices are all apparent in the naming patterns of members of four generations born from about 1726 to 1886. Naming infants for the day of their birth was a common African practice. The Ashanti names Kwesi Kwande, Kwamma, and Kwame were names for children born on Sunday, Tuesday and Saturday respectively. Versions of these names may be found in Quash Quandry (or Quandy Quash) and his son Quamony. According to one late-nineteenth-century account, Quash (there identified as Quasho Quando) insisted on keeping his African name even though LaBaron, his master, wanted to call him Julius Caesar. An intriguing cultural hybrid occurred in the third generation of this family when the sons of Quamony Quash and his wife Ellen Stephens were identified in official records as Winslow S. Quash and Charles H. W. Quam.[5]

Naming patterns among the Parting Ways settlers illustrate the combination of cultures in another way as well. Studying the names of white colonial New Englanders and Thomas Jefferson's slaves, historians have noted that both were likely to name children for lineal kin. The African Americans, however, were more likely to name children for grandparents, uncles and aunts, while white New Englanders were more likely to be named after their parents. Evidence available for the family of Plato and Rachael Turner of Parting Ways over four generations suggests that children were as likely to be named after parents as for other relatives, but that the African naming patterns persisted as well. Two of Rachael and Plato's four children carried their names. In the third generation their daughter Sarah's son, James Thurston Burr, carried his father's name, while their son James' daughter was named after her grandmother Rachael. Of five children identified in the fourth generation, one was named for her mother, while two were named for grandparents. The Turner family illustrates one other kind of American adaptation as well— the mixing of cultures within families by the inclusion of people from different groups. The Turners included two white women (Plato's wife Rachael and their son James's wife Nancy) and one Gay Head Indian, a man named Peter Johnson who married James's daughter Rachael.[6]

The townspeople of Plymouth were sympathetic to the years of economic adversity suffered by their black Revolutionary War veterans. In 1792 Cato Howe, Prince Goodwin, Plato Turner and Quamany were given the rights to 106 acres of the town land where they were living in return for the labor it would take to clear it. These families lived simply in their small settlement, accumulating few possessions beyond some livestock (chickens and a pig or a cow), a few pieces of furniture, and some tools. They raised their children and saw some of them move to nearby towns or to Boston to find work and to marry. Contrary to his hopes as a young free man, Cato Howe did not prosper but was forced to rely on public assistance in his old age. He applied for the pension to which his wartime service entitled him when Althea was seventy years old and bedridden, just a few years before her death. The year after Althea died Cato married Lucy Prettison, a local widow twenty years his junior. They were married only two and a half years when Cato died, leaving Lucy a widow once again.[7]

Cato Fisk, a younger man than Cato Howe, was only seventeen when he enlisted as a drummer with the Second New Hampshire regiment in 1777. He courted a young free black girl named Elsa Huso who lived with a black woman known as Aunt Sellars in Brentwood, New Hampshire. Not long after peace was declared in 1783, Cato Fisk, then twenty-three, took a furlough and married sixteen-year-old Elsa. Their marriage ceremony was performed by abolitionist minister Nathaniel Trask whose family lived half a mile down the road from Cato's bride. After the wedding the groom returned to his regiment to serve out the three months remaining before the army disbanded.[8]

After the war Cato and Elsa moved to the nearby town of Exeter where he could find work mainly as a laborer and sometimes as a fiddler. By the time he applied for his pension at age sixty in 1820, age and disability had curtailed his ability to work. According to his pension application, he had few resources and many responsibilities. His wife Elsa continued to help support the family with odd jobs. Their daughter Nancy, age thirty, had left the family home, but two sons still lived with them. James, age twenty-eight, had been diagnosed as mentally ill and Ebenezer, age twenty-four, was suffering a long illness and confined to bed. The entire family including a three-year-old granddaughter lived in a "small hut." All they had managed to accumulate was a few farm animals and sparse household furnishings. Despite his destitution, Cato Fisk was well respected in his community. After he died in 1824, his daughter Nancy remembered that the minister had preached a sermon on his death and the death of Revolutionary General McCleary, mentioning Cato Fisk's death first, to the annoyance of some of the parishioners.[9]

The precarious position of the black war veterans was extreme, but economic uncertainty and an unstable currency created problems for all Americans during the postwar period. Although they were politically independent, the economies of America and Europe were still inter-twined. Cycles of war and peace in Europe were reflected in economic fluctuations in the United States. The situation was especially difficult for newly freed slaves and indentured servants who had no property and had been unable to accumulate any savings as a hedge against hard times. Farmers like Cato Howe and Cato Fisk were hit particularly hard since prices for farm commodities lagged behind recovering business prosperity during most of the 1790s.

Of course, not all African Americans in the North had been freed by the Revolutionary War; many continued in slavery for many years (Table 4.1). In states where freedom evolved through programs of gradual emancipation, some masters attempted to circumvent manumission laws by selling or transferring their slaves to slave states before emancipation took effect. Children and young adults were often most vulnerable, since in some states like New Jersey and New York they could be held in servitude until they reached their mid- to late twenties. Faced with the loss of these young slaves, northern slaveholders were often tempted to sell them for the handsome prices they would bring in the rice-growing and tobacco-growing Carolinas or in the newly emerging cotton-growing territories of the deep South.

To forestall such circumventions of state emancipation provisions, laws were instituted to prevent transferring slaves out of state against their will, but they were not always effective. One Connecticut slaveholder was brought to trial in 1792 for violating state law by "exporting" two slave children before they were to be freed. There is, however, no record of the violator being convicted.[10] Many slaves in New Jersey were sold to travel-ing slave traders before they could be set free under provisions of the 1804 state law. Sometimes slaveholders used subterfuge to trick young

Table 4.1 Slave Population in the North, 1775–1790*

	1775	1790
Connecticut	5,000	2,648
Delaware	9,000	8,887
Massachusetts	3,500	0
New Hampshire	629	157
New Jersey	7,600	11,423
New York	15,000	21,193
Pennsylvania	10,000	3,707
Rhode Island	4,373	958
Vermont	NA	0

*For population figures for 1775, see George Washington Williams, *History of the Negro Race in America 1619–1880*, vol. 1 (1883; reprint, New York: Arno Press and *The New York Times*, 1968), 325; for population figures for 1790, *Negro Population in the United States, 1790–1915* (1918; reprint New York: Arno Press and *The New York Times*, 1968), 56. Note that New York's and New Jersey's slave population increased between 1775 and 1790. Vermont abolished slavery in 1777.

inexperienced slaves, promising them early release in return for "short-term" work and residence in the South. In 1818 Harey, an eighteen year old from Middlesex County, New Jersey, agreed to service in Louisiana. By the time he learned the truth it was too late.[11]

Some scholars contend that such violations of the laws were common and that hundreds of New York slaves were sold between 1810 and 1820 as masters sought to beat the emancipation deadline. As had been true since the beginning of the African slave trade, the labor of young male slaves was in greatest demand. Thus they often brought the highest prices in the South and had the greatest risk of being sold away from the freedom they had been promised.[12] In this way the personal tragedies of slavery continued long after the emancipation laws had been passed. Isabella had been born a slave in a Dutch-speaking area of New York State after the Revolution. When she was ten years old her master died, and Isabella, her brothers and sisters, and her elderly parents were put on the auction block. The children's mother tried to ease the pain of their separation by explaining that wherever they were, each member of the family would always be under the same moon and stars. She told Isabella that she could always talk to God and ask Him to make her new masters "good." Later, when it became obvious to the young girl that her entreaties were ineffectual, and her masters "didn't get good," the pragmatic Isabella spoke to God again, saying, "God, maybe you can't do it. Kill them."[13]

After New York's emancipation law was passed but before they were freed, Isabella's own young son was illegally taken from her, given as a wedding present to his master's daughter who was leaving New York to live in Alabama.[14] When the anguished mother learned that she had lost her child, she confronted her mistress, but the white woman was not moved. "A fine fuss to make about a little nigger! Why haven't you as many of 'em left as you can see to?" Isabella was heartsick, angry, and determined that she would not lose her son. "I'll have my child again," she vowed, and eventually she was able to recover her son. The painful memory of her losses in slavery gave power and passion to her later work as an antislavery speaker and women's rights advocate, when she was known as Sojourner Truth.[15]

Continued suffering under slavery even after the war fought for American freedom led to especially frustrating conditions for slaves in states where gradual emancipation laws had been passed but who themselves had no legal right to ever be free. Such was the case for Silvia Dubois, the strongly built Pennsylvania slave who could no longer abide her mistress's abuse and knocked her unconscious in the presence of several customers in her master's tavern. Realizing the seriousness of what she had done, Silvia then fled to a nearby town, but returned when summoned by her master. He apparently understood his wife's temper and her long history of conflict with the slave, and he made Silvia an offer. He would set her free if she would agree to leave Pennsylvania and never return. She agreed and set off on foot, carrying her eighteen-month-old child through the wilds of northeastern Pennsylvania to New Brunswick, New Jersey.

Silvia's mother in New Brunswick, Dorcas Compton, had tried a different route to freedom. Her mother had bought her freedom from her master, Richard Compton, with a loan from Minical Dubois. Unable to earn enough money to pay off the loan, Dorcas and her children, including two-year-old Silvia, had become Dubois' slaves. When Dubois treated her badly, she arranged to be sold to another master with whom she made a similar arrangement for the promise of her freedom. Dorcas Compton tried to buy her freedom in return for future payment at least one other time before she finally died a slave in New Jersey around 1838.[16]

Since northern emancipation was gradual, abolitionists continued to work against the cruelty and injustices of the institution in the North as well as the South. In 1809 the New York Manumission Society charged upholsterer Amos Broad and his wife with assaulting and beating Broad's slave Betty and her three-year-old child. Prohibited from testifying on her own behalf, Betty relied on the testimony of white servants formerly in Broad's employ to expose her master's cruelty. Their testimony catalogued the abuses which this slave suffered: being whipped, stripped naked and made to go about her work or stand outside in the winter, having boiling water poured on her hand, and being tied up and deprived of food. The child was kicked, beaten, and suffered a severely cut head when Mrs. Broad threw a knife at her. Amos Broad's voluntary manumission of the

Table 4.2 Black Population Increase, 1790–1820

	From 1790–1800 Only	From 1790–1820
Philadelphia	210 %	418 %
New York	84	214
Boston	53	125

slaves under the constraint of the court proceedings did not save the Broads from substantial fines or avert his four-month prison sentence.[17]

Thus, the hardships of slavery continued even as the institution waned or disappeared. Even before the Revolution northern blacks had been substantially an urban population with concentrations in the cities on the coast. As they achieved their freedom, many more African Americans joined the growing urban populations in search of family members, jobs, and the sociability and protection of developing black communities. As a result of both emancipation and in-migration, the free black population of New York City, for example, increased over 600 percent between 1790 and 1810.[18] The black populations of the major northern port cities experienced an especially dramatic growth in these years. Gary Nash has estimated a total black population increase for three of these cities (Table 4.2). He linked the unusually rapid growth of Philadelphia's black population to the city's proximity to Maryland and Virginia. Many slaves manumitted in these large slaveholding states during the first generation after the Revolution came to Philadelphia. Some from these southern states also made their way to Boston and New York City. By 1800 the major cities of the Northeast had substantial and increasing black populations. Blacks also moved to smaller urban communities with sizable free black populations and small slave populations (Table 4.3).[19]

As northern blacks emerged from slavery and settled in black communities, they also moved out of the homes of former masters and formed independent family and household units. New York's black children, born into slavery after July 4, 1799, were required to serve their masters into

Table 4.3 Black Urban Population, 1800

	Slaves	(as percentage of total Blacks)	Blacks	(as percentage of total population)
New York	2,868	(4.74)	6,367	(10.53)
Philadelphia	55	(0.13)	4,265	(10.33)
Boston	0		1,174	(4.71)

Source: Leonard P. Curry, *The Free Black in Urban America, 1800–1850* (Chicago: University of Chicago Press, 1981), 244–248.

adulthood even though they were technically free, and many of the city's black adults remained enslaved until 1827. Thus, the formation of independent black families and households in New York lagged behind those in Boston or Philadelphia, where emancipation came decades earlier. In 1820 almost four out of every ten free blacks in New York City lived in white households, compared with less than three in ten in Philadelphia and less than two in ten in Boston.[20] Household formation was also impeded by the special problems African Americans faced. John Moranda gained his freedom late in 1795 when Samuel Jones, Jr., a New York lawyer and politician, paid his owner $200. A few months later he had managed to save the $50 necessary to purchase his four-year-old daughter from her owner in New Jersey, but it was another three years before he managed to save $160 to buy his wife and son and finally unite his small family in freedom.[21]

Freedom gave blacks greater control over choosing a marriage partner. Evidence on how this choice was made is scarce, but there are a few very important clues. The choice of partners in black marriages, as in all marriages, was influenced by a range of factors, from convenience and practical social and economic considerations to intangible human qualities. Shades of skin color also seem to have affected choices, however, since African Americans were likely to have spouses of approximately the same skin color.[22] For the almost three thousand marriages listed in eight cities for 1850 and 1860, 82 percent of the African-American men listed as black were married to African-American women listed as black, and 87 percent of those listed as mulattoes were married to women listed as mulatto. These percentages are far too high to be a matter of chance, especially in light of the fact that African-American men listed as "black" who were married to mulatto women were more likely to be skilled workers, business operators, and property holders than other "black" men. This pattern suggests that lightness of color, especially for women, provided a wider array of marriage choices. The few mulatto women who married darker men were likely to choose economically secure men. This corresponds with notions in nineteenth and twentieth century black-authored novels that attributed great beauty to the "high yellow" woman, celebrated in many sea shanties and popular folk songs like "The Yellow Rose of Texas" and "Shallo Brown," a song that related the story of a sailor leaving his girlfriend for a "bright mulatto . . . from Cincinnati." "Sally Brown," the shantie "sung in all the ports of the world," featured a "bright mulatter [sic]," a "very pretty . . . Creole lady" from New York City who chewed tobacco, drank rum, spent a man's money, and teased, but "wouldn't marry" a sailor. One version of this song lamented that after seven years of courtship, the singer was unable to win Sally who finally had a baby and married a "nigger soldier."[23]

Marriage choices provide important clues to regional variations, indicating that social institutions adapted to local conditions and were shaped by the demography of the local community. The folklore of certain regions of the deep South gives particular support to the idea that the lighter color resulting from a racially mixed heritage both reflected and conveyed a distinct social and economic advantage for African Americans, especially for African-American women. Especially, though not exclusively, in New Orleans, "Creole ladies" were often the "acknowledged daughters of wealthy [white] American and Creole fathers [and] educated with all of the style and accomplishments" money could buy.[24] Color differences were not as important among northern blacks, but they did seem to play a role in the selection of a mate. Although the general pattern held throughout the North, the significance of color is especially striking when analyzed by region and city. In cities with a high proportion of southern-born residents, both black and white, shade of color appeared to be more important in African Americans' selection of a spouse than in cities with a high proportion of northerners. Cincinnati, with its overwhelmingly southern-born population, had an extremely high rate of same-color marriages, higher than any of the cities studied with predominantly northern-born black populations (Table 4.4).

The evidence for men's color preference in choosing a mate is apparent in all northern black communities, but the fact that it was strongest in Cincinnati suggests the influence of the southern status system on northern relationships during the nineteenth century. In the South, where blacks had little protection from the law, they were sometimes able to call on the paternalistic protection of influential whites. Thus, light skin and its implied or acknowledged familial connection to white society often proved extremely important, and mulattoes who might convey this connection became valuable mates.[25]

As the black family evolved gradually from slavery, the majority of independent households, like most American households, established two-parent families. In his thoughtful analysis of free black family forma-

Table 4.4 Marriages of Mulatto Men by Color of Spouse, 1860

	Cincinnati	Detroit	Buffalo	Boston
Mulatto woman	226 (88%)	58 (82%)	30 (81%)	109 (80%)
Black woman	27 (11%)	5 (7%)	1 (3%)	7 (5%)
White woman	5 (2%)	5 (7%)	6 (16%)	21 (15%)
Percentage of total population born in the South	72	65	37	29
Total black population	3751	1459	845	2261

tion during this period, historian Gary Nash traced the family's emergence in Philadelphia, New York City, and Boston. He noted several stages of development as blacks moved from living in white households during and immediately following slavery, to the establishment of extended families and expanded black households, and finally to the predominance of the nuclear two-parent family by the second decade of the nineteenth century. By that time the average black household contained about four people in Philadelphia and Boston and six people in New York, where slavery still existed.[26]

Throughout the antebellum period the vast majority of black households consisted of families headed by couples, but a substantial minority were headed only by women. In 1820 Nash found women heading 12 percent of the black families in Philadelphia, 15 percent in Boston, and 19 percent of the free black families in New York.[27] Furthermore, there were increasing proportions of single-parent households among free blacks during the first half of the nineteenth century. In 1830 only 11 percent (16 of 149) of Cincinnati's black households were headed by women, but that proportion had more than doubled by 1850. Similarly, by mid-century over a quarter of Boston's black households were headed by women. Historian Paul Lammermeier also found an increase in female-headed black families in the seven Ohio Valley communities he studied. There the proportion of families headed by women increased between 1850 and 1860, a trend not reversed until after the Civil War.[28] Although the majority of black families continued to be headed by couples, the general decline in their proportion may indicate the difficulty of maintaining stable two-parent families in the urban North during the first half of the nineteenth century. In Boston just under two thirds of the black families were headed by couples at mid-century, decreasing to 60 percent by 1860. There was a similar pattern in Cincinnati and Philadelphia, and although smaller black communities like Detroit had proportionately more couple-headed families, there too they declined from 80 percent to 70 percent during the 1850s. In his study of Philadelphia, historian Theodore Hershberg interpreted the growing number of single-parent families as an indication of increasing socioeconomic hardships faced by Philadelphia's free blacks and generally deteriorating conditions for black people during this period.[29]

Although a decrease in couple-headed black families in many cities between 1820 and 1860 seems apparent, its causes and effects on the community, and especially on the children, are less obvious.[30] An analysis of available U. S. census data for 1820 suggests that high mortality rates accounted for many of the missing members of black families. First, the younger black children were, the more likely they were to live with both parents. Families with children under the age of fourteen were much more likely to be headed by a couple than those with older children. Even though New York City had a smaller percentage of two-parent families overall, if only families with children under the age of fourteen are compared, New York (81.5 percent), Philadelphia (88.4 percent), and Boston (77.5 percent) all had similarly high proportions of two-parent families.[31] The fact that the age of the child, and by extension the age of the parents, is one significant predictor of family composition is an indication that the mortality of parents was a factor in producing single-parent families. Family data also suggest that black children were likely to have two parents in residence for their years of maturation.[32] Of the more than 5,000 children under the age of fifteen living in the eight cities studied here, over 60 percent lived with two parents in 1850 and 1860.

Another indication that mortality was an important factor in creating single-parent families is the age of the surviving single parent. Single men and women who headed families were likely to be older than couples who headed families. Most single parents were women, but unlike the young single mothers of the late twentieth century, female heads of families during the first half of the nineteenth century were disproportionately older women who assumed that role in their mid-thirties or early forties. In the Ohio Valley, black women heading families were likely to be over the age of forty, that is, several years older than the general female population in that region. In Boston in 1850 their average age was forty-six, more than a decade older than other adult black women in the community. The gap narrowed by 1860 but was still considerable, with female family heads averaging forty-three years of age while other adult women averaged thirty-five years. In Cincinnati female family heads were on average five years older than other women in 1850 and more than four years older a decade later. The pattern was the same in other communities, with female heads four to six years older on average in the other communities studied. Moreover in Boston, Cincinnati, and in the communities that Lammermeier studied in the Ohio Valley, black female family heads were likely to be older than black males who headed families either with their wives or as single parents. Their relative maturity is an important consideration in assessing the meaning of female-headed families for the lives of black children in the nineteenth century. This evidence all supports the likelihood that single women who headed families were widows.[33] Clearly, higher mortality for black men was an important factor in creating one-parent families, and many husbands and fathers did not leave their families voluntarily. Many men worked at dangerous jobs as seamen or laborers and were vulnerable to life-threatening injuries.[34]

Some scholars have believed that families headed by women were more common in black society because of the lasting destructive effects of slavery that undermined the traditional family structure. Under this argument, the authority of slave masters made black men irrelevant as husbands and fathers.[35] Our findings and most recent scholarship refute this contention. In his thorough and succinct critique of this perspective, Orville Vernon Burton points out the irony that this argument began with an abolitionist critique of slavery. Our data does suggest a correlation between southern birth (and probably a more recent link to slavery) and single parenthood for women. A close examination of the data, however, indicates that the southern-born adults in the cities studied tended to be older than those born in the North.[36] In Cincinnati, Buffalo, and Chicago the southern born black women were on average from three to seven years older than their nonsouthern-born counterparts. Since older women were more likely to be single mothers, what appeared as a correlation between region of birth and a woman's status as a single mother, may in fact have been a correlation between that status and advancing age.[37] Thus, single parenthood was as likely to be the result of the older southerners' greater risk of losing a spouse to death as it was to reflect the hardships of slavery.[38] Other studies have found families who emigrated from the South to be especially durable. In her study of the black community in Boston during the second half of the nineteenth century, a community expanded by the postwar migration of many southern ex-slaves, historian Elizabeth Pleck found that the predominantly couple-headed rural southern black family made the transition to northern urban life with relatively little disruption. These families were most likely to become single-parent families only after being in the city for a decade or more. Pleck's findings support Theodore Hershberg's conclusions that it was the city with its attendant problems of poverty and racial discrimination, rather than the effects of slavery, that was most damaging to black families during the nineteenth century.[39] Hershberg found that nearly one third of black families in Philadelphia by 1860 were headed by a single person, but concluded that ex-slaves seemed to have been better adapted to the pressures of a free but racially prejudiced society than blacks who had never been slaves. He speculated that the same qualities that enabled slaves to achieve liberation, often through buying their freedom or escaping, served them well in freedom.[40]

Further evidence for the effect of urbanization is provided by other studies in both the South and the North. In the rural community of North Hempstead, New York, at mid-century a county of 5,000 residents with 703 free blacks, both the proportion of southern-born blacks and the proportion of black female-headed families was extremely low.[41] In his study of a South Carolina community, Burton found that the proportions of single female-headed black families were higher in urban areas than in rural areas. Furthermore, during the antebellum period southern-born blacks living in northern cities were likely to have had some urban experience before moving to the North.[42] Perhaps that southern urban experience, and not slavery, contributed to their overrepresentation among single female parents. This is not to discount cultural factors that may have arisen as an adaptation to slavery. Jacqueline Jones, for example, has suggested that slave women may have been more likely to be single mothers because it was "socially acceptable to the slave community" and because having a child proved a woman's fertility, increased her value to her owner, and made her sale less likely. Burton concluded that the acceptance of the children of unwed parents in black society was an acceptance of reality.[43] The preponderance of evidence therefore indicates that advancing age and urban life contributed to an increase in single-parent black families, and that black male mortality was certainly a most important factor.

Black male mortality rates were particularly high, but death was a nearly constant presence threatening family and community stability for all poor blacks. Zilpha Elaw, a young girl growing up on a farm near Philadelphia, was acutely aware of its menace. Born free in about 1790, she was a member of a small and devout family composed of her father and mother, Zilpha, her brother who was six years older, and her younger sister. Family life was marked by devotional songs and prayers each morning and evening, and the family had frequent need to call on God's help and comfort. It seemed that Zilpha's mother was always either pregnant or burying another child. By the time Zilpha was twelve, her mother had had nineteen children die in infancy, leaving her with only three of the twenty-two she had borne. It was that year that her mother died in childbirth.

When her mother died, Zilpha was the only one left at home with her father. Her brother had gone to live with their maternal grandparents on a distant farm west of Philadelphia six years before, and her sister had recently been placed with a nearby aunt. Zilpha's father found a position for her with a Quaker couple with the agreement that she would stay with them until she was eighteen. Adapting to the Quaker style was difficult for her, as the "religious exercises" of her guardians "were performed in the secret silence of the mind." Less than two years later her father died. The weight of so much sorrow competed with her generally happy day-to-day life. Without the constant reminder of daily devotions, Zilpha often felt guilty about her childish exuberance and the joyful times she shared with the other children in the household. Despite the kindness of her guardians and her inclusion in their home, Zilpha was periodically overcome with grief, and remembering her father's death she felt abandoned and lost.[44]

The emotional and economic consequences of high mortality were shared by all who lived in the eighteenth and nineteenth centuries, but death records make it abundantly clear that they fell especially heavily on African Americans. This is partly explained by the high proportion of free blacks living in Atlantic port cities. Throughout the eighteenth century, seaports provided entry to slaves, settlers, and disease. Increasing urban populations and the nearly total lack of sanitation measures made cities breeding grounds for disease. One study of mortality in colonial Pennsylvania illustrates the urban danger—whereas the death rate for blacks and whites in the countryside was 15 per 1,000 each year, in Philadelphia it ranged from 34 per 1,000 to 52 per 1,000. The most feared early scourge was smallpox that frequently reached epidemic proportions in cities like Boston and Charleston, South Carolina. African medical traditions played an important role in addressing this problem which continued to menace colonial settlements until just before the Revolution, when inoculation began to be accepted as a preventive measure. As early as the 1720s, Boston physician Zabdiel Boylston acknowledged the role played in the development of a smallpox vaccine by Oneissimus, a slave who explained the inoculation procedure used in West Africa that protected Africans from the disease. Still, the pre-Revolutionary smallpox death rate in Philadelphia was twice that of London and accounted for 18 percent of the deaths in Christ Church's cemetery between 1750 and 1775.[45]

Yellow fever, a tropical viral disease, swept through many cities during the eighteenth century, hitting Philadelphia in 1793, New York in 1794 and 1795, and Philadelphia, New York and Boston in 1798 and 1799. Fearing the fever, those who could afford to fled from the cities to suburban or country homes each year in the late summer and early fall. In 1805 one third of the population of New York left the city in September and October. City authorities provided temporary housing in tents and barracks in the more desirable locations of Greenwich Village and Bellevue for some people. The danger of yellow fever was especially great in the South, and many prosperous southerners went North to spend the "sick season" in a more healthful environment. The well-to-do traveled to resort areas like Saratoga Springs, New York, where, years before, Native Americans had discovered the health-giving properties of the waters. The increasingly crowded urban poor, unable to leave the cities and often living in marshy areas or on filled-in swamps, were most likely to suffer from the yellow fever epidemics recurring until the mid-1820s.[46]

The 1793 yellow fever epidemic in Philadelphia was the most serious. It started in late July, and by mid-September more than half the city's residents had left for the countryside. Terrified of contracting the disease, families abandoned ailing relatives, nurses refused to care for the sick, and grave diggers would not bury the dead. As Gary Nash described the situation, "the poor were starving and the dead lay everywhere in the streets, while thousands of middle- and upper-class Philadelphians took refuge in the countryside." When the eminent doctor Benjamin Rush approached free black minister Richard Allen asking for aid, he assured Allen that blacks were immune to the disease and therefore, he argued, obliged to perform those services many whites refused to offer. At a meeting called by Allen and Absalom Jones, African Americans determined to offer their aid, not because they were immune—a claim that was soon amply proven to be false—but because they saw it as their Christian duty and an opportunity to prove that they were capable of rising above their animosity toward whites who had formerly enslaved them. Assisting Rush, these blacks nursed the sick, cared for children whose parents were afflicted or for orphans whose parents were killed by the fever, and carted the dead to cemeteries and buried them. By the time cold weather in November ended the epidemic (killing the mosquitoes which transmitted the fever), over four thousand Philadelphians, nearly one-tenth of the population, had died. Proportionately nearly as many blacks as whites had succumbed, yet they had not abandoned their service.[47]

Whatever immunity may have afforded African Americans a slight protection from yellow fever, they certainly had no advantage in the face of other epidemics that raged through the poorer sections of cities in the first half of the nineteenth century. Historians have noted the increasing residential segregation of the classes in cities like New York and Philadelphia between 1790 and 1820. Such segregation was by no means complete, especially since there were many live-in servants in the homes of the wealthy, but economic development and class differentiation led to increasingly well-defined upper- , middle- , and lower-class neighborhoods during this period. In Philadelphia there was a general movement of the poorer population to the edges of the city, though many still lived in crowded alleys and lanes in the central city. In New York a housing shortage prompted the use of the dank, unfinished cellars, formerly kitchens, as residences for poor tenants in working-class and middle-class neighborhoods. In Boston many African Americans moved to the lower slopes of Beacon Hill to be near their employment in the grand homes of affluent families who lived at the top of the hill. Inadequate sanitation, contaminated water, and increasingly overcrowded conditions for the poor contributed to nearly continual outbreaks of bacterial diseases. Typhoid fever, dysentery, typhus, and cholera killed both blacks and whites, but since blacks were more likely to be poor, they suffered a disproportionately high death toll. During the 1820s in New York and Philadelphia, the black mortality rate was almost twice the white rate.[48]

One doctor in Philadelphia observed that the epidemic of 1818 was almost totally limited to the city's black population which "inhabit[ed] the narrow streets, courts, and alleys of the southwestern parts of the city and suburbs." In the same year the "Banker-street Fever" hit blacks who lived in New York's cellars especially hard. Nearly twenty years later, poor blacks still lived under deplorable conditions. One New York physician described what he found at one residence where he was treating a patient for typhus. The dwelling was situated in a yard that had been boarded over to cover the filth resulting from the animals kept there. Even so, the muck oozed up through the boards, creating an aesthetically unpleasant setting and a breeding ground for disease.[49] A reformer was appalled by the conditions he found in black residential areas in Philadelphia. To reach one group of buildings, he reported having to traverse dark cavelike passageways so narrow that "a stout man would have found it tight work to have threaded it." Having reached the apartments inside, he was horrified by "dark, damp holes, six feet square, without a bed in any of them, and generally without furniture, occupied by one or two families."

Although public health advances gradually helped to lower mortality rates even in the poor black community, blacks' rates remained higher than whites'.[50] In Boston during the 1840s the black mortality rate was almost sixty percent higher than the white rate. A Boston city official contended in 1855 that the death rate among blacks was "greater than that of the whole city" even though more than half lived on Beacon Hill in what was generally one of the healthiest wards of the city.[51]

In the face of epidemics and unhealthful living conditions, the weakest members of society were the most vulnerable, and this often meant a high death toll for children. Although the case of Zilpha Elaw and her family is undoubtedly an extreme example, throughout the colonial period and well into the nineteenth century, infant mortality was high in America. Susan Klepp's study of a forty-year period for colonial white Philadelphia found an infant mortality rate of one in four; by age fifteen, one half of the children had died. There is little direct evidence that allows a comparison of black and white infant mortality. Yet, indirect evidence indicates that infant mortality was even higher among African Americans. Northern urban black families had fewer children than their white counterparts, although evidence suggests that the black birth rate was at least as high. According to a study of the 1820 census returns for Boston and New York City, the ratio of children to adult women was more than twice as high for whites as for blacks. The differential was not quite as great in Philadelphia, but the white rate was still substantially higher. This ratio continued to be low among blacks throughout the antebellum period. Two studies in Boston in 1848 and 1854 showed that although the birth rate among African Americans was the highest in the city, the number of black children remained disproportionately low.[52]

The tribulations of Cato Howe and Zilpha Elaw exemplify the threats to the family posed by disease and the deaths of loved ones. The story of the family of Tobias Wornton of Gloucester, Massachusetts illustrates many of the difficulties families faced and their continuous struggle to find an adequate means of support. Tobias Wornton, sometimes known as Backus, was an African who had been the slave of Captain Winthrop Sargent of Gloucester. He was a veteran of the Revolutionary War, had fought at Bunker Hill, and was a faithful member of the Congregational Church. He married an Indian woman whose people had been captured by the English and who worked as a domestic for a white family in Gloucester.[53] Early in the 1790s Tobias' daughter, already a widow, married Thomas Gardner, an African American from Nantucket. When Gardner died in Newburyport in December 1799, she returned to her father's home with her two children, five-year-old Silvia and three-month-old Nancy. After about a year the widow married a sailor employed by Captain Fitz William Sargent named Money Vose—the African who had earned his freedom by jumping off a slave ship anchored in a northern harbor.

During the next twelve years Money Vose and his wife had six children. He was frequently away at sea, and Silvia and Nancy later remembered being mistreated by him when he was home. The children did have a close relationship with their grandfather Tobias who lived nearby. He was adamant that his children and grandchildren receive the proper religious and moral training. Tobias took his children with him to church on Sunday mornings, and in the afternoon cared for the smaller children so his daughter could take her own. It was hard to support such a large family, and when the children reached seven or eight, places were found for them in town or in the surrounding area with families who would "bring them up" in exchange for their labor.

When war broke out again with Britain in 1812, seaman Money Vose was captured and pressed into service by a British privateer. Only three months after her father Tobias' death, Money's wife learned that he had sickened and died in British service. Only one of the children, Silvia, was an adult; the other seven ranged in age from thirteen years to six weeks. With the family patriarch and her husband both gone, the grief and responsibility were too much for the thrice-widowed Mrs. Vose, and she broke down under the strain. The older children then faced the necessity of providing support and care for the younger children and their mother. For the next ten years Nancy Gardner and her brother George Vose struggled to keep the family together. Silvia stayed with the family she worked for in the countryside seventy miles away. Thirteen-year-old Nancy and eleven-year-old George returned home from their domestic jobs and found places for the two older children. One was not easy to place—he had been suffering from consumption for about a year. His death a short time later grieved the family, but also lightened their economic burden a little. To support their mother and the three youngest children at home, Nancy and George gathered berries and sold them in Gloucester. George also fished and took a three-week job on a ship that paid him three dollars and four feet of wood, an important resource for the New England winter. Nancy and George then took jobs together with a family eight miles from town and sent their wages home to their mother.

A few years later in an attempt to find higher wages, Nancy left for Salem, promising to send for George. She stayed with her mother's friends in Salem, and when their daughter became ill, Nancy replaced her as the domestic servant of a demanding family with five children. Three months later she too was sent home exhausted and ill. After recuperating at home, Nancy returned to Salem the next spring with her older sister Silvia to find domestic work. Silvia soon left for a better position as a "nursery girl" in Boston, but in less than a year had turned to prostitution. Immediately on hearing of her sister's occupation, sixteen-year-old Nancy set off for Boston and with the help of friends there rescued her sister from the house of prostitution. With Silvia safely in domestic jobs closer to home, Nancy and George concentrated on bringing in enough money to get their four-year-old brother off of town support and back home. To earn more Nancy went to Boston and found a job as a chamber-maid, and George returned to sea. When Silvia came to Boston, too, Nancy got her a job as a chambermaid where she worked, hoping to keep an eye on her and prevent her from returning to prostitution. The money George was paid when he returned from sea enabled them to bring their mother and the younger children home together again.

About five years after Money Vose's death, their mother married again and settled in Salem. The children were not happy with this development, even though the new stepfather should have been a source of support. They were right to be distrustful, however, since the man refused to take any responsibility for the children. When George returned from a voyage and learned of this new arrangement, he shipped out again, this time leaving home for good. Their new stepfather refused to allow the chil-dren to live in his house when they left a place of employment, so Nancy became the effective head of the family. By the time she was eighteen, Nancy had assumed responsibility in Boston for one sister and two broth-ers, ages seven to fifteen. Theirs was not what might ordinarily be consid-ered a household, since all lived in different residences, but this was an arrangement demanded by economic necessity. The expansion of house-holds beyond dwelling walls was not unique, for the practice of informal adoption and placing kin in households of other community members was often necessitated by inadequate family resources. When she could, Nancy found places of employment for the children in wealthy homes. When she could not, she found friends in Boston to take them in or paid $1 a week for their room and board. At mid-nineteenth century, just under 10 percent of the black children were living in black families in Boston with which they did not share the same last name.[54] When her brother John decided to go to sea after several months of unemployment, Nancy spent two months' of her wages to outfit him for the five-week trip on a ship bringing Irish immigrants from Liverpool. Occasionally she moved closer to her mother in Salem for a time to care for her during periodic bouts of illness and insanity.[55]

Finally after ten years of struggling to support the family, and only rarely relying on Gloucester's public relief for the children, Nancy's life underwent dramatic changes. Since the youngest child was then ten years old and all were placed, she was able to quit her job and undertake train-ing as a seamstress. At age twenty-four she married an old family friend who came from a background much like her own, but whose life had taken a far different course. Mr. Prince had worked in domestic service with families in Massachusetts from the time he was a young boy. In 1810 he moved to Gloucester and sailed for Russia with Captain Theodore Stanwood. Upon their return he remained as a servant to the Stanwood family, during which time he visited the Vose household. When the cap-tain's son was placed in a school in St. Petersburg in 1812, Prince was sent along to work as a servant in the imperial court. After more than ten years in Russia, he returned to make Nancy his bride; they embarked for Russia a few months later. In the summer of 1824, Nancy Prince was formally presented to Emperor Alexander I and Empress Elizabeth at the imperial court in St. Petersburg.

In Nancy Prince's early life she made remarkable efforts to fulfill her responsibilities to her family. The responsibilities she undertook illustrated those recognized in both African and European cultures but greatly emphasized in her African heritage. The social and economic conditions under which Africans were brought to America and under which African Americans lived generally made it impossible for them to follow African familial traditions, but even under slavery, people managed to maintain their values and adapt traditional customs. Despite cultural variations, in West Africa the family was generally an expanded family including a variety of kin clustered together in a compound that often extended beyond the walls of a single dwelling. The entire group provided support for individual members, so that when a woman lost her husband, she was not alone but simply remained a part of this extended household until she remarried. Her new husband then became a part of the compound and the couple took their places within a larger household unit. Family organization of this type often included polygamous marriages where a man could have several wives. European culture, on the other hand, carried strong prohibitions against polygamy, condemning the practice as immoral and generally overlooking the utility of relationships between the women in these families. Although there were various ranks among African wives, each performed some necessary function within the household. The female companionship and shared household duties and child care were especially important for the women in these marriages.[56]

For those Africans and African Americans who married Native Americans, the importance of the expanded family was reinforced by shared cultural traditions. With Indians, too, the kinship group, connected by lineage traced through the mother, was the center of residence, political organization, household maintenance, and social identity. For both the Africans and the Indians with whom they came into contact in the Northeast, sustenance and survival depended on the cooperation of a large number of family members who lived together in the same house or in a cluster of nearby houses. Although free blacks living in the nineteenth-century North may not have consciously recreated the West African or Native American compound, this architectural structure was functional for their political and economic situation.[57]

Kinship was so important among most of the nations of West Africa that a system of fictive kinship was developed to ensure that those without relatives had a family to live with and thus were part of a kinship system. Scholars have argued that the institution of slavery established by the Dahomey and the Ashanti, termed "Odinko" by the Ashanti, was actually one means by which those without family were taken into an Ashanti family where they were of lesser rank, but were allowed to improve their place through good character and hard work. Among the West Africans of the Niger Delta region, where life was seriously disrupted by the Atlantic slave trade, the "House System" became an important organizing method, forming a traditional family-like grouping of nonkin. The head of the house was called "father" and his wife was referred to as "mother." Through this system of expanded household living, these Africans, without kin of their own available, could live in a family setting and maintain, to some extent anyway, the traditions of their ancestors.[58]

The extensive network of support so characteristic of African kinship systems was equally important among blacks in the Americas. For blacks living under the disruption of the slave system, fulfilling responsibilities to the expanded family meant accepting obligations to those related by blood and to others who were unrelated but who played kinship roles. Expanding their households by taking in relatives and friends enhanced the prospects of survival, especially for children separated from their parents, and was compatible with African-Americans' historical and cultural traditions. Historian Herbert Gutman found such family and household structures in such geographically varied North American communities as St. Helena's Island, South Carolina; Township, South Carolina; Issaquuena County, Mississippi; and the Jackson Ward section of Richmond, Virginia. During the last decades of the nineteenth century, after slavery had ended there, black households in these communities became increasingly complex with more kin and nonkin added. By the end of the century, for example, fewer than half of Jackson Ward's black households consisted of only nuclear families; five out of every seven contained single boarders or boarder families. According to Gutman, such households contained a "core nuclear family and either nephews and nieces or brothers and sisters of the household head." He speculated that the increase in these expanded households was a response to urban poverty and remarked that they "may have been closely related to the extended kin groups that had developed prior to emancipation." Gutman was referring mainly to the kin groups he had studied among southern slaves, but he could just as well have been describing similar groups among northern free blacks of the same period. Beset by economic problems and limited by discrimination, antebellum free blacks responded similarly, creating expanded household structures.[59]

In northern cities a sizable proportion of black adults boarded in the households of other African Americans. In the mid-nineteenth century, about one-third of black adults in Boston, Buffalo, and Chicago were boarders, and in Detroit the proportion was slightly higher. Available evidence indicates that boarding was one way of coping with hardship and unfortunate circumstance. Robert Johnson worked his way to Boston

from Maryland during the 1840s. By the 1850s he ran a small used clothing shop, a potentially lucrative business in the era before ready-made
clothes were generally available. When a national depression in 1857
affected local businesses and forced his customers to rely on the generosity of friends or to acquire fewer garments, Johnson went out of business.
He gave up his rented rooms and boarded with friends who were fellow
migrants from Maryland.[60]

In Cincinnati almost one-third of black adults were boarders in 1850, a
proportion that increased to 46 percent by 1860. The rise in the number
of African Americans being sheltered in the homes of others reflected
both the impact of the economic downturn which struck the city's economy in the late 1850s and the increased numbers of migrants entering the
city during the decade. Regional birthplaces within households taking in
boarders illustrate the typical chain migration pattern resulting from the
tendency of migrants to move to communities where friends and family
members have gone before. Hosts and boarders were often born in the
same region, most in the same state, indicating the likelihood that
migrants sought out friends and kin from home with whom to board in
their new cities. Cincinnati's location between the North and South
brought it black migrants from both regions, but most[61] were from Virginia and Kentucky, and most of these lived with people born in the same
states. During the 1850s, an increasing number of blacks from the North
migrated to Cincinnati, and they often lived in households headed by
other northerners. When John Hatfield came to Cincinnati from Pennsylvania in the mid-1830s, he used his skill as a barber and opened a shop
on Walnut Street between Pearl and Third. After a few years he was
joined by several relatives from his home state, including a brother and
sister-in-law who lived with him for a number of years. By 1850 the Hatfield household included his relatives and at least three friends from
Pennsylvania who also worked as barbers.[62]

Although there were families who boarded with other families, most
boarders were single men and women, new residents seeking a temporary
home and in need of help settling into their new communities. Since men
were more likely than women to be able to travel in the nineteenth century, more of the migrants who became boarders were men. They were
also likely to be young adults, an average of five or more years younger
than the general population. If he had good prospects a man might board
for only a short time before striking out on his own. Lemuel Burr, a
young man in his twenties, was born in Virginia. He was a barber by
trade, and when he arrived in Boston, he found lodging with Henry
Thacker, a waiter, and his family. Burr stayed with the Thackers for less
than a year; as he prospered in the barbering business, he moved into his
own residence.[63]

In 1850 more than half of the boarders in Cincinnati were men, even
though men were less than half of the black population. By 1860 more

migrants had entered the city, many of them young men, and men were over half of the African-American population and over 60 percent of the boarders. They found lodging in boarding houses run by African Americans or in private homes in the black community. While this influx of young male migrants mainly from the Northeast lowered the average age of Cincinnati's boarders from thirty-one years to twenty-nine years, the average age of male household heads increased during this period.[64] Increasing economic pressures on black families during the 1850s were evident in these changes in household composition. Not only were there more boarders moving into the households, but more adult children remained at home instead of establishing separate households. Since any adult sheltered by other adults was counted here as a boarder, this contributed to a rise in the boarder populations calculated in this study.[65]

The characteristics of black female boarders showed a similar pattern, although they were a bit older than the male boarders throughout the antebellum period. Like their male counterparts, female borders were an average of three years younger in 1860 than in 1850, and more new female migrants came from northern states. At the same time, like the men's, the average age of all black women in Cincinnati increased. Unlike the men, women were more likely to board in private homes, often with relatives or friends they had known at home.[66]

Boarding was an important social and economic institution in nineteenth-century black communities. The opportunity to rely on friends and family for shelter enhanced the mobility of poor people who were often forced to move to find employment. It provided financial assistance when people were unemployed; it provided social supports for people who faced discrimination; and it saved those who had left home or run away from slavery from social isolation.

Mary Liverpool came to Cincinnati from Virginia and apparently had difficulty securing work during her first few years in the city. By 1850 she was boarding with a family from Virginia, a morally acceptable arrangement for a single woman and a financially useful one, since she still was not working regularly. After Mary secured a job as a dressmaker, she left this home and went to live with her sister.[67]

In the early 1830s William Hodges, a free black man, left his home in Virginia, went to Canada, and finally made his way to New York City. Although he was far from home, he had frequent contact with his brother Willis still in Virginia through letters and messages delivered by friends. Shortly after William settled in New York, five of his nephews arrived; Willis and his wife soon followed. Their father Charles also traveled to New York but remained only long enough to purchase a family home and enroll the children in school, an opportunity they could not have received in Virginia. The travel between the Hodges' households in Virginia and New York was so frequent that various members of the family might be found living together in either location at any given time. As was true of their family home in Virginia, so too in New York, "the Hodges household seems to have rarely been without several friends and relatives on protracted visits." They not only depended on one another for room and board during their extended stays, but William, who lived in New York most permanently, also helped other members of the family find employment. Willis remembered that he received his first impression of the city when William accompanied him on an urban tour, pointing out the various jobs open to blacks.[68]

The Hodges household was not unusual. African Americans in the antebellum era could count on the presence of friends and kin in their home often and for long-term visits. Generally, black households were expanded by relatives and friends who contributed in various ways. The special utility of boarders in a household is illustrated by the family of Julia Foote. Julia's mother had been a slave; her father was born free but was kidnapped into slavery. After purchasing his own and his wife's freedom, her father settled the family in Schenectady, New York where the family's fourth child, Julia, was born. The Foote household was composed of family members and unrelated borders, including, "an old colored lady living in a part of [their] house" whom the children came to consider part of the family. As was often the case with fictive kin, they referred to her as if she were a relative, calling her Aunt Giney. All knew that she could be counted on to care for the children during the day, while Julia's mother and father worked. This was occasionally an onerous task, as on the day when five-year-old Julia got into her father's store of liquor and got "stupidly drunk." As Julia recounted the story, Aunt Giney aided by the other children, "walked me around and blew smoke in my face, to bring me to." Aunt Giney performed an important service to her host family and was part of the broader community that was expected to look out for its members.[69]

Although many boarders offered extra income to a household, the evidence suggests that in most cases the boarder got at least as much out of the arrangement as did host families. Clues are revealed in the special census taken by the Quakers of Philadelphia in 1847. In that unique document, census takers recorded several items not recorded in the state or the federal census of the time. One of these items was wages for members of free African-American households. Although this information is only available for one city and lists wages for less than half (45 percent) of the households, it does provide the best indication available of resources that boarders contributed to the income of their host family. This data indicate that the average border contributed only about 3 percent of the household income, with male boarders contributing almost twice as much as female boarders. There were some households, probably the poorest ones, that depended on boarders for a considerably higher proportion of their total income. In these, the earnings of male boarders constituted as much as 70 percent of the household income, while a female boarder's wages constituted up to 56 percent of the total household economy. Since black households were so often poor, even a small contribution might make a significant difference for survival. Boarding was, therfore, an important institution for both boarder and host family.[70]

As African Americans in the North moved from slavery into freedom, traditional family and household forms, many based in African cultures, were adapted to their needs, their new conditions, obstacles, and opportunities. The social and economic pressures encouraged a mutually supportive structure. This did not constitute a monolithic unity or a society free of community conflict, but it did place great importance on the social relationships among free black people. Generation after generation extended the family and household to shelter and nurture kin and nonkin, creating a complex set of social and economic relationships. These families and households formed the basis for cooperative arrangements to meet the problems associated with poverty, hardship, illness, and prejudice. It was on this foundation that African Americans built other institutions to create free black communities.

5

Coping with Urban Life:
Poverty, Work, and Regional Differences

The abolition of slavery in the North raised twin fears for officials in the free states of the new republic—dependency and disorder. Although many African Americans possessed skills and had a long history of doing the work for which they were brought to America, many whites saw slavery as the only way to make blacks productive. The apprenticeship arrangements that accompanied gradual emancipation in some northern states were, at least in part, an attempt to counter the imagined slavery-induced dependency. Bostonian Jeremy Belknap, who had supported immediate emancipation in Massachusetts, later feared that "many [free blacks were] in a far worse condition than when they were slaves, being incapable of providing for themselves the means of subsistence."[1] In the early spring of 1788, the Massachusetts legislature adopted a familiar solution to the problem of dependency. Assuming blacks to be incapable of supporting themselves, it passed a vagrancy law that required the expulsion of all African Americans who were not citizens of the state. Officials identified 158 blacks and 76 Indians and mulattoes by their city or country of origin and warned them out of Massachusetts. The list included fourteen Africans and thirty-three West Indians. If those identified did not leave the state within two months, they could be confined in the house of correction at hard labor, held there for trial and, if convicted, whipped.[2]

Relatively few whites believed that blacks could find a place in the new democratic society, a society regarded as particularly vulnerable to social disorder. Lacking the restraints imposed by the monarchy, the orderly progress of the society depended, in large measure, on the internalized values and the personal abilities of its citizens. Even antislavery advocates assumed that free blacks were incapable of fulfilling the responsibilities of citizenship. In 1798 several antislavery men in Burlington, New Jersey were distressed by what they saw as the "Idleness, Frolicking, Drunkenness, and in some cases . . . Dishonesty" of the free blacks in their vicinity. In Philadelphia one abolitionist believed that although there were many "useful and respectable" African Americans in that city most were "degraded and vicious."[3]

Many northern states seriously considered ways to rid themselves of blacks altogether. In 1821 the Massachusetts legislature established a committee to investigate the possibility of prohibiting blacks from migrating to the Commonwealth because they were believed to be dangerous to order and a burden to public charity. This attempted exclusion was unsuccessful, and all such efforts were discontinued in Massachusetts, but its serious discussion in this liberal state was illustrative of the inclination throughout the North to replace slavery with other racial controls and restrictions or to banish blacks completely. New Jersey was also concerned about free blacks becoming a drain on the local welfare system and in 1798 required former masters to be responsible for the support of any slaves they freed by posting a bond of $500 for each emancipated slave.[4]

Other regions of the country, especially the Midwest, established exclusionary provisions. In the Northwest Ordinance of 1787, Congress had banned slavery in the territories north of the Ohio River, the region from which the north central states were carved. Although slavery had technically never existed in this region, a rigid system of black servitude greatly limited the freedom of African Americans living there during the eighteenth and early nineteenth centuries. Many whites who migrated to this region were anxious to limit the black population. Ohio, Indiana, Michigan, and Illinois either banned black immigration outright or imposed heavy bonds to ensure "good conduct" from those blacks allowed to enter the state.[5]

Many people along the borders of slave states were especially afraid that southern free blacks would migrate to their areas or that slave masters would "dump" old and feeble slaves deemed unfit for plantation service in their states. Such concerns prompted Ohio's 1804 requirement that blacks who planned to settle in Ohio first register with the county clerk to ensure that they were not fugitives from slavery and obtain a certificate allowing them to secure work in the state. Those hiring a black person without such a certificate were subject to a ten- to fifty-dollar fine compounded daily for each day of illegal employment. Should the worker be found to be a fugitive slave, the employer could be required to pay the slave's master fifty cents a day. These "black laws" were strengthened three years later by provisions that required a black migrant to Ohio to post a $500 bond of solvency, raised the fines for hiring a black person without proof of free status or for harboring a fugitive to $100, and offered a fifty-dollar reward for informers.[6]

Despite the black laws, some southerners viewed the West as a suitable refuge for newly freed African Americans. One curious example stemmed from the actions of the North Carolina Yearly Meeting of Quakers early in the nineteenth century. The laws of North Carolina made it nearly impossible for Quakers prompted by conscience to free their slaves. Therefore, beginning in 1808, they settled on placing the ownership and care of slaves in the hands of the Yearly Meeting, hiring and protecting those who wished to stay in North Carolina, but intending mainly to aid all who would agree to move out of the jurisdiction of slavery. According to one report, the Yearly Meeting at one time had as many as 1,500 African Americans under its care. Some were transported to Africa or, with the help of prominent Quaker abolitionist Benjamin Lundy, sent to Haiti. The agents of the North Carolina Yearly Meeting assisted hundreds of other ex-slaves who settled in Pennsylvania, Indiana, and Ohio.[7]

Laws with economic sanctions designed to discourage black immigration into the north central states were supplemented by limitations on black political rights. The Ohio state constitution of 1802 denied black residents the right to vote, hold public office, or testify against a white person in court, and in 1803 blacks were barred from service in the state militia. In 1831 jury eligibility was changed so that only qualified electors could be considered, effectively excluding blacks from such service. These laws were not repealed until 1849.[8]

Ohio's legal restrictions were not unique; several other western states passed such laws. The legislature of the Illinois territory passed a law in 1813 prohibiting any black person from residing in the state, with violations punishable by repeated public lashings. The provision was carried over into the state legal system which threatened bondage for blacks who attempted to live permanently in Illinois. Michigan, Indiana, Wisconsin, and Iowa barred African Americans from their states, and the Oregon territory prohibited black immigration, entering the Union with this exclusion built into its state constitution. But restrictive laws on black immigration did not prevent the growth of the western free black population. By the 1820s, especially in border cities like Cincinnati, the free black population was substantial. Although they made up only about 2 percent of Cincinnati's population in 1820, the city directory listed over 2,000 African Americans, or nearly 10 percent of the population, by 1829. In those states, like Oregon, where the black populations were extremely small, exclusion was supported by popular sentiment and a popular vote. Yet, there were black residents in every one of these states, and the laws were enforced irregularly. So long as whites did not feel threatened, they tended to look the other way as blacks settled in many areas of these frontier states (Table 5.1).[9]

The remarkably rapid population growth on the western frontier during the 1820s was fueled by commercial opportunities stimulated by the opening of the Erie Canal in 1825 and, more generally, from economic

Tabel 5.1   Black Population in the Western States, 1800–1840

	1800	1810	1820	1830	1840
Ohio	337	1,899	4,723	9,574	17,345
Michigan	—	144	174	293	707
Illinois	—	781	1,374	2,384	3,929
Indiana	298	630	1,420	3,632	7,168
Wisconsin	—	—	—	—	196
Iowa	—	—	—	—	188

Source: Negro Population in the United States, 1790–1915 (1918; reprint, New York: Arno Press and *The New York Times*, 1968), 45.

recovery following a postwar depression. Cities like Pittsburgh, St. Louis, Cincinnati, and Buffalo acted as business outposts for the development of the surrounding territory. Cincinnati located in a free state but just across the river from a slave state attracted a growing number of African Americans, both free blacks and runaway slaves, and a white population of decidedly divided opinion about the institution of slavery. By 1829 the rapid increase of the black population precipitated a crisis that prompted town officials, acting in their roles as Overseers of the Poor, to decide that black laws should be enforced and to declare that all blacks in the city had thirty days to register and comply. In the ensuing months of extensions, petitions, and debate, African Americans were subjected to harassment and sporadic attack by the bands of white ruffians ever-present in early nineteenth-century cities. As a consequence of this reminder of the precariousness of black freedom in Ohio, contemporary reports estimated that over half the black population, well over 1,000 people, left Cincinnati during that year. Many fled to Canada, settling near York, Ontario in a place that came to be known as Wilberforce, named for a famous British abolitionist.[10]

Another Wilberforce, this one in southern Ohio, demonstrated the utility of neighboring free territory for conscience-stricken slaveholders. Settlement in Wilberforce, Ohio began as white planters visiting the summer resort at nearby Tawawa Springs established homes for their mulatto children there. The fathers helped guarantee their childrens' right to reside in Ohio by depositing money for them in Cincinnati banks. Many other Ohio settlements had similar origins. Chillicothe was settled in 1793 by sixty freed slaves who were brought to the area by their Berkeley Springs, Virginia master. Milton Township in adjoining Jackson County was founded in 1830 by Thomas and Jemima Woodson, mulatto offspring of plantation masters, who had bought their own freedom.[11]

The story of the Langston/Quarles family illustrates the complex ways the western free state of Ohio served the needs of the southern aristocracy and their freed slaves throughout the period of settlement. Ralph

Quarles was a wealthy bachelor Virginia planter and Revolutionary War veteran from Spotsylvania County who bought land in Louisa County, Virginia after the war. Like many of the gentry of the upper South in his time, he reportedly had questions about the morality of slaveholding. Nevertheless, he amassed land and slaves over the course of the years, and among the slaves he acquired in the early 1800s was a mulatto woman twenty years his junior named Lucy Jane Langston. Lucy was the daughter of an Indian slave woman and a black man. Available evidence indicates that she was probably the granddaughter of one of eight Indian men who attended the College of William and Mary during the 1750s, although she herself was illiterate.[12]

With his ownership of Lucy, the middle-aged bachelor began to build a family unusual among Virginia slaveholders not so much for its racial amalgamation as for its lack of concealment. Ralph Quarles and Lucy Jane Langston had their first child, a daughter named Maria, in 1806. The quality of the relationship which had developed between them by that time is attested to by the fact that Quarles granted Lucy and her daughter their freedom shortly after Maria's birth. Quarles took this action just a month before the deadline established by a new law requiring that freed slaves leave the state. Lucy took her freedom from her former owner seriously, and over the next six or seven years had one son, William, and two daughters, Harriet and Mary, who were not Quarles's children.[13] Then she began to make provisions for her family and her children's futures. She moved from the separate cabin she had maintained into the plantation house with Quarles, and by 1817 had given birth to two more of his children, Gideon and Charles. Quarles brought her elderly Indian mother to the plantation, and Lucy acquired title to 290 acres of land. When their daughter Maria expressed her desire to marry a slave named William Powell, Quarles bought Powell and gave them a nearby farm to manage. Since Virginia law forbade freed slaves from continued residence in the state, Maria maintained ownership of her husband, providing in her will that he be freed should he wish to leave the state. Curiously, her will directed that six other slaves she owned be sold for her estate.

Ralph Quarles was ostracized by all but one of his white neighbors, a man named William Gooch. Quarles created his own society, running a relatively benevolent plantation with no overseer and a task-oriented division of labor with the position of foreman rotating among the slaves. He taught his children to read and write and instructed them in the fundamentals of plantation business, tutoring them in the early morning before their work. It was into this life that Lucy and Ralph's last child, John Mercer Langston, was born in mid-December 1829, the pampered child of his parents' old age with the run of the plantation.

In the early 1830s the Virginia legislature, frightened by a slave rebellion in Virginia led by Nat Turner, faced the constant threat of slave revolt and passed new restrictions on free blacks. When Quarles died in the spring of 1834, the loss of his protection made the Langstons' precarious position more dangerous. By the time Lucy died later that year, she had made arrangements to assure her children's security. Quarles' will left some land and twelve slaves to his three nephews and freed the rest of his slaves, leaving enough money to each of four freedmen to buy a small tract of land in the West. The rest of his estate was divided equally between his sons Gideon, Charles and John, each to receive his inheritance at age twenty-one. Lucy Langston left her own property to her three other children, arranging for William Gooch to safeguard the money for the youngest daughter who was not yet an adult. Gooch also promised her that he would take four-year-old John into his home and see that he received an education.

By the fall of 1834, William Gooch and his family, the four freed slaves, and all of the Langston sons and daughters except Maria Langston Powell had made the difficult trip by wagon and horseback over the mountains through slave territory into southern Ohio. William, Lucy's oldest son, obtained a position as servant to the former governor of Ohio, Duncan McArthur, in Chillicothe. The freedmen and one Langston daughter located in the black settlement of Milton Township in Jackson County. Gideon and Charles settled nearby in Chillicothe and eventually enrolled in the preparatory department of Oberlin College. Young John was established as a member of the family of William and Matilda Gooch and their three daughters, the youngest of whom was responsible for his education until he was old enough to enroll in public school. Both Charles and John were registered under the guardianship of Gooch who, in accordance with Ohio law, posted a $20,000 bond for them.[14]

Despite the many advantages of liberty and security that African Americans found in the western states, capriciously enforced exclusionary laws were always a shadow cast over the lives of black residents. They could be called into play whenever any white person needed a weapon against a black job competitor or business rival. Although they were modeled on laws aimed at preventing the dependency of poor strangers on public charity, all African Americans, both affluent and poor, were vulnerable. Black laws were also variably enforced within states, with the northern regions of western states, generally peopled by white migrants from the North, being most hospitable to African Americans. In Cleveland, for example, blacks were allowed to vote in direct violation of state law, while in Cincinnati restrictive regulations were much more likely to be enforced. Chicago was the most tolerant area of Illinois, whereas Cairo on the state's southern boarder was far more hostile to black settlement.

These differences generally reflected the strength of the influence of southern economics, politics, and social connections on the regions involved. Although Oregon bordered no southern state, its white settlers were heavily southern in origin. Many had joined wagon trains assembled in St. Louis, Missouri, hoping to leave slavery behind. Often believing that the presence of free blacks endangered the peace and harmony of white society, they resisted including blacks in the "new" region. Ironically, several black settlers were already in Oregon before most of the original white settlers arrived. One African-American businessman and land speculator named George Bush, who had come west with $3,000 hidden in the false bottom of his covered wagon, had even helped finance some of the early wagon trains that brought whites to the territory. In recognition of the important role that he played in the early settlement, Oregon's legislature specifically exempted Bush and his family from measures prohibiting black people from becoming residents.[15]

Cincinnati had a predominantly southern-born population and was tied to the South as a port and trading center for goods traveling up and down the Ohio and Mississippi Rivers. In contrast, northern Ohio had fewer southern trade connections and was settled by New Yorkers and New Englanders. Thus, despite political restrictions, John Mercer Langston became one of the first African Americans to hold elective office in America when he became clerk of Brownhelm Township near Oberlin in north-central Ohio in 1855.[16] Despite Michigan's exclusionary laws, blacks settled in the frontier outpost of Detroit; its black population of 126 people in 1830 grew to almost 600 by mid-century. In the south-western corner of the state in Cass County near the Indiana border, a small farming community of almost 300 ex-slaves from Virginia was established in the 1840s on land provided by the estate of their former master, Sampson Saunders. By 1850 Saunders Colony had a population of almost 400, more than half of whom were voters.[17]

Although local sentiment sometimes allowed blacks to circumvent restrictive laws, especially in isolated areas, they could not totally escape legal restrictions or popular opposition. One plan to settle some 500 ex-slaves from Virginia in southern Ohio was abandoned when whites in Ohio threatened armed attack. Even in the East where efforts to legally exclude blacks were not successful, there were severe limitations on black rights, and sometimes formerly granted rights were withdrawn. Between 1822 and 1842, New Jersey, Pennsylvania, Connecticut, and Rhode Island revised their state laws to exclude black voters technically previously allowed to vote. In New York State blacks voted on an equal footing with whites until 1821. Liberalized property requirements for white voters in New York during the 1820s established separate racial standards for voting and effectively barred most black men from the franchise.[18]

The contention that African Americans were not able to support themselves and would drain society's resources was but one part of a broader argument presented by white authorities to justify restricting black civil and political rights. The supposed African-American inclination toward criminal behavior was another. Indeed, blacks were overrepresented in the jails since they were far more likely to be poor, and the most common

crimes were inextricably linked with poverty. Additionally, the crime of
running away from slavery only applied to blacks and tended to inflate the
numbers of black criminals. Nearly half of the thirty-six blacks imprisoned in Philadelphia between January and September 1795, for example,
were runaways. Then too, the poverty of most ex-slaves as they ran away,
were freed, or finished their indentures made them more vulnerable to
arrest and imprisonment for debt or vagrancy.[19]

Historians have noted an increasing concern with property and its
security in the developing new nation, and the nature of the prison population during the last decades of the eighteenth century reflected these
concerns. Property crimes accounted for at least 80 percent of the arrests
in Philadelphia during that period, and members of the neediest groups
were most likely to commit those crimes. Billy G. Smith found that rob-
beries in the 1790s in Philadelphia were committed mainly by African
Americans and Irish immigrants who often stole clothing or food. G. S.
Rowe found that nearly three quarters of the crimes committed by black
men between 1780 and 1800 were property crimes. Fewer than one third
of white men's crimes were property offenses, while over one third were
crimes against persons (compared with only 17 percent of black males'
crimes). Whites were much more likely to be arrested for crimes against
the public order like rioting or keeping a drinking house or a house of
prostitution, crimes nearly nonexistent among blacks. Such differences
may partially reflect the opportunity structure of criminal activity, with
African Americans located at the lowest, most desperate, position.[20]

The pattern was the same in all the growing eastern cities with their
developing class structure and increasing concentrations of wealth.
Leonard Curry found that blacks were from two to three times more
likely to be incarcerated than would be expected from their proportion of
the population in New York City during the 1820s. Blacks were vastly
overrepresented in the house of correction in Boston by the late 1830s
and early 1840s. About four times the number of blacks were incarcerated
there in those years than would have been expected from their numbers in
the total population.[21] Comparing all those incarcerated with those convicted of serious crimes further illuminates the importance of poverty in
determining the criminal population. One study of the prison population
by Noel Ignatiev found that from the late 1780s to the mid-1820s about
one third of those incarcerated in the Walnut Street Jail in Philadelphia
were black, well over their proportion in the population but roughly
equivalent to their representation among the poor. Ignatiev calculated
that about the same percentage (3.5 percent) of the black poor and the
white poor were incarcerated. Incarcerations, however, included those
arrested for both petty and more serious offenses and those awaiting trial
who might not be found guilty of any offense. In fact, three times as many
people were arrested in Philadelphia as were convicted. When only felony
convictions are considered, between 1787 and 1795, for example, blacks

were only 15 percent of those convicted. The role of poverty is apparent among these more serious crimes as well. Among convicted felons almost two thirds of whites and nearly three quarters of blacks were foreign born; immigrants were among the poorest of both groups.[22]

One group of black immigrants was seen as a special threat to law and order. Blacks from St. Dominigue were suspect because of their extreme poverty, their color, their strange customs and beliefs, and the reason for their immigration. Slave unrest on the plantations of the French-held Caribbean island drove some slaveholders to seek refuge in the United States as early as 1787. By the time a full-scale revolution for freedom from slavery and independence from France developed, many had escaped and brought their slaves with them. By 1793 an estimated 10,000 had made their way to the mainland. Most sought refuge in the South, but many French royalists settled in the northern cities, where they added the French language to the English, German, and Dutch already spoken there.[23]

In 1792 French refugee slaveholders petitioned for an exemption from the abolition laws, arguing that congressmen attending legislative sessions in Philadelphia were not required to free the slaves they brought to the city, even if they stayed beyond the legal limit of six months.[24] In refusing their petition the authorities declared that slavery was "obviously contrary" to the state constitution of 1790 and referred the matter to a legislative committee that recommended immediate and total abolition in the state. Although an epidemic interrupted action on the issue, the diverging paths of the state and the federal governments were clear.[25]

French-speaking slaves from St. Dominigue were conspicuous in the northern cities. Slavery on St. Dominigue was notoriously brutal, and these scarred and branded blacks were harshly treated by their masters. Once freed, they were among the poorest of the population and settled together in the cheapest, least desirable sections of the city. They practiced the religion called voodoo that predominated on the island, an adaptation to Catholicism of African religion dominated by Dahomean forms. The divinations, sacrifices, spirit possession, and trances that were part of the practice of this religion were strange indeed to the white Protestants of New York and Philadelphia. The most disturbing aspect of this religion, however, was undoubtedly its association with the organization of the long and bloody slave revolt in Haiti. These poverty-stricken French blacks with their especially alien ways, coming from an area associated with violent social upheaval, were among the most threatening of the "dangerous classes."[26]

The actions of a group of "French negroes" in New York City in 1801 further fueled such fears. When a white immigrant from the island tried to sell her slaves out of the state, twenty people attempted to stop the sale and a street fight erupted. They confirmed their willingness to use violence against the holders of slave property by threatening to "burn the house, murder all the white people in it and take away a number of the black slaves." Local sympathies were demonstrated by evening when hundreds of blacks congregated at the house and clashed with fifty watchmen. Contrary to the wishes of the rioters, the slaves were not released, and twenty-three rioters served time in jail for their participation.[27]

Foreign blacks were often the objects of suspicion. Spanish blacks were believed to be the instigators of waves of arson in New York City in the eighteenth century. The thwarted massive slave revolt led by Gabriel in 1800 outside of Richmond and the dread of the possibility that the Haitian Revolution might spread to the United States reinforced apprehension about blacks from St. Dominigue in the early nineteenth century. Although the focus of concern about Haitian refugees was often on their feared propensity for revolutionary violence, the greatest problems were associated with their extreme poverty. They were, in fact, more likely to be involved in the types of disorder and criminality associated with poverty.

Ironically, the racially restricted system of employment practically guaranteed that many free blacks would become poor, dependent and, perhaps, criminal. In most cases, African Americans were excluded from all but the most undesirable, lowest paid jobs in society, although the specific employment open to them depended on the local economy. From two thirds to three quarters of African Americans who were employed in antebellum northern cities worked at jobs requiring little skill or education. Port cities offered opportunities as sailors and boatman on seagoing or river vessels or as dock workers on the crews that tended cargo ships while they were in port. These jobs employed large numbers of black men who had few other work choices. Dock labor was often short-term day labor. Each day a foreman took stock of the work to be done, the number of ships to be loaded or unloaded, or the volume of cargo to be transported from the dock to city merchants or farmers in the surrounding areas, and hired a crew accordingly. In Boston's harbor, Buffalo's lakefront, or Cincinnati's riverfront, men gathered each morning on the docks where the work was apportioned. Commonly, black workers were selected last and for the least desirable jobs. A regular at the job site might get work day after day, but there was little stability. Even a slight decrease in port business resulted in an immediate decline in jobs for blacks.

Dock work was hard and sometimes dangerous. Since northern ports remained active so long as the weather allowed, winter cold and wet clothing often added to the rigors of the work as longshoremen sloshed about carrying huge loads. Onlookers were impressed by the phenomenal strength and skill of some workers who were able to handle as many as three of the immense barrels called hogshead at one time. Hulking seamen, they noted, could barely handle just one hogshead. As one observer commented, "I have known several instances of middle-size Negroes who from . . . practical skill would turn three hogsheads . . . upon their ends at once, each . . . weighing one thousand pounds net weight."[28]

Some stevedores acted as independent contractors, taking jobs on long-term agreements with merchants and shipping companies. Not many of these contractors were black, but there were a few. James Gardner was one who worked out of the port of Boston. He supplied his own crew and the handcarts, blocks, tackles, and winches to load or unload vessels and to move cargo between ships and warehouses.[29] Although most African Americans were common laborers, a few worked at skilled jobs on the docks. Some had even had experience in slavery as shipbuilders and carpenters. At harbors in the East there were a small number of blacks who held important jobs as stowers. An improperly loaded cargo could contribute to the sinking of a ship in even a light storm; it was stowers who ensured that the cargo was distributed in a way that maintained the craft's balance. Skilled jobs were more highly paid and harder for blacks to acquire.

Seafaring was an important source of employment for African Americans, although generally at sea, as on the docks, only the least desirable jobs were available to them. Most were deck hands who did dangerous and strenuous work—climbing the rigging, repairing sails, setting rope, and the like. A privileged few served as pilots who guided ships and smaller boats through inland waterways and harbors. Since blacks were more likely to serve aboard river or coastal boats and barges than on larger oceangoing ships, black pilots and even navigators were more likely to be used in river, lake, and bay transport. One historian reported that "many barges and sloops had all black crews; schooners and brigantines tended to have sixty to seventy percent of their crew black, and large ships tended to have thirty-four percent of their crew black."[30]

African Americans who crewed these ships and worked the docks were among those most vulnerable not only to the vagaries of the local economy but to national and international market fluctuations. As the new government took shape and established financial mechanisms to deal with debts incurred in the war, new economic initiatives promised future jobs. In 1789 British immigrant Samuel Slater recreated the latest English textile machinery in Massachusetts, and in that year the first charter for a manufacturing company was granted by the state, but few blacks obtained jobs in the factories. Of greater importance to them was the opening of trade with China in 1785 by American merchants freed from the British Navigation Acts. Boston traders initiated a new triangular trade, bartering trinkets, clothing, and hardware for sea otter pelts with the Indians in the Pacific Northwest and trading these pelts for teas and silks in China.

As American business and its merchant fleet moved into Asia, black sailors moved with them. Anthony D. Allen ran away from slavery in German Flats, New York near Schenectady in the late eighteenth century and became a sailor. He sailed to Europe, to the Pacific Northwest, and in 1806 was one of a number of black seamen who filled out the crews that brought American goods to the lucrative Chinese market. Allen's travels

brought him new opportunities, and he eventually became one of many
black sailors who jumped ship in the Hawaiian islands. He worked as a
ship's steward in the islands, received a grant of six acres of land on Oahu
(in present-day Waikiki), and took two Hawaiian wives, as he reported, in
accordance with "the custom of the country and the practice of some of
[his] white neighbors." He raised a family in Hawaii and for many years
operated a farm, trading station and hospital serving the many ships
which stopped there.[31]

The expanding sea trade, growing economic prosperity, and the
promise of economic stability represented by the ratification of a federal
Constitution in the summer of 1788, attracted many laborers, seamen,
merchants, servants, and artisans to the rapidly growing coastal cities.
Another seaman who took advantage of the new trading opportunities
was a Massachusetts native of African and American Indian ancestry
named Paul Cuffe. Paul was the seventh child of the ten children of
Cuffe Slocum, also known as John Cuffe, and Ruth Moses. The Ashanti
called Kofi had been captured when he was about ten years old and
shipped to America where he was bought by Quaker merchant Ebenezer
Slocum of Dartmouth (later Westport and New Bedford), Massachusetts.
Ebenezer Slocum's nephew John bought Kofi fifteen years later, but after
a few years was convinced by growing Quaker opposition to slaveholding
and gave the slave his freedom. Freed in the mid-1740s, Cuffe Slocum
soon married Ruth Moses, a local Wampanoag woman whose people
were farmers, seafarers, and long-time whalers.[32]

For many years Cuffe Slocum and Ruth Moses and their growing family lived on an island off the coast, plying the waters of Buzzard Bay to
maintain commercial and familial ties with Dartmouth on the mainland
and with the large Indian settlement at Chilmark on Martha's Vineyard.
After nearly twenty years of freedom, including living for a few years in
the Indian community at Chilmark, Cuffe Slocum had saved enough
money to purchase a 116-acre farm in Dartmouth. The large family
moved back to the mainland when Paul was eight years old and lived
together there until the patriarch of the family died six years later in
1772. After his father's death, young Paul shipped aboard whalers sailing
out of Dartmouth for the Bay of Mexico and the West Indies. The outbreak of war meant that sailors faced the danger of being captured, and
in 1777 Paul Cuffe and black Bostonian Prince Hall were among the seamen from the ship *Charming Polly* who spent three months in a British
prison in New York. During the war Paul Cuffe used his years of experience sailing the waters around Nantucket and New Bedford to trade
between the mainland and the islands in a small boat, risking capture by
running the British blockade.[33]

Once peace was established in 1783, Cuffe married Alice Pequit, an
Indian probably from the Pequot community on Martha's Vineyard. His
older sister Mary had also married an Indian, seaman Michael Wainer,

who joined forces with Paul to begin a life-long business partnership. They acquired a schooner in 1787 and began fishing and whaling in the Northeast off the coast of Newfoundland. When trading opportunities increased in the early 1790s, Cuffe and Wainer acquired a second schooner and outfitted it with a ready-made crew, as five of the Wainers' six sons were old enough to go to sea. The Cuffe men were not the only members of the family to be involved in the business. Paul's youngest sister, Freelove Slocum, was an important partner in the family enterprise, helping to finance many of their voyages, selling many of the goods they imported and advising her brothers on the family's investments.[34]

In 1796 Cuffe and Wainer launched a new sixty-two-foot schooner, the *Ranger*, financed by the sale of their other two ships and built in the shipyards at the family farm in Westport. That same year Cuffe took the *Ranger* and its all-black crew into dangerous territory, sailing up the Nanticoke River through slave territory to Vienna on Maryland's Eastern Shore to pick up a cargo of Indian corn for sale in New Bedford. The appearance of this ship and its unusual captain and crew in the slave South created a sensation during the several days they spent at the dock. They were protected, according to Cuffe biographer Lamont Thomas, by the good conduct of the crew and the impeccable credentials of its captain. During this period Paul Cuffe built a profitable business as a seafarer and businessman, a business with its basis in his extended family and in an extensive international Quaker merchant trading network.[35]

Cuffe was exceptionally successful, but there were a few other black sailor entrepreneurs who owned and commanded ships. Absalom F. Boston, the son of Seneca and Thankful Micah Boston, was born free in 1785. By 1800 he had begun his life as a mariner and laborer. He ended his life in 1855 as a businessman operating a public inn and a retail store. Before he left the sea he captained a whaling ship, the *Industry*, which sailed out of Nantucket in the spring of 1822 with an all black crew bound for the Bay of Mexico.[36] Another free man of color who commanded and financed trading voyages was Paul Cuffe's son-in-law, Richard Johnson of New Bedford. Johnson served as captain of various trading ships during the 1820s. In 1824 he commanded and helped finance the trading vessel *Rodman* in partnership with a white man, Peleg Crowell. The two sailed their ship into southern waters putting in at Charleston harbor where Johnson was threatened with prison under the Negro Seamen Act which provided that black sailors must be incarcerated for the length of their vessel's stay in port. Johnson's status as an owner and captain was considered only to the extent that the local magistrate allowed him to leave the state rather than be jailed. As a result, they lost the trade they might have done in Charleston.[37]

Unlike Allen, Cuffe, Boston, or Johnson, most black sailors suffered great hardships and gained little prosperity. Their families were without husbands and fathers for months, sometimes years, while their men were at sea, often going without their incomes until the ship returned to port and the proceeds of the voyage were divided. Under these circumstances black women played vital roles in the production of family income. The majority of black women were gainfully employed throughout the first half of the nineteenth century, most as domestic servants in the homes of upper- and middle-class white families.

Domestic labor was demanding, undesirable, and poorly paid, and many native-born white women found other opportunities in sewing, dressmaking, or teaching. During the 1830s and 1840s work in textile mills was quite respectable for young single women from New England farms, but Americans had such a distaste for domestic service that it was often noted by foreign visitors. Thomas Hamilton, an Englishman touring the country in 1834, reported that such work was "considered as degrading by all untainted with the curse of African descent." For black women there were few options—most other forms of work were closed to them. In 1860 in Boston over three quarters of the black female workers were employed in domestic work, Buffalo reported about the same proportion, and Cincinnati was slightly higher.[38]

Black women and their families needed the meager wages these jobs produced. During the 1840s in Philadelphia, a female servant could make from fifty cents to one dollar and a quarter for a day's work, but black women's wages averaged sixty cents. This was much lower than the average one dollar and fifteen cents per work day that black male laborers made. These figures underestimate the importance of a black woman's wages, however, since she was likely to hold a job longer and work many more days than her male counterpart. Thus, although her pay was less than one fifth of the man's per day, her contribution to the family income was significant and might account for half or more of the family income. Many male laborers were engaged in seasonal work, as seamen, dock laborers, teamsters, or porters, and were laid off in the winter when the ports were iced in. When declines in the economy curtailed commercial business, unskilled black laborers were likely to be laid off. At least until the massive immigration of very poor Irish women in the 1850s, black women had little competition for the domestic employment that helped provide some economic stability for many black families.[39]

Not only private families but hotels and boarding houses sought employees for the often arduous housekeeping services. Large hotels or the very wealthy often looked for male servants, a more prestigious choice. Male domestic workers, like butlers and doormen, made twice the salary of female workers, but their opportunites for employment dwindled during the nineteenth century. In Boston only a few dozen black men in 1830 and twenty-two in 1860 worked as live-in domestic servants,[40] and by 1860 only twenty-six of all two hundred black domestic workers in Boston were men. Men were still desirable servants, status symbols for their employers and, as one expert on staff for catering special occasions advised, "A respectable colored man will be found most efficient for this purpose." Those of more modest circumstances, seeking only one or two servants, generally chose female employees.[41]

In New York City, Boston, Philadelphia, and other large cities, employment agencies called intelligence offices specialized in finding domestic workers. Before 1850, several of these agencies provided the preferred black domestics, and employment ads in newspapers often stated a desire for American-born servants rather than foreign born. In Boston some wealthy Yankee families were distrustful of Irish workers and favored the more familiar black workers they termed "our good colored citizens." There was similar sentiment in other northern cities, but by mid-century this situation was changing. Black women were losing their advantage and Irish women were becoming the dominant group in domestic service in Atlantic coast cities.[42] According to one observer, Boston's restaurants and hotels were served by "corps of Irish chambermaids," and in middle-class households "Bridget became a familiar, indispensable figure."[43]

Still even after 1850 the shortage of domestic help provided opportunities. The story of Henry Watson's desperate search gives some indication of the demand for women willing to undertake such employment. In 1860 Watson traveled to New York City looking for a good cook who was also willing to do some washing. He managed to interview several prospects but had little success and claimed to have walked the streets of New York for six hours one day looking for an employee. Those he found acceptable would not take the job either because his family was too large or because, as accomplished cooks, they demanded job specialization. Some were unwilling to leave the city to work in his household. Finally, he located a cook willing to take the job, a bargain was struck, and a time was arranged for departure for the Watson home. Unfortunately, Watson fell ill with fever, was unable to meet the cook at the appointed time, and finally arose from his bed to find that his new employee had given up on him and taken another position.[44]

Although most black workers could find employment only at the bottom of the occupational ladder, about one quarter of those whose occupations were recorded in the census filled the middle occupational ranks of free black society. These workers included small shopkeepers and merchants who sold clothing, groceries, and dry goods, and others operating modest concerns that provided personal services like barbering, hairdressing, or tailoring. There were also skilled craftsmen, like blacksmiths, carpenters, and shoemakers, and a few entrepreneurs whose sailmaking, trading, or furniture-making afforded them relative affluence. Although property holding was not strictly distributed according to occupational position, and most held no property, workers in this middling group held more property than semiskilled and unskilled workers. Within this group barbers and clothing dealers were most likely to hold property, and many had the independence that came from owning their own homes and shops.[45]

The line between the relatively affluent and the very poor in black society was never fixed. Very successful entrepreneurs, like James Forten and Paul Cuffe, began in humble circumstances. Few blacks achieved such wealth, and success was often temporary, but there were hundreds of successful black businessmen. Peter Scudder was a familiar figure on the campus of the College of New Jersey at Princeton, where he shined the shoes of the white students and faculty and peddled apples and ice cream. By the 1850s his ice cream business flourished, and he purchased a shop on Nassau Street where he sold ice cream and candy.[46] Scudder's achievement gave him a respectable position as an independent businessman in the black community of Princeton. Anthony Simmons, who ran an oyster house and confectionery store near Scudder's, also belonged to the group of black entrepreneurs located in this small central New Jersey town. Simmons's thriving catering business enabled him to accumulate several properties in and around Princeton by the time he died in 1868.[47]

There were African-American entrepreneurs in every region of the North. In Boston Peter Howard operated one of a number of successful barbering and hairdressing businesses and Emilius Mundrucu, a political refugee from Brazil, was one of the city's most successful black clothiers. George Downing the caterer in Providence was even better known for his baths and water cure resort in Newport. John Jones migrated from North Carolina in the mid-1840s and established a lucrative tailoring business in Chicago. Farther west, William Alexander Leidesdorff, one of San Francisco's most prominent merchants and land speculators, left property worth $1,500,000 shortly after his death in 1848. Successful black craftsmen and businessmen were often cited by early black historians attempting to combat theories of racial inferiority. Stories of black achievement became a powerful argument against slavery.[48]

Although they received less attention from contemporary reporters, black women were also important to the business life of free black society. In 1816 Freelove Slocum, Paul Cuffe's sister, ran a small school and operated an import-export business in New York City. She also invested in her brother's shipping business and advised him on marketing the merchandise he imported. About the same time Grace Bustill Douglass ran a millinery shop in Philadelphia. By 1860 black women operated an impressive variety of enterprises. Sarah A. Tilman advertised herself as a fancy hair braider who made her services available to the ladies of New York. In Boston Nancy Ruffin, assisted by her children, became an independent retailer, marketing the fish and fruit that her husband in Richmond, Virginia shipped to her.[49] One of the most ambitious undertakings was the short-lived Female Trading Association established by over one hundred black women in New York as a grocery cooperative that sold everything from rice, meat, and spices, to brooms and brushes. Believed to be the first of its kind in the city, it was a source of great pride well beyond the borders of the local community. Many of its female managers later operated independent enterprises, and one member, Elizabeth Gloucester of Brooklyn, later used the business experience she had gained to make a great deal of money in real estate speculation.[50]

Hairdressing and sewing were the most common business activities of black women during this period. Most were able to manage only a modest living from their skills, but a few were extremely successful. Elizabeth Keckley was probably the best-known black dressmaker of her time because her designs were worn by First Lady Mary Todd Lincoln. Keckley, born a slave in Virginia, ran an elegant dressmaking shop in Washington, D. C. where she served the city's elite, including the wives of congressmen and senators. It was one of these clients, Varina Davis, wife of Jefferson Davis, who introduced Mary Todd Lincoln to Keckley.[51] In the North, through Hamilton, Newton, and Hamilton "Fashionable Dress Making," three black women partners provided their services to clients in Brooklyn, offering "Ladies and Children's dresses cut and made in the most fashionable style and warranted to fit." Mary Backous and Alice Wilkins designed and made mantuas for a select clientele in Cincinnati, Ohio during the 1850s, and at least seven dress shops in Buffalo, New York during the 1840s and 1850s displayed fashions by black women.[52]

Opportunities for free black skilled workers seemed limited in the North in some ways that they were not in the South. Slaves did virtually all types of work, and partly because almost all labor in the South was considered "nigger work," free blacks were employed at many levels, even in skilled jobs. It was not unusual to find black carpenters, blacksmiths, and coopers working in Charleston or New Orleans, for example. One observer reported that in New Orleans skilled work was performed by some white workers but also by a substantial number of blacks, "and of the negroes employed in those avocations a considerable proportion are free."[53] One black Virginian reported in the 1840s that in Virginia "both bond (slaves) and free (blacks) had trades." and he "had expected to find the people of color in free New York far better off than those in Virginia." Instead, he found that "many tradesmen [he] knew from the South were . . . cooks and waiters." Thus, northern blacks' occupations reflected both their job skills and the prejudice and discrimination which prevented many from using those skills.[54]

Official records paint a dismal picture of black opportunities for skilled work in Philadelphia. In 1859 they reported, "Less than two-thirds of (black workers) who have trades follow them," and "the greater number are compelled to abandon their trades on account of the unrelenting prejudice against their color." The exclusion of black artisans was even worse in Boston, where one foreign visitor reported seeing almost no skilled black workers in 1833. The few exceptions were "one or two employed as printers, one blacksmith, and one shoemaker."[55] White workers in New York City pressured authorities to exclude black workers from jobs requiring special authorization. The city regularly denied African Americans licenses as hackmen or pushcart operators, and although local officials announced that they would "issue licenses to all regardless of race," very few black men succeeded in obtaining them.[56] As a slave in Baltimore, Frederick Douglass was a skilled ship caulker. After he escaped slavery and moved to New Bedford, Massachusetts, he was unable to find employment as a caulker because, as he was told, "every white man would leave the ship, in her unfinished condition, if I struck a blow at my trade." Douglass was forced to take unskilled work at a fraction of the wages he would have made if he could have followed his trade.[57]

White workers in the North generally saw black craftsmen as competitors and tried to exclude them from the work force. Henry Boyd had been a carpenter in slavery, but he found that freedom in Cincinnati offered him few opportunities to work at his trade. There was work available, but employers would not hire him because, they said, white workers would never work with him. The one white employer willing to take him on was dissuaded when his white workers walked off the job. Boyd's experience was typical for blacks in Cincinnati. Blacks were barred from membership in the trade associations, dominated by German and some Irish immigrants, which pressured white businesses to hire black workers only for "appropriate" menial employment. One mechanic was reprimanded by the Mechanical Association of Cincinnati for taking on a black apprentice, and in 1830 one leader of a local trade group was tried by his organization for helping a young black man learn a trade.[58]

A few black craftsmen found work within Cincinnati's black community, but the general poverty there, as in all northern communities, meant that such work was scarce. Sometimes white abolitionists patronized black skilled workers, and a few like Boston newspaper publisher William Lloyd Garrison took on young black apprentices. One newspaper called on white friends of colored people to "encourage their industry" as a part of the "great duty of abolitionists," and complained that "few abolitionists ever call upon them" to do anything but menial work. One black Cincinnatian complained that "we have among us carpenters, plasterers, masons, etc., whose skill as workmen, is confessed—and yet they find no encouragement—not even among [white] friends."[59]

Beginning in the late 1840s and continuing through the 1850s, the difficulties of pursuing a skilled trade were further complicated by intensifying competition from increasing numbers of immigrants entering the port cities of the East and working their way to Buffalo, Cincinnati, Detroit, and Chicago. Competition was especially keen at the lower end of the occupational scale, but skilled workers and small business operators also felt the effects. Frederick Douglass noted the dramatic growth in the number of Irish barbers and hairdressers by 1853. "A few years ago," he observed, "a white barber would have been a curiosity—now their poles are on every street." Douglass lamented that white workers were becoming "porters, stevedores, wood-sawyers, hod-carriers, brick-makers, white-washers . . . so that the blacks can scarcely find the means of subsistence."[60] As immigrants filled out the ranks of developing craft unions, they increased the pressure on employers not to accept black artisans.

Occupational classifications provided by official records sometimes make it difficult to differentiate between skilled workers and entrepreneurs. James Forten, for example, was listed in the official documents of Philadelphia as a sailmaker, yet by the early years of the nineteenth century, he managed a business that employed a substantial work force and was a real estate investor and business financier.[61] The same was true for Cincinnati's Henry Boyd, classified in the city directories of the 1840s as a carpenter or cabinetmaker and in the 1850 federal census as a bedstead manufacturer. In 1836 Boyd established a small bedstead-making business, and by 1842 he built a factory, fitted out with the latest steam-powered equipment, in downtown Cincinnati. By the late 1850s, Boyd's business made many types of furniture, employed more than fifty blacks and whites, occupied two buildings, and was worth at least $40,000.[62] In 1859 Boyd's factory was destroyed by fire, and lacking adequate fire insurance, he could not rebuild. In 1860 he was still listed in the census as a furniture maker, a designation that had described his occupation throughout the great fluctuations of his fortune and changes in his occupational roles.[63]

Most artisans and skilled workers did not own their own factories or places of business, but all faced economic uncertainty. William Woodroff operated a successful small shop in Boston where he sold used clothing, but he could not weather the recession in 1837. He went out of business, never recovered from his misfortune, and died in the poorhouse in 1839.[64] With such a short step from solvency to destitution, rigid divisions between occupational levels did not develop in nineteenth-century northern black society. There were few barriers to associations between the relatively affluent and the masses of blacks. The laborers at the bottom were not isolated from the artisans and shopkeepers or from the relatively few black professionals.

Black professionals were slightly more secure, but not necessarily more affluent. This tiny group consisted primarily of ministers and teachers and included a few lawyers, doctors, and dentists. One study of black elites in Philadelphia between 1787 and 1848 found fewer than thirty holding professional positions, mostly teachers and ministers.[65] By 1860, when the census recorded the largest number of black professionals, there were fewer than 100 in all the cities we studied. Generally they represented less than 2 percent of all black workers, ranging from less than 1 percent in Cincinnati in 1850 to just over 2 percent in Boston in 1860.[66] Although few in number, professionals were extremely influential in the communities and esteemed as models of black success.

Blacks, some trained in African medicine, had worked as physicians in America from the early colonial period. Lucus Santomee was educated in Holland and in the 1660s brought his skills to New York City, where he served an interracial array of British and Dutch patients. In the 1740s in Connecticut, Primus, slave and medical assistant of Dr. Alexander Wolcott, was so respected that he was able to carry on his medical practice after he was freed. In 1792 a Massachusetts black named Caesar was a physician of such accomplishment that the *Massachusetts Magazine* published the formula for several of his medicines, adding that his snake bite medicine "never hath failed." Throughout the eighteenth and early nineteenth centuries, a few blacks received formal training in Western medicine, either in foreign institutions or in the United States. In 1848 David James Peck of Philadelphia graduated from Chicago's Rush Medical College, receiving the first medical degree ever awarded to an African American by an American institution.[67]

No black women were formally trained in Western medicine during the first half of the nineteenth century, but many women provided medical services to the black community. Many were midwives; some had learned their skills in slavery providing care for black and white women on the plantation. Sarah Douglass, of Philadelphia, studied anatomy and took classes at the Female Medical College of Pennsylvania and Pennsylvania Medical University during the 1850s. Not allowed a degree, she embarked on a series of lectures in Philadelphia and New York instructing black women in anatomy. She was criticized by those who believed the subject not suited for "the delicacy of woman's character," but the *Weekly Anglo-African* praised her lecture on the "Origin of Life," especially the "modest and dignified manner in which it [had] been given."[68]

Both black men and women faced obstacles to formal medical education. Commodore F. Buckner of Cincinnati attended medical school classes but was not allowed to formally enroll in any local institution. In 1850 Isaac Snowden and Daniel Laing of Boston were accepted to Harvard Medical School, but the hostility of white students and faculty forced them to withdraw.[69] The difficulties of obtaining an American professional education led some blacks to seek an education abroad. James McCune Smith was born in New York in 1813 during the period of gradual emancipation. His father was freed by the emancipation law, and his mother was able to purchase her freedom. Smith attended the African Free School in New York City and later entered the University of Glasgow in Scotland, where he earned a masters degree in 1832 and his medical degree in 1837. He practiced medicine in Paris before opening a medical office and drugstore on Broadway in New York City.[70] A small number of African Americans did manage to gain professional credentials in America. One study found over 400 black doctors practicing in the United States by 1860.[71]

In contrast to doctors, lawyers in the nineteenth century could receive credentials either from a school of law or from reading the law with an established attorney. When John Mercer Langston, honors graduate of Oberlin College, was refused admittance to J. W. Fowler's law school in Ballston Spa, New York, unless he was willing to pass himself off as a Frenchman or a Spaniard, Langston protested, "I am a colored American and I shall not prove false to myself, nor neglect the obligation I owe to the negro race." Instead, he read the law with a white attorney and was admitted to the Ohio bar in 1854.[72]

The strength of the antislavery movement in Boston provided opportunities there for a few African Americans to become qualified by studying with white lawyers. Robert Morris, born the son of an ex-slave father and a free-born mother in Salem, Massachusetts in 1823, gained his training reading the law with the prominent Boston attorney and abolitionist, Ellis Gray Loring. Admitted to the bar in 1847, Morris became a well-known lawyer with an integrated clientele. His success inspired African Americans who crowded the courtroom for his first trial. The trial was fraught with symbolism—a black man had brought suit against a white man for failing to fulfill contractual obligations, and the opposing counsel treated Morris with contempt—and his victory was especially thrilling. Macon B. Allen and John Rock were two other black lawyers who practiced law in Boston during this period. Allen was the first black man admitted to the bar, admitted in Portland, Maine in June 1844. John Rock was a man of many accomplishments. He was a dentist and a doctor, then studied law in Boston and was admitted to the Massachusetts bar in 1861. In 1865 he was the first black lawyer admitted to practice before the Supreme Court.[73]

The greatest number of black professionals were ministers, highly respected and influential men, and sometimes women, in black communities. Most served black congregations, some had integrated congregations, and a few led white congregations, but virtually all wielded both religious and political power in black society.[74] Teachers were another group of black professionals who were important community leaders. Their standing rested largely on the commitment of African Americans to education as the most promising route for the advancement of their children and the race. Most public schools were closed to black children, and the vast majority of black teachers worked in private black schools.

Some black teachers during this period were self-taught, many had just a few years more schooling than their students, but a few had college degrees. Peter H. Clark, one of Cincinnati's most influential educators and educational administrators, was trained at Oberlin. Clark expanded

the educational opportunities for Cincinnati's young people by conducting special sessions for advanced students after hours so that they might
become teachers. William Allen was educated at Oneida Institute in New
York State and became the nation's first black college professor, teaching
Greek and German at Central College in McGrawville, New York.
Although John B. Russwurm and Thomas Paul, Jr. had no college training when they taught at the private Smith School in Boston during the
early nineteenth century, both went on to graduate from college. Russwurm, finished Bowdoin College in 1826 and Paul graduated from Dartmouth College in 1840.[75]

Teaching was a low-paid and insecure profession, but it was one of the
few respectable fields open to black women. It was also the most common
occupation among professional women, and some like Mary Ann Shadd
of Pennsylvania made a reasonable living at it. Shadd was educated in
Quaker schools, started teaching when she was sixteen, and taught in a
wide variety of schools throughout the Middle Atlantic states and in
Canada. She served the cause of black education in the classroom and
combined this profession with her work as an antislavery editor and
activist.[76]

Black craftsmen, entrepreneurs, and professionals made up an important segment of black society. Their network of associations reached
beyond local and regional boundaries to black communities in the East,
the Midwest, and even to the West Coast. As the most literate segment of
black society, they were able to communicate through letters and the
pages of black newspapers which served local areas and functioned as a
national press. In this way community news was spread, and personal ties
were maintained. These upper-level workers were also tied together by
similar backgrounds and experiences. In every northern city studied, they
were more likely to be migrants who had been born in the South, reflecting the generally higher skill levels of free blacks in that region. They
were also likely to be lighter in skin color than African-American workers
at the lower end of the occupational scale. Mulattoes made up only 40
percent of the total black work force in all the cities we studied, but they
constituted 52 percent of the skilled workers, entrepreneurs, and professionals and were spread fairly evenly among these categories. Upper-level
workers also were more likely to be married, probably reflecting their
greater occupational stability and indicating greater security for their
families. Age differences between the groups were slight, and age was not
so important a factor for black workers' occupational level as it was for
white workers' during the 1850s.[77] For African Americans, working
longer did not generally lead to a higher-level job; their best chance for
having an upper level position was having a parent who was a skilled
worker, an entrepreneur, or a professional.

Upper-level black workers did develop associational networks, but they were not isolated from workers at other occupational levels. There were also residential concentrations; unskilled and semiskilled workers did tend to congregate near the docks in Boston's North End, for example, while upper-level workers were more likely to live on the lower slopes of Beacon Hill. Unskilled workers were also likely to be found in Cincinnati's Bucktown, with its less than satisfactory drainage conditions, but restrictions on where blacks were able to live and the relatively small number of upper level black workers contributed to the occupational integration of black neighborhoods, and individual dwellings, in every city studied. The residential patterns that facilitated associations between blacks at all economic levels reinforced community values, stressing the responsibility of individuals to other community members and to the race.

Successful blacks contributed to the welfare of their communities through their active involvement in and support of churches and community organizations and by providing aid to individuals in need. Catherine Dorham, a single woman, lived modestly after migrating from Kentucky to Cincinnati, where she boarded with John and Cassandra Taylor. When Catherine died, her will divided $10,000 between various relatives and friends and donated fifty dollars to the city's Colored Orphan Asylum.[78] Cincinnati's Charlotte Browning willed most of her modest holdings to the New Street Methodist Episcopal Church.[79]

Robert Gordon, a successful Cincinnati coal dealer, left a trust fund of $100,000 to the Colored Orphan Asylum and gave $25,000 to establish Gordon House, for "poor, indigent and aged colored women widows less than 40 years of age."[80] In Boston, Lewis and Harriet Hayden used the resources of Lewis's clothing store and their home to aid and shelter fugitive slaves. When Lewis died, Harriet donated several thousand dollars to Harvard Medical School for the establishment of a scholarship fund for black youth.[81]

The occupational structure among free blacks provides clues to the class structure of black society—although class is a difficult term to understand in this regard, and common economic need, limited opportunity, and boarding patterns tended to mute class distinctions. Yet there were important status distinctions, such as color. As illustrated by the census occupational data, there was a significant link between skin color and occupation. Mulattoes tended to hold a disproportionate share of skilled employment among African Americans and were most likely to run their own businesses. But the relationship between color and occupation was not direct, nor was it uncomplicated. It is an oversimplification to see lightness of skin color as the critical factor in greater employment opportunity. Mulattoes tended to have been born in the South, and since southern blacks were most likely to have been skilled workers before they migrated north, they were also most likely to hold skilled employment in their new homes. Thus, region of birth and skin color were related to one another and both affected occupational level. This finding, combined with earlier evidence indicating that color was also taken into consideration by African Americans in their choices of marriage partners, suggests that color was significant not only in economic terms but as a personal criterion as well. These issues also influenced the institutional and political structure among free blacks during this period.

The typical workers in black communities were not artisans and entrepreneurs, and black professionals were extremely rare. All, however, were expected to contribute to their communities and to the progress of the race. Community expectations for those who were most economically successful were especially great, but churches, mutual aid societies, fraternal organizations, and antislavery activities depended on the participation of those from all occupational levels. In a public lecture in Boston during the early 1830s, Maria W. Stewart exhorted black men to learn trades and establish themselves as businessmen as living proof of their manhood and of the worthiness of African Americans for freedom.[82] In 1858 John Rock, a doctor, dentist, and lawyer, reiterated the call to community responsibility and emphasized the importance of work in answering that call, declaring,

> The colored man who by dint of perseverance and industry, educates and elevates himself, prepares the way for others, gives character to the race and hastens the day of general emancipation.[83]

6

Sustaining and Serving the Community: Building Institutions for Social and Spiritual Welfare

When the French traveler Alexis de Tocqueville toured the United States in the 1830s, he reported on those things he believed distinguished Americans from the French and from other Europeans. American society, he observed, was characterized by a multiplicity of associations formed for myriad purposes by people of every station. "Wherever at the head of some new undertaking you see the government in France, or a man of rank in England, in the United States you will be sure to find an association."[1] Tocqueville was describing white American citizens primarily, but his remarks captured the mood and strategy of African Americans emerging from bondage every bit as accurately. Throughout the late-eighteenth and into the nineteenth centuries black Americans joined together to address their common problems. Associations varied in their specific purposes, but each was aimed at promoting the welfare and survival of its members and the civil rights and freedom of African Americans generally.

Blacks in Philadelphia and Boston had formed many organizations by the end of the first decade of the nineteenth century, while New Yorkers organized slightly later as the free black population gradually emerged from slavery.[2] Many of the earliest black organizations included mutual aid to ensure members against the adversity associated with poverty. This was one of the multiple functions of black freemasonry. When the British brought the Masonic Order to America in the 1730s, blacks' initial efforts to join were rebuffed. Finally in 1775, after repeated rebuffs, a British lodge within an Irish army regiment initiated fifteen Boston blacks led by

Prince Hall and authorized them to meet. After the Revolutionary War the American order refused to charter the black masonic group, and Prince Hall and his fellows resorted to gaining their charter from the British order. On January 4, 1787, three years after his written request, Hall received an affirmative reply and the African Masonic Lodge was finally established in Boston and given permission to hold masonic processions and burial rites. It was the first in a network of lodges providing fellowship and mutual support for members and status and training for community leaders in northern black cities.[3]

In 1791 Prince Hall was designated the "Provincial Grand Master of North America and Dominions and Territories there unto belonging." As the black Masonic movement radiated outward from Boston to other northern cities, lodges were chartered in Philadelphia in 1797, with ministers Richard Allen and Absalom Jones as officers, in New York City in 1812, and in several smaller communities in Massachusetts, Rhode Island, and New York State before the 1820s. Hall was influential in this development, and black Masons called the African Grand Lodge of North America they organized in 1808, the year of Hall's death, the "Prince Hall Masons." Most American lodges received their charters from the Prince Hall Grand Lodge in Boston; one Philadelphia lodge founded by black seamen in 1798 received its charter from a lodge in Germany.[4]

Since the organizational origin of the black American Prince Hall Masons was in a European institution, there is some irony in the fact that the elaborate rituals of the Masons claimed the order's genesis to be in Africa. The masonic doctrine in Europe and America contended that their principles originated in ancient Egypt and that Egyptian teachers brought the Greeks and Romans the knowledge base of their civilizations. European and Anglo-American Masons may have been able to divorce themselves from these mythologized Egyptians, but African Americans understood that the Egyptians celebrated by Masonic lore were Africans connected to the West and Central African societies of their heritage by centuries-old trade routes. The veneration of African roots was undoubtedly an important part of the Masons' appeal for African Americans.[5]

Although the Masons pledged to serve their membership, their commitment to freedom and racial uplift delivered a message of community-wide relevance. Their formal structure, prescribed hierarchy, and operation as a secret society, however, set them apart from the benevolent societies common in early urban black communities. Postwar hardships coupled with racial discrimination made organization for mutual support an economic necessity. The communal ethic of mutual responsibility that was a part of blacks' African heritage, and for many part of their Native American heritage, made such cooperative organization a cultural imperative. Typically, support for widows and orphans, and food, shelter, clothing, and firewood for the needy were provided by dues collected from the membership. Newly freed slaves in Philadelphia founded the first organization, called the Free African Society, with the cooperation of antislavery Quakers in 1787. Its purposes included mutual aid, the development of leadership for the growing free black community, and charity work among ex-slaves. Its articles of incorporation described its members as "the free *Africans* and their descendants, of the City of Philadelphia."[6]

Among the many other groups formed in the North were the African Humane Society of Philadelphia in the 1790s, the African Society of Boston in 1796, the African Benevolent Society of Newport in 1808, and the African Society for Mutual Relief of New York City in 1808. A few organizations like New York's African Marine Fund targeted specific occupational groups.[7] The use of African in organizational titles was not incidental, these were African people, some born in Africa but most only a generation or two removed, and the form and function of the early societies reflected this connection. Perhaps the strongest link between the African societies in America and the African heritage of their members was the centrality of burial benefits among their various functions. Many scholars have noted the importance of a proper burial in the religious customs of African cultures. "Funerals," Robert Harris observed, "characterized an extremely important element of African society" since "African cosmology held that life must have both a good beginning and a proper ending." Folklore and archeological evidence in America indicate that many African Americans also assured an amiable relationship with the deceased by carefully observing proper burial customs.[8]

In Africa and in America, black funerals and burials were often occasions for elaborate gatherings characterized by singing and eating as well as religious observance. When Primus Jacobs died in Boston in the winter of 1817, Dinah, his widow, spent four days cooking for the mourners she expected. The Jacobses had been married in Danvers, Massachusetts in 1776 and moved to Boston shortly before Primus went off to fight in the Revolution in 1777. They lived in Boston for almost forty years but maintained relationships with friends and family members in Danvers and Salem, so that when Primus died Dinah expected a large number of out-of-towners to attend the funeral. Dinah's efforts and the benefits provided by the African Society made an impressive service and an extended gathering possible.[9]

Most white communities denied blacks access to public graveyards, so black mutual aid groups worked to establish their own. In 1790 the Free African Society of Philadelphia petitioned the city for land to be reserved for a black cemetery in the Potter's Field. By 1797, one New York society owned its own cemetery, a property worth $1,500, adjacent to the future building site for its church.[10] Although some African societies included both men and women, most were all male and it was common for women to form their own groups. The reason for separate groups was probably a complex combination of cultural heritage, gender discrimination, and gender affinity. In Africa the "secret societies," on which the political and social organization of the community rested and into which every adolescent was initiated, were divided into male and female associations. In Philadelphia two of the oldest societies were the Female Benevolent Society of St. Thomas formed in 1792 and the Daughters of Tapsico of Mother Bethel Church established in 1805. By 1830 there were almost twice as many female benevolent groups there as male groups. Although the Free African Union Society of Newport, Rhode Island was open to "any person of colour whether male and female," women's participation was restricted, as only men were allowed to vote or hold office. In 1808, twenty-eight years after the group's founding, black women in Newport withdrew to form the all-female African Benevolent Society. Their break from the male-dominated society was apparently without rancor, and the men sent a delegation to the women to wish them well and to offer assistance. In return, the women sent a polite letter thanking the men and contributed ten dollars to the male society.[11]

Writing about early American voluntary associations, Richard D. Brown observed that joining such organizations was reserved for men, but from the 1790s onward women began to participate in charity clubs and social libraries. Presumably, Brown's remarks applied primarily to white women, but with some variation they describe the development of black women's organizations as well.[12] Unlike the generally middle-class white women of the charity clubs, black working women needed the unemployment payments and sick benefits their benevolent societies provided. African Americans, too, formed and joined the civic and self-improvement associations that Tocqueville found to be ubiquitous in America by the 1830s, but the precariousness of their lives made benevolent societies of at least equal importance. The Women of the African Dorcas Society formed in New York in early 1828 served the black children of their community providing them with clothing and other articles that they needed in order to attend school. The Afric-American Female Intelligence Society of Boston sponsored political lectures and discussions and provided health insurance and other forms of social welfare to its members during the early 1830s. Through these organizations black women not only contributed to the welfare of their communities, they also participated in the political discussions of the day, a role unfamiliar to most American women of the time.[13]

Although not all blacks could afford to join benevolent societies, the number of groups and their different levels of fees made widespread membership possible. In the 1830s initiation fees generally ranged from one to eight dollars, and the monthly fee from twelve to twenty-five cents. Some societies were short-lived, but others had a long prosperous existence. The New York African Society even rebounded from the theft of its treasury by one of its officers in 1812. By 1820 the society had not only replenished its accounts but had purchased bonds and real estate.[14] In the first half of the nineteenth century, six black benevolent societies in New York City were solid enough to have been formally chartered by the state. One study of black benevolent societies in Philadelphia found that almost fifty societies paid out almost $6,000 in benefits in 1830. Eight years later there were reportedly one hundred groups with 7,448 members—a remarkable number, even allowing for membership overlap, in a city with a total black population of 10,507. These groups had paid out $14,172 in benefits that year and had an additional $10,023 in their treasuries at the time they were studied. Typically such groups paid $1.50 to $3.00 a week to sick members and paid death benefits of $10 to $20. The extraordinary commitment to mutual aid shown by the existence of so many groups may help to explain the common observation of authorities that African Americans in northern cities were less likely than would have been expected from their status and condition to rely on philanthropy or public assistance.[15]

The early organizational life of free black communities demonstrated African Americans' economic concerns, their spiritual concerns, and their commitment to work for a better future. Mutual aid societies worked to provide some measure of economic security for members. These societies, however, cannot be divorced from the more informal often family-based mutual aid illustrated by the practice of taking in boarders, providing employment and community introduction. They were all part of the organized community assistance on which a person in need could draw. And they were often associated with the organization of religious meetings and churches or the educational institutions. All of these activities were intertwined in black communities, often sharing common origins, members, resources, and meeting places. The close relationship between the Philadelphia Free African Society and the Quakers has been noted; in its first years the society met in the Friends' Free African School. The society also contributed materially to the formation of independent black churches in Philadelphia in the early 1790s. Like the benevolent societies that were sometimes outgrowths and sometimes forerunners of the churches, church organizations ministered to physical, spiritual, and social needs. The lack of clear divisions between different types of organizations reflected the fact that African Americans did not generally make strong distinctions between practical concerns of this world and the divine concerns of the next. In Philadelphia one church society's prayer illustrated this view:

> Oh that the lord would help protect and defend
> this Society. May she increase in members, in
> harmony with god and man and in money also.[16]

The black church was the center of the free black community, and the spirituality it expressed was a this-worldly faith. Formal black churches began with small informal groups meeting for worship in peoples' homes, with Sunday school classes, with a core of black worshipers relegated to a corner or gallery in predominantly white churches, or in the camp meetings or revival weeks held by evangelical sects. The black church became a sanctuary from oppression where the spirits of God and the ancestors who had suffered through two hundred years of slavery and discrimination in America could be called on to give guidance, strength, and support to members of the congregation. Like the African cosmologies that came before it, black Christian theology tended to minimize the separation between sacred and secular, and the black churches were concerned with both the spiritual and the physical well-being of their members.[17] In carrying out their sacred ministries, black churches provided opportunities for spiritual worship and guidance, political forums, social and family aid associations, and facilities for community meetings, cultural preservation, entertainment programs, and education and training. For black ministers and congregations, working against slavery and promoting civil rights were also important ways to fulfill their Christian mission.

Christianity developed slowly among Africans in America, very gradually supplanting or supplementing the many religious faiths and practices people brought from Africa and taught to their children in America. White efforts to convert slaves were sporadic and sometimes controversial, especially in the South. Blacks in the North were more likely to be exposed to the teachings of Christianity, but they were subject to discrimination in white churches. Established white churches often provided African Americans with a second-class membership, restricting their seating to a black section, limiting the offices they could hold, and requiring them to take communion only after all white congregants had been served. Christianity had made significant inroads among blacks in the relatively egalitarian settings of the First Great Awakening before the Revolution, and the evangelical sects of the camp meetings continued to be the most popular forms of Christianity among African Americans.

There was a wide range of religious practices among American blacks. Some Africans enslaved in America were Muslims, having come in contact with the religion through trade in North Africa. They had a long tradition of education and religious study; many read and wrote Arabic, had been trained in professions, and were far more cosmopolitan than their kidnappers and owners. In the 1730s they included men like Job, a merchant trader who was reported to have written out three versions of the Koran from memory, Solomon, an office clerk, and Lamine, a translator. A generation later they were joined by such men as Abdul Rahahman, a soldier and heir to his nation's throne, Cochrane, a doctor, and Bilali, a law student. Though most landed in the southern regions, some found their way north in the late eighteenth and early nineteenth centuries.[18]

For decades after their enslavement, many Muslims retained their facility with Arabic and were able to correspond in the language with other Muslims. Some married Christian spouses, but they were not generally converted to Christianity, and some maintained what elements they could of strict Moslem religious observance, including the regimen of daily prayers, even in slavery. Many descendants of the African Muslims were converted to Christianity, however. Philadelphia's Robert Purvis, James Forten's son-in-law, was the grandson of a Muslim woman brought to South Carolina in 1766. Purvis was a Christian, but he knew about his grandmother's religion and was conscious of his African roots. Although he remained in the United States, he often expressed an interest in emigrating to the West Indies or to Africa.[19]

The smaller slaveholdings in the colonial North meant that slaves there were more likely than southern slaves to be regularly exposed to local Christian religious practices. Then, and later as servants in households, they would be included in household devotions, as Zilpha Elaw participated in the Quaker devotions of the Mitchels. A few African Americans like Paul Cuffe and the Bustill family adopted the quiet Quaker faith, but such integration into strictly European forms of the Christian religion was relatively rare. Most Africans in America practiced traditional forms of spiritualism, practices that continued for many generations. Even the occasional African Christian descended from those who had been converted by European traders or missionaries to the coastal nations of West Africa by the fifteenth century professed a Christianity incorporated into African ways. The survival of African religious practices was most significant among the large concentrations of West Africans in South America and the West Indies. Writing in the early eighteenth century, one English observer described the elaborate "lamentations, mournings, and howlings about their expiring" at a black funeral in the British West Indies. He reported that the blacks of Jamaica believed that after death their spirits would return to West Africa "and therefore regard death but little," probably a commentary on both the harshness of Jamaican slavery and on African religious belief. Another funeral witness detailed the ritual as Africans in America bore their dead with song through their community, pausing at the homes of those with whom the deceased had associated in life, then continuing on to the grave. Maintaining their ancient traditions, mourners buried articles of clothing or food and drink with the dead and danced and chanted to the rhythm of the drum.[20]

Such specific African practices were less likely to survive intact among the smaller African slave populations of North America than in the large African concentrations in the West Indies. The syncretic Christianity which developed as a result of European and African contacts in North America by the second quarter of the seventeenth century varied widely, depending on the size of the black proportion of the population and on social class differences. Christianity influenced African religious beliefs and African faiths affected the beliefs and practices of the formerly European Christianity.[21] According to historian Charles Joyner, in a slave community in South Carolina's low country, "They worshipped this new Christian deity in traditional African ways and they made European religious forms serve African religious functions."[22] Blacks in parts of South Carolina and in the New Orleans region of Louisiana into the nineteenth century and beyond belonged to voodoo or hoodoo cults transplanted to North America directly or through Martinique, Guadeloupe, Haiti, and elsewhere in the West Indies.[23] Hoodoo magic included the use of roots and herbal medicine, the belief in the power of the ax as a defense against storms, the use of charms, and the belief in the supernatural power of twins. Some beliefs were easily adapted—the ability of witches to leave their bodies at night and to cast spells and the power of red pepper as a defense against witches were elements of both African and European belief systems. White Christians not only incorporated elements of African religions into their own traditions, they used the black presence as a symbol in the struggle between good and evil. In eighteenth- and nineteenth-century New England the devil was said to have appeared to many white Christians in the form of a "small black man."[24] Respectable Christianity became increasingly intolerant of pagan beliefs and discouraged their public display, but it never succeeded in eliminating them.

In northern cities and towns blacks found it more difficult to maintain Old World communal religious practices. Widely separated and few in number, they were more quickly converted, but even there not all blacks adopted Christianity. Missionaries complained to the New York headquarters of The Society for the Propagation of the Gospel in Foreign Parts that many blacks refused to be instructed in the Christian religion. At Parting Ways in Massachusetts, the graves of nineteenth-century African Americans contain items indicating the continuation of African burial traditions. On rare occasions there were reports of voodoo being practiced among northern blacks even in the second half of the nineteenth century.[25]

Christianity made its earliest inroads among northern blacks and became especially popular with them in its evangelical forms during waves of religious revivalism. White elites often noted and sometimes disapproved of Methodist meetings in which multiracial congregations sang and prayed aloud in an expressive and frightening display of interracial fellowship and class consciousness.[26] A New England churchman concluded that such revivals seemed to provide valid religious conversions, observing that many blacks exposed to the evangelical spirit "appear[ed] to have been truly born again in the late remarkable season." Similar enthusiasms were reported among blacks in Philadelphia, New York City, and throughout the North, but their conversion from African beliefs was gradual from the seventeenth century into the nineteenth century.[27] Although African-American Christians subscribed to many different forms of the religion, from Roman Catholicism to Quakerism, and to virtually all Protestant denominations, they also retained many of their traditional African (and Native American) beliefs and were most likely to be converted by those congruent with African spiritualism, evangelical denominations emphasizing the workings of the spirit in believers' daily lives.[28]

A Second Great Awakening in the early nineteenth century brought the spirit of popular democracy into the churches and the spiritual lives of the common people. Spearheaded by strongly evangelical Methodists and Baptists, the principles of this "upsurge of democratic hope" had great appeal to African Americans and to lower-class whites. Historian Nathan O. Hatch's analysis of this populist religious movement clearly explains the great success these sects had in converting blacks to Christianity. Hatch described them as having a "passion for equality," a passion that led them to seek converts without consideration of race, to include blacks and whites, slave and free in their camp meetings and periodic church revival meetings.[29] A commitment to equality led their leaders to speak against slavery, to attack authoritarian church leadership, and to open the ranks of the clergy and church leadership to the uneducated, including black men and women. Unlike the more formal requirements of the Episcopalians, the Presbyterians, and the Congregationalists, early Baptist and Methodist ministers did not have to know Latin and Greek or to have an institutionally sanctioned education in theology. A famous evangelist from New England named Lorenzo Dow denied the right of the church hierarchy to pass judgment on the suitability of an individual to preach. The power to preach, he believed, demonstrated the spiritual fitness to preach. "[E]dducation [sic] don't give a man the power of the Spirit."[30] The Methodist and Baptist commitment to racial equality and antislavery principles in the first few decades of the nineteenth century were the necessary conditions for addressing the masses of blacks, but it was undoubtedly their spirituality that made these sects so appealing to African Americans.[31]

The styles of worship expressing this spirituality easily incorporated African traditions. Anglicans spoke condescendingly of the religious excitement that periodically inflamed the lower classes, judging it improper and inappropriate for a refined and intelligent religious sensibility. Many scholars have commented on the similarities between the highly emotional behavior encouraged at camp meetings and the "ecstatic behavior" brought on by spirit possession which was an integral part of the religious practice of West African peoples. The "shouting," physical gyrations, "holy laughter," the dancing, and the singing that was common at camp meetings would have been familiar to the West African ancestors of the blacks who took part in this religious ritual. The body movement that accompanied singing, the jumping and shouting of what African Methodist Episcopal Bishop Daniel A. Payne called "fist and heel worshipers," was especially important as a connection to the African tradition, specific movements common in the villages of sub-Saharan Africa and in the bush meetings of North America.[32] For blacks movement was a natural part of singing, and verbal participation was a natural part of communal worship. Ministers conducting evangelical meetings often found that the active presence of African Americans helped to build emotional excitement, to bring down the spirit, making the religious experience more intense for blacks and for whites in attendance. In this way African Americans helped to shape American evangelical religious practice.[33]

Although the revival meetings delivered thousands to denominational membership, some respectable white churchgoers were offended. Writing to her husband in the summer of 1806 just after attending a camp meeting in Pennsylvania, Budget Cary described a disturbing scene. She and her two female companions arrived on a Monday morning just in time to witness the conversion of a black woman who lay "stretched on a board apparently dead or dying [with] three or four [people] in the greatest distress imaginable weeping & wailing on their knees & over them stood three or four black fellows some preaching, some singing, & others clapping their hands & laughing att [sic] the joy they experienced by the conversion of so many sinners." After a while, Cary continued, the black woman rose from the board and "began to jump and clap her hands." Apparently shaken by this experience Cary was even more distressed to learn that this camp meeting would grow to more than 500 by the time it reached its apex on Sunday. "[T]o me it is an awful sight," she wrote, "such as I would never have any desire to witness again."[34]

It was not only the emotional style of the camp meetings and revivals that they were helping to fashion that appealed to African Americans, many other aspects of the services would have been familiar to them. The practice of baptism would not have seemed strange to followers of the water cult priests of coastal Dahomey or their descendants. The African call and response of musical worship was congruent with the common practice called "lining out," where the leader sang a line or two and the congregation responded in tuneful variation repeating the line.[35] Perhaps it is too much to say that these religious practices were transplanted directly from West Africa, but they were influenced by African traditions. As early as the seventeenth century, there is evidence that New England blacks greatly influenced the way the psalms were sung as singers and song leaders at predominantly white evangelical religious services. Indeed, by the end of the seventeenth century, reformers trying to change the common way of singing the psalm tunes complained of such typically African innovations as improvised embellishments, "the alteration of pitch and time values, the anticipation of the next tone, the sliding from one note to another and the sounding of harmony with the final pitch which was produced by sliding up in falsetto to the higher octave."[36] Although it is difficult to gauge with precision the ways and the extent to which African practices inspired evangelical worship, white worshipers were affected, and the cultural memory of African Americans embraced the familiarity of that worship style and established a basis of common ground between white and black evangelicals.

The evangelical sects that had the greatest success with blacks during the Second Great Awakening stressed the spiritual possibility of a direct relationship with God and God's agents. Seeking to return to a "primitive" form of Christianity before the development of elaborate church hierarchies and doctrines, the appeal of this faith was its simplicity and its power. The Methodist faith and spirituality appealed to Zilpha, a young teenager, in the first decade of the nineteenth century. She had a vision of Jesus while singing hymns and milking a cow and marked that experience as her conversion to Christianity. She was received into the Methodist church by a traveling preacher, attended religious classes, and was baptized into membership. A few years later, in 1810, she married Joseph Elaw, a man who had been disowned by his church and did not subscribe to the Methodist ban on dancing. The Elaw family moved to Burlington, New Jersey, and although her husband disapproved, Zilpha continued her active involvement in Methodism and had a remarkable series of spiritual experiences. On a visit to Philadelphia in 1816, Zilpha heard her dying sister Hannah sing in what she interpreted as a strange spiritual language. Before she died, Hannah said that she had seen angels and Jesus who instructed her to tell Zilpha that she must preach. The next year Zilpha attended a week-long camp meeting with thousands of worshipers, rising before dawn for devotions, attending preaching and testimonials during the day, and singing and praying by the light of bonfires and lamps and candles in the trees well into the night. There with a vision of light she became convinced of her salvation, and began a five-year "family or household ministry" visiting families in their homes.[37]

Occasionally, for several years, Zilpha reported hearing voices, and experiencing angel visitations and fortuitous events that she interpreted as signs of her call to preach. Finally, at another enormous camp meeting with an estimated seven thousand participants, supported by the ministers in attendance, she decided to answer the call and returned home to preach every Sunday to blacks and whites in her church. When her husband died of consumption in 1823, Zilpha incurred heavy debts to give him a proper burial, and she worked for two years, first as a domestic servant, then running a school, to pay off the debts. She then placed her daughter with a relative in Philadelphia and embarked on a life as an itinerant preacher, following the messages of her dreams and supported by the generosity of those to whom she preached. Zilpha Elaw spent the better part of fifteen years as a very successful preacher in the eastern United States, staying periodically at the home she established on Nantucket Island in the early 1830s. She made two trips to the slave states and preached to large crowds in the South, the middle states and throughout New England. She was well received by white congregations in New

England and by black congregations and mixed gatherings even in the South. On her first trip to the South early in her ministry, she impressed many of the elite in Washington, D. C. and nearby Virginia, and General Lee's wife invited her to their home to preach. Her second trip to the South in 1839 strengthened her resolve to leave for England where she continued her preaching for five years before publishing her autobiography. During her long and successful career as a preacher, Zilpha Elaw had faith in the guidance she felt from the leading of circumstance, dreams, the visitations of angels, and the voice of God.[38]

It was common for ardent believers in evangelical religions to report encounters with angels who advised them, hearing the voice of God, prophetic dreams, spiritual signs and omens. Many literally saw the light at their conversions; others felt the touch of the spirit on their shoulders. A people whose ancestors traditionally played a role in their everyday lives found the immediacy of such spiritual power believable. People enslaved or oppressed were sustained by the promise of such power. Baptists and Methodists motivated by such beliefs and proselytizing through camp meetings and revivals were phenomenally successful with African Americans. The number of black Methodists grew from under 2,000 in 1787, to almost 20,000 in 1800, and over 40,000 in 1815, by which time there were also 40,000 Baptists. By 1848 there were reportedly fewer than 300 black Presbyterians but 125,000 black Methodists and Baptists.[39]

The theology developed by black Christians was shaped by the circumstances of their lives in America. They identified with the children of Israel who endured slavery but who eventually gained their freedom and claimed the promised land. One foundation of black religion was the conviction that all humans would face God's judgment. The good may suffer the wicked's injustice, but "sooner or later, . . . we reap what we sow." The realities of black life tested this faith. In 1827 black minister Nathaniel Paul asked a question often on the minds of black Christians—

> And oh thou immaculate God, be not angry with us [for this] bold inquiry in this thy holy temple, why [didst] thou . . . look on with thy calm indifference of an unconcerned spectator when thy holy law was violated . . . and a portion of thine own creatures reduced to a state of mere vassalage and misery?[40]

Former slave minister, Francis J. Grimke, gave the answer that expressed their faith, saying,

> God is not dead—nor is he an indifferent onlooker at what is going on in the world. One day he will make restitution for blood; He will call the oppressors to account. Justice may sleep, but it never dies.[41]

This theology formed a worldview that directed the actions of the black church and its leaders. Doing God's work meant working against worldly injustice and hastening the triumph of good over evil. During at least the first third of the nineteenth century, especially at the informal camp meetings, Baptists and Methodists in the South and the North recognized the power and the right of slaves and free people, men and women, to be chosen by God to preach the gospel of freedom and justice.[42]

Richard Allen, one of the most important black religious leaders of the nineteenth century, had been a slave in Delaware who was converted to Methodism in a camp meeting. He was born in 1760 the slave of Benjamin Chew, a prominent Philadelphia lawyer who served for a time as attorney general of the colony of Pennsylvania. During the closing years of the decade, Chew fell on hard times and sold Allen and his family to a farmer near Dover, Delaware. For nine years the family worked the soil and tended the home of their new owner, until economic need prompted him to sell Allen's parents. Allen and his older sister and brother remained in Dover.[43] In the period after this painful separation, Allen experienced his conversion and joined a Methodist society. As he later recounted, "I cried unto Him who delighteth to hear the prayers of a poor sinner, and all of a sudden my dungeon shook, my chains flew off, and glory to God, I cried, My soul was filled."[44]

Allen was still a slave, but his owner allowed him to hire out his time. After three years, one year after the start of the Revolution, he had saved enough money to purchase his freedom, and the slave "Richard Negro" became the free man "Richard Allen." Twenty-two-year-old Allen then became an itinerant Methodist preacher, traveling through western New Jersey, Pennsylvania, and Delaware, supported by odd jobs and by the donations of the whites and blacks to whom he preached. After preaching for a time in Baltimore, Allen moved to Philadelphia where he held religious meetings for blacks at St. George Church and ministered to them in their homes and community meeting places. Another former slave, Absalom Jones, joined him in his ministry, a ministry that also included worship time in the meetings of the Free African Society. The society gradually adopted Quaker practices, such as a period of silence before meetings, and Allen, a thoroughgoing Methodist, withdrew. A few years later, in early 1791, the society under the leadership of Absalom Jones began to hold formal religious services in a schoolroom provided by their Quaker allies.[45]

Meanwhile, the enthusiasm of the black worshipers at St. George prompted Allen to approach the church's white leaders about establishing a separate black church. Twice they refused, and finally he was removed from his preaching duties by those who saw his request as troublemaking. Although Jones's group had included Quaker elements in their services, the Quakers remained uncomfortable with the Free African Society's worship, especially their singing of psalms, and soon the society moved their services to a blacksmith shop. By the end of 1791, Allen and Jones had again joined forces, decided to establish a nondenominational school and church, and began the difficult task of raising funds for an ambitious new building.[46]

Although many blacks grew progressively impatient with their inability to control their church life, most continued to attend regular services at St. George. Allen believed that a few of the "most respectable people of color" were uncomfortable with the idea of forming a separate black church and encouraged black members to bear even the segregated seating arrangements at St. George.[47] In 1792 when the building was enlarged, the black seating area was relocated from the main floor to a new gallery. One Sunday morning, by confusion or design, Richard Allen, Absalom Jones, and others took places in the white section of the gallery. While the congregation was kneeling in prayer, a white church official demanded that the blacks move. They refused to move until the prayer was completed, and other whites were summoned to physically remove them. Before the task could be accomplished the prayer was over, and the group, thoroughly disgusted and out of patience, walked out of St. George, never to return.[48]

Their determination renewed, blacks continued their fund-raising campaign, despite the setbacks of the yellow fever epidemic and philanthropists' redirection of promised contributions to support needy slaveholders who had escaped to Philadelphia from the revolution in Haiti. Donations from the city's blacks, aid from local white reformers, and donations from others like British abolitionist Granville Sharp finally allowed them to complete a large church building in the spring of 1794. Jones and Allen favored affiliation with the Methodists, despite the discrimination they had faced at the St. George Church. Allen believed the Methodist brand of worship served the needs of a broad spectrum of the community. As he later explained, "I was confident that no religious sect or denomination would   suit the capacity of the colored people so well as the Methodists, for the plain simple gospel suits best for any people, for the unlearned can understand, and the learned are sure to understand."[49] But the majority of deacons and elders favored affiliating with the Episcopalians (formerly the Anglicans), and Allen withdrew, leaving the leadership of the new church to Absalom Jones. Thus, established in 1794, St. Thomas Episcopal Church became the first black church in the United States. To help maintain its independence, Jones negotiated an agreement with the denomination that all the church's officeholders except its ministers must be Africans or descended from Africans. In 1804 the Pennsylvania Episcopal convention ordained Jones as the first black Episcopal priest in America. He remained pastor of the church until his death in 1816.[50]

After their withdrawal, Allen and a small group of followers worked quickly to establish their own church. They moved the blacksmith shop to a lot on Sixth Street near Lombard, renovated it, and opened the Bethel Church in a matter of months. Methodist Bishop Francis Asbury officiated at the dedication of Mother Bethel, as the church came to be called, just a few days after the doors of St. Thomas Church opened. In 1799 Allen was ordained a Methodist deacon, the first black so designated, but not empowered to exercise the full functions of an ordained Methodist minister. Bethel and St. Thomas were rivals, but it was not a hostile rivalry. As if to demonstrate that their theological difference did not prevent cooperative effort, Allen and Jones agreed not to simultaneously seek funds for their building campaigns from identical donors.[51]

All was not smooth sailing for the Bethel congregation. Philadelphia's white Methodists had opposed the establishment of the black Methodist church and presented many obstacles. Bethel was continually at odds with the Methodist hierarchy that sought to control the property and ministerial appointments. At its inception, Allen declared Bethel Church independent from the city's white Methodists and limited its membership to "descendants of the African race."[52] The next year, however, St. George's Church paternalistically listed Bethel's membership of 121 on its congregational roster, thereby increasing its own membership by more than one-third. During the first decade of the nineteenth century, Allen and his congregation resorted to legal action to block control by the white Methodists. By 1810 Bethel's black congregation, with almost thirteen hundred members, was one of the largest Methodist congregations in the country.

The great success of the Bethel Church is evidence of the power of Richard Allen's ministry and the appeal of his brand of Methodism. Allen retained the style of the itinerant preacher, believing that black people were not likely to be attracted to sermons that were formal treatises. "Reading sermons," he argued, "will never prove so beneficial to the colored people as spiritual or extempore preaching."[53] Allen also encouraged informality in the music for his services, and in 1801 he assembled a collection of hymns, selected because they were the favorites of his congregation. These were not all the traditional Methodist hymns, and white Methodists generally disapproved of the songs being sung in Allen's church. One complained about the "growing evil" of "merry airs, adapted from old songs" or of songs "composed and first sung by the illiterate blacks of the society."[54]

The remarkable similarity of these complaints to whites' criticism of the psalm-singing styles of seventeenth-century New England blacks attests to the African roots of the black Philadelphians' musical style. One visitor to the Bethel Church spoke of the chanting of "psalms in chorus, the men and women alternating." Eileen Southern, a scholar of African-American music, explained that

the choral response given by the congregation to the reading of each psalm, and the singing of the psalms in alternation by the men and the women ... [were] typically in the African tradition—the singers singing with all their might and becoming totally involved in the experience.[55]

To the European-trained ear, some of the music sounded like a "loud, shrill monotone" or "heart-renting moaning." Another observer was shocked at the way the black Methodists used music in their services, saying, "After [the] sermon they began singing merrily, and continued, without stopping, one hour till they become exhausted and breathless." Unlike in white churches, music did not merely punctuate a black worship service; it was a major component of worship. Observers commonly reported that the singing lasted anywhere from twenty minutes to more than an hour.[56]

Historians have generally attributed the appeal of simple hymns and spiritual songs to the illiteracy and lack of education of most blacks during this time, but this tends to confuse illiteracy with low intelligence. As a people with an oral tradition, Africans were certainly capable of maintaining a vast unwritten literature. Captain Paul Cuffe was astounded to encounter a Muslim man in Sierra Leone who had memorized the Koran, what he himself revered as the Old Testament.[57] Among African Americans, stories, songs, and bits of family and national history were passed down from generation to generation. Once the complexity of an oral culture is acknowledged, a clue to the importance and meaning of the use of simple, repetitious songs may be found in their context and use. Singing these songs for extended periods of time, improvising variations and harmonies on simple tunes, keeping time with hands and feet, and responding to the song leader and other singers served the same spiritual functions for black Christians as the ring shouts served for celebrants of African religions. Such singing was a cooperative activity that created a connection between participants, reinforcing the bonds of community. It was also an ecstatic activity, inducing the spiritual state which created a connection between the physical and the spiritual world. In the camp meetings blacks stayed up all night singing and dancing; there the connections to the ring shout were even clearer. Preachers at camp meetings recognized the importance of black participation to "bring down the spirit," and white participants too were moved by the power of the camp meeting hymns and spiritual songs.[58]

One white observer was critical of what he called the "extravagant" emotional and physical customs of the Methodists generally, but particularly disapproved of the African Methodists. Even in the churches, he believed, the emotional style of blacks had had a detrimental effect on white congregations.[59] Such reactions may have contributed to the continuing efforts of white Methodists to control the black Methodist church. On two occasions Richard Allen's black congregation in Philadelphia actually physically prevented white churchmen from taking the pulpit and managed to stop Methodist officials from installing their hand-picked black minister.[60]

The issue of control was a source of continuing tension. Richard Allen had negotiated a remarkable degree of independence for his church, since the national Methodist authority routinely maintained control over church property and appointments. Black Methodists did have some power in this matter—by 1815 there were more blacks than whites among Philadelphia's Methodists, and the number of black Methodists was growing more rapidly. Additionally, they were influential at the National Conference, since Bishop Francis Asbury had decreed that only itinerant ministers could attend, and blacks were well represented among the traveling preachers. On the other hand, as the evangelical denominations became more established, there was some effort to control the earlier excesses of their religious practices in a bid for respectability. Methodists, whose power was centered in the middle states, were under the greatest pressure from white southerners to oppose independent black Methodist activities in Philadelphia.[61]

The movement to establish separate black Methodist churches was widespread. After considerable communication, a conference was called in Philadelphia, and in the spring of 1816 delegates representing congregations in Maryland, Pennsylvania, Delaware, and New Jersey established the African Methodist Episcopal Church (AME), the first black Christian association of its kind.[62] Allen's Bethel Church and the Rev. Daniel Coker's African Methodist Church in Baltimore were the largest and most influential congregations in the new denomination, and these two men became rivals for its leadership. At first joint leadership was proposed, but Allen declined, saying that the small group did not need two leaders. Then, in a telling move, many, who described themselves as "pure blacks," objected to Coker's leadership. They complained that Coker, born of an English indentured servant mother and a black slave father, was too "light" in complexion to lead this premier black organization. With a man as light as Coker as its head, the membership was afraid that they would not be perceived as having an "African Connection."[63] Bowing to the pressure, Coker declined the position, and Allen became the first African Methodist Episcopal bishop.[64]

In 1822 branches of the AME church were formed in New Bedford, Massachusetts and White Plains, New York. By the end of the decade, AME missionaries reached Cincinnati, Pittsburgh, and cities in western New York. Allen's establishment as the leader of the AME church ensured greater influence for the Philadelphia black community among free blacks, as AME churches were added on the East Coast, in the Midwest, and as far south as Charleston, South Carolina. By 1830 the AME claimed more than 10,000 members, mostly in the Middle Atlantic states and in western Ohio.[65] It faced substantial white resistance in the South, where white fears seemed to be confirmed by the fact that many of those involved in the 1822 Denmark Vesey slave conspiracy were associated with Charleston's AME church. The church, which boasted a membership of almost two thousand, had been the meeting place for the conspirators. South Carolina focused on Philadelphia as the source of a radical

trend that incited its slaves to violence, and the state's official investigation named Allen as leader of this dangerous religious movement. After
the mid-1820s the AME was prohibited from organizing openly in the
states south of Maryland, but the denomination remained strong in the
North. In 1828 Morris Brown, a former member of the Charleston congregation who had fled to Philadelphia, was ordained a bishop. In 1831
when Allen died, Brown became the head of the AME Church.[66]

The appeal of the African Methodist Episcopal denomination for black
Christians was enhanced by its increasing contrast with the predominantly white Methodist Episcopal denomination. During the 1820s, the
antislavery stance of the denomination was muted to accommodate hard-
ening southern attitudes. In 1829 the South Carolina Methodist Conference established a mission designed to eradicate African religions among
plantation slaves. Especially repressive legislation made the churches a
special target after slave preacher Nat Turner's 1831 rebellion in Virginia.
White oversight of black churches and Sunday schools was strengthened,
and some black churches were closed. These changes in the South
affected Methodism nationally and made it less likely for black
Methodists to be granted the independence they desired.[67] In Philadelphia, the establishment and growth of the AME increased the prestige of
Mother Bethel, which soon eclipsed St. Thomas in size. Its freedom from
white control attracted new members and opened the way for leadership
positions for blacks at various levels in the denominational hierarchy. By
1820 Mother Bethel claimed a membership of approximately 2,000 while
St. Thomas served only a few hundred. Yet, as one of its later ministers
explained, winning "the mass of our people ... to her standard" was
never St. Thomas's primary concern, and St. Thomas saw itself as a more
exclusive church of "taste, order and intelligence."[68]

The religious division of Philadelphia's black community was partly
the result of the growth and accompanying diversification of the black
population there. There were similar developments elsewhere in the
North during the first decades of the nineteenth century as the black
communities grew. Unlike Philadelphians, in Boston blacks first turned to
the Baptist church, a denomination with its roots and strength in New
England. Like Philadelphians, black Bostonians who attended the city's
white churches faced discrimination. During the service at First and Second Baptist churches, they were limited to special "Negro Pews ... where
they could hear [but] not see the preacher or be observed by him or the
white congregation." Blacks tolerated this treatment until shortly after
emancipation in Massachusetts during the 1780s, when a small group
withdrew to hold their own services in private homes. By 1789 they held a
weekday afternoon meeting in Faneuil Hall and later met in a schoolhouse for Sunday worship. Finally, in 1805, with the support of the predominantly white First and Second Baptist churches, the African Baptist
Church was organized. In 1806 the African Baptist Church met in its

newly constructed meetinghouse in a black section on Beacon Hill and installed Thomas Paul, a free-born ordained minister, as their pastor.[69]

Since Baptists lacked the Methodists' centralized authority structure and allowed independence to their individual churches, blacks found little need for an independent association. They could form churches within the loose confederation of Baptists yet retain complete control of their congregational affairs, including certifying ministers for ordination. Boston's African Baptist Church was active in the movement to establish black congregations, sending Thomas Paul to New York City in 1808 to help organize what became the Abyssinian Baptist Church. Yet it also maintained close ties with white Baptist churches and became a charter member of the Boston Baptist Association when it was formed in 1812. The church also supported the denomination's foreign missions and the American Baptist Home Mission Society, and Thomas Paul conducted successful revival tours under their auspices. Two of Paul's sons followed him into the ministry, Benjamin served as pastor to the New York congregation his father had organized, and Nathaniel became the first minister of the First African Baptist Church in Albany, New York. In the Boston church, a period of internal dissension followed Thomas Paul's resignation in 1829, culminating in 1840 with the breaking away of forty-six members to form the Twelfth Baptist Church.[70]

An aggressive missionary campaign working through camp meetings and revivals led to the establishment of many other black Baptist churches. In Philadelphia in 1810, thirteen black members of a largely white congregation left to form their own church, and in 1819 a more amicable separation between white and black Baptists in Providence, Rhode Island created the African Union Meeting House as the first black church in that city. By 1820 the Baptists claimed about 40,000 black Americans in their membership.[71] Other denominations attracted smaller numbers. Black Presbyterians emerged as independent congregations in Philadelphia in 1807, in cooperation with the white Presbyterians of the city and under the leadership of John Gloucester, a former slave from Tennessee. Gloucester had come to Philadelphia with his master, a Tennessee evangelical preacher named Gideon Blackburn. Both men became part of the Presbyterian Evangelical Society in Philadelphia, and Gloucester, who had made a name for himself in Tennessee converting whites as well as blacks, became a popular preacher among Philadelphia's African Americans. The large crowds who came to hear him preach spilled over into the street when he conducted services in a vacant lot at the corner of Seventh and Shippen Streets. In the spring of 1811, the African Presbyterian Church opened the doors of its new building on that site. With Gloucester as its head, though interrupting his preaching to raise money to free his wife and six children, the congregation of 123 rose to over 300 within two years. Allen attempted to lure him to Bethel, but the popular minister continued to hold forth at Seventh and Shippen,

drawing some of the city's most prominent African-American businessmen, until his death in 1822.[72] Samuel E. Cornish, a free man from
Delaware who had studied under Gloucester and taught for a short time
at his African School, established the First Colored Presbyterian Church
in New York City in 1822, which later took the name Shiloh Presbyterian
Church.[73]

Presbyterians and Episcopalians were more likely than Baptists or
Methodists to be the churches of elite whites in both the North and the
South and "well into the nineteenth century [they] were still wringing
their hands about their failure to Christianize [free blacks or] their own
slaves."[74] They were less willing to be influenced by black styles of worship and more insistent on linking conversion to "order and decorum."
They stressed formal catechism, which in the South always emphasized a
slave's duty to the master, solemn and sober church music, "intellectual,"
often very dry sermons by dignified ministers who generally reinforced
the social and political message of white authority and black inferiority.
John Thompson of Maryland gave an oblique indication of the differences in appeal for blacks, saying, "preaching [at the Episcopal church]
was above our comprehension, so that we could understand but little that
was said." The Methodist religion, on the other hand, "brought among
us, and preached in a manner so plain" that the "way faring man, though a
fool, could not err therein." Tellingly, he indicated the appeal of the
Methodists' message as well as their style, as he continued, "It was something which [slaveholders] could not understand. It brought glad tidings
to the poor bondman; it bound up the broken-hearted; it opened the
prison doors to them that were bound, and let the captives go free."[75]
Thompson used the term "understand" in a particular way. Slaveholders,
he said, could not understand the preaching of the Methodists, but surely
whites did understand the veiled antislavery message of Methodist
preachers and found it dangerous. By the same token, blacks undoubtedly
understood and profoundly disagreed with the conservative message of
Episcopal ministers. Thompson understood their differences, and after he
escaped from slavery, he traveled to Philadelphia where he joined the
Bethel African Methodist Episcopal Church.[76] While thousands of black
people flocked to the Methodist and Baptist faiths, there were only two
known black Episcopal churches and twenty-one Presbyterian churches
established in the northern states before 1860. This compared with at
least seventy-five black Baptist, forty-six African Methodist Episcopal
Zion and 192 African Methodist Episcopal churches.[77]

As the Baptist and Methodist denominations grew and began to search
for greater respectability, their leaders attempted to discourage the
extremes of emotionality in their camp meetings and revivals. Bishop
Allen was tolerant of some emotional display in the AME church. He
joined with Daniel Coker and other AME leaders to urge the membership to "retain the spirit of singing" for "when the spirit and the under-

standing are united, it is believed to be a service acceptable in the sight of God, and beneficial to the souls of the people."[78] He and other leaders, however, came to disapprove of the emotionally charged worship of the tent meetings and were especially upset when the shouting, ring-dancing, and groaning crept into AME services.

By the end of the second decade of the nineteenth century, the traditional call and response practice of "lining out" hymns was being challenged in many churches by the introduction of choral "singing by note," with the congregation led by a choir. Some churches even started using instrumental accompaniment, a practice seen as sinful by more conservative congregations. Philadelphia's St. Thomas Episcopal Church installed a pipe organ in 1828 amid great controversy. When, a decade later, Mother Bethel Church built a choir gallery and introduced choral singing as part of the regular Sunday worship, several older members walked out in protest. Elsewhere ministers were censured, even removed by their congregations, for such outrageous innovations. When an increasing number of southern black migrants filled Mother Bethel with their indecorous music during the 1840s, several members reportedly left in disgust. In 1841 the concerns of the AME church hierarchy about the prevalence of traditional African forms of music in their services prompted the annual conference to pass a special resolution to "oppose the singing of fuge [sic] tunes and hymns of our own composition in our public places and congregations."[79] In 1852 Daniel Payne, a former AME historian who was highly critical of the emotional display and loss of control inherent in this brand of worship, was elected bishop of the AME Church.

Black leaders' interest in respectability was influenced by their political concerns. In their efforts to advance the causes of antislavery and racial equality, African Americans had sometimes been aided by white allies. Changes in American politics during the 1820s led to a shift in these alliances, a loss of many white working class allies and the gain of potential allies among white middle- and upper-class reformers. Earlier interracial alliances had linked people of similar life circumstances with similar styles of worship. These new alliances linked people with profound social and religious differences, differences that embarrassed some black leaders. As one historian of the period phrased it, "Many black leaders seemed to assume that white people would treat black people more tolerantly if whites could be convinced that blacks were becoming solid, assimilated, English-speaking Bible-reading Americans."[80] Implicit in the differences over the proper approach to worship were the issues of class and region.

The independence of their congregations made class and regional differences even clearer among Baptists. Even though the Baptists, like the Methodists, rejected such seemingly worldly activities as dance, black Baptists recognized "holy dance" as an important part of their religious life, and many of their services were as emotional as the Methodists' services. Black Baptists "shouted," clapped hands, and were said to "get happy"—so full of the spirit that they lost control. As one of the faithful explained, "When the ole spirit hit you, honey, I'm gona tell you the truth, you're not of yourself. I've known it to trip people, send um to the floor."[81] The music at such services contrasted sharply with the sacred concerts the more established black churches began to sponsor in the 1820s. These concerts featured instrumental musicians, choral works, and performers singing solos, duets, and trios. Commonly the music they performed was by composers like Handel, Haydn, and Mozart, along with music by black American composers. The Baptist Singing Society presented a concert at the African Baptist Church in Boston in the spring of 1833 that included an arrangement of "The Overture to the Marriage of Figaro" for a small orchestra and some vocal selections. At a much grander concert at the First African Presbyterian Church of Philadelphia in 1841, a fifty-piece orchestra led by Frank Johnson and a 150-voice chorus conducted by choral director Morris Brown, Jr. performed Handel's entire *Creation* oratorio.[82]

During the Second Great Awakening, black women had found important roles in the evangelical churches, had been accepted as preachers, and had served as itinerant ministers. Although they continued to have important functions in the leadership of the churches and to preach in the informal camp meetings, with the movement for greater respectability, many were attacked by male ministers for preaching in the churches. Julia Foote had grown up in the AME church in Albany, New York and had experienced a dramatic conversion at age fifteen, when she fainted at a Sunday evening revival meeting. Shortly after, following a week of prayer and visions, she was "sanctified," that is, convinced of her salvation from all sin, and began to preach to anyone who would listen. The following year Julia married a sailor named George Foote whom she had met at her church and moved with him to Boston where she joined the African Methodist Episcopal Zion Church.[83]

The minister of the AME Zion church was Jehial C. Beman from Connecticut, the son of an escaped slave and active in black education, charity work with the poor, and the antislavery movement. In Boston Foote continued to experience angel visitations, spoke to a women's group about her sanctification, and once again fainted at a Sunday evening prayer service. After this experience, Beman visited her at her home and expressed his disapproval of her religious expression. Beman's opposition to her preaching created some dissension in his church, and after she continued to meet with and preach to a group of members in her home, Foote was dismissed from the church for violating "the rules of discipline by preaching." Julia Foote's letter of protest to the Philadelphia Conference received little response. While there for the conference meeting in the early 1840s, she joined forces with three other women preachers who had also been opposed by the ministers and hired a hall for a series of religious meetings. With these meetings Foote launched her career as an itinerant preacher, traveling through New York State, Pennsylvania, New Jersey, Connecticut, and Rhode Island for about fifteen years. Like Zilpha Elaw, whose American itinerancy ended a few years before Foote's began, she was a successful evangelist who spoke to large crowds in camp meetings, homes, and churches. Unlike Elaw, although many church members and leaders were enthusiastic about her ministry, she was often opposed by ministers who did not approve of women preachers.[84]

The disapproval of many black religious leaders did not stop women from preaching. Black women asserted their right to both participation and leadership, publicly challenging male authority as virtually no women did in nineteenth-century white America. Nor did the church hierarchy's disapproval eliminate African-Americans' emotional style of worship which both suited their cultural memory and satisfied their contemporary needs. Religious worship gave slaves in the South and free blacks in the North freedom of the spirit. Black churches provided a sanctuary from discrimination and the psychological hardships of daily life. Several Cincinnati blacks decided that they must establish their own church after a black man attempting to abide by the more circumspect conventions of an integrated congregation suffered a ruptured blood vessel. Many African Americans believed that the emotional expression peculiar to most black worship was essential for mental and physical health.[85]

· In addition to worship and religious training, the black church served many other functions and did not limit its activities to strictly religious gatherings. A few congregations banned certain types of music and entertainment, like the New Jersey church that punished a member for attending the theater and chastised another for "suffering his son to play the violin,"[86] but others were far more liberal on these issues. African Methodist Episcopal and Baptist churches in Boston provided meeting space for community drama groups and an orchestra. Singing societies for adults and school classes for children met in churches, and the church building was often the only place in the community available for meetings to discuss community concerns. Black churches ruled on issues of morality and attempted to oversee the lives of members and resolve disputes between them.

They performed many of the functions once the province of village elders in Africa or of the black governors and their advisors in colonial times. Not only was the church leadership invested with the power to arbitrate and enforce morality and responsibility among blacks, but they often acted as a judicial body. An analysis of church records reveals an institution deeply involved in the daily life of the community, as much concerned with secular relations as with the spiritual well-being of its congregation. In this regard the black church also functioned much like the Puritan church of colonial New England, having important social and political roles as well as religious responsibilities. It tried to control everything from petty personal disputes between members to more serious criminal acts. The black church attempted to handle internal problems within the community, without recourse to the formal white authority that was seen as unsympathetic, not trusted to render fair judgments or give equitable treatment to African Americans.

Church elders received complaints and formed investigative committees which set their findings before the church body or a trial committee for adjudication. Trials were held regularly in Philadelphia's Mother Bethel AME Church and judgments were passed on a broad range of offenses, from lying in public, to breech of contract, and assault. Punishments were meted out to fit the offense, ranging from probation to expulsion from the church. Morris Dubline was accused by his wife of refusing to allow her to care for his clothes and of selling their household goods without her permission. Apparently taking this as an insult to her performance as a wife, she complained to the church elders. Dubline defended his actions, saying that the family's destitute financial condition forced him to sell household goods to pay the rent. Furthermore, he said that his wife could not be trusted with his clothing, as she routinely refused to wash them, tore them, and threw them on the floor. Apparently Mrs. Dubline told the more convincing story, and the committee found Morris guilty of "imprudent conduct," placing him on six months' probation during which time he was not allowed to hold any church office.[87]

These disputes sometimes dealt with complicated moral issues. Joseph Bohen charged that his wife, Hannah, "oppos[ed] him in many things" and that when he asked his friend, Robert Wilson, to talk to her about her conduct, she became very attached to Wilson. Fearing that the two were spending too much time together, Bohen then asked Wilson not to visit his home. Wilson's wife had also complained about the time Wilson and Hannah Bohen were spending together. The church found both Robert Wilson and Hannah Bohen guilty of indecent conduct. Wilson was placed on probation but Bohen was rebuked for not being "willing to submit to her husband as a dutiful wife" and "disowned" (expelled from the church). "Disowning" was the most severe punishment the church could inflict, and this verdict is an indication of its commitment to male authority in the family. Likewise within the patriarchal tradition, the church was committed to the protection of women. Many of the criminal cases that came before Bethel's committee involved family violence in which wives were victims. Sentences for the offending husbands in those cases were strict. One man was expelled from the church for beating his wife and threatening to fight another church member. Another man was disciplined for striking his wife and threatening an officer of the law.[88] Conviction of adultery was enough to expel one man, especially when the woman involved became pregnant.[89]

These trial committees were commonly composed only of males, but often women played active roles.[90] Women's roles in community life were circumscribed by nineteenth century gender expectations, but they did exercise some power through their ability to influence the decisions made by male authorities. During the summer of 1828, a trial took place in an AME church in central New Jersey involving George White who was accused of wife abuse and slander. Three women of the church formed a committee to investigate the charges. The all male trial committee accepted the women's report, found White guilty, and silenced him in the church until such time as he was reconciled with his wife.[91]

Often, as was the case with one midwestern congregation, the church was called on to address issues peculiar to black people whose relationships were complicated by slavery. Henry Williams escaped from slavery in Louisiana during the 1830s. He went to Cincinnati where he was able to secure work and maintained his freedom for a number of years. While living in Cincinnati, Williams met and married a woman from a neighboring town. This outraged many of his fellow members of Cincinnati's Union Colored Baptist Church who knew that Henry was already married and that his wife, a slave who had not escaped with her husband, was living in New Orleans. At the church trial Williams was charged with bigamy. Even though the congregation was aware of the special problems involved, they determined that he "deserted" his wife in slavery, and demanded a signed release from her before the church would sanction a new marriage. This presented quite a problem for Williams, a fugitive whose own freedom was not assured. With great difficulty and the help of a covert communication network, he was able to secure the necessary signature. This incident illustrates the extent to which the church attempted to stabilize family relationships even under the extraordinary conditions of a slave society.[92]

There was strong community pressure on black Christians to use the authority of the church to settle internal disputes, and sanctions were imposed on those who did not. In the spring of 1837, William Walen of Trenton, New Jersey, was censured by the Mount Zion AME Church for bringing civil charges against "his Brother" (probably a fellow church member rather than a blood relation) without first bringing his grievance before the church.[93] Black churches of several different denominations continued their roles as community arbitrators throughout the antebellum period, though they were just one means of redress for grievances, and many cases were brought before local and state courts.

Thus, the black church was a powerful force in the community, stabilizing relationships, providing psychological guidance and emotional sanctuary, and symbolizing autonomy and community among African-American people. It is an oversimplification to say that the black church sprang exclusively from the unwillingness of black people to be second-class members of white-dominated institutions. Although this surely played a part in its creation, the black church was more than a shaded version of its white counterpart, and blacks who abandoned white churches wanted more than freedom from discrimination. They wanted power in church decisions, and they wanted religious expression that gave meaning to their experiences and reflected their culture. Much of the style of black worship was shaped by African cultures and by the experience of life in slavery. The theology of the black church promised liberty to the slave, relief to the oppressed, and the power of the spirit to believers. From the pulpit on Sunday morning, churchgoers were likely to hear denunciations of slavery and racial injustice and calls to community responsibility. In 1817 Philadelphia blacks at Mother Bethel debated and finally rejected the proposal of the American Colonization Society to send blacks to a colony on the West Coast of Africa. In New York City, Cincinnati, Detroit, Chicago, and Pittsburgh, black churches hosted antislavery meetings and were stations on an underground railroad smuggling fugitive slaves to freedom. Churches provided a forum for the expression of black political views and a training ground for black political leadership. They were a critical component of the network of black community institutions and organizations. As advocates for self-help and racial uplift, churches often led in educating black children.

For African Americans, as for Americans generally, education was both the foundation of freedom and one of its benefits. As blacks gained their freedom, they established schools, often building on the earlier efforts of white evangelical groups and Quakers. Quaker educational efforts in Philadelphia were especially extensive, beginning in the 1750s and continuing with the Friends African School established in 1770 and the Association for the Free Instruction of Adult Colored People organized in 1789.[94] Under their auspices, until the War of 1812, black men and women in separate classrooms received a basic education on Sundays and in the evenings during the week at three different locations in the city. In 1790 members of the Pennsylvania Abolition Society formed a Committee on Education to support black education. They funded several schools started by blacks, including one begun by Eleanor Harris, a free black woman, in the 1790s, and assisted schools run by Absalom Jones, Cyrus Bustill, Ann Williams, and Amos White. The committee led efforts to raise funds for the construction of a permanent black school. Clarkson Hall, named in honor of British abolitionist Thomas Clarkson, opened in 1813, educating black children during the day and adults in the evening. For thirteen years, according to its abolitionist sponsors, this school provided "a decided refutation of the charge that the mental endowments of the descendants of Africa are inferior to those possessed by their white brethren."[95] Although the Clarkson school could not withstand competition from the public schools, many African Americans believed their success in maintaining the private school helped encourage the establishment of public schools.[96]

Black churches in Philadelphia had housed and sponsored several elementary schools since the 1790s. Absalom Jones opened a school in the parish house of his African Episcopal Church of St. Thomas in 1800. Mother Bethel supported day and night schools and a Sunday school, as did the First African Presbyterian Church. Some blacks formed the Pennsylvania Augustine Society for the Education of People of Colour that maintained a grammar school between 1822 and 1826. Black educator Prince Saunders set forth the philosophy of the Augustine Society from the pulpit of Mother Bethel in 1818: If black people were to prosper as a race, they must educate their children. He emphasized the paramount importance of education, saying, "we . . . are convinced that it is an unquestionable duty which we owe to ourselves, to our posterity, and to our God, who has endowed us with intellectual powers."[97]

By the fall of 1822, the new Mary Street School presented Philadelphia's blacks with their first opportunity for public education. Initially one school with 199 students, there were eight schools by 1850, but this was always segregated public education, where blacks expanded their classroom space by taking over formerly white schools after white students moved on to newer buildings. The city provided white teachers, and although a few were popular with black parents, by the 1830s the community took concrete steps to get black teachers in the public schools. They supported the move of the Institute for Colored Youth, a normal school training black teachers, to Philadelphia from just outside the city. The city, however, refused to hire black teachers, even after an 1854 law authorized the establishment of black schools throughout the state. African-Americans' efforts met continual failure until John Quincy Allen was hired as Philadelphia's first black public school teacher in 1862.[98]

Despite its low pay and job insecurity, the importance of education led many black men and women to become teachers. Teaching became the most common occupation among professional black women, as it was one of the few respectable fields open to them. Grace A. Mapps of Philadelphia taught at the Institute for Colored Youth. Sarah Mapps Douglass ran her own private school, the only one in the city offering a high school education to black girls. In 1853 she too taught at the Institute for Color Youth heading the girl's preparatory department and teaching science, a rare offering in women's curricula. During the late 1850s, after attending courses at the Female Medical College of Pennsylvania and Penn Medical University, Douglass taught medical classes in her home to black women. In black communities throughout the North, black women started and maintained schools for children and adults.[99]

In Boston during the eighteenth century, the instruction of black children and illiterate adults took place in private homes. A few black children were admitted to private white schools before 1800, but they endured ridicule and mistreatment by white teachers and students. Led by Prince Hall, blacks petitioned for their own public schools, and when that effort failed they organized the African School in 1798. Financed by small sums collected from black parents, the school first met in Primus Hall's home. By 1806 a white teacher had been engaged, and classes were meeting regularly in the basement of the African Meeting House, home of the African Baptist Church. Among the school's teachers during its early years were Thomas Paul, Jr., son of the minister, and John Russwurm, one of the first black college graduates in the country.[100] In 1815 Prince Saunders, then teaching at the school, convinced Abiel Smith, a white Boston merchant, to contribute funds for black education. Smith's donation combined with the twelve-and-one-half-cents-per-week tuition paid by black parents provided a more stable basis for black education, and the African School was renamed the Smith School in his honor. By 1820 Boston established a public school for blacks, and although the number of public schools dedicated to black education expanded throughout the antebellum period, they remained segregated, with curricula and facilities inferior to white schools. Boston's black children did not receive an education comparable to that enjoyed by white children until 1855, when public schools were integrated.[101]

In most black communities private school ventures were short-lived for want of students who could afford to attend. The staggering economic need of black families often meant that the income from a child's indenture or employment was crucial, and education, though its importance was acknowledged, was a luxury that many could not afford.[102] Black education in New York was additionally hindered by the gradual emancipation plan that kept large numbers of black children in servitude and under the control of masters often unwilling to release them during the school day. After a few short-lived efforts to open black schools in the eighteenth century, abolitionists of the New York Manumission Society finally founded a school there in 1786, hoping it would be an argument for emancipation. The African Free School opened in 1787 and fairly soon enrolled about one hundred black students. More students could be accommodated after 1809, when the school adopted an innovative new teaching method—the Lancastrian method, whereby more advanced students acted as instructors for the less advanced—believed by its principal to be used by only one other school. After the school was destroyed by fire five years later, the city was persuaded to donate land on William Street for a new building for two hundred students. A second school, the African Free School No. 2 capable of housing five hundred students, was opened as the boys' school on Mulberry Street in 1820. Enrollment continued to expand as slavery ended in New York, and by the early 1830s, four additional schools were in place. Black abolitionists in New York City, led by Thomas Downing, William Hamilton, and Henry Sipkins, became dissatisfied with the white principal of School No. 2, Charles C. Andrews, for his paternalism and his support of African colonization.[103] Though Andrews was supported by some of his former students and respected by many as a conscientious teacher and stern disciplinarian, when blacks took control of the African Free schools in 1832, they replaced the white staff. During the next few years enrollments grew to 1,400 students, beyond the capability of the Manumission Society to administer. When the Public School Society took over the schools in 1834, most of the black teachers were dismissed and education was reduced to primary grade level.[104]

Most schools in New York State were operated as segregated institutions. This was based on custom, not law, and some small towns and rural communities with few blacks and a degree of local racial tolerance operated integrated schools. In 1841 and 1847, the state superintendent of public schools declared, "Colored children are entitled equally with all others to the Privileges and advantages of the district schools."[105] Yet, school integration in New York remained uneven and problematic. One observer contended that "up to a certain age the boys [black and white] are all the greatest of friends and make no distinction of colour, but after that the poor blacks feel themselves badly looked down upon, and their spirit is quite broken by feeling themselves despised."[106]

White parents complained about their children being forced to share schools, although not always classrooms, with blacks, and black parents complained about the hostility their children faced from white students and teachers. Dutchess County officials reported racial harassment; in Kinderhook whites threatened to withdraw their children from the public school, and in Queens County many whites refused to attend the public schools. White teachers often expressed the racial prejudice that characterized the general society, maintaining segregated seating even when their classrooms were integrated and threatening delinquent white children with being seated among black students as a form of punishment.[107] Generally, black children found it much more comfortable to attend black private schools or public schools maintained for black students. Public school officials were also more comfortable with separate schools. The superintendent in Buffalo contended that integrated classrooms were impractical because black children required "greater patience on the part of the teacher, longer training and severer discipline than are called into exercise in the district schools." He believed that it would be many generations before integrated schools were a realistic possibility, "before [black children] will possess the vigor of intellect and the power of memory and judgement, that are so early developed in the Anglo-Saxon race."[108]

Racially-segregated public or private education generally meant lower teacher salaries and inadequate facilities. In New Haven, school buildings for blacks were "excessively crowded and destitute of some of the first requisites." Blacks in Rhode Island had similar complaints, and one white teacher in Providence was so embarrassed by the stigma of teaching black students that he threatened to punish any who greeted him in public.[109] Midwestern states either made no provision for public support of black education, as in Indiana and Illinois, or supported only segregated and inferior black public schools, as in mid-nineteenth-century Ohio. There were a few exceptional areas like Ohio's Western Reserve, where black children were admitted to white schools.[110] In Cincinnati there was stiff opposition to blacks' attending the public schools and even to the private instruction of African Americans not of very light complexion. Cincinnati whites were outraged during the 1830s when white students with abolitionist sentiments from Lane Seminary began to teach in four black schools, instructing children during the day and adults in the evening. A few years later a British minister, Hiram S. Gilmore, established Cincinnati's Gilmore High School for Negroes as a private institution with five teachers and at least three hundred students.[111] This private school was tolerated, but opposition to educating blacks at taxpayer expense prevented the establishment of public schools for blacks until the 1840s. Although Ohio's 1825 authorization of public funding for education did not specifically exclude blacks, Cincinnati officials ignored black citizens' petitions until the state forced them to institute a system of separate black public schools with a board of directors elected by black taxpayers. The state mandate was in 1849, but the first black school building was not constructed in Cincinnati until 1858.[112]

As black communities developed and grew, community members created a multitude of organizations and associations, including mutual aid societies, fraternal organizations, schools, and churches. African Americans generally formed their own separate groups, some affiliated with white institutions. They differed in specific detail from region to region and city to city, but all addressed the shared circumstance of poverty and all were aimed at overcoming social and political disadvantage. Like all social institutions, they served many purposes, but all were intended to serve and sustain black people and, as black leaders continually reiterated, to "uplift" the race. With black families, these institutions formed the foundation of black community life and sustained its social and political activism. Though responsive to local conditions, they were joined in regional, national, and international networks, and such networks, along with family ties, gave African Americans in the North the incentive and the opportunity to work against the greatest disadvantage African Americans faced—the institution of slavery.

7

Culture, Politics, and the Issue of African-American Identity

In 1787 Philadelphia physician and patriot Benjamin Rush gave voice to Americans' assurance that their new nation stood on the brink of a great adventure. "The American war is over," he observed, "but this is far from being the case with the American revolution. On the contrary, nothing but the first act of the great drama is closed."[1] America had won its political independence but had not yet established a national identity. During the next two generations Americans struggled to articulate a unique identity and to create lasting institutions. What did it mean to be a democratic nation? What were the implications of expanding rights and individual liberties? How could a national identity be forged from a diverse population with increasingly important racial distinctions? These were difficult questions for a nation which could not admit, even to itself, that racial diversity was integral to its identity or that Africanisms had become part of American culture, shaping it in particular ways. Almost all white Americans believed and reassured themselves that, as one historian put it, "America was meant to be a homogeneous white nation, inhabited chiefly by members of the Anglo-Saxon and closely related races." Yet, in reality, the emerging American identity of the late eighteenth and early nineteenth century was increasingly fashioned not of a single Old World European tradition but of many Old World traditions, traditions that included those of Africa and the ancient "New World" cultures of Native Americans, mingled and merged in various proportions in different locations.[2]

For blacks, more than for other Americans, an American identity was built on the African foundations of old continent beliefs and values. The African peoples brought to America to supply labor needs, wove their traditional cultural styles into the American fabric. Their style of speaking helped to shape an American spoken language that was infused with distinctly African words and expressions. Their food was integrated into the national cuisine and their style of worship helped to shape an American religious form. For hundreds of years after the arrival of the first African captives, Americans nourished themselves with okra and sweet potatoes and adapted regional favorites like gumbo and fried chicken. In the South, where African influences were strongest, common white people played the African banjo, which they regarded as an American instrument, used the African word "tote" to mean carry, and sang *Polly-Wolly-Doodle All Day* without the slightest thought or recognition that in doing so they were confirming the multicultural–multiracial character of their folk traditions.

Central to the multicultural creation of America was the infusion of African music into everyday life.[3] Wherever groups of Africans worked, in the fields of the plantations, as stevedores on the docks, or on ships' crews, they accompanied their toil with traditional melodies and complex African rhythms suited to their tasks, improvising words to fit their circumstances. In the rural regions of large plantations, the breeze carried their work songs across the countryside during the day. Their musical celebrations and lamentations drifted out from the slave settlements in the stillness of the night. In the cities African musical forms were almost as familiar. Street vendors called potential customers out of their houses with practical and entertaining songs creatively invented to promote interest in their wares. On the docks laborers sang the cadence of their most difficult tasks and even the streets were cleaned to the rhythms of Africa.

Black writer Martin Delany described both the ubiquity and the multifaceted meanings of black watermen's songs:

> In the distance, on the levee and in the harbor among the steamers, the songs of the boatmen were incessant. Every few hours landing, loading and unloading, the glee of these men of sorrow was touchingly appropriate and impressive. . . . If there is any class of men anywhere to be found whose sentiments of song and words of lament are made to reach the sympathies of others, the black slave boatmen are that class . . . they are seemingly contented by soothing their sorrows with songs apparently cheerful, but in reality wailing lamentations.[4]

Traditional music, new compositions, and endless variations were carried by sailors and watermen and trudging slave coffles between the islands of the West Indies and the mainland, along the rivers and coastal waterways, and from the established settlements of the upper South to the newer plantations of the lower South. Contemporary accounts indicate that Africans and their descendants sang alone and together to accompany their work, to express their joys, their sorrows, their longing for home, and the pain of partings caused by death or slave sales, to remember and teach their cultural history and ideals, and simply for their own entertainment.

Although the chants and hollers were sometimes strange to the uninitiated ear, the appeal of most black music to European Americans was clear in the accounts of travelers who often gave detailed descriptions of the slaves' singing, dancing, and musical instruments in the South. Slave musicians were enlisted to perform for plantation social functions; river boat stewards and waiters served as performers for evening entertainment, and song collectors began to record this music even before the Revolutionary War. Blacks were sometimes trained in the European musical tradition to which they often brought a special African style. One African musician, Newport Gardner, was a slave singer and composer formally trained in America by the white minister and singing master Andrew Law. When Gardner bought his freedom and opened his own singing school in Newport, Rhode Island in the 1790s, his former mistress became one of his pupils.[5]

Many black musicians were widely known and popular with both black and white audiences during the first half of the nineteenth century. African Americans were members of the military bands called into service during the War of 1812, as they had been during the Revolution. As freedom came to former northern slaves, musicians were able to take advantage of a postwar cultural renaissance. All-black brass bands were organized in New Orleans, Philadelphia, New York City, and in New England; black string orchestras performed at the increasingly popular balls and cotillions of the growing urban high society. These musical performances were popular and offered lucrative employment for black musicians, many of whom found it possible to make a living by playing at concerts and society dances. Teaching in and operating music schools and composing and arranging music often provided supplemental income.

The most famous society band leader was Frank Johnson of Philadelphia. Reportedly a West Indian, who had migrated to the United States just before the War of 1812, Johnson began his musical career as a leader of military bands, playing for parades and patriotic functions and giving formal band concerts after the war. Johnson's versatile musicians also played string instruments, transforming their military band into a dance orchestra as the occasion demanded. During the gala celebrations to honor Lafayette's visit to America in 1824, Johnson's orchestra was hired to play at the Lafayette Ball in Philadelphia. According to one account, Johnson was the first to play on the resort circuit at Saratoga Springs, New York. "The band, composed of colored men and led by Frank Johnson," William L. Stone remembered, "first played at 'Congress Hall' until the completion of the 'United States' when they played at each hotel on alternate evenings."[6]

Beginning in late 1837, Johnson and four men from his band went on a six-month tour of England, giving concerts from their varied repertoire that included operatic and classical European pieces as well as patriotic and popular songs. Upon their return, they introduced the promenade concert to America where it enjoyed such success that it became a regular part of the social season in Philadelphia. In the summers Frank Johnson and his musicians toured throughout the North and into Canada and played in fashionable resorts like Saratoga Springs, Cape May, New Jersey, and Sulphur Springs, Virginia. Johnson's illustrious career was cut short by his death in 1844, but the popularity of the Frank Johnson Brass and String Bands continued until the 1860s under different leaders.[7]

Popular though they were, African-American musicians and music did not meet with universal acclaim in America. One contemporary observer was critical of what he called Frank Johnson's "remarkable taste in distorting a sentimental, simple, and beautiful song, into a reel, jug, or country-dance."[8] Such "distortion," along with the inclusion of words and syllables incomprehensible to English speakers, seems to have been fairly typical of African-American music. Musical innovation, spontaneity, and the translation of European music into an African idiom, the source of much of the appeal of black music, often met with approbation. One white Georgia minister hoped that training in traditional European religious music would persuade African Americans to be more conventional in their singing. "One great advantage in teaching them good psalms and hymns," he asserted confidently,

> is that they are thereby induced to lay aside the extravagant and nonsensical chants, and catches and hallelujah songs of their own composing; and when they sing, which is very often while about their business or of an evening in their houses, they will have something profitable to sing.[9]

Twenty citizens of New York complained about the graphic expressions and discordant tones of certain black urban workers, calling them "savage yells" and "detestable cries." In the late summer of 1817, they petitioned the city about the "vagabond negroes who have taken upon themselves the business of nightmen" negotiating the streets and collecting the refuse from the city's privies. The petitioners conceded both the unpleasantness and the necessity of the work, but urged that steps be taken to discourage the "bawling out [of] such expressions as are most shockingly indecent" adding that the workmen "commonly go in pairs and perform a duet of this description."[10]

Disturbing as some whites found these musical performances at the time, they formed the African-American basis for an emerging American music. Nearly a century later, a scholar collecting sea shanties was struck by the unique aspects of folksongs that had begun among African-American sailors before 1850. The "genuine Negro shanties were not esteemed so highly by mixed crews as were those of English and American origin," she found. Her suggestions for why such black-originated extemporaneous songs did not become more generally popular among sailors are familiar—"perhaps because their words were even more trivial and meaningless than the general run of shanties, perhaps because their rhythms and cadences were difficult for white sailors to execute."[11]

Although black music may have been difficult for white performers, considered less cultured or civilized, or associated with an immoral or heathen way of life, it provided the basis for an extremely popular entertainment in nineteenth- and early twentieth-century America. African music, collected in Africa and America, had found its way to English and American concert stages and opera houses even before the Revolution, but a new popularity began with performances by minstrel troops in the 1820s. Almost entirely composed of white performers, these minstrel companies ostensively recreated southern plantation scenes with performances of songs and dances. The music derived from slave songs was adapted to the abilities and sensibilities of white musicians. Whites, performing in blackface, presented African Americans as comic figures, the objects of ridicule. Many American songwriters, like Stephen Foster, gained their fame by writing so-called Ethiopian songs for the minstrel stage. Jim Crow, a caricature of the plantation slave made popular by white performer Thomas Dartmouth "Daddy" Rice, and Zip Coon, his foolishly pretentious urban counterpart, became stock figures in the American theater. By the 1840s hundreds of minstrels, including the famous Virginia Minstrels, William Whitlock, Daniel Emmett, Frank Bower, and Dick Pelham, and the Christy Minstrels, E. P. Christy, George Christy, Lansing Durand, and Tom Vaughan, were presenting full-length shows in the best American theaters and touring in Europe. According to historian Eileen Southern, minstrel shows were the most popular theatrical entertainment in America for over forty years.[12]

White performers developed their material by observing blacks and embellishing, exaggerating, and caricaturing what they saw. Rice reportedly formulated his Jim Crow song and dance routine after watching a black stableman in Louisville sing and dance as he went about his work. Likewise, the first full-length touring minstrel show presented by the Virginia Minstrels, which played in New York City, Boston, and throughout the North, was based on the work songs and dances of Virginia slaves that the minstrels had observed. Although this popular American music was derived from African music, black performers were not generally included in minstrel groups. Dancer and musician William Henry Lane (known as Master Juba) was the only black performer to tour with an early minstrel company. Lane, believed to have studied with black "reel-and-jig" dancer Uncle Jim Lowe, performed in the dance halls of New York's Five Points district and was described by Charles Dickens as "the greatest dancer known." This was high praise from Dickens, who was well familiar with the great performers of Britain as well as America.[13] Thus, Lane performed for both black and white audiences. His exceptional career as a minstrel performer highlights the remarkable absence of blacks in this type of entertainment. Excluding African Americans from black-face minstrelsy assured white control, making the minstrel show a means for whites' experiencing what they wanted to believe was authentic black culture while rendering it so ridiculous as to be benign. Despite its distortion, a form of African-American culture influenced popular American culture through these shows. As Eric Lott has observed, minstrelsy "continually acknowledged and absorbed black culture even while defending white America against it."[14]

African Americans created many different types of music and drama for the theater and concert stage in northern cities. Philadelphia was the hub of black entertainment, but New York became the most important center for black theater. As individual acts and in large companies, African Americans established themselves and their virtuosity within the structure of American performing arts before 1820. One popular black performance group called the African Company, a dramatic troupe organized by Henry Brown, gave their first performance at the African Grove, America's first black theater. Black businessman Allen Royce opened the establishment on Mercer Street at the corner of Bleeker, to serve a primarily African-American audience in 1821. It became a popular gathering place for blacks and a point of curiosity for whites. Ballet, opera, song and dance shows, drama including Shakespearian tragedy, and elaborate musical productions entertained audiences at the theater for the substantial admission price of 75 cents for a box seat, 50 cents for seats in the pit, and 37½ cents for gallery seating.[15]

The black patrons often arrived elegantly dressed and caught the eye of at least one foreign visitor to New York who reported "the very superior air of gallantry assumed by the men when in attendance on their belles, to that of the whites in similar circumstances." Foreign travelers whose stereotypes of black life were shaped almost exclusively by accounts of slavery and destitution were at once amused and surprised by well mannered, apparently prosperous segments of African-American society. The sight of smartly dressed blacks was remarkable to one traveler who contrasted them with a group of white youths standing about smoking in public. One "young negress," dressed in the "extreme of the fashion," was "accompanied by a black beau, whose toilet was equally studied; eyeglass, guard-chain, nothing was omitted; he walked beside his sable goddess uncovered, and with an air of most tender devotion."[16] A Scottish traveler wrote after his visit, "One of the theaters is for black people of the city; it is really worth one's while to go there for a few nights for the novelty of the thing." The novelty may have brought many whites to the African Grove initially, but the quality of the productions attracted a loyal following. Whites who attended the African Grove performances were relegated to seats in a gallery reserved for them, "following," as one visitor observed, "with nice etiquette and equal justice, the arrangement of the white theaters, in all of which is a gallery appropriated solely to the use of the blacks."[17]

Two years after the theater's opening, Brown's company introduced his "The Drama of King Shotaway," the first play by a black writer presented on the American professional stage. A West Indian by birth, Brown based his play on a slave insurrection on the Island of St. Vincent. The lead role of King Shotaway was played by the popular James Hewlett, one of the most talented and well-known black actors and singers of his day. Plays by white authors were often specially adapted for the Grove's black audiences. When the popular English musical *Tom and Jerry* was performed, for example, special scenery was designed for the African Grove presentation, and extra scenes depicting a slave auction and a slave dance were incorporated. The African Grove gave many blacks their early training and performing there launched several international careers. Hewlett, who toured Britain as the "New York and London Coloured Comedian," and the great Ira Aldridge, renowned throughout Europe as a Shakespearian actor, appeared there often during the theater's early years. African-born Aldridge had been a slave in Maryland and studied acting in America under the visiting British actor Edmund Kean. Aldridge made his London debut when he was in his early twenties, became especially famous for his role in Othello, and was surely the best-known "Ethiopian" actor of his time.[18]

The uniquely American culture that emerged from the mingling of European and African styles was evident in the adaptations of European dramas and in the minstrel shows, but its most striking examples were in the development of American popular music. Music lovers who visited dance halls and music "dives," like Almack's in New York's Five Points, where "hot music" was played on trumpet, drum, and fiddle, or Philadelphia's Dandy Hall, where European visitors and well-to-do whites indulged in what a century later in Harlem would be referred to as slumming, recognized the creation of a uniquely American musical art form as early as the 1820s. Popular tunes like *Cooney in de Holler*, a favorite with the dance crowd, and *Opossum Up a Gum Stump*, packed dance houses up and down the Atlantic coast from Philadelphia to New York.

One contemporary observer who experienced a Saturday night at Pete Williams's hall, Dickens' Place, in Five Points described the music scene as "of no ordinary kind." He was particularly struck by the musicians. "[T]hat red-faced trumpeter . . . looks precisely as if he were blowing glass, which needles [of sound] penetrating the tympanum, pierce through and through your brain without remorse." He went on to portray other band members including "the bass-drummer [who] sweats and deals his blows on every side, in all violation of the laws of rhythm." Three quarters of the women who frequented Dickens' Place were "negresses, of various shades and colors," many of whom gathered around the bar while others thronged the dance floor as the band played at a frantic tempo. The dancers began each dance "in tolerable order," but by its conclusion they were "contorting their bodies and accelerating their movements . . . with shouts of laughter and yells of encouragement and applause, until all observance of the figure (the original steps) is forgotten and every one leaps, stamps, screams and hurras on his or her own hook."[19]

This was American music of the antebellum period, a blend of European and African music set to African rhythms and born of the spirit of innovation and improvisation at the heart of Africans' cultural adaptation. Africans in America were developing a culture that was more European than the culture of their ancestors in Africa but more African than the culture of European Americans. At the same time, European Americans were developing a culture that was more African than the culture in Europe. It was in music that a culture recognized in Europe as American found early expression, and African and European music forged a link symbolic of the multiracial society in which they existed. Simultaneously, however, the sociopolitical dynamic of the period encouraged the submergence and finally the denial of this intercultural reality. As America became more culturally amalgamated, it also became politically more racially exclusive.

In the North these contradictory developments coincided with the emergence of blacks from slavery during the first third of the nineteenth century. Abolition in the northern states did bring freedom, but it was a gradual and uneven freedom, a freedom that carried limited potential for political power and participation. Historians have argued effectively that law took on new meaning in America during the early national period as a significant number of white workingmen participated in its formulation. No longer simply edicts imposed from above, law became a contract that "established the framework of the social intercourse," an extension of the power of individual citizens acting together for mutual benefit. The participation of common people in lawmaking, albeit mainly propertied white men, exemplified America's unfolding political identity.[20]

One important consequence of these changes was the waning influence of the Anglo-American heritage that had provided a quasi-legitimate political role for mob action. Revolutionary mobs were perhaps the most extreme example of the expression of popular sentiment through "outdoor politics." The expansion of democratic institutions in the first decades of the nineteenth century called for a different form of mass political expression. In his study of New York City, Paul Gilje traced this gradual transition to a political system that proscribed mob action and provided legal means for political participation by "the people." The reorganization of political power in the early life of the nation brought with it a reconsideration of the concepts of citizenship and citizenship rights. By the 1820s "the people" connoted a far more racially exclusive constituency than it had in the 1750s.[21]

In the decades immediately following the formation of the nation, the mob still exercised its traditional role, redressing grievances and acting in defense of shared values. The Doctors' Riot in New York City in the spring of 1788 was one example. Rumors circulated that doctors and medical students were robbing graves to supply corpses for dissections, and a mob of four to five thousand people assembled to protest this "affront to the moral values of the community." They invaded the medical school, destroyed medical equipment, and captured doctors and medical students—actions tolerated by city authorities who shared their outrage. Continuing unrest, however, compelled the authorities to call out the militia who then acted forcefully to quiet the disturbances. The troops finally resorted to firing on the mob, killing three people and scattering the rest.[22]

Similar riots in many cities during the post-Revolutionary period were continuations of traditional attempts by working people to directly impose their will on a wide range of issues. In 1792 hundreds of angry New Yorkers demanded that authorities hand over a financial speculator whose banking scheme had driven him into debtor's prison and many others into bankruptcy. Houses of prostitution, often tolerated by the police, were popular mob targets in the late 1790s. Sailors engaged in violent protests against continuing impressment and in violent wage disputes in the early years of the nineteenth century. In the 1820s riots were triggered in New York when a hogcart driver attempted to enforce a new law against freely ranging hogs. The presence of African Americans as community members venting their displeasure in most of these mob actions demonstrated the continuing existence of a certain measure of interracial consensus and cooperation.[23]

Amid the population diversity of American cities, however, some mob violence expressed ethnic, racial, and religious conflicts. While African Americans were participants in interracial mobs, they were also the targets of racially motivated mob attacks. During the 1790s, Boston's Prince Hall challenged those mobs who attacked blacks to "face [them] man for man." The violence against blacks in that city was common enough to prompt Hall to declare, "We may truly be said to carry our lives in our hands." Hall accused the rioters of cowardice. "Helpless women," he said, "have their clothes torn from their backs . . . by a mob or horde of shameless, low-lived envious spiteful persons."[24]

New York City blacks complained to city officials as early as 1807 that whites were disturbing their church services with disruptions ranging from pranks by a few disorderly teenagers to more serious attacks by mobs. In many cities and towns white ruffians harassed, attacked, and played cruel practical jokes on black people. One young artisan, William Otter, told of a "spree" instigated by white Philadelphians. Apparently disturbed by the presence of a black church in their neighborhood, they "fell upon a plan to get the boys and let them make a set upon them." About sixty young white men (butchers, ropemakers, carpenters, plasterers, and bakers) armed with homemade weapons descended on the church during a worship service. They forced a blindfolded goat inside the sanctuary, barred the door, and assaulted the members of the congregation as they attempted to escape through the windows. "No particular regard was paid to sex," Otter recalled, the white attackers "levelled them indiscriminately."[25]

Black street vendors seem to have been a special target of racially motivated harassment. Otter gleefully recalled tying string to the produce-filled pots black women carried on their heads. At the appropriate moment the string was pulled, upsetting the pot and ruining its contents. On another occasion he and his companions poured whitewash on black-berries a vendor was selling. Such pranks were costly humiliations for very poor people struggling to make a living. Young working-class white males like Otter found sport in harassing blacks, but blacks were not their only targets. Old people, women of all ages, newly arrived immigrants, or anyone who seemed vulnerable might become the butt of their cruelty. Black people were always among the most vulnerable, though, often because officials tolerated and sometimes even sanctioned action against them.[26]

Poor black areas of the cities sometimes became special targets of another kind. When Mayor Josiah Quincy of Boston declared war on illegal drinking establishments and brothels in 1823, he personally led raids into the black section of Beacon Hill. Two years later, a mainly middle-class mob of Bostonians followed his example, though without legal authority. With blackened faces, carrying pitchforks and noise makers, they invaded brothels and gambling houses in the North End, another area of the city where many black people lived. They excused their unauthorized invasions of private property as citizen action against undesirable disorderly elements of society.[27]

Mob action was often motivated by a complex combination of concerns. From its inception the African Grove was frequently subjected to mob attacks. It is difficult to determine the mobs' motivations, but it is safe to say that they were partly racial and partly economic. Gangs of rowdies frequently attacked black churches and other establishments for sport, and a black theater that relegated white patrons to a gallery must have presented an especially tempting target. Some of this violence was engineered by white businessmen motivated by economic rivalry and professional jealousy. Often it was geared to cripple their competition. One competing theater, the white-owned Broadway Circus, was especially implicated in the frequent attacks that led finally to the closing of the African Grove in 1829.[28]

One aspect of the behavior of white mobs that targeted blacks provides an intriguing window on racial motivation and the meaning of color during this period. The blackface worn by the Boston mob in 1825 was not uncommon, and the patterns of its use indicate that it was more than a device to provide cover in darkness. David Roediger's analysis in *The Wages of Whiteness* draws on his own work and the research of others to initiate an explanation of the changing patterns of racial association in the early nineteenth century and the meaning of this change for the American psyche. The shifts which became apparent by the middle of the 1820s involved a complex interplay of forces. The racial theories gradually developed to justify the continuation of slavery assigned blacks an inferior intellectual and physical status. In the beliefs of the dominant culture, then, Africans gradually come to embody man's baser instincts, less civilized, sexually uncontrollable, and lacking the self-control demanded by the standards of republican virtue and a modern, industrializing society. Northern blacks were increasingly shut out of any hope of legitimate political power, and they faced rising economic competition from greater numbers of European immigrants. Racial rapproachment became less likely as public officials banned or restricted traditionally interracial black-initiated celebrations such as Pinkster and Negro election days, in efforts to control the working class' "lewd and lascivious behavior." As black performers were attacked and black celebrations disrupted, there were fewer opportunities for whites to participate directly in familiar aspects of black culture. It was then that white performers in blackface began to imitate and parody blacks on the minstrel stage, recapturing their ability to be a part of black culture but in a way that emphasized their differences while giving the minstrels permission to act out their fantasies of what it meant to be African American. Whites in blackface appeared on the streets as well as on the stage. Blackface crowds, according to Roediger, "overwhelmingly" young, male and working class, performed at militia days in New York, Philadelphia, and New England where black participation had been banned. They were at festivals and processions in Philadelphia, including the Christmas procession, where in the late 1820s young white men began dressing as black women they called "Aunt Sallys." Gradually during this period public celebrations shifted from black festivals and processions attended by whites, to some white participation in processions (sometimes in blackface), and finally to blacks being the target of white mobs, often white mobs in blackface. Whether on the minstrel stage, participating in festivals and processions, or attacking black performers or churchgoers, acting in blackface seemed to give young white men special dispensation from laws and moral strictures; it seemed to allow them to act out their impulses and fantasies under the cover of darkness.[29]

Harassment and mob violence against African Americans became more blatantly racially motivated in the East and the Midwest throughout the 1820s and into the 1830s. The most notable mob actions were a short-lived Philadelphia riot in 1829, a more serious one in 1834, and the infamous Cincinnati riot of 1829 which reportedly drove many African Americans from that city. These race riots conveyed the message that free blacks were not welcome in American cities, especially after 1820, when there was a surplus of laborers that brought blacks into more serious competition with white workers. Black Americans might still be included in the occasional nonracially inspired mob, but their involvement became less common as the broadened franchise offered a more generally accepted means of political expression.[30]

The racial composition of the mob changed as the acceptable grounds for mob violence narrowed. Earlier mob action had frequently centered around moral issues or political controversies. An unpopular tax, a law thought to be unfair, or the failure of the law to protect some shared community value had traditionally generated a mob. Such grievances shared by the politically powerless of all races produced eighteenth-century mob action; consequently such actions were interracial. As white workingmen gained access to other forms of political participation, mob action gradually lost its acceptability as a form of political expression. The franchise and organizations centering on party politics were becoming more legitimate political vehicles, and these were increasingly racially restricted.

The republican ideal that animated the leaders of the Revolution anticipated the formation of a society of independent, propertied, virtuous citizens, a society in which opportunity was based on individual merit rather than family background or social connections. Theoretically, independence and self-sufficiency would allow citizens to forego selfish personal interests and to act for the good of the community. In such a society there would be no legitimate need for mob action, since social and political change would be created through the use of the ballot and representative government. The central figure in this society was the independent citizen assumed to be the patriarch of a family. As David Roediger put it, "the heritage of the Revolution made independence a powerful masculine personal ideal."[31] Indeed, citizenship was synonymous with manhood, but it was mature manhood, distinct from the boyish actions of the mob. For unlike a boy, a man was self-controlled, able to restrain his aggressive emotions, his enthusiasm, and his "brutish" nature.[32] Masculine traits were also sharply distinguished from feminine characteristics. Linda Kerber's analysis has demonstrated that the ideal of the citizen—that is the autonomous male—was counterposed to the dependent female, and "women's weakness became a rhetorical foil for republican manliness."[33] The emphasis on mature manhood and independence as the preeminent qualifications for full citizenship in the republic provided the logical basis for the denial of such rights to dependent population groups such as women, children, and blacks.

The presence of black people in America posed two problems for the defenders of republicanism. First, slavery and the opulence that often accrued to slaveholders from the labor of their human property disturbed some who feared that the institution would lead the planter class to dependence on slaves and to character-endangering excess. The Virginia planter was rebuked: "he sets up two carriages instead of one; maintains twenty servants, when a fourth part of that number are more than sufficient to discharge the business of personal attendance." Second, a black presence in America raised critical questions about the nature of African Americans in connection with the possession of citizenship rights. In the estimation of the powerful, the republican citizen was male and white, since blacks were assumed to lack the capacity for the autonomy and self-restraint required of a citizen. The assumption that blacks could not be citizens was common even among those whites who questioned the legitimacy of slavery. Thomas Jefferson believed that blacks like whites were endowed with natural rights and did not accept slavery as the rightful condition of Africans even though he was a slaveholder. Partly because he feared retaliation from slaves, he was convinced that blacks could be incorporated into American society only under the most controlled conditions. Slavery was necessary if blacks were to remain in American society, Jefferson concluded, even if the institution itself was evil. He asserted that blacks were not the equal of whites in their ability to reason, in their capacity for imagination, or in any intellectual ability. Never had he found, he wrote, "that a black had uttered a thought above the level of the plain narration; never [had he seen] even an elementary trait of painting or sculpture." Jefferson's conclusions were consonant with evolving scientific theory in which biological explanations were supplanting the environmental theory that explained racial differences as responses to physical and social conditions. A biological basis for racial differences meant that black inferiority was immutable.[34] If this were true blacks would never be granted citizenship and would remain separated from the white workers who might gain such rights.

The expansion of citizenship began during the late eighteenth century as urban workers transformed fraternal organizations into political action groups through which they exercised power in the economic and political life of the city. As workingmen organized, the number of voters doubled in Philadelphia in the 1790s. Property requirements were lowered for voting and office holding, and the number of eligible voters increased. In Massachusetts, New Hampshire, New York, and New Jersey, where colonial assemblies had been largely the preserve of the economic elite before the Revolution, the number of yeomen farmers and mechanics in the legislatures increased dramatically in the early years of nationhood.[35] Jefferson had provided the theoretical foundation for the participation of the yeoman farmer, and though he had never portrayed himself as a common man, he symbolized the true republican. Although perhaps more comfortable with traditional outdoor politics than the Federalists, even he saw a need to guard against the excesses of the mob. The popular unrest of outdoor politics was increasingly unsettling to the growing middle class and to most elites who identified the interests of the new nation with the role of law and the preservation of order.

The growth of republicanism and a democratic spirit in most states during the early nineteenth century resulted in the extension of the right to vote to virtually all adult white males by the mid-1820s. State constitutions in 1800 had generally tied voting rights to minimum property holdings. Since urban artisans, for example, possessed very little property, they were generally not eligible to vote. The removal of some property quali- fications for voting during the early nineteenth century was an effort to channel the energies of dissent into party politics. The expansion of the franchise for white men, however, was often accompanied by the restric- tion or elimination of the franchise for black men. The New Jersey con- stitution only limited voting with property requirements until an 1807 state law added racial restrictions. African Americans were allowed to vote in Connecticut until an 1814 law incorporated into the state constitution four years later denied the vote to all blacks who had not voted up to that time. In 1822, Rhode Island's legislature disenfranchised blacks in that state for the first time.[36]

In New York the constitution of 1777 had guaranteed all men who could meet the property restrictions, including free blacks, the right to vote. New York Republicans tried repeatedly through the early years of the nineteenth century to disenfranchise black voters, but Federalists defended black voting rights and foiled several attempts to institute racial restrictions. The War of 1812 was a turning point for Federalist political power in New York as elsewhere. Discredited by their opposition to the war, Federalists lost control of state politics and were unable to stop Republicans first from limiting the black vote in New York City in 1814 and changing the state constitution in 1821. Property qualifications for white males were removed, but black males were required to have lived in the state for three years and have more than $250 in property before they could vote. This so limited the number of qualified black voters that by 1825 only 298 of a total state black population of almost 30,000 and only 16 of New York City's more than 12,000 blacks possessed the property needed for voting.[37]

As the roster of eligible white voters expanded in every state, even in the South, a new political grassroots style brought General Andrew Jack- son to the presidency in 1828. Political parties vied for the votes of com- mon working people, and candidates portrayed themselves as ordinary men. Jackson's frontiersman image and William Henry Harrison's "log cabin and cider" campaign of 1840 (and Abraham Lincoln as "rail-split- ter" by 1860) were the products of this new populist politics. "Jacksonian democracy" was both a symbol and a product of this change. This "age of the common man" was the age of the common white man, as black men (and all women) lost the franchise in many states. Party politics became a struggle between white men for the support and loyalty of other white men. Although the Jacksonians' political ideology was populist in that it attacked a somewhat vague "privilege," its incorporation of a growing belief in white superiority and its distinctly racial orientation helped make it populism with a class consciousness limited by racial exclusivity. As race became a more powerful determinant of political participation among common people, it became more difficult for nonwhite Americans to assert their rights (Table 7.1).[38]

Political rights in America included much more than the franchise. The Revolution had injected egalitarian values into an existing body of English legal precedent and custom which dictated that citizens, even if they were without the right to vote, were entitled to the protection of their person and property and were required to give allegiance to the state and obey its laws. The political task of the post-Revolutionary period was to reconcile existing beliefs and practices aimed at maintaining an orderly society with the expansion of rights for the common people that Revolutionary values implied. As a result, some of the traditional powers of the government were curtailed, and the formal rights of the common man were expanded. The definition of rights for blacks and women, however, presented special problems. Women had achieved some recognition of their right to an education, and there was even some debate in the courts of their right to control their own property, but in

Table 7.1 Black Rights to Vote By State

	1830	*1860*
Maine	Yes	Yes
New Hampshire	Yes	Yes
Vermont	Yes	Yes
Massachusetts	Yes	Yes
Connecticut	No	No
Rhode Island	No	Yes
New York	Restricted	Restricted
New Jersey	No	No
Pennsylvania	Yes	No
Ohio	No	Restricted
Indiana	No	No
Illinois	No	No
Michigan	No	Restricted
Iowa	No	No
Wisconsin	No	No
Minnesota	No	No
California	No	No
Oregon	No	No

Restrictions: New York—property requirements for black voters; none for white voters. Ohio 1860—only mulattoes could vote (defined as more than half white); Cincinnati blacks could vote in school board elections for black schools. Michigan 1860—blacks could vote in school board elections; there was some other voting at the discretion of election judges.
Source: Paul Finkelman, "Prelude to the Fourteenth Amendment: Black Legal Rights in the Antebellum North," *Rutgers Law Journal* 17 (Spring and Summer 1986): 415–482, 424, and 425.

the paternalistic ideology of the time they were still essentially a dependent population, little different from children in the power structure of the household and society.[39] For African Americans the definition of their status was complicated by the long history of slavery and its continuing existence in the South. A primary set of rights maintained under the new political system concerned the protection of property, and the vast majority of African Americans were still property. Even in the more liberal North, blacks had been a dependent population, and fears of their continuing dependence persisted into freedom. The developing justifications for southern slavery raised questions about their ability to function as citizens. The expansion of political participation in the nineteenth century reinforced the identification of politics with power, and thereby with manliness. In this way, maleness became linked to "power, independence, and freedom of action."[40] As this link strengthened in the 1820s, blacks' and women's claims to power in the public arena became even more difficult to defend.

The political ideology of Jacksonian America also reinforced the belief that American culture rested on an entirely European foundation. If black cultural forms were acknowledged, they were burlesqued, as in the minstrel shows, or rendered primitive curiosities, as in white parodies of black religious customs or fraternal organizations. Still, African cultural forms and their American variants were maintained in the communities of African Americans. Despite the growing racial exclusivity of American politics, America's African heritage was deeply embedded in American culture and was also preserved in the customs and habits of all Americans. The uncertain status of African Americans was one by-product of America's unwillingness to acknowledge African influences on American culture. Although there had been black people in America for more than eight generations by the end of the eighteenth century, the acknowledgment of their American identity after the Revolution was even more uncertain than was the acceptance of more recently arrived European Americans. Despite the strength of their African memories, blacks claimed America too. Not only had they provided much of the country's labor, they had fought for its independence and, white dismissals notwithstanding, blacks understood their contributions to the building of the nation. Yet their status was ambiguous. Free blacks still voted in several states, and Congress safeguarded African-American seamen in foreign ports by issuing them protection certificates that declared them "Citizen[s] of the United States of America." On the other hand, they were excluded from the federal militia, and the Constitution explicitly limited naturalization to white immigrants.[41]

Federal officials sent mixed messages—blacks were prohibited from carrying the mail, but an African American carried the mail through New Jersey on the route connecting Philadelphia and New York City in the early nineteenth century. In 1817, a "skillful black driver" delivered mail in Virginia, though officials employed the fiction of white supervision by sending along a ten-year-old white boy. During the 1820s, at least one slave served in the Richmond post office, and as late as the 1830s, blacks were illegally subcontracted as mail carriers. Comments by Postmaster General Gideon Granger indicated that while he felt that such restriction was "justified" by the fears of the authorities, it was illegitimate by America's own principles. Writing to the chair of the Committee on the Posts, who was also the senator from Georgia, Granger rationalized his support for firing free blacks from the mail service. The extensive travel of a mail carrier might prove dangerous, he observed, as it would allow the acquisition and dissemination of knowledge among free blacks and slaves. "They become acquainted with each other on the line. Whenever the body, or a portion of them, wish to act, they are an organized corps, circulating our intelligence openly, their own privately." Granger especially feared that African Americans carrying the mail would "learn that a Man's rights do not depend on his color."[42]

African Americans knew the injustice of laws and customs that limited their rights all too well. They faced restrictions in many aspects of their everyday lives, often excluded from public education and segregated in public entertainment, accommodations, and transportation. Blacks often found travel a humiliating and sometimes dangerous experience. Most railroad cars, steamships, and stage coaches were racially segregated. Henry Highland Garnet reported that on a trip through New York State to Niagara Falls, the conductor informed him that even though he had paid for a first-class ticket he was not allowed to sit in the first class car. "Colored people cannot be permitted to ride with the whites," he was told, "for Southern ladies and gentlemen will not tolerate it." When Garnet protested, he was dragged off the train and severely beaten while white bystanders, though offering no assistance, pleaded that his life be spared.[43] Neither class nor gender protected black travelers from mistreatment. Elizabeth Jennings, a school teacher in New York City, was assaulted by a conductor and a driver when she attempted to board the horse drawn cars.[44] The Reverend Theodore S. Wright was forced to remain on the deck of a steamboat, while the special accommodation to his wife's illness only allowed her to sleep in the cook's quarters, "a dirty little apartment near the machinery."[45] When a businessman, frustrated at having to pay full fare to shiver on deck, confronted the ship's captain, he was put ashore for his audacity. "I was landed on one of the most desolate spots on Long Island (Crane Neck) at midnight, amid wild cattle who had, probably, not seen the face of a man for a [year]," he recalled.[46]

Rather than endure continual affronts, many blacks avoided potentially discriminatory situations, making black community organizations, personal associations, and kinship networks especially important. Sarah Forten of Philadelphia explained how her family minimized insults—"We never travel far from home and seldom go to public places unless quite sure that admission is free to all." Despite the fact that she had several white friends, Sarah admitted that she went out of her way to avoid unfamiliar whites and advised all blacks to follow her example in order to spare themselves "some very painful realities."[47]

In eating houses, in public parks, at public gatherings of all descriptions black Americans were turned away or relegated to the most undesirable places. As Frederick Douglass recalled the refrain familiar to every African American who ventured out into a public facility, "We don't allow Niggers in here." These were shared experiences that served as another tie binding African Americans in a common American experience. Many blacks protested these situations, sometimes individually and sometimes through organized efforts. Frederick Douglass refused to be segregated in the train to Lynn, Massachusetts, and made it as difficult as possible for the conductor to bodily remove him from the train. Other African Americans tested the custom of segregated seating in places of entertainment by purchasing tickets to the theater and bringing suit against the owner who refused them their seats. Some white abolitionists, especially Garrisonian integrationists, joined blacks in demonstrating their opposition to racial discrimination, mounting petition campaigns, memorializing legislatures, and traveling in integrated groups on public conveyances.[48]

By the time Jacksonian democracy ushered in the era of the common man, race was the defining limit of African-American life. Facing daily discrimination and racial insults, generally removed from the formal arena of politics, and restricted economically, their hold on citizenship was becoming increasingly tenuous. In the face of this assault, some blacks called for a general uprising of black people to reassert African Americans' natural right to independence, power, and autonomy, what some called the manhood of the race. Not willing to suffer racist theory or disenfranchisement without protest, blacks spoke out strongly. One of the most militant statements of this period was given by David Walker, a Bostonian who had been born to a free black woman in North Carolina in 1785 and had grown up in the South. Walker never knew his slave father, who died before David was born. He spent the first forty years of his life in the South where he had the opportunity to become familiar with the horrors of slavery in many states. By the time he arrived in Boston in the mid-1820s and established a clothing business there, he was a man in his forties, six-feet tall, slim, with "loose hair," and a dark complexion. He joined Boston's African Masonic Lodge, the African Methodist Episcopal Church, and a black antislavery group called the Massachusetts General Colored Association. It was before this latter body that Walker gave a fiery speech in the winter of 1828, a speech later printed in New York's *Freedom's Journal*, the first black newspaper in the country. One year later he published an expanded version as his *Appeal to the Coloured Citizens of the World*, a ringing condemnation of slavery, of Thomas Jefferson's racial beliefs, of prejudice, and of any black person who refused to stand for black citizenship rights, what Walker and others called manhood rights. The *Appeal* scandalized southern politicians and occasioned secret meetings of the Georgia and Virginia legislatures. Rumors circulated in the South and the North of large rewards offered for Walker's death.[49]

Walker's *Appeal* asserted the right of black people to American citizenship by virtue of the contributions of their labor and sacrifices to the establishment of the nation and to its prosperity. He took issue with Jefferson's suggestion that blacks were inferior to whites, the theory that created a basis for the denial of rights to blacks. Walker wrote that Jefferson, who had died a few years before, "was one of as great characters as ever lived among the whites" and therefore had a unique power not only in America but throughout the world. He noted that many white men like Benjamin Franklin, Benjamin Rush, and Alexander Hamilton had already questioned Jefferson's racial views, but he believed it was critical that the challenge come from blacks. "We and the world wish to see the charges of Mr. Jefferson refuted by the blacks themselves, according to their chance; for we must remember that what the whites have written respecting this subject is other men's labours and did not emanate from the blacks."[50] Most important, only by the efforts of their own intellects could African Americans refute Jefferson's intimations that they were a lower order of humanity not worthy of full freedom. His challenge to fellow blacks was clear. "Are we MEN!!—I ask you, O my brethren! are we MEN? Did our Creator make us to be slaves to dust and ashes like ourselves?" Slavery, the kidnapping of "loads of men, women and children," must be opposed and should be opposed on the grounds that African Americans were human beings naturally the equals of whites. "We are MEN, and not brutes as we have been represented, and by the millions treated."[51]

David Walker asserted the humanity of black men. Walker, too, accepted the nineteenth century republican ideal equating citizenship and a manhood defined by power and autonomy. He believed black men had special responsibilities to protect their families and to publicly represent the race. He wrote that a father must educate his son so that as an adult the son might gain the power to defend and forward the race. Moreover, Walker demanded that black men be ready to defend themselves and their families with violence if need be. He challenged them to refuse to be slaves and reject the authority of slave masters. If this leads to violence, "kill or be killed . . . had you not rather be killed than to be a slave to a tyrant, who takes the life of your mother, wife and dear little children?" Walker's argument suggested that ultimately the achievement of individual manhood and the manhood of the race might well come through violence. The most primitive assertion of manhood might be needed to acquire the more humane and socially acceptable manhood associated with republican citizenship.[52]

David Walker died in late June 1830, just a few months before his son was born. His body was found on Bridge Street in Boston; the cause of his death was uncertain. Walker's death did not end his influence. His

Appeal continued to be circulated, and his theme was taken up in Boston by a black woman named Maria W. Stewart. Like Walker, Stewart framed her message in a religious imperative, speaking equally to the condition of slaves and free blacks. Stewart had been inspired by Walker's message and his martyrdom and declared her readiness to follow his fate in service to the cause of freedom and racial progress. Stewart had been born Maria Miller in Hartford, Connecticut in 1803. She was orphaned at age 5 and bound out until age 15 as a domestic servant in the household of a minister. She had moved to Boston in the 1820s and in 1826 was married by the Reverend Thomas Paul to James W. Stewart, an older man who was a naval veteran of the War of 1812 and a successful ship outfitter. After only three years of marriage her husband died, leaving the twenty-six-year-old Maria once again without family support. The year of Walker's death Stewart experienced an intense religious conversion. The following year she made a public profession of her faith and began her short career as a writer and public speaker.[53]

With the assistance of antislavery editor William Lloyd Garrison, Stewart published a pamphlet in 1831 and religious meditations in 1832. In the next few years she gave four public lectures in Boston, launching this highly unusual occupation for a woman with a speech to the Afric-American Female Intelligence Society. She defended herself against criticism by emphasizing her religious motivation, assuming the role of speaking for God in the manner of the Old Testament prophets. Speaking to the society, she called on the examples of various revolutionaries including the French, the Haitians, the Greeks, and the Poles, urged an end to treachery and envy among blacks, and called for unity in their struggle to achieve black rights in America. In this first talk, Stewart appealed to the women in terms congruent with the ideal of republican womanhood, arguing that the progress of the race depended on them because their "spirit of Christian love and unity" would have a strong influence over their husbands and children.[54] In another speech later that year to a mixed audience of men and women, Stewart continued her previous themes and forcefully claimed the right of blacks to their American heritage, saying, "for I am a true born American; your blood flows in my veins, and your spirit fires my breast." Denouncing blacks' relegation to menial labor and ignorance, she urged her audience to emulate the pilgrims and the patriots, to actively demand their rights.[55]

In February 1833, speaking before the African Masonic Lodge in Boston, Maria W. Stewart may have carried her role as a prophet too far. Like Walker, she recalled the glories of Africa's ancient history and called on her listeners to act in "the spirit of men." She was standing in the hall that was home to the Masons organized and led by men like Prince Hall, Primus Hall, and James Barbadoes, men who had fought in the Revolution, had been the first in the state to speak out against slavery, had won freedom for Massachusetts' slaves, and had organized black groups including an antislavery society. After a brief recognition of the role blacks had played in the Revolution and the War of 1812 and of the late David Walker's bravery, she asked a question that could not have endeared her to the men in her audience. What was it, she asked, that caused the Revolutionary and post-Revolutionary generation, "our men who are 60 or 70 years of age, never to let their voices be heard, nor their hands be raised in behalf of their color?" Was it "blindness of mind, or stupidity of soul, or want of education," or "fear of offending the whites?" Perhaps in an attempt to strengthen her justification for giving public lectures in violation of rules of feminine propriety, she contended that she was forced to speak out because the men had failed to do so.[56]

With stinging attacks Stewart tried to goad the men to greater achievements. There were no illustrious blacks, she charged, not only because of white prejudice and oppression but also due to a "want of laudable amibition and requisite courage." "Have the sons of Africa no souls?" she demanded. "Feel they no ambitious desires?" She was especially critical of "our rising youth," who she believed squandered the resources of the community. They must "flee from the gambling board and the dancehall; for we are poor, and have no money to throw away." She instructed black men to turn to temperance and build institutions to serve community needs and act as a foundation for black economic and political power. Maria Stewart, like David Walker, saw the fate of the race in the hands of black men. The elevation of the race depended on their achieving their own personal manhood through vigorous self-assertion. For her outspokenness and for what some members of the audience perceived as unwarranted criticism rather than divinely inspired prophesy, Maria Stewart was hooted and jeered and pelted with rotten tomatoes.[57]

Under attack and feeling isolated and alone, Stewart decided to shake the dust of Boston from her shoes and move to New York. Before she did, though, in the fall of 1833 she gave her "Farewell Address to the People of Color" in the schoolroom of Thomas Paul's church. Stewart had been criticized, she said, for talking so much about religion and had been urged to tell her listeners something they didn't already know. She interpreted this as an attack on her right as a woman to assume this role. "What if I am a woman?" she asked. A person should be judged no more by gender than by race, "for it is not color of skin that makes the man or the woman, but the principle formed in the soul." She gave a lengthy defense of the special place of women as seers and prophets in the Bible and in the history of great European civilizations. As a further defense of her public role, she cited examples of accomplished female "divines and scholars." In this speech she not only gave her audience new information, she gave them precedent and justification for expanding acceptable women's roles in society. The greater part of the responsibility for advancing the race still fell to black men, but Stewart also defined specific roles for women. She argued that black women should promote their own welfare, the strength of their families, and the elevation of their race not only in the private world of the home but also in the public world. Women must "strive, by their example both in public and private, to assist those who are endeavoring to stop the strong current of prejudice that flows so profusely against us at present."[58]

In her written work in late 1831, Stewart had urged women to practice "prudence and economy," to "excel in good housewifery," as a way of accumulating the wealth to promote black education. Working together, she argued, women could raise the money, build, and staff the schools. She still gave men the primary responsibility for defending the race, challenging them to "prove to the world that you are neither ourang-outangs, or a species of mere animals but that you possess the same powers of intellect as the proud-boasting Americans." But the place she envisioned for black women in this struggle went beyond their roles as models of virtue or, as one black male organization put it, "the God-given help-mate[s] of man."[59]

In her farewell address she began to create an argument for women's central role in the public struggle for the progress of the race, but Jacksonian politics and combating justifications for slavery kept the focus on the rights of men and the issue of black manhood. Although Stewart still envisioned women's tasks as extensions of their traditional duties as women, supporting roles in the achievement of manhood rights, she expanded their roles and widened their arena. As Americans developed their national identity, the strong gender prescriptions delineating womanhood and manhood were integral to that identity. Thus clearly defined gender roles gained importance in the politics of American society during the 1820s, and what Mary Ryan called the "newly feminized civic values" of "chastity, sobriety, passivity, domesticity" characterized the proper female reformers of the 1830s and 1840s. By 1833 Maria Stewart gave public notice that black women would not be constrained by the dictates of all the gender ideals of Jacksonian politics.[60]

Only a minority of women questioned their place in the American polity during this period, but black protest against the growing political exclusion of African Americans was widespread. Yet, while African Americans' role in electoral politics was circumscribed, African and African-American cultural forms continued to shape America's cultural identity. Of this period, novelist Ralph Ellison later observed that the American vernacular expressed a "natural" Americanization process that defied "the social, aesthetic, and political assumptions" of its leaders, creating a culture "more 'Democratic' and 'American' than the social and political institutions in which it was emerging."[61] Ever aware of these simultaneous and contradictory trends, blacks continued their protest sometimes believing in the ultimate triumph of America's principles and sometimes despairing of their realization in the nation they were helping to create.

8

Ambivalent Identity:
Colonization and the Question
of Emigration

Paul Cuffe, sailor, captain, shipowner, and businessman from Westport, Massachusetts, acknowledged many professional and personal
identities. He was American Indian through his mother's heritage, African
through his father's heritage, and American by birth. He maintained his
personal allegiances throughout his life, emphasizing each identity at one
point or another but never abandoning any. Soon after Massachusetts
abolished slavery he joined with other African Americans and successfully
petitioned the Commonwealth for black political rights. They claimed
taxation without representation and acquired the vote, that basic manhood right of citizenship. His role in this campaign established Cuffe's
identity within the state.[1]

The American identity that many blacks like Cuffe asserted was a complex one since Africa and different Americas called on their loyalties.
African Americans took the rhetoric and the spirit of the Revolution and
the assumptions of republicanism seriously. They were drawn to America
as a symbol of freedom and equality and ready to give it their loyalty, but
they were realistic about the ways in which the nation fell short of that
symbol. When the protests of Daniel Shays and the angry farmers in
western Massachusetts threatened to close local courts, and the federal
and state governments could not raise sufficient troops to enforce the law,
veteran Prince Hall volunteered to lead a contingent of 700 Boston area
blacks to put down the rebellion. Massachusetts officials refused Hall's
offer, turning instead to wealthy Boston merchants who contributed
funds to raise a sufficient force of white troops to quiet the revolt. Hall

and his followers took the rejection of their offer as an insult. Shortly thereafter, in June of 1787, over seventy Boston blacks, under Hall's leadership, petitioned the Massachusetts General Court asking for funds to transport to Africa all blacks who wished to go.[2]

Many felt a connection to Africa based on racial heritage, but some had more direct ties. Cuffe's link to Africa through family connections was reinforced by his business ventures that included trade with West Africa. African Americans maintained a strong attachment to African culture, but they also participated in the American culture they had helped to create. Still, there were a great many blacks not so committed to their emerging and still indistinct American identity that they were unwilling to leave America and reclaim Africa. The Massachusetts constitution had abolished slavery, but many believed that they could not experience true freedom under the degraded circumstances they were forced to endure even in this progressive state. "[W]e find ourselves, in many respects, in very disagreeable and disadvantaged circumstances; most of which must attend us as long as we and our children live in America." Thus, some asked "to return to Africa, our native country, which warm climate is much more natural [and] agreeable to us . . . and where we shall live among our equals and be more comfortable and happy, than we can be in our present situation."[3]

The issue of African identity for African Americans was strongly influenced by the fact that there were many African-born blacks in the generation growing old during the late eighteenth and early nineteenth century. The majority of slaves brought to America arrived between 1760 and 1810, many of them directly from Africa. Quash Quande and many of his neighbors at Parting Ways, Massachusetts arrived from Africa during that period. Newport Gardner, named Occramer Marycoo, was brought to Rhode Island in 1760 and lived there to a very old age, but he never forgot his African tongue. Tobias Wornton of Gloucester and his son-in-law Money Vose were members of the last generations of Africans whose personal connection with Africa as a birthplace colored the identity of free African Americans and encouraged their perceiving Africa as home.

There is ample evidence that substantial numbers of American black people saw themselves as Africans in America through the first decades of the nineteenth century.[4] When the Constitution officially ended the African slave trade in 1808, blacks held mass celebrations in northern cities. The crowds joined in prayer and song, and speakers addressed "Beloved Africans." Even a brief, incomplete listing of organizations is sufficient to make the point: the African Union Society in Newport, Rhode Island, founded in 1780, the Free African Society in Philadelphia in 1787, Boston's African Masonic Lodge a month later, the African Free School established that fall to educate New York City's black children, before the turn of the century, the African Church of St. Thomas and Bethel African Methodist Episcopal Church in Philadelphia, and the

African Society in Boston. In 1794 the Newport association helped Philadelphia's blacks start the African Humane Society. Throughout the first generation of the nineteenth century, the names of most black churches, schools, social and mutual aid societies, and intellectual associations included the designation "African." New York City's African Grove was just one of many examples.[5]

For those who saw themselves as America's African people, the thought of African emigration was often appealing. Even before Massachusetts blacks petitioned for transportation to Africa, blacks in the Newport African Union Society, with the encouragement of minister Samuel Hopkins, had discussed the feasibility of obtaining clear title to land somewhere in Africa where they might start a Christian settlement. Before the Revolution, abolitionists, critics of the slave trade, and ministers like Hopkins with evangelical ambitions for Africa had contemplated the resettlement of African Americans. Some Quakers, too, continued to have personal reasons for interest in proposals for African settlements. A young white Quaker architect and physician, William Thornton, the son of a West Indian sugar planter, inherited seventy slaves in 1785 and immediately began contemplating possibilities for participating in a settlement experiment somewhere in Africa. Thornton became committed to the dream of his friend, Henry Smeathman, who had explored West Africa and was gathering support in England for the establishment of a free colony in Sierra Leone.[6]

Smeathman had already found 400 potential emigrants before he died in 1786. His work was carried on by British abolitionists, Quaker merchants, government officials, and private philanthropists concerned about the rising costs of assisting the many thousands of very poor blacks in the city of London. Most of the emigrants were destitute sailors who had come to London from America during the Revolutionary War. Meanwhile, William Thornton pledged his own slaves to the Sierra Leone venture and set out for America to recruit more participants. He visited and spoke to mass meetings of blacks in northeastern port cities where his enthusiasm was received with cautious respect. Despite their interest in African settlement and their petition to the state legislature, the African Company in Boston expressed their reservations in a letter to the African Union Society in Newport, Rhode Island. "We do not approve of Mr. Thornton's going [to] settle a place for us," they wrote. "We think it would be better if we could charter a vessel and send some of our own blacks."[7]

Philadelphia blacks, already lukewarm on the topic, rejected Thornton's plan outright. This is surprising because there were many African-born blacks in the city, and blacks there had a long-standing relationship with white Quakers. In fact, Philadelphia's blacks may have given Thornton little support precisely because of increasingly aggressive efforts by Quakers and other progressive reformers in the city on behalf of black freedom in America. Just at the time that Thornton was attempting to recruit African Americans, the Pennsylvania Abolition Society reorganized and expanded its work. Fired by the efforts of zealous men like Benjamin Rush, it is likely that many blacks were convinced of Philadelphia's progressive possibilities.[8]

African Americans were also aware of the serious problems involved in the founding of the colony in Sierra Leone—Thornton wasn't their only source of information. The association of the famous English abolitionist Granville Sharp with the project and the enthusiastic report to the Rhode Island Yearly Meeting from William Rotch, Sr. were promising. Rotch, a prominent New Bedford Quaker, returned from England just as the ships were readying their departure from London for the colony. Yet, disturbing rumors flew around the Atlantic maritime world. Departure had long been delayed, and many colonists had spent cold months on ships in port under conditions rumored to be coercive. The purpose and administration of the planned colony were ambiguous, there was even talk that organizers were considering setting up a trading station. For many this was too reminiscent of British slave-trading ports in Africa. The loading of a convict ship at a dock next to an emigrant vessel seemed to provide support for newspaper accounts that convicts were to be included in the colony. The dismissal of the African supervisor of supplies for the emigrants, Gustavus Vassa (also known as Olaudah Equiano), raised new questions. Vassa was an experienced seaman and navigator who had been a steward on an American ship just before being hired as a clerk by the committee for Sierra Leone. A former slave, he had gained his freedom with the help of a Philadelphia Quaker. News of his problems and his complaints about the inadequacy of provisions made their way to America where Vassa had strong ties. This kind of notoriety did not promote the colony among America's blacks.[9]

Members of the African Union Society of Newport corresponded with blacks in Providence, Boston, and Philadelphia in an effort to establish a regional association to promote and support African emigration. "We are waiting," wrote Anthony Taylor for the Newport society in the fall of 1787, "and longing to hear what has been the success of the attempt made in England to make a settlement of blacks in Africa." He expressed the hope that Massachusetts would provide the funds for emigration, said Newport blacks would like to join Boston blacks in emigrating, but lamented the fact that they were too poor "to do much." Finally, in 1794 the Rhode Island societies with the backing of some white merchants interested in establishing an African trade managed to gather the resources to send emissaries to negotiate with officials in Sierra Leone. William Olney and James McKenzie from Providence and Newport Gardner from Newport were chosen, but by the time the ship departed in late 1795 only McKenzie was aboard. Sierra Leone officials promised McKenzie that twelve families from Rhode Island could emigrate and receive land but required that their character be vouched for by the Reverend Samuel Hopkins, white president of the Rhode Island Abolition Society. Hopkins would not provide the necessary endorsement for the Providence blacks.[10]

Although interest in emigration continued, especially among African-born blacks in America, there seemed little hope of gaining the necessary resources and trustworthy allies during the next ten years. Finally, Paul Cuffe became interested in the enterprise. By 1800 Cuffe, whose business relied mainly on family members as partners and workers, was one of the most successful black men in America. He and his partners owned a 200-acre farm in Westport, Massachusetts, a shipyard, a gristmill, a windmill, and a ship, the *Ranger*, which plied the coastal trade between Westport and Wilmington, Delaware. By 1804 he had built another ship, the *Hero*, and sent it on a whaling expedition off southern Africa. A respected businessman in the Atlantic Quaker trading network and a member of the Westport Quaker meeting, Cuffe was energetically recruited in 1808 by Friends in London's African Institution, the organization then promoting settlement in Sierra Leone, through their contacts in the American Quaker community. Cuffe attended the Yearly Meeting in Newport that fall and while in the city consulted with Newport Gardener who encouraged his interest in the African colony.[11]

Paul Cuffe was in a unique position to further the aims of African Americans interested in African settlement. His business ties gave him the credentials that gained the respect of the prominent Englishmen sponsoring African colonization. From their perspective, his character and financial resources made him the model settler who would draw other respectable settlers. Cuffe had friends, many of them Africans, in the black communities of the eastern seaport cities and was familiar with their long-standing interest in emigration. He had conducted successful whaling expeditions off the coast of Africa and was intrigued by the prospect of demonstrating that a profitable African trade could be established exclusive of the slave trade. Especially important to African Americans, Cuffe had the ships to transport settlers to Africa, ships with trustworthy black crews.

Maritime restrictions imposed by the U. S. government in 1807 limited trade and postponed any prospects for emigration. George Washington had warned Americans in his 1796 Farewell Address against becoming embroiled in European hostilities, but his successors found it increasingly difficult to remain aloof. John Adams had managed to avert war with France through negotiation, and Thomas Jefferson attempted to avoid a direct confrontation with the British, though England continued to impress American sailors and interrupt American shipping. As the precarious peace between Britain and France collapsed in 1803, America's neutral stance proved increasingly untenable. Jefferson's claim for neutrality was complicated by America's flourishing trade with the French

West Indies, a trade that enriched American merchants and brought West Indian sugar and coffee to Europe in American ships in direct competition with British merchants.

In a last effort to assert America's neutrality and to economically punish both France and Britain, Jefferson engineered the passage of legislation effectively closing American ports to foreign trade. Despite evasions and loopholes, which for example allowed American ships blown off course in a storm to put in at European ports, this embargo had a serious effect on American merchants and workers whose jobs depended on sea trade. Although several merchants went to debtors' prison, many managed to diversify their investments by moving capital into manufacturing. For some merchants and for the economy, then, there were long-term benefits as a result of the embargo, but workers were not so fortunate. Thousands of seamen and dock laborers, a large proportion African American, were thrown out of work in seaport cities, especially in New England.

When the embargo was lifted for a time in 1809 Paul Cuffe resumed sailing. A few days after Christmas in 1810 Cuffe set out on his brig *Traveller*, captained by his nephew Thomas Wainer and crewed entirely by black sailors, to personally investigate settlement conditions and trading opportunities in Sierra Leone. When they arrived in March 1811, the colony had a population of about 3,500 people: a few families from the original settlement, other people of African ancestry roughly equally divided between Nova Scotians, Maroons from the British West Indies, local Africans, Africans recaptured from slave ships, and the twenty-eight Europeans (less than 1 percent of the population) who controlled 60 percent of the property in the colony. Cuffe and Wainer rented houses and began to discuss trading possibilities with the black population of Sierra Leone. Leaving Wainer in Africa, Cuffe then sailed to England for discussions with the British businessmen and philanthropists with interests in the West African colony. In December Cuffe was back in Africa, where he stayed until February 1812. Samuel Hicks and Prince Edwards, two of his crew members who were not his relatives, decided to stay as settlers in the colony. Since English merchants monopolized the Sierra Leone trade, it was unclear whether Cuffe would be able to capitalize on the trading connections he had established with the Africans or whether trading licenses would be forthcoming.[12]

When the *Traveller* returned to port in Rhode Island in April 1812, partially loaded with British goods, customs officials seized the ship. As relations with England rapidly deteriorated, Cuffe journeyed to Washington, D. C. to successfully plead with President James Madison and Secretary of the Treasury Albert Gallatin for the release of his ship and cargo. He also discussed his interest in transporting Africans from America to Sierra Leone. Returning from Washington, Cuffe stopped in New York, Philadelphia, and Baltimore to report on the colony and to encourage the establishment of African Institutions to organize potential settlers. Once home he wrote to friends in Boston urging them to organize an African Institution as well. Although a correspondence continued between Cuffe and the African Institutions in America, President Madison's declaration of war with Britain on June 1, 1812 again postponed emigration plans.[13]

The War of 1812 prevented some black people from leaving America, but it also presented African Americans with opportunities for reasserting their claim to liberty. As in the early years of the Revolution, the southern states feared the consequences of arming slaves and resisted black enlistment. Once again the British issued a call for black troops, promising freedom to slaves in return for service, and once again slaves responded in large numbers. Blacks joined with British sea forces in battles on the Great Lakes and in the Chesapeake Bay, and they marched under the Union Jack with the British forces that invaded and burned Washington, D. C. In the South the specter of a general slave uprising like the Haitian Revolution haunted the populace and created sporadic panic.[14]

As in the Revolution, blacks fought on both sides of the war. After the British sacked Washington, Philadelphia seemed certain to come under attack, and New York was vulnerable too. When the British blockaded New York harbor in the summer of 1814, blacks responded, calling a series of meetings and offering their services to defend the city. Some Afro-New Yorkers argued that it was the "duty of every colored man resident in this city to volunteer."[15] New York officials replied by reinstating an old provision of the state law allowing black enlistment in the state militia, and that fall New York State authorized two regiments of black troops under white leadership. In Philadelphia, James Forten, Richard Allen, and Absolom Jones raised a "Black Brigade" of 2,500 men to fortify and defend the city from an anticipated British attack that never materialized.[16]

The patriotic actions of these black people bespoke their continuing identification with and commitment to America. In a time of crisis they were able, it seemed, to put aside the ambivalence created by racial restrictions. Many blacks simply refused to accept a second-class status and were determined to claim their right to act as full American citizens despite whites who rejected the idea of black citizenship. Some blacks carried their assertion of an American identity farther, refusing to fight on the British side even when such refusal jeopardized their freedom. Charles Black, an impressed seaman serving aboard a British gunboat, would not fight against the United States. Consequently he was held in irons, first as a prisoner aboard the British ship and then at the notorious Dartmoor prison near Plymouth, England.[17] Not all black sailors refused to serve against American forces, but they were far more likely to refuse than their white American counterparts. Historian William Jeffery Bolster estimated that of the more than one thousand American sailors serving aboard British ships at the start of the war, twice as many blacks as whites refused to fight on the British side and were imprisoned at Dartmoor. Bolster also described acts of patriotic protest among imprisoned blacks. On occasion, for example, the prison's black band defiantly played the popular American song *Yankee Doodle Dandy*.[18]

Once inside Dartmoor American sailors found that a patriotic attitude toward America was demanded, and that it could be dangerous to admit having fought with the British against the United States. A prisoner might be branded on the cheek with a TR (for traitor) or receive worse treatment for such an admission. Inmate prison enforcers like Richard Seaver of Salem, Massachusetts carried out sentences and maintained order in Dartmoor. Called "Big Dick" by his fellows, Seaver was well equipped for his role, standing well over six-feet tall (estimates vary from 6 feet 3 inches to a probably exaggerated 7 feet tall) and weighing 300 pounds or more. Seaver had entered the U. S. Navy in 1812 and was eventually captured by the British and sent to Dartmoor. He was said to be incredibly strong and commanded great respect in the prison. After the war he taught boxing in Boston, but local legend contended that his business was limited by his knocking out many of his students in practice sessions. Later he acted as special aid to the Boston police.[19]

At Dartmoor prison the number of inmates increased from 24 blacks and 226 whites in 1813 to over 1,100 blacks and five times as many whites the next year. It was an all-male, relatively young population who shared a common profession and the maritime culture. Initially, American prisoners were housed together, but as the black population grew, whites accused blacks of stealing and petitioned for segregated facilities. The charge was probably true, since stealing was widespread among white and black prisoners. African Americans were moved to building number four where they established a distinctive community. Their political system, continuing African-American colonial practice, was based on the designation of a charismatic leader called the governor or king, the role assumed by Big Dick (also called "King Dick"). Whites, who elected committees and presidents to conduct their internal affairs, complained that the blacks were undemocratic.

The cultural life of the black barracks was also distinctive. Blacks seemed generally quite religious; Simon, a black seaman and Methodist minister, preached for frequent church services. Since there were no regular religious meetings in the other barracks, several whites with religious inclinations were attracted to Simon's services. Number four also had recreational activities ranging from card games and boxing to dramatic productions. Inmates' performances of Shakespearian plays like Romeo and Juliet and the ever-popular Othello entertained African Americans and the white Americans who joined them in their section of the prison. Fencing matches which pitted the best of the prison population against one another were entertaining and potentially profitable for gamblers. With the variety of activities in the black section of the prison, Bolster believed that it became the focal point of the entire prison population. The music and dancing so impressed white prisoner Nathaniel Pierce, for example, that he spent much of his time there. In his diary, Pierce commented on the band, the choir, Seaver's boxing classes and the school that offered instruction in reading and writing.[20]

In Dartmoor black and white Americans temporarily breached the barrier of race, but it was never permanently broken down. Available evidence suggests that almost all interracial association took place in the black section. Though predominant, race was not the only source of identity. Nationality, region, and locality also determined comradeship and mutual interest. Men shared their mess with others from their hometown. After a lucky streak at the gambling table, one black man from Newburyport shared part of his winnings with his white hometown mates as well, making them the handsome present of "a two penny loaf and a pint of Coffee." Although their living conditions were far from egalitarian, confirmations that they shared a national identification with their white comrades and blacks' active commitment to the patriotic American cause made the consideration of schemes for African colonization less likely for these black sailors.[21]

The Treaty of Ghent brought a negotiated end to the war in late December of 1814, but word of the peace had not yet reached Louisiana, when General Andrew Jackson and his troops, including at least six hundred free blacks, repelled a British attack. At the Battle of New Orleans, they inflicted more than two thousand casualties and provided America with its greatest victory of the conflict. The motivation of many of the black troops who stood at New Orleans seems clear. The slaves Jackson recruited from area plantations were promised their freedom if victorious in battle. In an "Address to the Free Coloured Inhabitants of Louisiana," General Jackson's perception of their status seemed unambiguous. He seemed to believe that American blacks were Americans as he declared, "As sons of freedom, you are now called upon to defend our most inestimable blessings. *As Americans*, your country looks with confidence to her adopted children for a valorous support." Jackson promised equal treatment, equal provisions, and equal pay to blacks who would volunteer. The reward pledged to them was $24 and 160 acres of land, just as was provided to white troops.[22]

One slave, James Roberts, who fought with Jackson at the Battle of New Orleans, had risked his life before in service to the United States. Roberts was born a slave in 1753 on Maryland's Eastern Shore, and in the Revolution he accompanied his master Francis DeShields, a colonel in the Revolutionary army. After DeShields died, Roberts returned home to his wife and four children, hoping to be set free in return for fighting for American liberty. "But, instead of freedom," he recounted, "I was, soon after my return, sold to William Ward, separated from my wife and children, taken to New Orleans, and sold at auction sale to Calvin Smith, a planter in Louisiana, for fifteen hundred dollars."[23] Nor did Roberts receive his freedom after the Battle of New Orleans. At war's end, when black troops were no longer needed, General Jackson seemed less sure of their status and of his responsibility to free those who had fought with him at New Orleans. He was extravagant in his praise for the fighting abilities and "noble enthusiasm" of the black soldiers but said he could not free those who were slaves—that was up to their masters. James Roberts was returned to slavery, greatly embittered and feeling he had once again been "duped by the white man."[24]

The end of the war and the lifting of maritime restrictions enabled Paul Cuffe and his associates to resume their efforts to transport American blacks to Sierra Leone. Immediately Cuffe notified his friends and correspondents in the African Institutions, James Forten and Richard Allen in Philadelphia, Perry Lockes and Prince Saunders in Boston, and Abraham Thompson and Peter Williams, Jr. in New York, of his intentions. So much interest was expressed that Cuffe was convinced he could send one ship a year with settlers if financial arrangements could be made. For the first expedition, the African Institution in London agreed to pay some of the settlers' expenses, a few could finance their own move, and Cuffe agreed to take care of the rest.[25]

Finally, on December 10, 1815, Captain Paul Cuffe put out to sea on the brig *Traveller* loaded with cargo for trade, a crew of almost all Cuffe relatives, three passengers, and thirty-four settlers bound for Sierra Leone. The passengers were Charles Columbine, an African who intended to make his way to the Congo, and Anthony Survance and his wife. Survance from Senegal had been enslaved and sold to the French in St. Domingue. He had come to America during the Haitian Revolution, obtained his freedom and some education, and acquired property in Philadelphia that he was selling to pay for supplies for his return to Africa. The settlers ranged in age from eight months to about sixty years, and by April 1, 1816, two months after their arrival, Cuffe reported to William Allen at the African Institution in London that he had successfully obtained homesteads for the settlers. Samuel Wilson and his wife from Philadelphia and William Guinn, his wife and daughter from Boston were working separately, but five families from Boston had decided to work a ten-acre farm together. This group of twenty-nine people included Perry Lockes, age thirty, his wife and four children, Samuel Hughes, age fifty, his wife and four children, Thomas Jarvis, about fifty, his wife and five children, Peter Wilcox, about forty, his wife and five children, and Robert Rigsby, about thirty-six, his wife and one child. Cuffe himself had considered the possibility of moving to Sierra Leone, but his American Indian wife refused to leave the land of her ancestors. Although some blacks found the idea of emigration promising, most feared the hazards, had ties with family and friends in America, or were hopeful about the future and did not intend to leave.[26]

Paul Cuffe was not always sure of a positive outcome for his African ventures. Commerce was central to his purpose, but even though he had invested $8,000 in settlement and trading in Sierra Leone, he had been unable to obtain the necessary trading permits from the British authorities. Consequently, he was concerned about the financial feasibility of his undertaking, but the prospects for settlement seemed somewhat more promising. Cuffe's successful trip to West Africa in 1815 generated a good deal of publicity, and members of the African Institutions read his account of the voyage in black churches in America.

Cuffe's trip encouraged another even more ambitious African colonization effort with very prestigious supporters. In late December 1816, the American Colonization Society (ACS) was formally established in the United States Capitol building in Washington, D. C., and Supreme Court Justice Bushrod Washington was elected as its president. Following Britain's example in the Sierra Leone colony, the organization aimed to promote a similar colony in West Africa, to encourage free blacks to emigrate there, and ultimately to convince slaveholders to emancipate their slaves and send them. The effect of this would be to remove black people from America and to establish an American Christian foothold in West Africa. Organized by Virginian Charles Fenton Mercer, New Jersey minister Robert Finley, and Francis Scott Key, its membership included Andrew Jackson, William Thornton, the Reverend Samuel J. Mills, Henry Clay, Daniel Webster, John Tyler, and John Randolph of Virginia. African Americans were quick to note that most of the distinguished members of this society were slaveholders.[27]

Cuffe and his knowledge of Sierra Leone were valuable to the American Colonization Society, and they proposed returning him to Africa to explore the Guinea coast in search of a location for an American colony. With Cuffe's assistance, they hoped to interest Congress in financing African colonization. The goal of the ministers who founded the society to Christianize Africa certainly agreed with Paul Cuffe's desires for African colonization. It was probably Cuffe's already substantial personal investment of money and time that led him to support the ACS despite its slaveholding members. He had visited Sierra Leone for extended periods and had spent several frustrating years negotiating with the British for trading rights. He had used his own money to finance some of the expenses of the settlers he transported; he had encouraged the establishment of black colonization groups. In answer to a request from the society, Cuffe suggested they contact the African Institutions in New York and Philadelphia. He then wrote to Forten advising him to expect the society to contact him.[28]

Despite Cuffe's willingness to accept the participation of the ACS in African settlement, most free blacks were vehemently opposed. Even many of those who had organized the African Institutions were extremely suspicious of the new society's motives. Within a year Philadelphia blacks held a mass meeting at Bethel Church at which more than 3,000 people registered their strong objections to the society's plans. They asserted their rights as Americans based on military service in the Revolution and the War of 1812. They also explained that they were unwilling to leave America while their friends and relatives remained in bondage in the South. They were afraid that slaveholders were motivated by a desire to remove free blacks, the strongest voices against slavery in the nation, and they had strong suspicions that should colonization become government policy, free black people would be forced to emigrate whether they wanted to or not. Resolutions denouncing the society and rejecting its plan were adopted unanimously at the Philadelphia meeting.

Even supporters of colonization found they could not withstand the strength of community opinion. James Forten who presided over the meeting at Bethel Church doubted that blacks could ever be free from impediments to their progress if they remained in America. He confided in a letter to Paul Cuffe that "my opinion is that [black people] will never become a people until they come out from amongst the white people." Although Forten said he would express his opinion to any who asked, opposition to colonization society plans among the overwhelming majority of Philadelphia's blacks encouraged him to "remain silent" on the issue.[29]

When Robert Finley visited Philadelphia for the ACS, he sought both James Forten and Richard Allen's support. Finley later wrote that Forten was very receptive, arguing that since neither education nor money could place black people on the level of equality with whites in America, there were few alternatives. Furthermore, Finley quoted Forten as favoring Africa as a place for a colony over a separate colony in the United States. Apparently Allen agreed, remarking that if he were a younger man he would emigrate himself. "He considered the present plan of colonization as holding out great advantages for the blacks who are now young," Finley reported. Regardless of their personal opinions, however, it became increasingly difficult for Forten and Allen to publicly support the ACS.[30]

Paul Cuffe's interest in Africa never wavered. He suggested locations for the establishment of the new African colony and accommodated objections to African colonization by contemplating two colonies, one in Africa and the other in the United States. Just before his final illness Cuffe encouraged Forten to stand fast. "Don't be uneasy," he urged, "but trust in God who hath done all things well." Until he died in September 1817, at the age of fifty-eight, Cuffe remained convinced that colonization was the surest way to improve the condition of the free people and "a great help towards liberating those who remained in bondage."[31]

Although strong black opposition to the ACS continued throughout the antebellum period, some African Americans were attracted to its program. Early in 1820, the society and the federal government sent the first settlers to an area just south of Sierra Leone. Eighty-six African Americans informally led by African Methodist Episcopal minister Daniel Coker sailed for the new colony on the *Elizabeth*, the "Mayflower of Liberia." Educated in New York, Coker was born about 1785 in Maryland to a white English mother who was an indentured servant and an African father who was a slave. As a teacher and minister in Baltimore, Coker had been one of the community leaders who encouraged Paul Cuffe's interest in African colonization.[32]

The primary strength of the American Colonization Society among blacks was in the upper South, particularly in Baltimore and Richmond. There opportunities for free blacks were extremely limited, and suspicions were growing among whites that they presented a danger to slaveowners' control of their slaves. The second group of settlers who migrated to Liberia in 1821 included Lott Cary, who played an important role in establishing a measure of self-determination for the black settlers. Cary was born in slavery in Virginia around 1780 and worked in Richmond until he was eventually able to buy his freedom. Cary was sent to the colony as a Baptist missionary from the interracial First Baptist Church of Richmond. Christian evangelism may have been Lott Cary's primary motivation for emigration, but he also had other motivations. "I am an African," he said, and he explained that emigration alone would allow him to find opportunity based on his ability. During the next decade, 1,400 blacks, most already free, followed the original settlers from America to Liberia.[33]

African memories and African identities remained strong in the early nineteenth century. African-born blacks in the North still gathered by nationality during Pinkster, governors' election days, and on other festive occasions. William Wells Brown, born a slave in Kentucky in 1814, recognized "Kraels, Minahs, Congos and Mandringas, Gangas, Hiboas, and Fulas," among dancers gathered by ethnic group in a New Orleans square during the early 1830s.[34] Abdul Rahahman, a slave taken from a wealthy and politically powerful family in Timbo (now part of Guinea), was one of those anxious to return to Africa. In 1788, at the age of twenty-six, he had led 2,000 soldiers against military and economic rivals in defense of his nation's coastal trade. On his return home, he and fifty of his men were ambushed, captured, and taken to the Gambia River where he was sold to British slave traders. After several weeks in transit across the Atlantic, through the Caribbean, and on to the North American mainland, Rahahman arrived at New Orleans, a city smaller than his home city in Africa. This educated man formerly of high social standing was sold to Thomas Foster, a planter in Natchez, Mississippi, who on learning of Rahahman's background from a Mandingo translator, named him Prince. Rahahman remained a slave for almost forty years, becoming the informal overseer of the plantation. His life changed, however, in 1807 when John Cox, a white man who had known him and his father in Timbo, saw Rahahman selling vegetables in the Natchez market. As a young seaman,

Cox had been aided by Rahahman's family, when he was separated from his ship in West Africa, and so he knew Rahahman to be of royal heritage. He attempted to get Foster to free him, but he refused. Finally, in the late 1820s, after a local newspaper editor became involved, Secretary of State Henry Clay arranged to pay Rahahman's passage back to Africa, and Foster agreed to free him.[35]

Rahahman's prospective repatriation was complicated by the fact that he had married Isabella, an American-born slave who was the midwife of the Foster plantation, and had a family of nine children. He would not leave the country without his family, including grandchildren, and thus faced the necessity of raising funds to buy their freedom and pay for their passage.[36] For a year he toured many northern states, telling the dramatic story of his life and soliciting contributions. "The appearance of the aged Moor is dignified and imposing," wrote one newspaper in New England. "He is said to be well versed in the Arabic language and in our presence traced several lines of the Arabic characters with apparent ease and facility."[37] In Washington, D. C. Rahahman met with Henry Clay, John Quincy Adams, Francis Scott Key, and others associated with the American Colonization Society, lodging at Williamson's hotel, although Clay invited him to stay at his home. In Boston, prominent merchant Charles Tappan[38] headed his contribution fund, and during his five-week stay, the city's blacks held a dinner in his honor at the African Masonic Hall on Cambridge Street. The dinner was preceded by a grand procession with four marshalls, including David Walker, from the African Meeting House to the African Masonic Hall. George B. Holmes sang an original composition written for the occasion, and toasts included salutes to Rahahman, African evangelism, Haitian independence, and worldwide freedom.[39]

In Hartford, Connecticut, Rahahman met a former slave, an elderly man from the Fula nation, who had been in the military in Timbo under Rahahman's father. He was also introduced to Thomas H. Gallaudet, who headed the Hartford asylum for the deaf and dumb. Gallaudet became an ardent supporter of Rahahman's cause, arranged gatherings on his behalf in New York City, and put him in touch with New York financier and colonizationist Arthur Tappan. Rahahman became both a celebrated cause for the American Colonization Society and its valuable exhibit. Gallaudet urged the society to gain his friendship in hopes that he would provide access to Timbo, the fabled wealth of Timbuktu, and "the other great cities of Central Africa," where the profit on $5,000 invested over a year or two was said to be $20,000. From his tour and the added assistance of Cox's son, Rahahman raised the money to purchase at least eight members of his family. Under the auspices of the American Colonization Society, he and Isabella returned to West Africa aboard the *Harriet*, landing in Liberia in 1829.[40] Word of Rahahman's coming reached his nation ahead of his arrival, but he was delayed by illness and the rainy season and never made it all the way home to Timbo. The *New Bedford Mercury* reported on November 13, 1829, "the Black Prince Abduhl Rahman [sic], for whom subscriptions were raised a short time since, is dead."[41] Rahahman died on July 6, 1829 at the age of sixty-seven. His final act was to have his writings transported to Timbo to be archived in the library of the school where he had been educated as a child. In 1830 two of Rahahman's sons, a daughter-in-law, and five of his grandchildren, joined Isabella in Liberia. They managed to live their father's dream of freedom in Africa, but other family members remained in slavery in America.[42]

Although blacks born in Africa, like Rahahman, were likely to be among those who wanted to emigrate, some Africans were unwilling or unable to give up the life they had made in America. African Boston Crummel, a slave in New York, was from the region of Sierra Leone. He had conveyed his love of Africa to his family, but his wife, who had been born on Long Island, refused to migrate to Africa, especially under the colonization society's sponsorship. The opposition of most African Americans demonstrated their distrust of the motives of the American Colonization Society, but it also signaled a watershed in black identity in the 1820s. As the generation of African-born Revolutionary era blacks grew old and died, they were replaced by a great majority born and raised in America. For these African Americans, Africa was more their heritage than their home.[43]

Yet Africa was not the only alternative to the United States that blacks were willing to consider. While their opposition to the ACS plan had intensified by the 1830s, the interest of many northern blacks in Caribbean or Canadian colonization grew during this period. African-American reactions to plans for immigration to Haiti illustrate the ambivalence and complexity of their national identity, since it involved an appeal to their racial pride on the one hand and to elements of their Americanness on the other. The northern urban population included many Afro-West Indians and some Africans who had come to North America by way of the Caribbean. Many American blacks were especially proud of Haiti, the first independent black nation in the Western Hemisphere. In addition to the slaves brought by French planters from Haiti during the revolution, many mulattoes who had sided with the French against the rebels fled to East and Gulf coast cities. After the revolution, Jean Jacques Dessalines' promise of amnesty and financial support lured many of the mulattoes back to Haiti, and the active trade with the West Indies made it possible for them to maintain contacts with their friends and relatives in North America. The support of the Haitian Revolution by the Federalist administrations of the 1790s had helped win free blacks to the Federalist banner. After 1801 when Jefferson took the White House, the federal government acquiesced to the pressure of the proslavery South and prohibited all trade with Haiti. Federalist opposition was not strong enough to overcome southern fears of the Haitian export of slave revolt, and the official anti-Haiti stance was maintained throughout the antebellum period. For African Americans Haiti remained an important symbol of black freedom.[44]

Haiti was interested in attracting African-American immigration as early as 1804 as part of a broader interest in Pan-African ideals. Toussaint L'Ouverture planned to sail an armed force to West Africa to end the slave trade and slavery and had set aside millions of francs to finance his project. Although this venture never materialized, Toussaint did invade Santo Domingo City in the Spanish colony that shared Hispaniola with Haiti and freed the slaves there. He abolished the institution from the entire island in 1801.[45] Always in danger of French or British invasion, Haiti needed an increasing supply of soldiers and settlers, men with skills who might hold and cultivate the land. To encourage the emigration of African Americans to his nation, Dessalines, after his assent to power following the French capture of Toussaint, issued a proclamation offering American ship captains $40 for each "native black or man of color" brought to Haiti. He stressed that emigrants would be free citizens of his country, not slaves or forced laborers. Dessalines died in 1806 and his call went largely unheeded among black Americans. Indeed, it was over a decade after the establishment of Haitian independence before American blacks began to consider it as a serious alternative to Africa for colonization.[46]

Meanwhile, Haiti continued to support slave liberation efforts in the West Indies and in Latin America. When "The Liberator" Simon Bolivar led an unsuccessful rebellion against Spanish authority in Venezuela in 1815, he and his men were granted asylum in Haiti. The eventual success of Bolivar's revolution rested in part on supplies provided by Haiti and on a number of Haitian troops who served under his command. Bolivar's victories throughout Spanish South America brought an end to slavery in that region in keeping with an agreement worked out with the Haitian government. Thus, Haiti had come to symbolize not only independent black national power, but also the strong and active advocacy of black freedom around the world. In the late teens the Haitian government again attempted to attract black Americans, this time with greater success. In direct communication with New York City's black community, it offered to pay passage and provide land to those who would settle in Haiti. When Prince Saunders introduced the idea at the 1818 meeting of the American Convention for Promoting the Abolition of Slavery in Philadelphia, it was enthusiastically received.

James Forten, Richard Allen, Peter Williams, and many other supporters of Haitian emigration had backed Paul Cuffe's African emigration plans but were even more comfortable with the idea of nearby Haiti as an alternative. Prince Saunders himself had been one of Cuffe's original correspondents in the Boston African Institution. Saunders, a native of Vermont who had been educated at the Moor and Indian School attached to Dartmouth College, was ill and on leave from teaching at the African School in Boston. His doctor advised him to take a long trip to a warmer climate and in 1815, acting partly on this suggestion, Saunders wrote to Cuffe informing him that he and several families from Boston were interested in emigrating to Sierra Leone. In preparation for emigration to Africa, Saunders went to London for training as a missionary. At that time British abolitionists were exploring the possibility of Haiti as a destination for freed American slaves, and Haitian ruler King Henri Christophe had expressed a need for teachers. Consequently, William Wilberforce persuaded Prince Saunders to go there to help establish schools.[47]

For the next few years Saunders recruited teachers and promoted interest in Haiti, dividing his time between England, the United States, and Haiti, where Christophe appointed him minister of education. Saunders, British abolitionist Thomas Clarkson, and the king developed a plan for Haiti to provide asylum for emancipated American slaves as an alternative to the American Colonization Society plan. Saunders' efforts on behalf of Haiti were interrupted by personal conflicts with Christophe, a coup against the king, and Christophe's death in the fall of 1820. Internal struggle in Haiti was brought to an end when the new president Jean Pierre Boyer brought the eastern and western halves of Hispaniola under Haitian control for the first time in a generation in 1821. Finally, in 1823 Boyer recalled Saunders from Philadelphia and appointed him attorney general of Haiti. The following year Boyer revived efforts to attract settlers from America, offering at least thirty-six acres of fertile land, four months of provisions, and other financial assistance to each emigrant in hopes of stimulating the economy of his war-torn country and staving off French threats to retake their former colony.[48]

Saunders was one of many who sought to convince African Americans of the wisdom of Haitian emigration. Boyer dispatched Jonathan Granville, a mulatto, a dashing military officer, and man of grand style, as his official representative to assist in recruitment. Upon his arrival in the United States, Granville became an instant celebrity. The story of his encounter with an American naval officer in a New Brunswick, New Jersey eating house was told and retold in the pages of newspapers all over the North as evidence of his graceful dignity. Insulted by the American who refused to sit at the dinner table with a black man regardless of his station, Granville consented to leave the table but insulted his adversary with such genteel subtlety that the American quickly became the laughing stock of the restaurant. "Sir, the Haitian began, "I am an officer also in my own country, and if I were there, it would be part of my duty, sir, to take into custody those Haytians who insulted strangers." As Granville rose most of those who had been seated with the American officer accompanied the Haitian to an adjacent table. When the American later apologized to Granville for his remarks the Haitian responded, "Sir, I write insults in sand; favors, on marble."[49]

Granville's reputation preceded him as he traveled and lectured on behalf of Haitian emigration. His black audiences in New York, Boston, Philadelphia, Baltimore, and elsewhere were large and enthusiastic, and his words were printed in many newspapers. Granville's efforts and Prince

Saunders' years of promoting Haitian emigration bore fruit—the Haitian Emigration Society was formed at a mass meeting in Philadelphia in 1824. The gathering was encouraged by a letter endorsing emigration from the Reverend Thomas Paul who had recently spent time in Haiti as a Baptist missionary. In a few weeks sixty black Philadelphians set sail for Haiti, ten days later 120 embarked from New York City, and a week after that twenty-one sailed from Baltimore. Soon they were joined by other blacks from Providence, Cincinnati, New York, and Philadelphia. By 1826, more than 6,000 American blacks had emigrated to Haiti; estimates of the number of African American immigrants who had gone to Haiti by the end of the decade range from 8,000 to 13,000.[50]

Initial reports of the conditions in Haiti were favorable. Letters to Richard Allen from his son John who had emigrated with the Philadelphia group were encouraging. Letters from other emigrés, however, indicated trouble. Haitian officials wrote to Allen that the new settlers were not willing to work hard enough to earn their keep, but they were optimistic that in the long run this experiment would "unite the great family" of African peoples in the Western Hemisphere. The minister of Philadelphia's First African Presbyterian Church, Benjamin Hughes, who had emigrated in 1824, believed that many American blacks had gone to Haiti with unrealistic expectations and looked to the government there to provide for all their needs. Many American blacks had difficulty adjusting to the new climate, and some became sick. Hughes believed that the Haitian government had been "liberal beyond any reasonable conception." Others wrote praising Haitian support and chastising settlers for unwillingness to "bend to a hoe or . . . an ax."[51]

Unrealistic expectations of an easy life and ready wealth held by many emigrés may have been encouraged by subversives, plants working on behalf of the American Colonization Society deliberately attempting to scuttle Haitian emigration efforts. The tendency of blacks, people with an oral tradition, to ignore the Haitian literature explaining the details of emigration and rely instead on word-of-mouth reports made them especially vulnerable to these tactics. Often subversive agents deliberately painted an overblown picture of what emigrants might expect in Haiti, hoping to encourage the disappointment that might then be publicized to discourage others from emigrating. The American Colonization Society opposed Haitian emigration both because it was a competitive alternative to African colonization and because many of its southern slaveholding members strongly objected to the expansion of a black national power so close to the American mainland.[52]

There were other reasons for the difficulty that many African Americans had adjusting to Haitian society, and some of them illustrated just how American these African Americans were. Many American blacks arrived in Haiti as urban poor people, and, despite their common racial heritage, they found Haitians an unfamiliar people. As one observer pointed out, "These unfortunate people [found] a new country which so little resembled the one they just left, a population whose language they did not understand, although the same color as themselves, and on whose faces they notice a mocking smile, aroused by their sorry dress, in spite of all the good-will that it showed them."[53] Beyond the strange language and unfamiliar customs Haitian Christians were primarily Catholics. Many of the settlers disapproved, believing, as David Walker said, that Haiti was "plagued with the scourge of nations, the Catholic religion." Walker hoped that in time Haitians would become a Protestant people, and, although he did not state it explicitly, more like Americans. Haitians, on the other hand, regarded many American blacks as unrealistically ambitious and too impatient for success. They claimed that emigrés were lazy, ungrateful and uncooperative, "idle vagabonds," and "enemies of all industry." Haiti needed stable, skilled farmers, but too many African Americans were unwilling to work the farms given them by the government. They sold or rented their land and moved to the cities where they were confronted by the strangeness of Haitian society with greater intensity, and many were unable to cope. Anticipating that their adaptation would be difficult, Granville had recommended that Americans settle together in small "American" communities where there would be shared language, religion, and customs. He promised religious freedom, although Boyer had made his disapproval of missionary ambitions clear in his pledge that immigrants would "not be meddled with . . . in their religious belief, provided they [did] not seek to make proselytes." Granville also suggested that African Americans could become familiar with Haitian French over time. After all, he suggested, "the acquisition of a new language adds to the dignity and to the pleasure of existence."[54]

One of the most successful settlements of African Americans in Haiti was made up of several hundred who followed Granville's advice and formed what amounted to an American agricultural community on the eastern section of Hispaniola on the isolated Samana peninsula. Their language was English, their religion Protestant, and their political and social customs American. Their isolation cushioned the cultural shock of emigration, they retained their American identity, and their descendants remain an English-speaking enclave in the Dominican Republic today.[55]

Although there were successes, most African-American emigrés did not make a satisfactory adjustment. The common African heritage, shared racial identity, and heroic revolutionary history made Haitian emigration attractive to black Americans. But their divergent social and cultural development made the transition difficult. In early 1825 the Haitian government, troubled by the settlers' complaints, began to reconsider the project. Charges of attempted fraud by some American blacks prompted the Haitian government to stop paying settlers' passage. At the same time, the country's deteriorating rural economy and Boyer's determination to pay off debts to France led him to institute laws designed to curtail idleness, increase productivity, and keep rural people on the land. The laws, especially the Rural Code of 1826, drew popular opposition and were not enforced. Within a year many African Americans returned to the United States with horrifying stories of hardship and slave-like plantation labor. By the spring of 1826, about one third of the emigrants had returned to America; few original settlers were left to work the homestead land grants.[56]

The emigration experience in Haiti dampened interest in all colonization schemes and fueled the already considerable antagonism toward African colonization, a consequence members of the American Colonization Society had not anticipated when they worked vigorously against Haitian settlement. Still, there were steadfast supporters of emigration, and a small number of free blacks emigrated to Liberia under the auspices of the American Colonization Society during this period. Thirty-two emigrants set sail for Liberia from Rhode Island in 1826, among them two aged Africans, eighty-year-old Newport Gardner and seventy-year-old Salmar Nubia, originally from Africa's Windward Coast. Finally, going home nearly ten years after his friend Paul Cuffe's death, Gardner said: "I go to set an example to the youth of my race. I go to encourage the young. They can never be elevated here. I have tried it sixty years—in vain. Could I by my example lead them to set sail, and I die the next day, I should be satisfied."[57] Both Gardner and Nubia died a few months after they arrived in Africa.

Other African Americans, like John Russwurm, were less consistent in their opinions of colonization. Russwurm was born in Jamaica, the privileged son of a slave woman and a white planter from Virginia. He was sent to school in Quebec, and when his father moved to Maine and married, Russwurm moved there too. After his father died in 1815, he lived with his stepmother and continued his education. As a young man, he returned to Jamaica but after a brief stay returned to teach at African Schools in Philadelphia, New York, and Boston. In 1824 he enrolled at Bowdoin College in the small town of Brunswick, Maine, and two years later became one of the first blacks to graduate from an American college. After his disappointing stay in Jamaica, his stepmother had advised him to consider emigration to Liberia, but he was also interested in and had given a commencement speech praising Haiti. While he considered the alternatives and discussed a position in Liberia with the American Colonization Society, he took classes in the medical college at Bowdoin. At one point he offered his services to the ACS and even received an offer from them to travel to Liberia in early 1827, but friends persuaded him not to accept an offer from the ACS in early 1827. When a meeting of New York City's black leaders, including several powerful clergymen, decided to establish the country's first black newspaper, *Freedom's Journal*, under the editorship of minister Samuel Cornish, Russwurm agreed to become junior editor. Although based in New York, this newspaper served black communities all over the North, and it received support from those in other cities. Before it was published, black leaders assembled in Boston to discuss and ultimately to endorse the venture, and David Walker became a Boston agent for the newspaper. At a second meeting a year later, the Boston group pronounced it a success in the "defence and support of the African cause." Those attending the meeting agreed that the newspaper was "well worthy of our unremitted exertions."[58] From the first issue of *Freedom's Journal* in 1827, the paper became the national voice of African America. It took up the causes of black self-help and antislavery, and it strongly criticized the program of the ACS, giving voice to the black opposition that had been mounting over the past decade and had been virtually ignored by the white press.[59]

As senior editor, Cornish encouraged black pride and racial advancement and infuriated the influential leaders of the ACS with his scathing attacks on colonization society officials and their efforts. In a public declaration he accused the ACS of being chief among those who slandered the race. Cornish wrote editorials praising the Haitian revolution, and although the euphoria associated with Haitian emigration was fading among the black leadership, he published several articles that pointed with pride at the independence of the Haitian people. Blacks were encouraged to look to improvements "at home," to establish businesses, to educate their children, even to take up farms and leave the city for the independent, rejuvenating existence of the country.

Cornish railed against the racist attacks of New York journalists like Mordecai Noah who argued that African colonization would rid the society of a large criminal element and a many undeserving poor.[60] Others in support of colonization claimed that the jails were "crowded with coloured convicts" and asserted that "beyond a doubt their moral character is far more debased than any part of the white population." Arguing that the ACS encouraged such thinking as a means of building white support for its plans, Cornish struck back at those who attacked African-American character and those who assumed that blacks and whites could never live together. He reaffirmed America as the rightful home for black Americans and declared arguments to the contrary to be "the very stronghold of slavery and oppression."[61]

Colonization society officials worried that Cornish's editorials would lower the organization's already tarnished reputation among free blacks. Faculty members at Princeton Theological Seminary cancelled their subscription to *Freedom's Journal* and urged their colleagues and students to do the same. "If I were a coloured man," wrote one of the school's most prestigious professors, "I would not hesitate a moment to relinquish a country where a black skin and the lowest degree of degradation are so identified that scarcely any manifestation of talent, scarcely any course of good conduct can entirely overcome the contempt which exists."[62] After just six months as the scourge of the colonizationists, Cornish resigned, perhaps in part for health reasons but probably also because of the pressures of the job and the vacillations of his junior editor.

Although Russwurm had appeared to take an anticolonizationist stand in the summer of 1827, asserting that African Americans were "all to a man, opposed, in every shape, to the Colonization Society," he had been intermittently interested in emigrating.[63] Shortly after Cornish's resignation, Russwurm took a more centrist editorial position on the question of colonization, publishing articles in favor, usually by white society officials, and ones opposed, generally written by blacks. Many blacks felt the paper's policy had become too accommodating to the ACS. Then in the fall of 1828 Russwurm met Rahahman, who was then in New York City on his fund-raising speaking tour. Russwurm was impressed with this African and his story and became interested in emigration once again.[64]

By the spring of 1829, Russwurm advocated colonization, warning that blacks could never find freedom or dignity in America. He urged all African Americans to go to Africa as free men and prepare a place for slaves who might be set free by slaveholders who might see the African colony as a place to send emancipated slaves. Although some prominent black leaders in New York encouraged him, most black New Yorkers were not ready to have the only black newspaper in the country operated by a colonizationist, even a black colonizationist. Rahahman, then in Liberia, advised black Americans not to come to the colony as he believed that it was "not fit for people like you." He warned Russwurm that it would endanger his health to come to the colony, but Russwurm was not discouraged and remained an advocate of colonization.[65] Finally, black community disapproval forced Russwurm's resignation, and the last issue of *Freedom's Journal* was published on March 28, 1829. Shortly thereafter Russwurm sailed for Liberia complaining of the "violent persecution" that he had received from "the most influential of our people."[66]

African colonization continued to be a controversial and divisive issue throughout the antebellum period. By 1830 there were fewer Africans in the northern black population as the distance in time increased from slavery and the slave trade. As their direct memory of Africa as a home diminished, and the American Colonization Society was identified with slaveholders' plans to rid America of free blacks, few proponents of African colonization could be found among African Americans in the North. By the 1830s, the ACS had become a powerful organization with substantial support from officials in the federal government. Much of its campaign was through churches and religious organizations in the North, appealing to missionary impulses for the Christianization of the heathen continent. Some blacks were attracted by the mission, but few could support the ACS.

The campaign of black leaders to blunt the influence of the American Colonization Society included efforts to persuade white allies of its dangers. One of their greatest successes and eventually one of the most outspoken white advocates of immediate emancipation was William Lloyd Garrison and his crusading Boston newspaper, the *Liberator*. Garrison's close alliances with black leaders and his paper's reliance on black subscribers and supporters helped to make the *Liberator* a voice for the black community. James Forten, one of his earliest and most important supporters, expressed his confidence in a letter to Garrison that even in the face of the "weight, numbers, and unbounded influence of the colonizationist . . . ours is the cause of justice—and though feeble, despised, and the victims of a cruel prejudice, we are not overlooked by Him who suffers not a sparrow to fall without his notice."[67]

In a continuing effort to raise their collective voice against colonization, free blacks initiated local meetings in 1831 to address the question once again. The resolutions passed and speeches offered left no doubt of their vigorous opposition. They also indicated that black attitudes toward Africa and the society's colony there were becoming more negative. Perhaps reflecting the dwindling numbers of Africans in the population and changes in black education, the views of Africa they expressed were closer to the dominant attitudes and stereotypical views held by white Americans. Some spoke of the unsuitability of the African climate for American black people; others expressed fears of the "wild animals" and the "uncivilized" natives. In stark contrast to statements just over a generation earlier that described Africa as the homeland, these black people seemed to feel separated from Africa. A Brooklyn meeting compared Canada with Africa, calling it a "place far better adapted to our constitution, our habits and our morals." In Columbia, Pennsylvania, they decided to "support the colony at Canada, the climate being healthier, better adapted to our constitution, and far more consonant with our views than that of Africa." Those attending these meetings were expressing typically "American" views of Africa.[68]

By this time, racist interpretations of Africans and their history had gained currency in America and Europe as justifications for slavery and the exploitation of Africa. Earlier interpretations had recognized ancient Egypt as the cradle of mathematics and a major source of classical Greek culture and religion. Moreover, classical Greek writing had affirmed that the culture of the pharaohs derived from the cultures of "inner Africa" south of the Sahara, indicating a strong black African cultural influence through the Greeks on northern Europe.[69] In 1830 German philosopher G. W. F. Hegel expressed a contrary view, claiming that Africa was "no historical part of the World; it [had] no movement or development to exhibit." Further, he argued that the African people had no culture or civilization but represented "the natural man in his completely wild and

untamed state." This view became popular in the United States, supporting emerging theories of racial inferiority.[70] The American Colonization
Society's use of the older more positive view of ancient Africa to attract
black emigrants was gradually eclipsed by arguments that declared
ancient Egypt to be non-African, detached from the continent and the
civilizations and peoples of Africa. Some American blacks like David
Walker continued to stress Africa's ancient glories to argue for the dignity
and proud heritage of African Americans; the attitudes of others reflected
the dominant American view of Africa.

Despite their cultural roots in Africa or their pride in Haitian independence, the overwhelming majority of free people of color decided to
remain in the United States. Most African Americans in the early nineteenth century continued to assert their claim to the rights of American
citizens. In one of the most militant statements of the period, black
Bostonian David Walker spoke against African colonization and for the
rights of black Americans. "Let no man of us budge one step," he commanded, "and let slave-holders come to beat us from our country. America is more our country, than it is the whites—we have enriched it with
our *blood and tears*."[71] Delegates to a national gathering of blacks opened
the meeting in 1830 proclaiming their commitment to the spirit of the
Declaration of Independence. The next year, they resolved that the Declaration and the Preamble to the Constitution be read at the opening of
each convention. The "truths contained in the former document are
incontrovertible," they declared, "and . . . the latter guarantees in letter
and spirit to every freeman born in this country all the rights and immu-
nities of citizenship."[72]

African Americans did not embrace their American identity uncriti-
cally, nor did they completely reject their African identity. At national
meetings throughout the antebellum period, resolutions expressed black
identity and commitment—both racial and American. They were committed to America's revolutionary values, values they charged the country
professed but did not practice. Black leaders saw themselves as the
guardians of America's ideals, functioning as the conscience of the
nation. In a Fourth of July speech in 1830 at St. Philip's Episcopal
Church in New York City to benefit the Wilberforce colony, Peter
Williams, the black rector of that church, contrasted the treatment blacks
received with the situation of recent European arrivals. He claimed
blacks' rights as Americans, saying

> we are NATIVES of this country; we ask only to be treated as well as FOR-
> EIGNERS. Not a few of our fathers suffered and bled to purchase its inde-
> pendence; we ask only to be treated as well as those who fought against it.
> We have toiled to cultivate it, and to raise it to its present prosperous condi-
> tion; we ask only to share equal privileges with those who came from distant
> lands to enjoy the fruits of our labor.[73]

Black abolitionists' anticolonization stance and their determination to remain in America, reform it, and demand full citizenship rights for African Americans led to a subtle alteration in black self-presentation after 1830. Clearly this debate was in response to the growing influence of the American Colonization Society during the 1830s. To use the word "African" in connection with the identity of American blacks seemed to reinforce the argument of the increasingly powerful group in the American Colonization Society who would use African colonization as a form of "free colored removal." Some argued that "oppressed Americans" was most descriptive of the status of the descendants of Africans in America. Significantly, in the midst of the debate over colonization, Russwurm and Cornish chose the name *Freedom's Journal*. When Russwurm decided to leave for Liberia, Cornish started another paper under the title *Rights of All*. Some blacks even opposed the term "colored" unless it was used in conjunction with the word "American." Accordingly, when New York City's *Weekly Advocate* changed its name, it changed it to the *Colored American*, and the editor explained that "we are Americans—colored Americans."[74]

Long-standing institutions also felt the impact of this identity debate. In the 1830s the African Baptist Church of Boston, founded in 1806, changed its name to the "First Independent Church of the People of Color," according to its members, "for the very good reason that the name African is ill applied to a church composed of American citizens."[75] In 1837 Samuel Cornish, by then the editor of the *Colored American*, made the political assertion involved in the name change very clear when he wrote:

> Many would rob us of the endeared name, "Americans," a distinction more emphatically belonging to us than five-sixths of this nation, one that we will never yield. In complexion, in blood and nativity, we are decidedly more exclusively "American" than our white brethren; hence the propriety of the name of our people, Colored Americans, and of identifying the name with all our institutions, in spite of our enemies, who would rob us of our nationality and reproach us as exoticks.[76]

After considerable debate, an 1835 national convention of blacks unanimously adopted a resolution calling for the removal of "the title of African from [black] institutions, the marbles of churches, and etc."[77] The periodic black national meetings that followed were termed "Colored Conventions," and in the minutes of those conventions blacks referred to themselves as "people of color." When blacks referred to themselves as colored Americans, they were not denying or rejecting their African heritage. They were, however, asserting their rights as Americans and vehemently rejecting any public or private efforts to force them to emigrate against their wills. They understood that culture and historical experience linked Africans and black people in the Americas, but the efforts of the American Colonization Society had forced them to publicly emphasize the ways in which they had participated in the American experience and the ways in which their culture was American. African Americans, like all Americans, were a complex and diverse people whose regional, gender, and class differences often sparked disagreement and debate. By the late 1830s most free blacks, while maintaining a delicate balance between seemingly conflicting identities, had declared themselves willing to stand together to demand recognition as colored Americans.

9

The Growth of the Antebellum
Antislavery Movement

African Americans had witnessed many ominous developments during the 1820s, including congressional compromises with slavery's power that brought the admission of Missouri to the Union as a slave state, the racial limits to Jacksonian democracy, and the violent attacks on Cincinnati's black community that forced many to flee the city and led some to seek safety in Canada. As slavery expanded and the importance of slave products increased, slaveholders seemed surer of their political power. When the Supreme Court ruled in 1823 that South Carolina's Negro Seaman's Law[1] was unconstitutional, the state refused to accept the contention that, as one South Carolinian paraphrased it, "South Carolina possesses no right to enact laws, guarding against the corruption and consequent insubordination of her slaves."[2] Such state laws created special hazards for free black sailors, as throughout the Deep South they were either confined to their ships or incarcerated for the duration of their stay in port. The lives of many northern blacks were touched directly by this practice, since seafaring was a common black occupation and about one fifth of those who shipped out of northern coastal cities and Philadelphia were blacks.[3] In 1830 in Savannah, Georgia, John Glasgow, a free-born West Indian serving aboard a British ship, was jailed under a black seaman's law, and when the ship's captain refused to pay for his release, he was sold into slavery. Some federal officials publicly sympathized with the plight of these sailors, but the federal government seemed unable or unwilling to compel southern states to obey the law where black rights were concerned. Massachusetts blacks petitioned state officials to take action, and state representatives went into the South with lists of incarcerated black sailors, but most northern agents were threatened with violence and forced to withdraw from southern ports. A congressman from Massachusetts introduced a resolution in the House of Representatives condemning the jailing of black sailors, but the measure was tabled. Although they often lacked the power to protect black sailors, northern abolitionists could regard southern efforts to isolate slaves from potential sources of antislavery information as evidence of their own growing influence.[4]

Sailors were most likely to be in jeopardy of losing their freedom, but all blacks faced discrimination and public humiliation. Education was less available to them, and even with the proper skills and qualifications, their employment was restricted. Segregated seating in public transport relegated all blacks, no matter how old, infirm, or prominent, to the tops of coaches and the decks of ships where they were exposed to the elements in all seasons and to separate cars or sections on trains. The experience of New York restauranteur and newspaper editor Thomas Van Renselaer was a familiar one. He boarded a steamboat in Boston bound for Providence after purchasing a ticket at the regular price of $3.50 that entitled him to a berth in the cabin. He remained on deck until dark and then retiring for the evening was accosted by a white man who asked, "Whose servant are you?" Van Renselaer replied, "I am my own Sir," whereupon the man demanded that Van Renselaer leave the cabin and remain on deck for the night. After a heated exchange the captain was called, and Van Renselaer was forced to leave the cabin. Only the kindness of the ship's waiters, who provided a place for him to sleep, saved him from having to spend the night on deck. Being forced out of a cabin for which he had paid was uncomfortable and maddening; the captain's later refusal to talk to him about the incident was even more humiliating.[5]

Virtually all blacks faced such treatment, but many whites resented black accomplishments and seemed to make successful blacks special targets. "If I earned property, I know not but my house would be pulled down over my head by a mob," reflected one black Cincinnatian.[6] In New York prejudice was said to be especially apparent in whites' irritation at black achievement. A successful black man contended that "it is with the colored man as a gentleman that they feel the most intense displeasure. They cannot bear it, and they must pour out their pent-up wrath, whenever an opportunity is afforded for doing so."[7] New York had a history of intense competition between white and black workers exacerbated by the apprenticeship system of gradual emancipation. Additionally, the large number of southern slaveholders who took advantage of the regular steamer service established between New York and southern ports to make cultural pilgrimages and commercial buying trips to the city had other reasons to be hostile to signs of black equality. As one historian put it, "Race mixing—by which southerners meant having any contact, however remote and impersonal, with [an African American] who was not in a servile position—was abhorrent to southern whites wherever they found it."[8]

Throughout the antebellum period African Americans of wealth and social standing suffered from such virulent prejudice. James Forten's son Robert sent his daughter Charlotte to live with abolitionist friends in Salem, Massachusetts near Boston so she could attend an integrated school, and after meeting her new classmates, she confided her feelings to her journal. "It is hard," she wrote, "to go through life meeting contempt with contempt, hatred with hatred, fearing with too good reason, to love and trust hardly any one whose skin is white—however lovable, attractive, and congenial." Although many of the white students were cordial to her within the protected confines of the school grounds, "they feared to recognize" her on the public street. Charlotte Forten acknowledged that the slights she suffered were trivial, "certainly [compared] to the great, public wrongs which we as a people are obliged to endure." Still, they caused her to regard her white classmates with suspicion, "scorn and contempt," and she too was angry at the injustice she seemed powerless to prevent.[9]

Anger at personal affronts and indignities and resentment of violent threats to personal safety and freedom adversely affected relationships. They also fueled the powerful sense of injustice in light of contradictions to American democratic rhetoric that helped animate much of African-American writing and activism. It was this anger and sense of injustice that were powerfully presented in David Walker's *Appeal*. Walker was aware that slaveholders feared slave retribution, a fear Thomas Jefferson had expressed a decade before. "We have the wolf by the ears," Jefferson had said. "We can neither hold him, nor safely let him go."[10] Walker confirmed the danger and was straightforward in his warning, "And wo, wo [sic] will be to you [slaveholding Americans] if we have to obtain our freedom by fighting"; adding, "You [white Americans] are not astonished at my saying we hate you, for if we are men, we cannot but hate you, while you are treating us like dogs."[11]

Walker wrote in a tradition of anger and reasoned protest that reached back at least into the last century. "Cruel that you are," wrote one unidentified former slave in 1789, "you make us slaves . . . then impiously impute to nature, and to God, the origin of vices, to which you alone have given birth; and punish in us the crimes, of which you are yourselves the authors." As Walker charged American republicanism with hypocrisy for tolerating slavery, this unknown author had castigated those who "exalted the martyrs of public liberty, the saviours of their country, and the deliverers of mankind" but simultaneously denied freedom to black people. Two generations before Walker, this anonymous writer had warned the nation's founders that the slave "feels the wrongs of his countrymen as deeply, and attempts to revenge them as boldly."[12] Periodically in the intervening years, Americans were reminded of the profound anger slavery engendered, and nearly fifty years after Walker's writing, Sojourner Truth put it directly in her autobiography. "When I was a slave," she remembered, "I hated white people."[13]

In his *Appeal* David Walker argued that Thomas Jefferson's charges of black inferiority could only be effectively refuted by blacks themselves.[14] In this view he joined the editors of *Freedom's Journal*, who explained that they began the newspaper because "We wish to plead our own cause." White allies were not always reliable, and many colonizationists who professed to have the best interests of African Americans at heart had "not hesitated to represent us disadvantageously."[15] Indeed, the American Colonization Society had accommodated, and almost seemed to countenance, American racism when it called it "invincible" and "too deep to be eradicated." Colonizationists saw no humane alternative to emigration, they said, because blacks could never rise above their degraded position in American society, "be [their] talent, [their] enterprise, [their] virtue what it may."[16] This assertion of the permanence of American racism seemed to encourage white acceptance of racial discrimination against free blacks. If blacks were excluded from restaurants and theaters, from first-class accommodations on trains and ships, from desirable jobs and residential areas, it was to be expected, and it was a situation that could not be changed. *Freedom's Journal* encouraged black people to use all means available to acquire and defend their rights as American citizens.

Freedom's Journal and the many other black newspapers that followed were part of an important social and political development in Jacksonian America. Andrew Jackson swept into the presidency in 1828 on the support provided by his national network of political news publications. Technological advances made printing cheap enough for newspapers and tracts to be practical as a popular form of communication, and advances in mass education expanded their audience.[17] Increased opportunities for private and some public education raised the literacy rate in free black communities as well and created a larger potential readership for black newspapers. By mid-century about two-thirds of black adults in six large and medium sized northern cities had at least a rudimentary reading ability.[18] African Americans published many newspapers in the decades before 1860 and, like the proliferation of newspapers published by whites at this time, they were plagued by continuous financial troubles, and most were short-lived. Together they were the voice of black America, carrying messages of political struggle, moral and social uplift, and general community news and providing a forum where blacks could speak for themselves. Although locally based, most were national rather than local in scope and readership. Local agents distributed *Freedom's Journal* in the cities and towns of the Middle Atlantic states, New England, and the Midwest, and others followed this example.

The *Rights of All*, which Samuel Cornish began editing in March of 1829, two months after *Freedom's Journal*'s demise, was financed by a group of black businessmen in New York and carried by agents into far-flung black communities. Unlike the weekly that preceded it, financial realities forced Cornish to publish this paper as a monthly. He carried on the opposition to African colonization, protested racial discrimination, and gave special attention to the mob attacks on blacks in Cincinnati, but only published six issues before it ended in October of 1829. Seven years later, Cornish joined with journalist Philip Bell and abolitionist minister Charles B. Ray, who had published a single issue of the *Weekly Advocate*, to launch the *Colored American*.[19] The longest-lasting of the early black newspapers, the *Colored American* provided information about general social and economic conditions in black communities across the North and even in parts of the South, as well as news of protest organization and antislavery activities. Ray traveled extensively promoting the paper and eventually replaced Cornish as its editor in 1840. Although beset by financial troubles, the *Colored American* was highly successful as a political and social link between black people across the nation, employed a corps of regionally based agents, and functioned as a national publication.[20]

One publication, the *Mirror of Liberty*, begun by antislavery activist David Ruggles in New York in 1838, was published irregularly for about three years and apparently occasionally for some time thereafter.[21] An enterprising young reformer born in Norwich, Connecticut in 1810, Ruggles operated a temperance grocery, a bookshop and cooperative library, and a printing business in addition to his newspaper.[22] In Boston, Benjamin Roberts, printer and social activist, started the *Anti-Slavery Herald* in 1838 and tried again in 1853 with another short-lived venture, the *Self Elevator*.[23] In 1842 Henry Highland Garnet and black educator and lawyer William H. Allan published the *National Watchman Clarion* in Troy, New York, and Stephen Myers edited the *Elevator* in Albany. Martin R. Delany edited the *Mystery* in Pittsburgh in 1843, and in Cleveland in 1853, William H. Day published the *Aliened American*, the first black newspaper in the Midwest. Day had been born in New York City in 1825, but after his father died, a white reformer from Northampton, Massachusetts adopted him. He attended school there, apprenticed in the print shop of a newspaper, and when refused entrance to Williams College, entered Oberlin College in Ohio in 1843. Day had years of experience in Ohio politics, antislavery work, and journalism before he started his own newspaper in 1853.[24] Also during the 1850s, Philip Bell moved from New York to San Francisco where he edited the *Pacific Appeal* with Mifflin W. Gibbs and J. H. Townsend in 1857.[25]

The increase in the number of newspapers in America and particularly the growth in the number of specialized publications, like religious tracts and reform society or political party periodicals, aimed at a mass audience beginning in the late 1820s, reflected both the formal participation of working men in the political process and more widespread opportunities for education in the northern states. Although African-American participation was more restricted and their opportunities more limited, the same factors created an audience for black newspapers. Given the extreme poverty among free blacks, it is not surprising that most of these publications were of limited duration; yet black newspapers helped build a national network for reform and activism. They informed and inspired their readers, served as a national arena for discussing and debating important issues, and facilitated the implementation of other strategies for working against slavery and promoting racial justice.

In 1827 *Freedom's Journal* called for a national meeting to consider actions to address the problems faced by black people in America. In 1829 the attacks on blacks in Cincinnati compelled black leaders to consider such a meeting, and in the spring of 1830, Hezekiah Grice, a butcher in Baltimore, sent a circular to "prominent colored men in the free States, requesting their opinion on the necessity and propriety of holding" a convention to consider their common concerns.[26] The issue was raised in August at a meeting in Philadelphia to hear reports on Canadian settlement, and a committee was formed to call for a convention to explore establishing a settlement in Canada as one immediate response to Ohio's enforcement of the restrictive black codes. On September 20th, twenty-six delegates and fourteen honorary members representing nine states gathered in Philadelphia's Mother Bethel Church and elected seventy-year-old Richard Allen president of that meeting. They met annually between 1830 and 1835, growing to a body of sixty-two by 1833, then shrinking to thirty-five in 1835, after which national meetings were temporarily suspended. The conventions were held in Philadelphia, except the 1834 meetings which were held in New York, and the largest delegations were from Pennsylvania and New York State. Although mainly from the North, there were also delegates from Virginia, Maryland, and the District of Columbia. Organizing themselves into "The American Society of Free Persons of Colour," delegates encouraged the establishment of local auxiliary societies and maintained a continuing interest in black settlement in Canada. They debated and ultimately maintained their opposition to African colonization and supported a proposal to establish a college for black men based on the manual labor system. The conventions also discussed, passed resolutions, and formed committees to deal with issues of civil rights, antislavery, the general defense of the race, and increasingly by the mid-1830s, moral reform.[27]

These national meetings were an extension of earlier organizational efforts like the Massachusetts General Colored Association organized in Boston as an antislavery group in 1826. They encouraged the continuation and expansion of the regional, state, and local conventions that had met sporadically for over a decade. They strengthened the network of communication linking African Americans from different regions to a common effort and encouraged a broad conversation on critical issues. The Cincinnati riot made the debate over emigration and colonization especially consequential. Both the Cincinnati mob and the American Colonization Society seemed to be trying to compel free blacks to leave the country. Federal discussions of an Indian removal policy that proposed forcing the Cherokee, Creeks, Choctaw, and other tribes to move west seemed to portend a frightening precedent.[28] If the federal government, a partial sponsor of the American Colonization Society, could force Indians out of the country, it might do the same to free blacks. Some refused to believe the federal promise not to move the Cherokee from Georgia without their consent, and one black speaker asked his audience in New York, "can they blame us if we attach the same credit to their declaration that they mean to colonize us only with our consent?"[29]

Austin Steward, an agent for *Freedom's Journal* and a convention delegate from Rochester, New York, argued that improving the condition of the free people of color depended on their becoming financially independent. To this end he urged blacks to leave the city and acquire farms. There was racial prejudice in rural areas, he acknowledged, but he believed that it was no worse in the country than in the city and that its effects were "less potent in the country, where a farmer can live less dependent on his oppressors." Sensitive to the fact that, as in Ohio, white hostility could drive blacks out, Steward supported Canadian settlements as one route to black independence.[30] Richard Allen concurred in the belief that through agriculture, blacks could "act with a degree of independence" and also endorsed a northern colony.[31] He asserted the importance of a shared language and lifestyle in British North America, suggesting such differences had been part of the difficulty American blacks had with Haiti. Canadian settlement seemed more practical; homesteads were relatively inexpensive and there was a ready market for farm produce.

When representatives of the American Colonization Society attended the meetings in Philadelphia to reassure the 1832 convention, their arguments were refuted by black abolitionist John B. Vashion from Pittsburgh and white abolitionist William Lloyd Garrison, a convention guest. The ACS was repudiated, most participants opposed plans for emigration to Africa or Haiti, and they expressed support for Canadian settlements.[32] Convention participants could not agree on a plan for financial support for Canadian settlers and left colonies to rely on the services of fund raising agents.[33] Blacks regarded successful Canadian settlements as proof of African Americans' fitness for freedom, and considered Canada a congenial society with relatively few impediments to their progress. Slavery had been only a minor institution there, and slave importation was outlawed in 1793. Within a decade, in 1803, the court severely limited the rights of slaveholders, and finally in 1833, Canadian slavery was abolished. Moreover, and most important for American blacks, Canada refused to return fugitive slaves unless they were charged with a crime other than running away from slavery. Shortly after slavery was outlawed in Canada, two Kentucky runaways, Thornton and Rutha Blackburn, escaped to Canada to avoid arrest in Detroit. The couple was pursued, but authorities refused to surrender them to slavery on the grounds that they had committed no crime punishable under Canadian law.[34]

In 1829 Ohio blacks had delegated charismatic ex-slave and Cincinnati resident Israel Lewis to negotiate the purchase of a township of eight hundred acres north of London in Upper Canada, where they established the community of Wilberforce. Lewis petitioned the Ohio state legislature for aid, received assistance from Ohio Quakers, and supervised the building of roads in the colony. He also angered the agent for the "Canada Company" by failing to provide payment for the land as agreed. Thereafter the agent reportedly refused "to sell a foot of land to any colored person whatever," limiting the possibilities for the colony's expansion and exacerbating its economic problems.[35] African Americans founded other settlements near Windsor, Chatham, and St. Catharines during the Jacksonian period. In the thirty years after the establishment of Wilberforce, more than forty thousand African Americans migrated to Canada. These Canadian immigrants faced prejudice and were generally restricted to segregated public schools, but they did find relative security and greater political and economic opportunities than they had in the United States. The Canadian government provided black settlers with the basic citizenship rights granted to few American blacks. They could vote, serve on juries, and run for political office, and they had the full protection of the law.[36]

Canadian settlement extended and strengthened African Americans' international networks and organization, and many convention leaders participated directly. Austin Steward, vice president of the 1830 convention in Philadelphia, was an early resident of the Wilberforce colony. Steward had been born a slave in Prince William County, Virginia in the early 1790s. When he was a young man, Helm, his owner, sold the plantation in Virginia and marched his slaves, including Steward, his parents, and his sister, north for twenty days to the dense forests of western New York. The slaves cleared farmlands in Bath, New York, built mills and a distillery, and Helm settled his family there. It did not take the slaves long to learn that they had more privileges in New York State. They refused to be whipped and drove the overseer away. When Helm faced financial difficulty, he hired his slaves out, and a lawyer informed Steward that being hired out entitled him to his freedom. Helm tried the subterfuge of a reunion party for his slaves in an abortive attempt to reestablish control, take them South, and recoup his loss by selling them on the slavemarket. During the ensuing struggle, Steward's father received wounds that later proved fatal. Although Helm managed to capture and return a few of his former slaves to southern slavery, most remained free in New York State. By the 1820s Austin Steward was an established family man, community leader, and businessman in the village of Rochester, New York. After the convention meeting in Philadelphia, Steward became determined to aid the settlement in Canada. He closed his business, and in the spring of 1831 moved his family to the Wilberforce colony, then a settlement of about fifty people, where he was chosen president of the board of managers. After about five years, frustrated by the colony's inability to expand

and embroiled in disputes with the colony's agents Israel Lewis and Nathaniel Paul over the disposition of the money they collected, Steward moved back to Rochester.[37]

There was ambivalence about encouraging emigration to Canada. Some were loathe to appear to be relinquishing the rights to which they felt entitled; others feared emigration might discourage white allies committed to their cause. Yet they recognized that emigration could mean an opportunity for independence and freedom from oppressive laws, especially for fugitive slaves.[38] Many fugitives did find a haven from slavery in Canada, although slave catchers made occasional forays into Canadian territory, and forty thousand emigrants to Canada in thirty years hardly constituted a mass exodus. Many more American blacks did go to Canada than to Haiti or Africa, but most blacks vowed to remain in the land of their birth and demanded that America recognize their right to citizenship.

There were encouraging signs in the early 1830s that this message was being heard by a few influential whites. On January 1, 1831, William Lloyd Garrison published the first issue of the *Liberator* in Boston, declaring his commitment to the immediate abolition of slavery in the United States. Garrison, descended from Puritan loyalists and Irish immigrants, had been raised in Newburyport, Massachusetts by a converted, strongly committed Baptist mother whose sailor husband had deserted the family when Lloyd was a small boy. As his mother struggled to support the family and finally moved to Baltimore to work as a nurse, Lloyd was placed in various apprenticeships until he settled in to be a printer's apprentice in Newburyport. Garrison had a succession of newspaper jobs for a few years after he finished his seven-year apprenticeship. In January 1828 he became the editor of the *National Philanthropist*, a temperance newspaper begun two years before by Boston's Baptist city missionary, the Reverend William Collier, who also ran the boardinghouse where Garrison lived. Garrison's interest in reform included opposition to slavery, and when asked to edit an anti-Jackson paper in Vermont during the fall of 1828, he agreed to do so if he could also write about temperance, antislavery, peace, and moral reform. At Collier's he had met the itinerant antislavery Quaker, colonizationist, and newspaper editor Benjamin Lundy, who later walked from Boston to Bennington, Vermont seeking Garrison's help in editing the *Genius of Universal Emancipation* in Baltimore. On his way from Vermont to Baltimore in 1829, Garrison gave a Fourth of July antislavery address at Boston's Park Street Church under the auspices of the American Colonization Society, expressing his view that "immediate and complete emancipation is not desirable. . . . No rational man," he said, "cherishes so wild a vision."[39]

It was in Baltimore that Garrison was converted to the cause of immediate emancipation. He moved into the boardinghouse run by two Quaker sisters where Lundy lived and met the Quakers and African Americans who lived there. Garrison credited some of his "good colored friends," primary among them undoubtedly his boardinghouse mates

William Watkins and Jacob Greener, with his conversion.[40] Once convinced, he took up the cause with passion, attacking the illegal slave trade
and earning nearly two months in jail in his conviction for libel after
accusing Newburyport shipowner Francis Todd of involvement in the
infamous trade. A letter written by Ephraim Allen, the man with whom
he had served his newspaper apprenticeship, and published in the Newburyport *Herald* defended Garrison in a way that helped explain why the
Quaker Lundy may have been somewhat uneasy with their coeditorship.
"Resolute in his convictions on subjects of higher importance, he may
seem (and no doubt sometimes is) hasty, stubborn, and dogmatic, rash
and unyielding, where patience and docility would have varied his views
and softened his temper."[41] It was just these characteristics that appealed
to blacks who had been fighting for their rights as Americans for half a
century. After New York reformer and businessman Arthur Tappan paid
his fine, Garrison was released from jail with the energy of a man newly
martyred for the cause. He spent the next six months giving lectures in
northern cities opposing slavery and colonization. In Boston he spoke to
audiences which included the intellectual luminaries of the time, men
like Lyman Beecher, Samuel J. May, and A. Bronson Alcott, and convinced a few of the desirability of immediate emancipation, a belief that
came to be known as "Garrisonianism." Beecher, however, considered
Garrison a fanatic for holding such a radical view.[42]

In the late fall of 1830, three young men in their mid-twenties,
William Lloyd Garrison, editor and publisher, Isaac Knapp, publisher,
and Steven Foster, printer, established themselves in an upstairs office in
Boston and prepared to put out a weekly paper. The enterprise was initially supported by donations at lectures, aid from Arthur Tappan, and
subscriptions from the black community. The trio outfitted the office
with a bed on the floor in one corner, ate simply from the wares of the
bakery across the street and the fruit and cake shop in the basement, and
worked while their cat perched on the table by a window. After a short
time, they put their principles into practice and hired a young black
apprentice, Thomas Paul, Jr., son of the minister of the African Baptist
Church.[43] Midway between the first and second annual meetings of their
national convention, black leaders were especially heartened by the
uncompromising stand the editor of the new paper took in his first issue.
He dedicated the *Liberator* to the struggle against slavery and the
"improvement of the condition of the free people of color." The paper's
banner declared, "Our country is the world—Our countrymen are
mankind." In the fight against slavery, Garrison said, "I will be as harsh as
truth and as uncompromising as justice ... I am in earnest—I will not
equivocate—I will not excuse—I will not retreat a single inch—And I
WILL BE HEARD."[44]

Garrison's words horrified slaveholders still reeling from David
Walker's distribution of his *Appeal*. In December 1829, for example,

Walker had sent thirty copies of his book to a correspondent in Richmond, Virginia, instructing him to sell them for twelve cents a copy to those who could afford it and to give them free to those who could not.[45] Slaveholders considered Walker's *Appeal* and Garrison's *Liberator* to be deliberate provocations, and their fears seemed confirmed when slave preacher Nat Turner led a major slave revolt in Virginia in the late summer of 1831.[46] Garrison's pacifist philosophy required him to repudiate Turner's uprising; neither had he endorsed Walker's call to resistance, although he had reprinted portions in his newspaper. Still, many believed Garrison and Walker to be at least partly responsible for instigating the revolt that left sixty white southerners dead. Slaveholders feared that Nat Turner's rebellion, following as it did a massive slave rebellion in Jamaica the previous winter, was the initiation of a new wave of slave violence.[47] Laws were passed in the South forbidding the circulation of the *Liberator*, rewards were offered for the arrest and conviction of white agents of the newspaper, and pleas were sent to the mayor of Boston asking for the paper's suppression. In November 1831 Nat Turner was hanged in Virginia, and the state of Georgia offered a $5000 reward for the editor, publisher, or agents of the *Liberator*.[48]

When Garrison attended the National Convention of the People of Color in June 1831, black leaders greeted him as a friend and champion of black freedom. A committee of white abolitionists, including Garrison, Lundy, and Arthur Tappan, came to this second convention to solicit support for a proposed manual labor school, an integrated institution of higher education they hoped to locate in New Haven, Connecticut.[49] The year before, Allen had argued that blacks needed greater access to the "mechanical arts," as another means to economic independence and, he said, "to the standing and condition we desire."[50] The combination of an education in the arts and sciences and the opportunity for students to earn their way by learning and practicing a trade seemed ideal. A resolution of support was passed, and Samuel Cornish was charged to head the fundraising effort. The convention acknowledged the important role played by white abolitionists by deciding that the board of trustees for the New Haven college should be integrated, although blacks should retain the majority.[51]

New Haven had been chosen partly because it was considered a liberal city, but local resistance was swift. Plans for the school were halted when whites called a town meeting in the fall of 1831 to "resist the establishment of the proposed College . . . by every lawful means." The proposed school, they said, would create disorder and was an insult to Yale.[52] Opposition was not confined to lawful means—a white mob attacked New Haven blacks and Arthur Tappan's home, removing his furniture and burning it in the street. Mob participants attempted to justify their actions by claiming that the school would encourage abolitionism in the city. Convention speakers the next summer denounced New Haven's reactions, charging that they shamefully "cast a stigma on the reputed fame of New England and the country." Although white hostility discouraged interest in locating the school in that city, it not diminish black commitment to the project. "We must have Colleges and High Schools on the Manual Labor system," declared one spokesman, "where our youth may be instructed in all the arts of civilized life."[53]

Convention support for a manual labor school forged another link between the black antislavery movement and the world of white reformers. The manual labor movement was part of the wide-ranging reform movement that grew out of the religious revivals of the 1820s, and it was through this part of the movement that African Americans gained another important white ally. Theodore Dwight Weld was the son of a Presbyterian minister and came from a long line of distinguished forbearers, including Jonathan Edwards, Timothy Dwight, and Aaron Burr. His family moved from New England to New York State at the height of the revivals and Weld was deeply impressed by the popular revivalist preacher Charles Finney and his perfectionism. In 1827 when Finneyite Presbyterians located a new academy on a 114-acre farm in Whitestown near Utica and close to his home, twenty-six-year-old Theodore Weld enrolled in the first class. The school, which a few years later became known as the Oneida Institute, was committed to the new manual labor system advocating a balance between mental and physical labor, and Weld found the system well suited to his temperament. The tendency for excessive study to the point of "overwork[ing] the brain" that was thought to plague many students was discouraged, and Weld discovered chopping wood to be helpful when he was "oppressed with [mental] fatigue."[54] Students at Oneida were active in virtually all aspects of reform and started temperance, colonization, and missionary societies even as they were physically building the school. At Oneida Weld met Lewis Tappan whose two sons were also attending, and when Tappan decided to establish an experimental national manual training institute, he chose Weld, the recognized leader of the student activists, as his agent.

Weld decided that the West was where the struggle for the nation's soul would be engaged and the crusade for salvation from the sin of slavery decided, and he chose struggling Lane College in Cincinnati as the site for their theological seminary. The Reverend Lyman Beecher relocated from Boston to Cincinnati to head the theology school, and twenty-four Oneidans entered the first class of forty students. In the meantime, while on an extensive speaking tour for the causes of temperance and manual labor, in discussions with Garrisonians Beriah Green, Elizur Wright, and Charles B. Storrs, Weld was converted to immediate emancipation. After more than a year of anticolonization agitation, in February 1834 in typical revival style, Weld and his fellow "Oneida boys"[55] organized the Lane Debates, five hours of lecture and discussion for each of nine evenings over the course of eighteen days. The programs drew on Garrison's phenomenally successful *Thoughts on African Colonization*, a 240-page tract published and circulated with Arthur Tappan's help in 1832, and included testimonials from a student who was a former slave and students from slaveholding southern families.[56] With revolutionary zeal, the Lane students conducted an intensive campaign in the black community, organizing schools, Bible classes, a library, and frequent public lectures; even boarding with local black families, attending black churches, and participating in social events in the black community. Finally, under threat of expulsion for political activities and for advocating and practicing social equality between the races, thirty-nine students left Lane in October 1834.[57]

White advocates of immediate emancipation were instrumental in opening higher education to African Americans on an equal basis, helping to provide opportunities for a generation educated in free schools, and expanding the educated black leadership group of the 1840s and 1850s. Beriah Green opened Oneida Institute to interracial admission when he became the school's president in 1832 and maintained the school's character until it fell victim to economic depression and the Tappan brothers' bankruptcy in 1844. Oneida was a small school with no more than 125 students at one time, but it enrolled six blacks in 1836, fourteen over the years of its existence, and had one of the most active student antislavery societies in the East.[58]

In 1834 the Noyes Academy in Canaan, New Hampshire announced that race would not be a barrier to admission. The national convention supported its fund-raising efforts, and the school registered at least fourteen black students, one of them female. The interracial and coeducational character of the school incensed local whites, however, and they destroyed it the following year, using ninety teams of oxen to drag the building into a swamp a half mile from its original site.[59] Henry Highland Garnet organized his black classmates to make bullets for their defense against the mob. Garnet was familiar with danger. His family had escaped from slavery a decade before and continued to face the risk of recapture. Once when Henry was away at sea, the family had narrowly escaped the slave catchers who invaded their New York City apartment. During the attacks at Noyes, his fellow students credited Garnet with saving them from assault by exchanging gunfire with night riders. Thomas Sidney, Alexander Crummell, Garnet, and the other black students were finally forced to leave, and their wagon was fired on by cannon as they made their departure. Back home in New York, they learned that Oneida was open to black students, and the trio set out for Whitestown to continue their education.[60]

Farther west, the students who withdrew from Lane Seminary had struck a bargain in 1835 with a new coeducational manual labor school called Oberlin Collegiate Institute in rural Russia Township in northern

Ohio. Oberlin was short of funds, in need of faculty and a president, and wanted to offer theological courses. The students agreed to come to Oberlin in exchange for freedom of speech and positions for their men as president and on the faculty, and a position teaching theology for Charles Finney. One additional condition caused a great deal of debate and division—that Oberlin admit black students on an equal footing with whites. After initial objections from students and trustees, but with strong support from Oberlin's founder and the promise of very generous financial assistance from Finney's friends, the Tappans, the advocates of equal access for African Americans won agreement to their terms. Theodore Weld came, along with the rest of the Lane rebels, and gave a series of lectures, but he refused an offered position on the faculty, deciding instead to devote himself to antislavery lecturing and organizing.[61]

Among the students who were able to take advantage of the greater opportunities for African Americans in higher education were many alumni of the African Free School in New York City, and they came well prepared. From its earliest years, students at the school were encouraged to express antislavery ideas, and public oratory at special events was filled with abolitionism. "Freedom will break the tyrant's chains," predicted twelve-year-old Thomas Sidney in his poem of 1828. During his years there Sidney's classmates included future abolitionist leaders Henry Highland Garnet, Alexander Crummell, and Charles Reason. Other African Free School graduates were George T. Downing, restaurant owner and reformer, the actor Ira Aldridge, Samuel Ringgold Ward, considered by some the greatest black orator of his time, and James McCune Smith, who studied medicine at the University of Glasgow and became a celebrated and influential doctor, educator, and reformer. Encouraged by their teacher Charles Andrews to believe that they "had as much capacity to acquire knowledge as any other children," the students were proud of their accomplishments and outspoken in their beliefs.[62] The young boys, aged thirteen to sixteen, formed a society to denounce slavery. "For years," recalled one, "our society met on [the Fourth of July] and the time was devoted to planning schemes for the freeing and upbuilding of our race." Young Garnet, it was said, led the group in their vow that after their education they would, "go South, start an insurrection and free our brethren in bondage."[63]

Young students in other cities were also active in abolition. Garrisonian abolitionists made a special effort to include the children in their campaign by creating youth groups and choirs like Boston's Juvenile Garrison Independent Society which they formed in the early 1830s.[64] The black schools in Cincinnati were particularly active, especially those run by Lane and Oberlin students. Teachers sponsored projects to educate their students about the need for abolitionist action, though not much education was needed on that score. In one essay contest black children were asked to write about the things they thought most about, and their thoughts were instructive and sobering. "I have two cousins in slavery who are entitled to their freedom," wrote one ten-year-old. They were about to be sold down the river to the Deep South. "If this is the case," he asked, "what would you do?" Another raised the question on many minds, "How [can] the Americans . . . call this a land of freedom where so much slavery is?"[65] Childrens' concern with slavery stemmed from the ties of family and friendship that bound free blacks to slaves. Like adults, they shared the slave experience through family and community folklore; some had been slaves themselves. Blacks of all circumstances and all ages were likely to have strong opinions and be involved in a variety of antislavery activities. The tradition of activism was passed from one generation to another and involved entire families in protest and reform work.[66] Thus, black children were engaged in the struggle for equality partly because they could not be sheltered from it. In freedom, they were often the targets of racial prejudice, and it was common for children to be harassed on their way to school.

Attempts to integrate schools made children special targets. In 1833 Sarah Harris asked to be admitted to the exclusive all-white private girl's academy which Quaker schoolteacher Prudence Crandall ran in Canterbury, Connecticut. Impressed with the young black girl's "respectability" and "earnest manner," Crandall agreed to allow her to attend classes. Crandall anticipated some opposition from the parents of her other students, but was unprepared for the vehement reaction of both parents and the local community. Parents protested the presence of this one black girl by withdrawing their daughters from the school. Her principles affronted, Crandall decided to transform her school into an academy for young ladies of color. Community reaction was swift and unmistakable. The local church excluded her students, opponents fouled her well with a dead cat, local merchants refused to sell her food and supplies, and mobs attacked her home and school. Townspeople disrupted classes by blowing horns, ringing bells, and firing guns. Crandall's efforts were supported by Garrison and his *Liberator*, but in response to a local petition, the state legislature ruled that a private school for nonresident African Americans was illegal in Connecticut. Attempting to continue her school even after the passage of this new regulation, Crandall was arrested, convicted, and sent to jail. Her conviction was reversed on a legal technicality, but the law stood. She was finally discouraged after townspeople launched further attacks, breaking windows with heavy iron bars and smashing and burning walls, and she moved out of the state. "Where is justice?" asked one of the students.[67]

Strangely, the white citizens of Canterbury saw themselves as the victims in this confrontation. Several resolutions passed in a town meeting were designed to justify their opposition to the school. In their attempt to do so, they contradicted history and justice, reminded African Americans once again of the intransigence of white prejudice, and warned white abolitionists of the strength of their opposition. Canterbury residents resolved that the nation and all of its institutions belonged to the "white men who now possess them." They asserted that these institutions had been "purchased by the valor and blood of their Fathers," and that they must be protected against all other nations or any other "race of men." They described Crandall's attempt to integrate the school as an illegal assault on the community and argued that the violence against the school had been provoked by the "oppression" of those who "declared as a matter of right that they would fix their establishment upon Canterbury in defiance of law."[68]

Efforts to provide advanced education for blacks continued, and by 1835 the national convention reported that "six colleges or high schools" admitted "colored students upon an equal footing with the rest of the community."[69] Another significant advance in black education came in the 1840s with the establishment of a college in New York State that prided itself on having both an integrated student body and an integrated faculty. New York Central College was founded by the American Baptist Free Mission Society as a manual labor school and located at McGrawville, New York near Cortland, south of Utica and Syracuse.[70] Cyrus P. Grosvenor, the abolitionist minister and friend of William Lloyd Garrison who had initiated the organization for the school in 1847, became its president. At its opening ceremonies in September 1849, the speakers included Samuel Ringgold Ward and Henry Highland Garnet. Ward, cousin of Garnet, had been called to serve as minister to a white antislavery church in nearby Cortland in 1846. Its faculty included Charles Reason, a graduate of New York City's African Free School, as professor of Greek, Latin, mathematics, and natural philosophy and two women, Eliza Haven and Sophie M. Lathrop. It was supported and addressed by a wide spectrum of the most prominent abolitionists of the day, from Henry Ward Beecher and Horace Greeley to William Lloyd Garrison, and received especially strong support from Quakers and antislavery churches in western New York.[71]

New York Central College pledged itself to "the morality of anti-slavery" and "the doctrine of the unity, common origin, equality and brotherhood of the human race." Not only did it propose to admit and educate African Americans, but it also intended to "contribute to the settlement of the equality of the sexes" by giving female students "equal advantages in literary, scientific, moral and physical education." Either one of these aims would have generated criticism; the combination alarmed both moderates and conservatives.[72] Like Oneida and Oberlin, New York Central came to be known as a "nigger school," even though the proportion of black students at each was relatively small. At Oberlin black students were at most 5 percent of the total students, and only 100 African Americans attended the college department before 1861. At both Oberlin and New York Central, black students were most likely to attend the academy or preparatory program. By far the smaller institution, New York Central had a higher proportion of blacks and women, probably at least 10 percent black and 30 to 50 percent women, though estimates vary widely.[73]

The character of the student body made fund raising more difficult for both of these schools, and they depended on the commitment of the abolitionists and the largesse of the Tappan brothers and Gerrit Smith. New York Central's task was made somewhat more difficult when a black professor and white student decided to marry, reinforcing opponents' of integrated schools fears of racial amalgamation. William G. Allen, the professor involved, had been born in Virginia in 1820 to a free mulatto mother and a white father. He was a graduate of Oneida Institute and had studied law in Boston in the office of Ellis Gray Loring before coming to New York Central. Allen and Mary King faced the disapproval of her family and the wrath of a mob before marrying in New York City and settling in Britain in 1853.[74] Allen's position at the college was filled by another African American, George B. Vashon from Pittsburgh. The final blow to New York Central was struck by a depression in 1857. White abolitionist Gerrit Smith tried to maintain the school after it declared bankruptcy by buying the main building and sixty-six of its 157 acres in 1858, proposing that James McCune Smith and Charles Reason take it over. They declined, unless a secure foundation could be established with a sizeable endowment; the school ended its operation in 1861.[75]

For black abolitionists educational efforts served many functions. Better education for free blacks was intrinsically valuable and would enhance the prospects for the independence of individuals and community institutions, but it also served the antislavery cause. More successful free black relatives and friends would give the slaves' most committed and tenacious allies more power. Black leaders also believed that black progress would refute allegations of black inferiority and colonizationists' contentions that African Americans could never be incorporated as equal citizens in American society. Lorenzo de Zavala, who toured the United States in the late 1820s, observed that the degraded condition of free blacks was frequently used as "an argument that discourage[d antislavery's] most ardent [white] supporters" and was "the great argument against the emancipation of the slaves."[76] Thus, many white reformers were convinced that the progress of free blacks was an argument for antislavery. Frances Wright, an English writer and reformer who came to America in the 1830s to establish a Utopian settlement and educational experiment in Tennessee, was motivated by this belief. Wright hoped to educate black children and white children on an equal basis in order to prove that race was no barrier to intellectual ability, working against both slavery and racial prejudice.[77]

One historian has argued that it was unrealistic to believe that racism that supported slavery could be overcome by logic and living contradictions. He believed that antebellum blacks must have realized that no amount of self-improvement and no logical argument would convince whites that African Americans deserved full citizenship rights. Although nineteenth century white attitudes may seem immutable from the perspective of the late twentieth century, it was not so for black leaders at the time. Interracial cooperation before and during the Revolution and in the nineteenth century in war, business, and reform proved that at least some whites could be convinced to work with blacks. Individual experiences like that of Lemuel Haynes, who ministered to a white church in Vermont at the end of the eighteenth century, or Paul Cuffe whose business was fostered by his connection to the white Quaker business community, or lawyer and effective black leader Robert Morris of Boston who was trained in the office of Ellis Gray Loring were only a few among many examples of white support in African Americans' progress. Even so, black leaders were concerned with more than influencing white attitudes. They also believed education, temperance, religious beliefs, and honesty improve social, political, and economic conditions inside African-American communities.[78]

It was clear that some white reformers, particularly those with close ties to the black community, understood the link between the elevation of African Americans and the fight against slavery. Theodore Weld, speaking from his experience with the Lane students in Cincinnati, argued that campaigns for black uplift deserved the support of white abolitionists because they would enable them to live out their antislavery principles. Additionally, he said, "it would show both to South and North that blacks are *men* and in every respect equal to whites. At least 3/5ths of the northerners *now* believe the blacks are an *inferior* race."[79] With this understanding, Weld included black education, school integration, and recruiting black students for Oberlin and Oneida in his antislavery work. Abolitionists were not naive about their opposition, and African Americans knew that progress depended largely on their own efforts. While blacks used the words and spirit of America's founding documents to argue for equal rights, some colonizationists interpreted them very differently.

In the fall of 1833, Joseph Tracy, editor of the *Vermont Chronicle*, lectured before the Vermont Colonization Society revising even Jefferson's moderate interpretation of the Declaration of Independence. It was dangerous, he argued, to think that the Declaration meant to imply a condition of pure human equality. This "naked doctrine of the equal rights of men," he asserted, would inevitably lead to a breakdown in government and the rule of law, a reasoning away of all property rights, and the abolition of male authority in law so extreme that women would be likely to take control of legal authority. Tracy concluded that immediate emancipation was foolish and dangerous; instead, the plantation system should be transformed into an educational setting gradually preparing blacks for freedom in Africa.[80] This approach was soundly rejected by the black national conventions and by the white abolitionists devoted to immediate emancipation.[81] Many white abolitionists were unwilling to advocate black voting rights, and few promoted the social integration of the races. In the 1830s William Jay, a white New York lawyer was direct in his misgivings about black suffrage.[82] Blacks often worked with white reformers, including ardent white Garrisonians, who displayed racially prejudiced views and treated blacks with paternalistic disrespect. Boston's Wendell Phillips confessed to feeling uncomfortable sharing a room with black fellow abolitionists on lecture tours, Abbott Lawrence refused to shake the hand of a black man, and Edmund Quincy insensitively told racist jokes at antislavery meetings.[83] Many blacks saw the prejudice of whites as the most important impediment to ending slavery and racial injustice. Indeed, one writer in the *National Reformer* expressed doubts that progress could come through self-improvement and concluded that the only way to improve the condition of black people was "the improvement of the white man's heart."[84]

The issues of racial progress through education, self-improvement, and moral uplift were related to a general moral reform movement that was organized to maintain the conversions of the evangelical revivals. Many moral reform societies were begun by ministers and were centered in the churches, and they linked the issues of moral reform, temperance, and the abolition of slavery. The societies proliferated in the 1830s and 1840s, especially in areas where evangelical religion was strong, and remained influential nearly to the end of the nineteenth century. The Female Moral Reform Society was organized in New York in 1834, for example, and seven years later had sixty-one chapters in New England, 3,000 subscribers to its bimonthly magazine, the *Friend of Virtue*, and counted many Garrisonians among its interracial membership.[85] In black communities the expansion of a general black reform movement stressed moral uplift and education, reinforced the tie between the call for black advancement and the abolition of slavery, and had a profound impact on the national conventions. William Whipper, a black Philadelphian and strong Garrisonian, made the connection explicit when he addressed the national convention in 1835. Advocating the creation of an American Moral Reform Society, he identified "four valuable subjects for rallying points . . . Education, Temperance, Economy, and Universal Liberty."[86] Perhaps some recalled the unpredictable cruelty of drunken slaveholders and overseers when the convention declared, "Intemperance and slavery are closely allied." They believed sober and successful black communities to be an argument for freedom and urged the formation of temperance societies to "facilitate the cause of immediate and universal emancipation."[87] The belief that moral reform would help bring about the "total abolition of slavery"[88] echoed the approach of those in the eighteenth century who gained their freedom hoping, as one former slave said, "to make my freedom, in some degree, the instrument of [slaves'] deliverance."[89]

Although there was broad agreement among African Americans on the desired goals of freedom and racial justice, there were strong differences on the route to these goals. Whipper proposed a moral reform society open to all regardless of race to meet annually in Philadelphia with auxiliary societies around the country. There was opposition, led by New Yorkers, who felt that a black organization was necessary and could be more effective, but the Philadelphians carried the day.[90] The formation of the society was approved by resolution during the 1835 convention that was controlled by the Philadelphia group. A national convention intended for the following year in New York City never took place.[91] Discussions at the meetings of the American Moral Reform Society expressed general agreement on expanded educational opportunities for black children, but disagreements continued over the issue of exclusively black organizations. Debates over black-identified organizations became focused on descriptive terminology, with Whipper, Robert Purvis, and their allies objecting to a call for educational societies formed by the "free people of color." Indeed, they sought a complete discontinuance of reference to race or color, and as this argument over language grew increasingly heated, some found it ridiculous and needlessly distracting. In March 1838 Cornish lost patience with the "contentions about NAMES," saying black people had no time for this. "The good sense of some of our brethren in Philadelphia, seems to have forsaken them," he wrote of the American Moral Reform Society debates. "They are quarrelling about trifles, while their enemies are robbing them of diamonds and of gold." Cornish saw no point in continuing the argument. "You are COLORED AMERICANS," he said, "The Indians are RED AMERICANS, and the white people are WHITE AMERICANS and *you are as good as they and they are no better than you.*"[92]

By 1840 the American Moral Reform Society meeting attracted only five delegates, all from Philadelphia; it held its last meeting in 1841.[93] In their concentration on strategy, Whipper and his associates had obscured the broader African-American agenda. They were too dogmatic in their stance against separate black organization and finally lost credibility as a result of a divisive, unproductive argument. Yet for Whipper, as for his opponents in this argument, it was never a matter of choosing between moral reform and abolition. A resolution passed at the 1837 meeting made their sentiments clear.

> Resolved that we will never voluntarily separate ourselves from the slave population in this country; they are our brethren by the ties of consanguinity, of suffering, and of wrong; and we feel that there is more virtue in suffering privations with them here than in enjoying fancied advantages for a season.[94]

Whipper's commitments were also related in practice. From his successful free labor and temperance grocery store in Columbia, Pennsylvania just outside Philadelphia, he ran an underground railroad operation for more than twenty years. Profits from his business and his considerable investments financed shelter and other expenses for hundreds of fugitives escaping from slavery in the upper South. Later, he came to believe that black organizations could successfully address questions of abolition and racial justice and changed his stand, even supporting all black schools and a black African colonization project.

Historians have sometimes argued that antebellum black leaders in the North neglected abolition and spent too much of their time fighting over issues of concern only to northern free blacks. Yet Whipper and his Philadelphia associates were committed to moral reform as a way of improving the condition of free people of color and also of abolishing slavery. In this they agreed with others who understood the relationship between the plight of free blacks and of slaves and believed the persistence of racial prejudice was connected to the existence of slavery.[95] Whipper, Purvis, and other black moral reformers urged free black people to improve themselves and live morally upright lives not only to better their lives and improve white perceptions of free black people, but as part of their antislavery duty. The negative racial stereotypes held by whites helped to justify slavery, they believed. "If we are lazy and idle," Richard Allen argued, "the enemies of freedom plead it as a cause why we ought not to be free."[96] "Prejudice, like slavery, cannot stand the omnipotence of Truth," another black spokesman argued. It would be "impossible for the bold, clear and discriminating mind" to believe the proslavery argument, the delegates of the 1835 convention had contended, if they saw living examples of successful free African Americans.[97] Throughout the antebellum period, black leaders in their speeches equated racial uplift with antislavery, and most agreed with the resolution passed at the Philadelphia convention of 1855 that "in our elevation lies the freedom of our brethren; in that elevation is centered the germ of our own high destiny, and the best well-being of the whole people."[98] In 1858, New Yorker James McCune Smith took white ally Gerrit Smith to task for a letter to the *Tribune* stating that "the mass of the blacks are ignorant and shiftless." The statement was untrue, he observed, and very damaging to blacks and their cause.[99] The black moral reformers were in a small minority in one respect, however. Although most blacks welcomed the assistance of progressive white reformers, they believed that by working together in black groups they could play an important part in the elevation of the race and the abolition of slavery.

There were practical and strategic reasons for maintaining black antislavery and reform organizations. White reformers were more likely to accept a gradualist approach to antislavery, and blacks sometimes faced discrimination or subtle prejudice in integrated organizations. Integrated meetings also exposed African Americans to the danger of mob attack. Although there were many attacks in the East, the danger became even greater as the antislavery movement advanced into western areas like Ohio, Indiana, and Kansas. When in the mid-1830s Theodore Dwight

Weld invited Ohio blacks to a series of antislavery lectures in Zanesville, the black community there paid dearly as a consequence of whites' antagonism to the prospect of integrated meetings. Many people were fired from their jobs, community members were threatened, and one man who attended a preliminary lecture was attacked. Black leaders decided they should not attend, as Weld explained in answer to Lewis Tappan's criticism:

> 1. If *they* attended, it would keep away that very class of persons which they wished to go—the *prejudiced* ones. 2. If they attended, it would expose them not only to insult and outrage while there, but it would be seized as ground for the pretence of mobbing them, tearing down their houses, etc.[100]

Despite the dangers, there continued to be integrated organization and action in the antislavery cause, though all-black organization continued, and the two parts of the abolition movement often moved on parallel courses.[101] Most blacks were encouraged by integrated action and believed that white hearts and attitudes could be changed. Such changes were apparent among antislavery whites. Abby Kelly, white abolitionist and later women's rights advocate, argued during the late 1830s that white reformers benefited from the interracial contacts in their work by having their prejudices challenged on the issues of race, gender inequity, and the general denial of civil liberties. Wendell Phillips undoubtedly exaggerated in 1851 when he argued that white reformers had overcome their own prejudice in the effort to abolish slavery. "If we never free a slave," he observed, "we have at least freed ourselves in the effort to emancipate our brother."[102] In fact, many whites credited their work with blacks as broadening their views and stimulating personal growth. Emily Howland, an educator, early feminist, and abolitionist who worked closely with black children, testified that "the Negro opened the book of life to me."[103] Although they were often dangerous for blacks and did not eradicate prejudices among white abolitionists, interracial efforts during the 1830s and 1840s did generate greater understanding and increased white reformers' respect for African Americans' abilities.

The most effective integrated abolitionist organizations were first organized in the 1830s by William Lloyd Garrison. Garrison and his supporters formed the New England Anti-Slavery Society in Boston in 1832 at the African Meeting House, home of the African Baptist Church, in the heart of the city's black community. Although all of its initial founders were white, blacks quickly became a large and influential part of the organization. At least one quarter of those who signed the society's constitution were black, and almost immediately the existing black abolitionist Massachusetts General Colored Association applied for and was granted affiliate status. Key members of both groups became active in the national American Anti-Slavery Society, founded by Garrisonians in 1833. The sixty-two delegates at the first convention included three

African Americans, James Barbadoes of Boston, and James McCrummill and Robert Purvis of Philadelphia. The interracial Philadelphia Female Antislavery Society, the first women's auxiliary, was formed the same year and included two black women, Margaretta Forten and Sarah McCrummill. Organization progressed rapidly, and by the end of 1833, there were forty-seven local antislavery societies in ten states from Maine to Indiana.[104] The AASS coordinated the work of state and local societies, hired and trained traveling speakers, published antislavery propaganda, and held national conventions.[105] The founders of the AASS conceived of their task as the awakening of the nation's conscience on the question of the sin of slavery. They believed at first they could place moral pressure on slaveholders through the churches and the press, and the meeting in Philadelphia in 1833 organized a committee to gather material designed to convince religious denominations in the South that slavery was immoral.[106] The resistance of the organized church denominations, and the intransigence of a Congress, where the South wielded great power, soon convinced abolitionists that their potential constituency resided in northern communities. Following the example of the evangelical revivalists, they blanketed the North with antislavery pamphlets, sermons and newspapers, and by 1836 began to send speakers to virtually any town or hamlet where they could gain a hearing.[107] Although antislavery speakers were often attacked, locked out of halls and churches, and sometimes run out of town by mobs, their oratory won converts. By the early 1840s, abolitionists discovered that their most effective antislavery weapon was the testimony of slaves and former slaves. Speakers supported by the American Anti-Slavery Society received wages of just over $400 a year plus expenses and a small stipend for those with families. These agents were expected to lecture, collect money to support abolitionist newspapers and organizations, encourage and help form local and state auxiliary societies, and help improve the conditions of free black people. The black speakers, especially the ex-slaves, faced the greatest danger of attack by antiabolitionist mobs for the very reason that they were the most effective.[108]

Local, state, and national authorities often gave indirect sanction to violence against abolitionists. President Andrew Jackson made no secret of his antiabolitionist sentiments and did little to discourage mob violence against blacks and their white allies in the movement. In his 1835 message to Congress, Jackson condemned abolition, declared its literature "unconstitutional and wicked," and supported calls for northern states to ban abolitionist activity.[109] When the American Anti-Slavery Society mounted a campaign to send thousands of antislavery newspapers and pamphlets from New York City into the South by mail, Jackson's postmaster general, Amos Kendall, unofficially approved of southern inspection and censorship of the mail. A proslavery mob in Charleston attacked the United States Post Office and burned sacks of mail thought to contain abolitionist literature. The mob then hanged Garrison and Tappan in effigy and formed groups to inspect future mail to keep the region free of "incendiary" material.[110]

In 1835 antiabolitionists disrupted a meeting of the Boston Female Anti-Slavery Society at which the British reformer George Thompson had been scheduled to speak. While on a lecture tour in Britain speaking against colonization a few years before, Garrison had met and befriended Thompson and invited him to lecture in America.[111] Thompson came for a one-year tour and withstood attacks wherever he spoke, but threats convinced him it was too dangerous for him to speak at the Boston meeting, and Garrison replaced him on the program. A mob of prominent "gentlemen" looking for Thompson invaded the meeting and focused their anger on Garrison. He fled to his newspaper office, but the mob broke in and captured him, put a noose around his neck and took him out into the streets. Before they could carry out their threats, he was rescued by a group of sympathetic Bostonians, a number of blacks among them, and taken to protective custody in the local jail.[112]

Three years later a mob attacked a meeting of abolitionist women at Philadelphia's Pennsylvania Hall. The mob stoned the building breaking windows, interrupted the meeting, and harassed the participants, forcing the women to run a "gauntlet of taunts and threats" at the end of the first day. Some suggested that black women not attend the second day, as their presence seemed to excite a particularly violent reaction, but white abolitionists Lucretia Mott and Abby Kelly disagreed, saying that "no one would be alarmed by a little appearance of danger." Black women attended the session, but at the end of the second day the situation looked even more dangerous. Angelina Grimké called on white women to "protect our colored sisters while going out by taking each one of them by the arm." The black women, the most vulnerable to the "fierce, vile-looking" mob, were surrounded by the white women and safely left the building. Later that night, Philadelphia's mayor addressed the mob and explained that he had not called out the militia to restore order because "you are my police." He needed to say no more; the mob burned the meeting hall to the ground. The next day, linking arms in an interracial parade of defiance, the women marched across town to a schoolhouse where the final day's meeting was held. At this last session Kelly urged the convention to stand for social integration, saying white reformers should visit African Americans "in their homes and encourag[e] them to visit us, receiving them as we do our white fellow citizens." Although her remarks were supported by the passage of a resolution, some whites worried they would be interpreted as a call for "amalgamationism." Black educator and reformer Sarah Mapps Douglass, however, praised Kelly for having "turned her back on prejudice."[113]

Attacks on abolitionists were frightening and undoubtedly discouraged some from attending meetings, but they also attracted attention to the cause and engendered some sympathy. Abolitionists gained some support from those who felt they were being deprived of their civil rights, and Garrison found that subscriptions to the *Liberator* increased after he was mobbed in Boston. Their most important conversion tool, however, was the antislavery speaker. In the summer of 1836, the AASS sent Theodore Weld through Ohio, New York State, and New England where he recruited fifty agents for the society. In mid-November many of them gathered in New York City for an intensive two weeks of training by Weld, Garrison, and other experienced antislavery speakers before being sent out into the field.[114] The earliest paid full-time black abolitionist, traveling agent was Charles Lenox Remond, the free-born son of John Remond, a successful Salem businessman, abolitionist and civil rights leader, who led the drive to integrate the public schools of Salem. Charles Remond was employed by the Massachusetts Anti-Slavery Society in 1838 after having addressed a meeting of the Rhode Island Anti-Slavery Society a year earlier. He toured New England raising money and organizing local societies, and later on a tour of Britain he was a "great favorite in every circle." He was so popular as an antislavery speaker that when a group of whites in Lynn, Massachusetts refused to allow him to address the Lyceum, "a majority united in the formation of another institution . . . in order that they might hear his speech."[115] David Ruggles of New York City was an effective fund raiser and traveling agent for the American Anti-Slavery Society and the society's newspaper, the *Emancipator*.

The most famous antislavery lecturer was Frederick Douglass, who began his speaking career as a fugitive just three years out of bondage. Douglass, son of a slave mother and a white father, had been born Frederick Bailey on Maryland's Eastern Shore in 1818. As a child on the plantation of Edward Lloyd, former governor of Maryland and United States senator, Douglass had taken advantage of opportunities to learn about the world. From a tutor from Greenfield, Massachusetts, provided for his young white playmate, he managed to glean the beginnings of the education that he completed himself. He had been hired out in Baltimore as a young man, and at age twenty, with the help of a free black woman named Anna and contacts in the underground railroad, had made his escape. Douglass made his way to David Ruggles's house in New York where Anna joined him and they were married. The couple continued on to New Bedford, Massachusetts, where they settled in the black community and where Douglass worked on the docks and became a lay preacher in the AME Zion church. During the next few years, Douglass attended local antislavery meetings where occasionally he told the story of his own bondage and escape.[116] In August 1841 he went to Nantucket Island just off the Massachusetts mainland, partly on holiday, the first he had taken since he had escaped slavery in Baltimore, and attended an antislavery convention. There he was spotted by white abolitionist William C. Coffin who had heard him speak to a small gathering at the Zion chapel in New

Bedford. The fugitive was prevailed on to address the antislavery audience as a living exhibit of slavery. He was nervous when Coffin asked him to address the crowded meeting, but his powerful story greatly moved the audience. He so impressed Garrison and the other prominent abolitionists at the meeting that they offered him a position as an antislavery agent for the Massachusetts Anti-Slavery Society. Late that fall, Douglass, his wife, and two children moved to Lynn, Massachusetts, a Quaker community they believed would be safer for a fugitive slave than Boston, and he began his career as an antislavery orator. Over the next two years, Douglass spoke in over sixty towns in New England and became an accomplished speaker. Few equaled his power to affect and inspire an audience.[117]

Douglass, Remond, and other abolitionist speakers continued to face attacks. Remond was pelted with eggs and stones and had his carriage vandalized in Hampton, Maine in 1839.[118] Later a club-wielding, stone-throwing mob injured Douglass and two companions and prevented them from speaking to an audience in Pendleton, Ohio, during a swing through the Midwest. A mob traveled sixteen miles from a neighboring town to disrupt an antislavery meeting and attack Remond in Noblesville, Ohio. In Indianapolis two hundred men on horseback vowed to prevent abolitionists from gathering, by murder if need be, forcing Remond to postpone his lecture. Apparently these antiabolitionist forces had some support from local authority. "Shame on the State of Indiana," declared Remond, "shame on the sentiment that permits the crying disgrace— much less the hands of those who elevate to office such men."[119] Such attacks curtailed but did not prevent Douglass's and Remond's western lecture tour in Ohio, Indiana, and western Pennsylvania, aimed at holding one hundred meetings in the year before the AASS meeting at the end of 1843.

Although violence and the danger of physical injury or even death was the most serious threat to abolitionist speakers, they also faced more continuous physical hardships, frustrations, and general inconvenience. Like evangelical revivals, these abolitionist meetings were community affairs attended by the old and the young. Former slave William Wells Brown was forced to postpone one lecture in western Pennsylvania for an hour because of the "music" of at least twenty-seven babies who attended his rally in their mothers' arms. Finally, after the babies fell asleep, he was able to begin his lecture. Crying children, mothers singing to their babies, "one . . . throwing her child up and catching it," challenged abolitionists' abilities to lecture. As Brown reported, "my head ache[d] . . . from the exertion I made to be heard."[120] In the West Henry Bibb, a Kentucky fugitive, traveled through Ohio and Michigan telling his story to small meetings in private homes, schoolhouses, and rural cabins, anywhere a few people gathered to hear him. He traveled through swamps, over log roads, and through axle-deep mud. He spoke to very poor frontier people, some of whom arrived on wagons pulled by teams of oxen and loaded with men, women, and children. Often he brought his own candles when his hosts could not afford to supply them for evening meetings.[121]

Proselytizing for antislavery was aimed at building a constituency for the eventual destruction of the institution of slavery. The underground railroad, another important part of the antislavery movement, provided more immediate and direct aid to the slave. African Americans were central to the work of interracial antislavery organizations, but they were even more important to the formation and operation of the underground railroad. The informal networks that aided slaves' escape and helped them maintain their freedom had existed for many years. Formal antislavery societies, Quaker meetings, churches, black communities, and sympathetic individuals had long been part of this underground, but in the 1840s a Supreme Court ruling gave their work added urgency. In 1842 the Court decided in the case of *Prigg v. Pennsylvania*[122] that Pennsylvania's 1826 law strengthening free blacks' legal protections from kidnapping, was unconstitutional because it contradicted the federal fugitive slave law of 1793. In response, abolitionists organized more vigilance committees.[123] Sometimes called slave refuge societies or fugitive aid societies, they were the most organized northern arm of the underground railroad, aiding fugitives passing through their local areas, protecting free blacks from kidnapping and attempting to rescue any captives. The New York committee headed by David Ruggles was especially alert for opportunities to rescue slaves brought to that city. When one ship from Brazil docked in the harbor in the late 1840s, a delegation of blacks boarded to search for slaves in need of assistance. One of the three young slaves they found was the ship's steward, Mahommah Baquaqua, a Muslim brought from northern Dahomey in West Africa in the 1840s to slavery in Brazil, where his third owner was the ship's captain. The three Portugese-speaking slaves were excited about landing in New York because they knew that blacks in New York were free, but the only English word they knew was "free," taught them by an Englishman aboard the ship. With the assistance of the vigilance committee, they were brought before the Brazilian Consul, held in the local jail, and, according to Baquaqua, finally rescued by "some friends who had interested themselves very much in our behalf." Baquaqua went first to Boston, and when the abolitionists gave him a choice between going to England or to Haiti, chose Haiti. There he was befriended by the Judds, American Baptist missionaries who helped arrange for him to enroll in New York Central College a few years later.[124]

In 1842, the year of the Prigg decision, a group of black men and women in Boston organized the Freedom Association. That fall when fugitive slaves George Latimer and his family escaped from Norfolk, Virginia to Boston, their owner, merchant James Gray from Norfolk, pursued them and had George arrested for larceny, a charge later changed to flight as a fugitive. Following an unsuccessful attempt by the Freedom Association to rescue Latimer, black and white abolitionists organized a massive effort that included publishing a daily newspaper, *The Latimer and North Star Journal*, posting signs denouncing the Boston police as "Human Kidnappers," and holding mass meetings protesting the fugitive's capture. Boston blacks turned to representative and former president John Quincy Adams for legal advice, but finally the local community raised the money to purchase Latimer's freedom. Efforts did not end there, however; an ambitious campaign produced a huge 150-pound petition bearing nearly 65,000 names which was forwarded to the Massachusetts State legislature. In response, lawmakers ultimately passed the state Personal Liberty Act of 1843 that forbade state officials from participating or state facilities from being used in the apprehension of fugitives from slavery. This victory reaffirmed Massachusetts' preeminence in the antislavery movement and reflected the growing power of Boston abolitionists. In 1846 the Freedom Association became part of the newly organized, integrated Boston Vigilance Committee.[125]

Vigilance committees were organized groups, generally able to provide financial aid and legal services and maintain connections between many communities in the United States, Canada, and Europe. They constituted the most structured aspect of the underground railroad, with conductors who moved fugitives from one place to another and participants who fed, clothed, and sheltered them. As historian Larry Gara pointed out more than two decades ago, this highly organized network run by altruistic white reformers has dominated the romanticized legend of the underground railroad. There was an organized underground run by black and white abolitionists, but at least as important was the loosely coordinated or individual efforts of thousands of blacks and many whites who acted out of personal compassion. Most runaways could not count on encountering organized assistance until they left the South, and initially, escape depended on the personal resources and inventiveness of the fugitive and the aid of the friends, relatives, and associates immediately at hand.

William and Ellen Craft, a slave couple from Macon, Georgia, planned a daring escape that depended on Ellen's fair skin, straight raven hair, and Roman nose for its success. With a face wrap feigning a swollen jaw from a toothache to hide her beardlessness and her arm in a sling to explain her inability to sign travel documents, Ellen disguised herself as a young southern gentleman traveling north for medical treatment. William acted as her personal servant as they boarded a train to Savannah in 1848 and made their way by train and boat to Philadelphia.[126] Finally, in Philadelphia the Crafts contacted William Still, their first connection with the formal organization of the underground railroad. Still, born free in New Jersey, was the son of a runaway slave. He moved to Philadelphia in the 1840s and became active in the city's vigilance committee. Philadelphia, fairly close to the southern border, with strong institutional ties to Baltimore and a long history of antislavery, was a major transfer point on the underground railroad.

In the beginning of August 1850, two men visited Still's office at the Pennsylvania Antislavery Society. One of the men, Peter Freedman, had recently purchased his freedom and was searching for his parents from whom he had been separated in slavery. As Still listened to Freedman's story, it became increasingly familiar. He was astonished to realize that Freedman was the older brother he had never met, one of two young boys their mother had left in slavery when she made her escape. Taking a closer look, he recounted, "I could see in the face of my newfound brother the likeness of my mother. My feelings were unutterable." After the family was reunited, Peter Freedman embarked on a five-year quest, speaking and collecting money to gain freedom for his wife and children still in slavery.[127]

Successful escape from slavery was arduous, and family ties sometimes discouraged slaves from attempting escape. Slave women were most likely to be the guardians of children and less likely to run away than men. When they escaped with children it was especially difficult, and William Still was always anxious about their prospects. He believed they took "three times the risk of failure that males were liable to." Some slaveholders encouraged their slaves to marry and have children because they too saw the family as an impediment to escape.[128] The punishment for being caught could be severe physical abuse or sale "down the river" from the upper South to the Deep South, where the work was harsher, the survival rate lower, and escape more nearly impossible. Many men with families or mothers with children elected to endure slavery rather than leave their children behind. The experience of a slave named William illustrates the difficulty of keeping families intact while attempting an escape. William was the son of Elizabeth, the slave of Dr. John Young of Lexington, Kentucky. William's father was Young's cousin, and William received special treatment because of their familial relationship. In 1827 Young moved his household to just outside St. Louis, and teenage William was allowed to hire himself out, first as a tavernkeeper's helper, then as a steward on a Mississippi steamboat, and as an office boy for Elijah P. Lovejoy, editor of the *St. Louis Times*. After members of his family were sold, and as his sister was about to be sold down the river to Natchez, William decided to attempt an escape. He convinced his mother, who was then the property of a man in St. Louis, to accompany him, though she was reluctant to leave her children in St. Louis.[129]

They did not make contact with the organized underground, but they found people who helped them and gave them food and advice. After they journeyed 150 miles and had reached the free soil of Illinois, they were stopped by three men on horseback who brandished a handbill offering a reward of two hundred dollars for the return of the slave mother and her son. The slave hunters were God-fearing men, William observed wryly, men who read the Bible in the evening after they secured him with ropes for the night. Under their control, the slaves "started [their] journey back to the land of whips, chains and Bibles." His mother was sold South, "to die on a cotton, sugar, or rice plantation," and William blamed himself for her fate, since he had convinced her to run away.[130]

William was also sold, but because his master had promised William's white father that the boy would not be sold farther South, he remained in St. Louis. First he was placed in the household of a tailor, then with a steamboat owner. Knowing a married slave was less likely to attempt escape, his new owners tried to find him a wife, even buying a woman they thought he liked, but William was determined to escape once more and refused to consider marriage. His confidence was strengthened by a visit to Uncle Frank, a seventy-year-old slave fortune teller with an impressive presence. He was over six-feet tall with a slender build, was popular with blacks and whites, and was a "great favorite of the young ladies, who would go to him in great numbers to get their fortunes told." For twenty-five cents, Uncle Frank predicted freedom for William, complete with the details of his escape. When nineteen-year-old William finally did escape in 1834, it was winter, and the hardships he faced included illness, frostbite, and the perils of discovery along country roads. He marked the kindness of the Ohio Quaker who sheltered a stranger for a few weeks by adding his name to his own and called himself William Wells Brown. He continued north to Cleveland where he stayed until the spring. He worked on a lake boat, tried his hand at barbering and banking in Monroe, Michigan, then settled in Buffalo, New York in 1836.[131] Like many others, Brown accomplished his escape from slavery with only informal assistance until he reached the North. Fugitives were most likely to seek assistance from black people if given a choice, and the historical record is filled with accounts of strangers providing informal aid to runaways. "We did not dare ask [for food], except when we found a slave's or free colored person's home remote from any other and then we were never refused, if they had food to give," one fugitive reported.[132]

Sometimes, however, the organized arm of the underground railroad did reach into the South to rescue slaves, taking them from southern cabins and fields and escorting them to freedom. On these instances the legend of the underground railroad was built, legendary tales featuring people like Harriet Tubman, "the Moses of her People." Tubman escaped from slavery in Maryland in the summer of 1849 and worked as a cook, a domestic servant, and a seamstress in Philadelphia. After she met William Still, she became one of the most active conductors on the underground railroad, reputedly making nineteen trips into the South and leading over three hundred slaves to freedom.[133] Called Mother Tubman or Aunt Harriet, she was said to be as strong as any man and smarter than most, compassionate but intolerant of the faint-hearted, and single-minded in her determination that once a rescue began it must end in freedom. A fugitive too terrified to continue was not allowed to turn back. "A finger around the trigger and a calm, 'Dead Negroes tell no tales' was all that was ever needed" to convince her charges of her seriousness.[134]

Occasionally rescues were arranged by abolitionists who did not go into the South themselves but financed others who did. Former slave John Tyler, of Cazenovia, New York related the story of his escape. Posing as cattle drovers, abolitionist agents employed by New York's Gerrit Smith had visited his plantation in eastern Maryland. They instructed Tyler and ten members of his family to leave their cabins after dark and meet them in the woods. By morning fifty men with dogs were searching for the fugitives. A few fearing capture decided to return to the plantation, but the abolitionists reached them first and were able to bring them safely through Pennsylvania to New York. Tyler revered Gerrit Smith for his efforts on behalf of the slaves. As he put it years later, "Massa Garry Smith was a great man."[135]

Gerrit Smith was probably also involved in an elaborately organized mass escape attempt from Washington, D. C. in April 1848 that came to be known as the "Pearl Affair." William L. Chaplin, a traveling speaker for the American Anti-Slavery Society who had helped to plan several earlier escapes, devised the initial plans for the escape. He wrote to Smith in March to tell him that he was waiting for a vessel to arrive from Philadelphia to take fifty or more passengers.[136] Early in April the slaves received the word to be ready, and on the evening of the fifteenth, slaves from different parts of the city made their way on foot or in carriages to a deserted wharf on the Potomac River. There, they boarded a wood-hauling schooner named *The Pearl* under the command of Captain Edward Sayres, which had been chartered by Captain Daniel Drayton, a veteran of other slave rescues. There were extra passengers—"a few friends" joined the escape—swelling the number of runaways to seventy-seven. A few free blacks like carpenter Daniel Bell also came along, accompanying family members who were not free. It was about 10 P. M. when *The Pearl* sailed out of Washington. They put in a short distance away at Alexandria, Virginia for the night and at dawn moved into the Chesapeake. A storm's severe winds forced them to wait in a sheltered port at Point Lookout about 140 miles from Washington. Meanwhile, back in Washington slaveholders had discovered the escape, and a large posse scoured the city for information. The escapees were betrayed by Judson Diggs, a free black hackdriver who had transported several of the fugitives to the wharf the preceding night. The immediate reason for Diggs's betrayal was apparently the failure of a fugitive to pay what Diggs considered a proper sum for his transportation to the wharf, but there were also more complex reasons for his actions. He had attempted to court one of the Edmonson sisters, attractive and intelligent light-skinned slave women who were the daughters of a successful free black landowner in nearby Montgomery County. His overtures had been soundly rebuffed, and it is likely that the social role that color played in the southern city of Washington made him feel his rejection more deeply. Diggs was a free, independent small businessman, but he was dark in complexion. For whatever the combination of reasons, his treachery proved decisive. The posse boarded a steamboat, overtook the *Pearl* before it could clear southern waters, seized it, and towed it back to the city. In Washington an angry mob attempted to lynch Drayton and succeeded in severing part of his ear before he, Sayres, and the fugitives were jailed for safekeeping. The frustrated mob then attacked the offices of *The National Era*, the abolitionist newspaper in the city. After their capture, many of the slaves were sold out of the city, some to the Deep South, and Drayton and Sayres were charged with "slave-stealing."[137]

Even the organized efforts of the underground railroad were often greatly decentralized, with informal groups providing aid to fugitives. In Cincinnati a group of black dock workers and boatmen recruited black travelers passing through the city to help them establish contacts further north. When Jim and Sam, the former slaves of North Carolina planter John Saunders, stopped in the city for the night, they encountered several black stevedores who asked them an unusual number of questions. These worldly wise dock workers were skeptically amused by the story that Saunders had freed his slaves and was transporting them to the land he had purchased in Michigan for their settlement. Jim produced freedom papers to support his account, and knowing these naive former slaves were vulnerable, the workers warned them not to show the papers to anyone and not to trust any white people. Later, ignoring the admonitions, Jim and Sam met a man posing as a minister, who took their papers and threatened to take them south as fugitives. Saunders saved the day, however, and the police arrested the would-be kidnapper. When Jim and Sam met the dock workers again at the stable where they gathered, the ex-slaves learned that they were hiding fugitives bound for Canada there. After they were settled in Michigan, Jim and Sam might provide valuable information about routes to Canada to aid the development of this branch of the underground railroad. In this informal way, small groups established links to other regions that allowed them to move fugitives from place to place. They also became at least indirectly tied to the more formal operations of the underground railroad and the antislavery movement.[138]

The most dramatic part of the underground railroad was the work of the highly organized vigilance committees in New York, Boston, Philadelphia, and many smaller cities and towns, especially in communities bordering Canada. In 1836 slave trader Bacon Tate from Nashville arrived in Buffalo searching for the Stanfords, a fugitive couple and their six-year-old child. Learning they were living in Saint Catharines, Ontario, he engaged four men to cross the boarder, kidnap the family and bring them back to the United States. The kidnappers struck late one Saturday night, bound their victims, and brought them into Buffalo in a carriage. They stopped only long enough to confer with Tate and proceeded southward before stopping again to change horses at Hamburg, New York, about eleven miles from Buffalo. News of the kidnapping reached Buffalo about noon on Sunday, and the antislavery underground swung into action. A group of about fifty armed men, one of whose leaders was fugitive William Wells Brown and most of whom were black, overtook the party at Hamburg and rescued the Stanfords. They returned to Buffalo, but as they were putting the Stanfords on a ferry bound for Canada, the sheriff and a posse of sixty or seventy men confronted them at the riverfront. Neither side was willing to negotiate to the satisfaction of the other, and a full-scale riot ensued, as Brown recalled, "one of the most fearful fights for human freedom that I ever witnessed."[139] Although one of the rescuers was killed and forty were arrested, the sheriff was unable to prevent the Stanfords from being escorted back to Canada amid the cheers of their Buffalo supporters. Twenty-five of Brown's group were prosecuted and fined, but the fugitives were saved.

The flow of fugitives and other black travelers was a critical component of the community network that provided information for the antislavery movement and helped free blacks maintain connections with those left behind in the slave South. Like the newspapers and the conventions, the underground railroad became an important part of the interregional information link. William Still remained aware of conditions in the South through the intelligence provided to him by the stream of fugitives who passed through Philadelphia. Frederick Douglass and many others collected information from fugitives. Black sailors and boatmen carried messages to slave parents from adult children living in freedom. Thus, one grandmother enslaved in Mississippi remained informed about her daughter's life in Cincinnati and followed her grandson's progress as a student at Oberlin.[140] Sailors, particularly black sailors and boatmen, often provided information, carried messages, and aided escape attempts for southern slaves and free blacks. Slaveholders' awareness of these activities was one reason black crewmen were jailed while their vessels rested in southern ports.[141]

The most spontaneous actions of the antislavery underground during the Jacksonian era were likely to be black efforts. When integrated groups acted, they were more likely to be part of a formally constituted organization. Responding in part to the assault on black rights during this period and in part to the perceived threat of colonization, organization was facilitated by the overt communication networks established by black newspapers and the national conventions and by the covert networks of an expanding underground railroad. By the late 1820s and early 1830s, antislavery action had a long history among northern blacks, and as a growing number of white reformers were willing to join them, integrated action promised to bring new resources, attention, and power to the struggle.

During the 1830s and 1840s the antislavery movement had many different aspects both within black communities and in integrated public forums, where blacks and whites joined in a sometimes uneasy alliance. In some ways this cooperative action was reminiscent of pre-Revolutionary interracial efforts, but there were important differences. Interracial cooperation in the antebellum period generally involved affluent, well-educated white abolitionists, many motivated by religious conviction and working as altruistic reformers on behalf of black people. Rare was the white abolitionist who recognized even the best educated, middle-class black as equal; interracial cooperation generally took place in the context of paternalism. By contrast, much eighteenth-century joint activism had brought people of similar social and economic ranks together to act against shared oppression. Black and white servants and slaves recognized shared problems and often acknowledged a common opponent. White elites tended to regard them as occupying the same low economic and social status, a perception they frequently shared.

The paternalism and prejudice of many antebellum white reformers limited the possibilities for individual and organizational cooperation in the abolition movement. Communication networks, newspapers, tracts and printed sermons, arguments for racial justice presented at public meetings, dramatic rescues, organized campaigns, and informal individual acts to aid fugitives from slavery were some of the myriad faces of antislavery activism. Within the framework of abolition, blacks and whites made different but equally important contributions. Whites brought financial power, reformist zeal, and the respectability of their color. Blacks brought their passion, the personal experience in slavery that mesmerized northern audiences, and their commitment to those remaining in bondage. Together they fed the fire of antislavery ardor.

10

The Widening Struggle,
Growing Militancy, and the Hope
of Liberty for All

Few understood the precariousness of African-American freedom better than Solomon Northup. He was the freeborn son of a former slave who had acquired enough land in Washington County to qualify as a voter in New York State, and spent his youth there, doing farm work with his father, cultivating a love for books, and playing the violin, what he called "the ruling passion of my youth."[1] In 1829 his father died and Northup married Anne Hampton, a local young woman of African, European, and American Indian ancestry who worked as a cook. He worked for a time on the Champlain Canal and then moved to the village of Kingsbury where he farmed a small plot of land and supplemented his income by playing the violin for local parties and dances. In the early spring of 1834, the Northups moved to Saratoga Springs, New York where Solomon drove a hack, worked on the Troy and Saratoga Railroad, and played his violin at resorts. He and Anne were both employed at the United States Hotel, and there he met slaves who accompanied their vacationing southern masters, puzzling over the power that could hold a human being in bondage against his will.[2]

In March 1841, Northup, looking for employment to last until the resort season, was approached by Alexander Merrill and Joseph Russell, two white men who offered him several days of work playing for their act in New York City. In return they offered him a handsome salary. Anne was on a trip to a neighboring town, and his new employers were in a hurry, so he left on the short trip without leaving her a note. The trio performed to a sparse audience in Albany where they stayed the night, but once in New York City the two convinced Northup that there were far greater opportunities for them with the circus opening soon in Washington, D. C. They took a carriage through New Jersey and Philadelphia to Baltimore and then a train on to Washington. During the trip into the South, Northup noticed his companions' anxiety but attributed it to their excitement about working with the circus.

The party arrived in Washington on the eve of President Henry Harrison's funeral and took residence at Gadsby's Hotel on Pennsylvania Avenue.[3] His new employers treated him well, giving him a considerable sum of money—a portion of his wages, they explained. The next day as they wined and dined him, one of the drinks made Northup ill. They set upon him, handcuffed him, and robbed him of his money and free papers, and sold him to Washington slave dealer James H. Burch for $650. Northup protested that he was a free man, but after more than an hour of vicious whipping, he fell silent.

Northup's case was not unique. Free blacks throughout the North faced the danger of kidnapping, and the danger grew with the growing need for slaves in the lower cotton-producing South and with slaves' increasing value. Northup estimated that hundreds of free blacks had been kidnapped and illegally held in bondage on plantations in Texas and Louisiana.[4] On his way to slavery in Louisiana, Northup was put in a slave pen in Richmond where he encountered another man who had been kidnapped—Robert, a free man with a family in Cincinnati. Like Northup, Robert had accepted a job from two white men and had traveled to the South with them. They sold him into slavery in Fredricksburg, Virginia, and he was taken to Richmond where he joined Northup and the party of slaves moving south. In Norfolk they met Arthur, another free man, a mason by trade and a resident of Norfolk who had been kidnapped by a gang which set upon him as he returned home one evening. The whole group was confined together aboard the brig *Orleans* bound for New Orleans, and the three men immediately began planning their escape. Robert contracted smallpox and died before their plan could be put into effect, and on landing in New Orleans, Arthur was rescued by friends who traveled from Norfolk to meet the ship. The best Northup could manage was to smuggle a letter to his family in Saratoga with the assistance of one of the sailors aboard the *Orleans*. In New Orleans Northup, now called Platt, was sold again, this time to a Louisiana planter who was also a Baptist minister.[5]

The danger of being kidnapped into slavery created another link between free blacks and those in bondage and was another reason, in addition to concerns for family members and friends, that the abolition of slavery was in free blacks' own interest. The increased danger added urgency to their antislavery work and made them more open to direct action, more amenable to party politics, and renewed their dedication to self-defense. It was however only the most blatant threat to black liberty.

Mob action, local laws, even federal policies and legal rulings all conspired to rob black people of the privileges and "manhood rights" routinely guaranteed to Americans.[6] In the two decades before the Civil War, African Americans debated the most effective approach to defending and asserting their rights and protecting themselves, their communities, and those bound in slavery. By the late 1830s, many more abolitionists, black and white, expressed their disagreement with William Lloyd Garrison's pacifism and disdain for party politics. Yet, prominent black Garrisonians like Boston's Robert Roberts, New Bedford's William Powell, one of the only black members of the New England Non-Resistance Society, and moral reformer William Whipper remained staunchly committed to his philosophy. At the 1837 meeting of the American Moral Reform Society in Philadelphia, Whipper strongly defended nonviolence, saying, "We must learn on all occasions to rebuke the spirit of violence, both in sentiment and practice." Furthermore, he argued that any person who resorted to violence for any reason, no matter how just, had "no just claim to being regarded as a christian [sic] or a good citizen."[7]

Violent attacks on free black communities and abolitionists tested the resolve of the pacifists. Between 1833 and 1838, the abolitionist press recorded 160 violent incidents. Samuel Cornish confessed that when faced with kidnappers or "a midnight incendiary with a lighted torch in his hand," he had trouble believing in the virtue of "using moral weapons."[8] Although many northern blacks stood ready to follow nonviolence as a general philosophy, they had difficulty eschewing violence in defending against kidnappers and slavehunters.

At a mass meeting in New York in 1837, blacks publicly challenged Garrisonian nonviolence, nearly passing a resolution stating "we cannot recommend non-resistance to persons who are denied the protection of equitable law, and when their liberty is invaded and their lives endangered by avaricious kidnappers."[9] Several black ministers, including Charles B. Ray and Theodore S. Wright, opposed the resolution as contrary to Christian principles, but other activists like David Ruggles argued that blacks should defend themselves, their families, and their homes. Garrison beat back another much broader challenge at the annual meeting of the integrated Massachusetts Anti-Slavery Society in late 1837 with the aid of abolitionist women and Massachusetts blacks. Abolitionist clergy and their allies attacked Garrison for "inexcusable egotism and religious heresy," decrying his attacks on the church, strong condemnation of the church denominations' failure to disavow slaveholding and slaveholders, and his endorsement of women's rights.[10] Although some blacks, especially ministers, were concerned with such issues, for most the important question was the issue of nonviolence. In the early winter of 1838, Ruggles's coworker in the underground, the West African born Augustus W. Hanson, wrote directly to Garrison expressing his reservations about the practicality of his pacifist philosophy, arguing that self-defense could be justified, as it was directed at stopping an attacker rather than carrying out an attack. He also suggested that his own activities had not been reported in the *Liberator* because he had disagreed with Garrison's doctrines.

Garrison did not seem to demand a commitment to pacifism. He had written admiringly of the abolitionist editor Elijah Lovejoy, who had armed himself in an attempt to defend the presses that angry mobs repeatedly destroyed, and who was finally murdered by a mob in Alton, Illinois in November 1837. On principle, Garrison could not take up arms himself, but he respected Lovejoy's bravery and declared that the antislavery movement must be open to a broad range of opinion on this issue. Many of his white antagonists in the movement never believed Garrison tolerated disagreement, but Garrison's acceptance of others' acts of self-defense was important to many blacks who believed it was their manly duty to use violence if necessary to defend themselves or their families. In the context of American slavery, aimed at emasculating the black man, it was difficult for most black men and women to accept the "feminizing" connotation of nonviolence. Garrison's more liberal stand on this issue allowed many blacks not completely committed to nonviolence to maintain their loyalty to Garrison.[11]

On two consecutive evenings in September 1837, large numbers of Boston's African Americans gathered in the black school on Belknap Street to discuss Garrison's position. They agreed with his attack on the organized white church for its lack of support for abolition, although not with all the particulars of his doctrine of nonresistance. They endorsed the *Liberator*, claiming it as "our great organ," and gave it and its editor their unwavering affirmation.[12] The black Philadelphia Female Literary Association published their support of Garrison in a letter to the *Liberator*.[13] In New York, Cornish worried about the effect of such endorsements. He saw the controversy raging in the abolition movement as one pitting Garrison against the white abolitionist clergy and warned that blacks should not take part in this quarrel, a disagreement that seemed to be largely on the "non-essentials of abolition." He refused to publish the report of the Boston meeting in the *Colored American* for fear it might encourage the "unseemly sight of bodies of colored men arrayed against abolitionists."[14] When John T. Hilton and other black Bostonians chided him for failing in his responsibilities, Cornish published a cutting rejoinder that questioned the sanity of those who challenged his editorial judgment. He professed respect and personal affection for Garrison, whom he referred to as "THE BELOVED EDITOR," but he also reiterated his view that blacks should not insinuate themselves into this internal struggle among white abolitionists. Furthermore, Cornish threatened to allow the paper to fold rather than be ruled by the "intemperate zeal" of his Boston detractors.[15]

These complex issues involved community rivalries, egos, and the loyalty of blacks in Boston, Philadelphia, and other areas to Garrison. To maintain black support and reaffirm his commitment to nonresistance, while not imposing it on the antislavery societies, Garrison established the separate Non-Resistance Society in the summer of 1838. With this separation, he hoped to remove one important point of contention from the abolitionist movement, but for most white abolitionists and some blacks outside of Boston, it was too late. At the next meeting of the Massachusetts Anti-Slavery Society the fight continued, and the Garrisonian forces again carried the day. The split finally came at the 1840 meeting of the American Anti-Slavery Society and focused on the issue of Garrison's stand in favor of full female participation in society affairs. Many white abolitionists and some blacks thought that a profeminist, antichurch, antigovernment stand would make the antislavery movement vulnerable to charges of radicalism and anarchism. Almost three hundred delegates withdrew to form the American and Foreign Anti-Slavery Society, a new organization governed by a male executive committee and relegating women to a female auxiliary. Even though Garrison supported women's rights within the antislavery movement, not all female abolitionists supported him. In an 1837 debate over Garrison in the Boston Female Anti-Slavery Society, only a minority of white members had stood with him, while a majority of black members supported him. When the American Anti-Slavery Society split came in 1840, the female society in Philadelphia remained Garrisonians, but the Boston group split and anti-Garrison forces formed the Massachusetts Female Emancipation Society. The dissenters emphasized their opposition to slavery but did not embrace Garrison's broader approach to reform. Black female abolitionists generally remained staunch Garrisonians, applauding his long-standing commitment to black civil rights and to abolition and expressing their gratitude for his willingness to speak out for black rights.[16] Boston's black abolitionists, both women and men, were generally loyal to Garrison and stayed with the American Anti-Slavery Society. Many blacks, particularly Cornish and other New Yorkers, attempted to remain neutral, not wanting to split the movement over religion, pacifism, women's rights, and other issues they believed were peripheral to abolition. In the end, many left the AASS to join the American and Foreign Anti-Slavery Society, among these were a number of black ministers including Cornish, Garnet, and Ray from New York.[17]

The Garrisonian position on women's full participation was immediately tested at the meeting of the World Anti-Slavery Convention that opened in London shortly after the stormy New York meetings. The American Anti-Slavery Society contingent included Garrison, Wendell Phillips, Nathaniel P. Rogers, Remond, and white feminist women Lucretia Mott, Maria Weston Chapman, and Ann Greene Phillips. Over their protestations, the female delegates were refused the right to vote and were relegated to the balcony. Garrison, Remond, and two other male delegates then refused to list their names among the official delegates and protested by joining the women in the balcony; other Garrisonians boy-cotted the conference.[18]

Garrison argued that abolition must stay clear of party politics, believing that factionalism and the compromises that political involvement inevitably required would dilute antislavery principles. Although some free blacks had been denied the vote in New York by the property requirements applied only to them, and the fear of violence kept many in other states away from the polls, blacks were loathe to give up the manhood right that political participation represented. Like white women, black women depended on representation through adult males, but black women were a part of the struggle for the manhood of the race at almost every stage, fully expected to be included in the politics of their community, and saw the ballot as community property, even if cast only by men.[19] When Sarah Douglass called for the "dignity of Manhood" for all African Americans, she assumed a role for women.[20]

African Americans were especially attracted to the Liberty Party, an antislavery party organized in western New York in 1839, and they were associated with it from its inception. The *Colored American* endorsed the party's national slate headed by abolitionist and former slaveholder James G. Birney, calling him "decidedly a better man in every possible respect to be President of the United States" than current Democratic President Martin Van Buren or Whig candidate William Henry Harrison.[21] John T. Raymond, a black Baptist minister, attended the party's first annual convention in Albany in 1840. Although this "third party" had "warm friends" in the 1840 New York State Convention of blacks, a resolution endorsing the Liberty Party was hotly debated there and finally withdrawn.[22] The Liberty Party attempted to broaden its appeal beyond antislavery circles by linking the evil of slavery with the injustice of poverty. "Pity not only the enslaved poor and the colored poor, but all poor," urged a broadside advertising its meeting in Peterboro, New York in 1846.[23] Still, self-consciously designed as an abolitionist alternative to Garrisonian nonresistance, its strongest stand was against slavery.

Some African Americans worked as stump speakers for the Liberty Party. In western New York State, one of the most successful was Jermain Wesley Loguen, an escaped slave from Tennessee, who became pastor of a small, financially struggling church in Bath, New York. In 1844 while in Cortland on a fund-raising tour, he met a number of Liberty Party men who asked him to speak to a political rally on behalf of the party's candidates. Loguen agreed, with the proviso that he could appeal for funds for his church at the same time. Most whites in attendance had never seen a fugitive slave, and they were captivated by Loguen's story. "No prayer ever made in Cortland melted the people like that," wrote one observer. He was so successful that the party asked him to represent it in that region of New York, and his efforts were credited with doubling Liberty Party votes there.[24]

African Americans searching for the most effective way to assert their rights and protect their communities debated the third party issue throughout the 1840s. Liberty Party officials recognized the potential power of black votes, and after his unsuccessful 1840 presidential candidacy, Birney wrote to Lewis Tappan suggesting a petition campaign to secure equal suffrage for blacks.[25] Partly as another attempt to enable blacks in New York to become qualified voters, in 1846 white abolitionist Gerrit Smith announced his intention of providing 120,000 acres of land in New York State for grants to temperate blacks of good character. Eventually, with the assistance of James McCune Smith and Charles B. Ray, Gerrit Smith distributed more than three thousand land titles for forty- to sixty-acre tracts, creating thousands of qualified black voters.[26] One group of grantees founded a settlement called Timbucto in 1846 in North Elba, New York near Lake Placid. A few professionals were included, but the settlers were mainly cooks, waiters, coachmen, and barbers. The land was poor, low, and swampy or rocky mountain slopes, and the winters were harsh, but the settlers established farms, raised sheep, and initiated a wool trade with Canadian towns. In 1849 white abolitionist John Brown paid one dollar an acre for a 244-acre farm on the outskirts of the settlement, settled his family there, and offered his surveying skills to the community. Eleven of Brown's twenty children grew to maturity on this family homestead.[27]

It was difficult for many blacks to adhere to Garrison's opposition to party politics, and his stand on nonviolence seemed increasingly impractical as white mobs continued to attack free black communities through the late 1830s and into the 1840s. Occasionally, as in the riots of the summer of 1834, gang violence in New York City expanded beyond the continually threatening white street gangs to include a broader range of working-class and middle-class whites. On the Fourth of July that year, a disturbance broke out when the Chatham Street Chapel was mistakenly reserved simultaneously for the New York Sacred Music Society and for a group of the city's blacks celebrating the anniversary of New York's emancipation law. On successive nights there were small disruptions in various parts of the city, and by July 9th the disturbances had become destructive and increasingly violent. Thousands of whites joined an assault on white abolitionist Lewis Tappan's home, mobs attacked several black churches, private homes, and businesses and beat blacks in the streets wherever they were found. According to contemporary accounts, "Throughout the night the screams of tortured Negroes could be heard."[28]

Similar violence occurred in Philadelphia and Boston during the 1830s, and began in the 1840s in March in Dayton, Ohio, where anti-abolitionist attacks escalated into a riot and the mob's destruction of black residences. In September 1841 racial violence in Cincinnati amounted to racial warfare.[29] Disturbances began with a clash between a white gang of youths who threw stones at "several well-dressed" black men and other blacks

who went to their defense. Late the next night other fights broke out
after an armed group of white men appeared at the Dumas Hotel and
demanded the surrender of a black man who had been involved in the
fighting the night before. Ominously, groups of white men from Kentucky began to gather in the streets. Threatened blacks armed themselves
and chose twenty-eight-year-old J. Wilkerson, a mulatto from Virginia
said to be the grandson of a Revolutionary War colonel, to lead them in
any confrontation. When a white mob moved toward the black residential area where young John Mercer Langston boarded near central
Cincinnati at eight in the evening on September 3, 1841, the armed
blacks were waiting in their homes, in the alleyways, and on the rooftops.
Before the violence was over, hundreds of whites fought battles in the
streets with local blacks. They used stones, clubs, and rifles; whites
dragged a cannon up from the river, and about fifty blacks drove the mob
out of the neighborhood under covering fire from a nearby house. To
bring the fighting under control, city officials declared martial law in the
black area and succumbed to white demands that the state's black codes
be enforced, that fugitive slaves be sought out and arrested, that abolitionism be repudiated, and that the city's blacks be disarmed. No whites
were arrested, but three hundred blacks were jailed; once disarmed, they
were attacked again by white mobs.[30]

Adhering to the principles of nonviolence under these circumstances
seemed to many both ineffective and unmanly. To be a man in the context
of nineteenth-century American society meant exercising manly privileges like voting, but it also meant asserting one's rights and protecting
one's family and community. As Frederick Douglass remembered it,
physically preventing a slave breaker from whipping him was the symbolic achievement of his manhood. Years later the memory of his successful resistance still evoked passionate pride, as he wrote, "My dear
reader this battle with Mr. Covey . . . was the turning point in my life as a
slave. . . . I was nothing before; I was a man now."[31] The black men of
Cincinnati who defended their families and homes against white mobs
were attempting to fulfill their responsibilities, defending their manhood
and the manhood of the race.[32] They stood "like men," reported the *Colored American* against an "inhuman blood-thirsty mob."[33] Many former
slaves incorporated their new manhood into the names they chose, names
like Freeman. Jehiel Beman, the Connecticut AME minister and temperance leader who was born a slave, chose this last name when he gained his
freedom and could finally *be a man*.[34]

The system of slavery and its justifications assaulted the humanity of
African Americans; slaves and free blacks alike suffered the stigma of its
degradation. Therefore, self-assertion and resistance were highly valued
in the black community, especially direct resistance to enslavement. In
this context, a revolt on the *Amistad* led by a strong, dignified, and manly
African named Cinque became a widely celebrated cause. En route to

Havana, Cuba aboard the Spanish slavery schooner *Amistad*, fifty-three Africans, including four children, revolted against the crew, killed the captain, and took over the vessel. They made an effort to return to Africa but were tricked by some of the crew and ended up on the coast of New England where they were taken into custody in the port of New London, Connecticut in August 1839. The Africans were imprisoned and charged with piracy and murder. Spain demanded the return of both the ship and its slave cargo. Abolitionists argued that because the Atlantic slave trade was illegal in the United States after 1808, and Spain had signed a treaty with England outlawing the trade in 1817, these Africans were the victims of kidnapping.

By the time the case arrived at the U. S. Supreme Court in 1841, it had become an international cause, with both Spain and England identified as interested parties. Former president of the United States, John Quincy Adams, acted as defense attorney for the Africans, with abolitionists including Lewis Tappan, Simeon Jocelyn, and Joshua Leavitt assisting him. A play produced in New York entitled *The Black Schooner or the Private Slaver "Amistad"* drew enthusiastic audiences and raised more than $5,000 for the defense. Abolitionist papers carried detailed accounts, printing communications from the Africans as they learned English, partly from the visitors who flocked to see them. "We want you to ask the Court what we have done wrong. . . . All we want is make us free," wrote one of the prisoners in a letter published in the *Emancipator*.[35] Among free blacks the *Amistad* rebels were revered as heroes. Philadelphia's Robert Purvis commissioned a portrait of Joseph Cinque, and copies were sold for $1.00 each to raise money for the African's eventual return home.[36] Prominent black abolitionists displayed Cinque's portrait in their homes, and William Wells Brown expressed his admiration by naming his daughter Cinque. Finally, the Court declared the Africans to be free, and on November 27, 1841 the thirty-five survivors of the fifty-three originally captured Africans left New York for Africa aboard the *Gentleman*.[37]

Just three weeks before the *Amistad* Africans returned to Africa, nineteen slaves being transported aboard the American ship *Creole* mutinied, killed a slave trader on board, wounded the captain, and captured the vessel. The leader of this rebellion was Madison Washington, a fugitive from Virginia who had been captured when he returned from Canada to free his wife. Once in control of the ship, the slaves forced the crew to sail to the Bahamas, hoping British authorities and the large black population might be sympathetic to their cause. The American consul demanded the slaves' return to the United States for trial, but British officials released the slaves after fifty boatloads of black Bahamians sailed to the *Creole* and threatened to free them by force if necessary.[38] News that the *Creole* mutineers were free in the Bahamas encouraged African Americans, and Madison Washington, "that bright star of freedom [who] took his station in the constellation of freedom," joined Joseph Cinque as a symbol of black manhood.[39]

Although African Americans often admired violence in defense of life, family, or freedom, their affection for their "beloved friend" Garrison remained. Yet, during the 1840s many were becoming increasingly disillusioned with the dogged racism even among white abolitionists and pressed for race-specific organizations freer from what seemed to be the restraints of integrated action. These controversial issues disclosed the political and philosophical differences among blacks. The *Colored American* issued a militant call for direct action, for a movement dedicated to "universal emancipation and universal enfranchisement" at all costs. "Should we die," read one editorial, "we will die virtuous martyrs in a holy cause." But the *Colored American* itself expired in 1841, publishing its last issue on Christmas Day.[40]

Left with no national standard save the fragmenting antislavery movement and an untested new national political party, some African Americans worked to rejuvenate the national conventions. In the *Liberator* in August of 1841, David Ruggles announced a convention to be held in New York to consider the condition of black people and to plot their best course of action. He raised the alarm against the "storm of colonization [which had] come upon our brethren in Maryland and threatens to visit us throughout this land." He appealed to the slaves, urging, "Rise brethren, rise! Strike for freedom or die slaves." Dismissing the Garrisonian emphasis on moral suasion, he ended his call saying, "In our cause, mere words are nothing—action is everything." Philadelphia blacks, hosts of the original convention, also called for a national meeting, but racial violence in the late summer of 1842 thwarted their plans. Finally, in the spring of 1843, New Yorkers announced that a national convention would meet in Buffalo in August. Philadelphia blacks, whose leadership was challenged by New York rivals, did not send a delegation. Additionally, perhaps, the militant New York call seemed at odds with their Garrisonian principles.[41] A month before the convention, Boston blacks, among the most committed Garrisonians, met at the Baptist church on Beacon Hill and denounced the proposed meeting for encouraging racial exclusivity. Despite strong opposition, Boston did send a delegation to the convention.[42] A gathering of New Bedford blacks also condemned the Buffalo meeting, expressing their support for Garrison's American Anti-Slavery Society.[43] The third party question was raised again in Buffalo. A resolution was offered that "it is the duty of every lover of liberty to vote the Liberty ticket so long as they are consistent to their principles." Douglass objected, arguing that no party could be trusted and that politics were "necessarily corrupt." He was supported by Remond and William Wells Brown. Garnet, Ray, and others from New York and Detroit spoke in support of the Liberty Party. The resolution that also condemned both the Whig and Democratic parties as proslavery and not deserving of black support finally carried.[44]

Garrisonians had been right in anticipating a militant 1843 convention. Samuel Davis of Buffalo, chair of the convention, had opened the meeting with a speech that set the tone. He did not want to discourage abolitionist friends, he said, but urged blacks not to wait for others to act. Using uprisings in Greece and Poland as illustrations of the need to strike for liberty, he asserted that "if we are not willing to rise up and assert our rightful claims, and plead our own cause, we have no reason to look for success."[45] In the afternoon of the convention's second day, Garnet gave a rousing address with militant echoes of David Walker's *Appeal*. Black people had been patient long enough, he proclaimed. They had waited for justice and liberty long enough. "We have hoped in vain. Years have rolled on, and tens of thousands have been borne on streams of blood and tears, to the shores of eternity." It was time for slaves to rise up and throw off their chains, he declared. Garnet urged slaves to refuse to be bound and to use violence if need be to defend their rights as free people. "You cannot suffer greater cruelties than you have already. Rather die freemen than live to be slaves."[46]

New York's Theodore S. Wright supported Garnet's position but Douglass, Remond, and other Garrisonians spoke against it, fearing that the resolution might expose blacks to retaliation from proslavery forces. Connecticut minister Amos Beman opposed the call for violence on moral grounds, saying "it had too much of the physical and not enough of the moral weapon about it."[47] The resolution failed by one vote, with mainly New York delegates providing its support, but the issue was debated again the next year at a meeting in Cortland, New York. Jemain Loguen, New York fugitive slave and a leader of the underground railroad in Syracuse, extended Garnet's argument, urging free blacks as well as slaves to fight for their rights. "Let blood flow without measure—until our rights are acknowledged or we [have] perished from the earth," he declared.[48]

African Americans saw the annexation of slaveholding Texas by the United States in 1845 and the outbreak of war with Mexico a year later as evidence of the expansion of slaveholders' power. When Texans had withdrawn from Mexico in 1836 to form an independent republic, the American Moral Reform Society had expressed opposition to its annexation, and the New York Vigilance Committee had circulated a petition denouncing it at the integrated Broadway Tabernacle.[49] Garnet had anticipated war with Mexico in his 1843 call for slave uprising, condemning the "propagators of American slavery [for] spending their blood and treasure, that they may plant the black flag in the heart of Mexico and riot in the halls of Montezuma."[50] When President James K. Polk asked Congress for a declaration of war against Mexico in 1846, Boston blacks expressed the general sentiment among African Americans by denouncing "any war which may be occasioned by the annexation of Texas, or . . . any other war . . . designed to strengthen or perpetuate slavery."[51] Sending

United States troops, including New England men, to fight and die in the Mexican War was a triumph for slave power, and Douglass scolded Massachusetts, "the brightest of every other state," for becoming "the tool of Texas."[52] When the war ended in the early spring of 1848, many blacks agreed with Douglass that those purporting to celebrate peace were actually rejoicing in the plunder of Mexico, since the war had been a hypocritical excuse to rob Mexico of her land.[53]

By the late-1840s slaveholding Texas was securely under the American flag, and new land had been added to the country in the Southwest, threatening to open another region to slavery. By the time of the national convention in 1847, the mood of many free blacks had grown pessimistic, angry, and decidedly more belligerent, and debate had shifted to resolutions urging black people to educate their sons in the "art of war." Those counseling patience, moral appeal, and faith in the power of truth still prevailed, but sentiment was clearly changing, and calls for violence as a means of dealing with the threat of kidnapping and with slavery became more common.[54] When the convention was held in Cleveland in 1848, a larger contingent of western black abolitionist leaders was able to attend. These western delegates included John Jones, a wealthy Chicago businessman, John Mercer Langston, his brother Charles Langston, and William H. Day of Ohio, Henry Bibb, fugitive slave and antislavery lecturer then residing in Michigan, and Pittsburgh newspaper editor and underground railroad activist Martin R. Delany. By the same token, the distance, and perhaps politics as well, prevented most of the New York and Pennsylvania leaders from attending.[55] The actions of this convention reflected a complex mix of Garrisonian and non-Garrisonian opinion, advocating moral suasion and women's rights on the one hand while endorsing the Free Soil Party on the other.[56] They also supported violent self-defense, authorizing the establishment of additional vigilance groups "so as to enable them to measure arms with assailants without and invaders within."[57] In 1849 a state convention of black Ohioans continued the militant stance and urged that "the slave . . . leave [the plantation] immediately with his hoe on his shoulder." They recommended the publication of five hundred copies of Walker's *Appeal* and Garnet's 1843 address on slave violence in a single volume.[58]

Frederick Douglass did not advocate slave rebellion, but now argued that slaves were justified in killing slaveholders. In the winter of 1849 he asked, "who dare say that the criminals deserve less than death at the hands of their long-abused chattels?"[59] His stand on the wisdom of black political involvement was also shifting. In the late 1840s the Liberty Party split between those who argued that their platform must remain focused on the single issue of antislavery, and those who believed that the party's future depended on its ability to attract a broader electorate by taking a stand on other contemporary issues like land distribution, tariff policy, and banking. This latter group met in Buffalo in June 1848, under the leadership of Gerrit Smith, calling itself the Liberty League or the National Liberty Party. This new political organization advocated such Garrisonian reforms as political rights for women, reforms that had split the abolition movement a decade before, but it also seemed to fulfill Garrison's prediction that politics would corrupt the antislavery movement by demanding too broad a platform in order to attract voters. Although abolition and women's rights were central to the program of the Liberty League, it also favored labor reform, the right of labor to organize, and the distribution of free public land in the territories. African Americans participated in the new party from the start. Garnet was a member of the business committee and spoke to the convention urging free blacks to shame slaveholders by being living examples of African Americans' abilities. He decried the fact that some blacks had voted for the Whig candidate Henry Clay instead of voting for the Liberty Party's James G. Birney. Douglass was also at this meeting in Buffalo, the first political convention he ever attended. Douglass insisted that he was still a loyal Garrisonian, but Garrison and other Garrisonians noted his presence at the convention disapprovingly.[60]

The relationship between white Garrisonians and Douglass had been strained for some time. Douglass was an effective and charismatic speaker from his first appearance on the lecture platform. With experience, exposure to the arguments of his fellow abolitionists, and travel in the United States and Europe, his presentations increased in intellectual sophistication. Experienced black abolitionists watched Douglass's development with admiration and some bemusement. In 1848 James McCune Smith commented on Douglass's writing, saying, "I love Frederick Douglas [sic] for his whole souled *outness*." Following his progress carefully, McCune Smith described Douglass as "one newly born among us. The church question, the school question, separate institutions," he observed, "are questions that he enters upon and argues about as our many but active young men thought about and argued about years ago, when we had Literary Societies."[61] Some white abolitionists worried that it was becoming more difficult for audiences to believe that Douglass was a fugitive slave. "Better have a little of the plantation manner of speech than not," he was told, "'tis not best that you seem too learned." They suggested that he confine himself to telling the slave's story simply and plainly. "Give us the facts," instructed one abolitionist, "we will take care of the philosophy."[62]

During Douglass's years of lecturing under the auspices of the American Anti-Slavery Society, the condescending attitude many white abolitionists displayed toward him changed very little. Proud of his accomplishments—having managed to negotiate treacherous financial arrangements as a young hired-out slave in Baltimore, having engineered his escape from slavery, and having supported a household and family with his labor as a fugitive slave—Douglass particularly resented Maria Weston Chapman's maternalistic oversight of his attitude and relation-

ships with other lecturers from her position as the manager of the antislavery office in Boston. He complained bitterly about inequities in pay
for black antislavery agents, and resented having to send Chapman
entreaties for money to support his wife while he was literally risking his
life on the antislavery platform in the West. Finally, when the publication
of his autobiography in 1845 placed him in greater jeopardy of being
captured and he was forced to leave the country, Douglass met what he
considered the final indignities from his American antislavery sponsors.[63]

On his arrival in Great Britain in the fall of 1845, Douglass spent a
month with a family in Ireland and reported that for the first time in his
life he was living in a setting free from racial prejudice. It was undoubtedly this new experience that made him especially irritable and impatient
with Nantucket Quaker James Buffum, his traveling companion for the
British lecture tour, when Maria Chapman put Buffum in charge of the
money. Douglass's new-found freedom and Chapman's determination to
maintain control of him led to an angry exchange of letters between
them with his threatening to resign from the American Anti-Slavery
Society rather than tolerate her condescension. Douglass considered settling permanently in Great Britain, but his family could not be persuaded.
Despite his differences with the white Garrisonians in Boston, he and
Garrison were still on good terms; they shared the speakers' stage in England and Scotland during the summer and fall of 1846. When British
friends formally purchased Douglass's freedom in December 1846 so that
he could more safely return home, it raised a storm of protest among the
Boston abolitionists who argued it was a violation of their principles and
a tacit recognition of slaveholders' rights, but Garrison supported Douglass and acknowledged the practical necessity of the arrangement. Douglass was affronted when some white abolitionists argued that as a free
man he would lose the moral power of a fugitive risking his freedom to
speak against slavery. It soon became clear that his appeal as an antislavery speaker was undiminished. When he returned to the United States
and appeared on the platform at the annual meeting of the American
Anti-Slavery Society in New York City on May 11, 1847, the crowd clam-
ored to hear him speak, drowning out Garrison's words of introduction.
That summer he and Garrison toured together in the West, but their
relationship was strained, and a short time later when Douglass
announced his plans to establish a newspaper, the Garrisonians tried to
dissuade him. They urged him not to found a newspaper because, they
argued, it would interfere with his antislavery lecturing. Although Garrison himself remained on the periphery of this controversy, he expressed
the concern that as an editor Douglass's special talent as a speaker would
be lost to the movement.[64]

Later that year Douglass moved to Rochester, New York and established a newspaper called the *North Star*, naming it after the celestial light
guiding slaves toward freedom. With this act, Douglass established his

independence from Garrison, the man who had been his mentor and the primary influence on his antislavery career. The ambivalent break between them was wrenching and tempered by admiration. Garrison treated Douglass's assertion of independence much like filial betrayal, and the gradual rupture of their relationship was not a repudiation on either side. The masthead of the *North Star* echoed the philosophy and the masthead of Garrison's *Liberator*, declaring, "Right is of no Sex—Truth is of no Color—God is the Father of us all, and we are all Brethren."[65] African Americans, including Garrisonians, rallied to support Douglass's new venture, and black women conducted a fair to raise money for his paper. Philadelphia's Sarah Mapps Douglass proclaimed Douglass's "talents and correct principles" worthy of "respect and confidence." "Sustain him," she urged, "because it is RIGHT to do so."[66]

In western New York Douglass was farther from the centers of Garrisonianism and within the sphere of the political abolitionists who were gathering strength during this time. Even in Boston some blacks held meetings to discuss establishing an auxiliary to the Liberty Party, justifying their involvement by arguing that African Americans must use every means, both moral and political, to fight against slavery. Meanwhile Garrison became ever more adamant in his denunciation of the churches and the federal government for their refusal to proscribe slavery. He burned copies of the Constitution, claiming that it was not worthy of respect because it accepted and protected slavery, and argued that free states should withdraw from the union with slaveholders. Blacks were reluctant to give up their claim to the Constitution and continued to use its words, especially the preamble, to argue for freedom and equality and to demand that America live up to its constitutional claims. There was one point of agreement between Garrisonians and political abolitionists—although African Americans were unwilling to concede the rights of slaveholders under the principles of the Constitution, most agreed that the Constitution was not protecting black rights. New York's Thomas Van Renselear attempted to resolve this dilemma by asserting that, unlike Garrison, "we do not wish to tear up anything," but proposing that so long as the government and the Constitution ignored black rights, blacks should in turn ignore them.[67]

Charles Lenox Remond stood closer to Garrison's call for disunion, reasoning that if the Constitution as the fundamental law of the land did not include blacks, then blacks should refuse to abide by American law. In 1841 Remond had anticipated Henry David Thoreau's 1845 "Civil Disobedience" and argued that African Americans should be willing to go to jail rather than pay taxes to institutions that discriminated against them. "Let our motto be—No privileges, no pay."[68] A few years later the Supreme Court's Prigg decision pushed the radical abolitionists farther along the path to disunion, and the American Anti-Slavery Society proclaimed, "LET THE CONSTITUTION PERISH."[69] During the society's

next meeting in 1844, Garrison declared, "NO UNION WITH SLAVE-
HOLDERS." Black leadership was split on this issue, with Remond and
most Boston blacks, Robert Purvis and many Philadelphia blacks, William Wells Brown and Frederick Douglass all supporting Garrison's position. New York blacks led by James McCune Smith, Cornish, and others
opposed disunion and refused to agree to the interpretation of the Constitution as a slaveholder's document. Remond and Smith clashed at the
1844 AASS meeting over this issue, and Douglass defended Garrison's
critique of the Constitution at the 1848 Liberty League convention.
Although Douglass remained convinced that in its original intent, "the
one given to it by the men who framed it, those who adopted it and . . . by
the Supreme Court of the United States," it was a slaveholders document. Within a year of the convention he wrote, "I am satisfied that if
strictly 'construed according to its reading' [the Constitution] is not a
pro-slavery instrument."[70]

For two years Frederick Douglass studied the questions of the Constitution and disunion and discussed them with abolitionists like Gerrit
Smith, William Goodell, and others from New York State. He pondered
the arguments of James McCune Smith, Samuel Ringgold Ward, and
other black abolitionist leaders. He considered the contention that the
Fifth Amendment guaranteed that no person could "be deprived of life,
liberty, or property without due process of law." Finally, at the May meeting of the American Anti-Slavery Society in 1851, he expressed his position. When longtime Garrisonian Samuel J. May suggested that the
Liberty Party Paper be placed on the society's recommended list, Garrison
objected on the grounds that the society should endorse only newspapers
supporting disunion. Douglass then rose to say that his *North Star* should
not be on the list because he "had arrived at the firm conviction that the
Constitution, construed in the light of well established rules of legal
interpretation, might be made consistent in its details with the noble purposes avowed in its preamble."[71] Thus, he contended, it might well be
called on to condemn slavery and to protect the rights of all Americans,
and the ballot could be a step toward full equality. He went on to appeal to
every "American citizen, whose conscience permits so to do, to use his
political as well as his moral power for [slavery's] overthrow." Garrison was
stunned and cried, "There is a roguery somewhere"; Douglass had made
the break public and had become a supporter of political antislavery.[72]

Events during the 1840s had driven many free blacks from nonresistance to militant rhetoric, and this trend accelerated in the next decade.
From the beginning of the 1850s, abolitionists and free blacks felt
assaulted. In the fall, President Millard Fillmore, a native of Buffalo,
New York who was formerly identified with antislavery, signed into law
the strictest fugitive slave measure ever enacted.[73] The law was so harsh
that the president himself had doubts about its constitutionality. It was
part of a broad compromise calculated by northern moderate and conser-

vative politicians to assure the southern states that the federal government would protect their human property. In this way, they hoped to quiet mounting sectional tensions.[74] The new law allowed slaveholders to more easily reach into any state to retrieve their runaways, and an accused fugitive need no longer be brought before a court. A slaveholder or his representative could simply present an affidavit with a physical description of the runaway from a court in his home state, and federal commissioners could turn over any black person presumed to be that slave.[75]

The new law also empowered federal marshals to compel bystanders to assist in the capture of a fugitive "when necessary to ensure a faithful observance of the . . . Constitution." There were stiff fines and imprisonment for those who obstructed the application of the law.[76] Furthermore, federal funds were provided to pay a substantial portion of the cost of recovering a fugitive. Fugitives were denied the right to speak in their own defense, no provision was made for habeas corpus, and counsels or jury trials were not required. Officials had incentive to find in favor of the slaveholder, as they were paid ten dollars if the accused was determined to be a fugitive but only five dollars if not.[77] This was a significant expansion of the 1793 fugitive law, and it made free blacks more vulnerable to kidnapping.[78]

The Compromise of 1850 also included the admission of California as a free state and the abolition of the slave trade in the District of Columbia. The necessity for this compromise and its fugitive slave law could be seen as evidence of the effectiveness of antislavery agitation and abolitionist resistance to southern attempts to reclaim fugitives, but African Americans' overwhelming reaction to them was anger. Throughout the North blacks held meetings to protest the law "so wicked, so atrocious, so utterly at variance with the principles of the Constitution."[79] They vowed never to allow fugitives to be taken from the North. "If the American revolutionaries had excuse for shedding one drop of blood," they declared, "then have the American slaves for making blood flow 'even unto the horsebridles.'"[80] In Chicago, abolitionist sentiment was strong; the Common Council denounced the law as unconstitutional, calling its supporters traitors. They refused to require the city police to assist in the arrest of fugitives.[81] In Boston, Douglass warned that if authorities attempted to enforce the fugitive slave law, the streets "would be running with blood." A broadside entitled "Read and Ponder the Fugitive Slave Law" reprinted the law prefaced by a condemnation of both the law and Massachusetts politicians who voted for it.[82]

It did not take long to test the resistance. On November 1, 1850, the *Liberator* reported "the appearance of two prowling villains . . . from Macon, Georgia, for the purpose of seizing William and Ellen Craft, under the infernal Fugitive Slave Bill, and carrying them back to the hell of Slavery."[83] Since their escape two years before, the Crafts had traveled the antislavery circuit telling their story and relating the horrors of slavery to audiences throughout the North. In Boston they had stayed at the home of Lewis Hayden, a fugitive from Kentucky who was active in the underground. It was there that they were tracked down by agents of their Georgia owner. The slave catchers obtained warrants for the fugitives' arrest but had trouble finding an officer who would serve them.

Boston's black community and white abolitionists, including a vigilance committee with over 100 members, went into action. They covered the city with signs alerting all friends of liberty to the presence of slave hunters. Local authorities arrested the southern men several times, charging them with slander against William Craft and conspiracy to kidnap him. Black Bostonians met to plan their strategy, vowing not to allow fugitives to be taken from the city. Hayden placed explosives on the front porch of his home, where William was hiding, and threatened to blow up the house and anyone who entered in pursuit of the fugitive. Convinced that recapturing the Crafts would be nearly impossible, the slave catchers left the city. It was clear, however, that the Crafts were only temporarily safe, and they were sent to England to continue their antislavery work.[84]

The next test of Boston blacks' ability to prevent the enforcement of the fugitive slave law came a short time later that winter. In February 1851 two white men charged Shadrach, a man working as a waiter at Taft's Cornhill Coffee House, with being a fugitive from Virginia named Fred Wilkins. The deputy marshal served a warrant and brought Wilkins before the commissioner. Wilkins's legal defense was interrupted when black abolitionist lawyer Robert Morris threw open the doors to the hearing room, admitting a crowd of blacks who surrounded the fugitive, rushed him from the building, and placed him in a carriage for his escape from the city. Shadrach found safe haven in Montreal, Canada, while Morris and Hayden were tried for their part in the rescue. The all-white jury, sympathetic to antislavery, fulfilled southerners' fears. Neither Morris nor Hayden was convicted. Indeed, it was later revealed that at least one juror, a blacksmith from Concord named Francis Edwin Bigelow, had actually been involved in Shadrach's escape.[85]

As part of the attempt to prevent a widened sectional conflict, the enforcement of the fugitive slave law had national significance. Henry Clay of Kentucky, 1844 Whig Party presidential candidate, considered slave rescues a threat to the rule of law and to the government itself.[86] Mississippi's Jefferson Davis believed the law was useless, since it could not be enforced in the North. Illinois Democrat Stephen A. Douglas saw evidence of a widespread abolitionist conspiracy centered in the dangerously radical city of Boston; the secretary of state called Shadrach's rescue, "an act of clear treason."[87] The strength of their reaction testified to the impact of abolitionist direct action. The federal government became more determined to enforce the law, both to assert its authority over the abolitionist underground and to convince the South that it could do so.

Boston remained a hotbed of antislavery action throughout the 1850s, although not all rescue attempts were successful. Thomas Sims was captured and returned to Georgia in 1851 despite abolitionist efforts. The show of force that prevented his rescue cost the government at least $2,400. It had a significant impact on Boston abolition, leading some blacks to flee the city and others to arm themselves "offensively."[88] The battle between federal power and the abolitionists, sometimes supported by state and local authority, was fought on the streets of many northern towns and cities. Shortly after the Sims's defeat in Boston, fugitive Jerry McHenry was arrested in Syracuse. Since the Liberty Party was holding its convention in the city at the time, the streets were full of antislavery reformers. In the first attempt to rescue McHenry, he was retaken by the authorities, but then a large crowd stormed the jail, overwhelmed the police, secured his freedom once again, and sent him on his way to Canada. Gerrit Smith, Jarmain Loguen, and Samuel Riggold Ward were part of the crowd that saved McHenry. Although Smith believed that the fugitive slave law might eventually be declared unconstitutional and McHenry freed, he favored the rescue for its propaganda value. The government indicted twelve blacks and fourteen whites for participating in the rescue. Most of the blacks escaped to Canada, and all of the whites were either acquitted or had their charges dismissed. Only one rescuer was convicted, a black man, Enoch Reed, who became a symbol of the government's feeble effort to save face.[89]

After Reed's trial, Gerrit Smith and other abolitionists brought charges against the deputy marshal who had arrested McHenry, claiming the arrest was illegal because the fugitive slave law was unconstitutional. At the trial before the state supreme court, Smith made his argument—holding forth for seven hours—but in the end the law was declared constitutional. Nevertheless, the trial focused public attention on the antislavery argument and continued the discussion of slavery's injustices. The Jerry Rescue was commemorated in Syracuse each year for the rest of the decade.[90]

Perhaps the strongest influence on northern public opinion came a short time later when Harriet Beecher Stowe published her wildly successful novel *Uncle Tom's Cabin* in 1852. Stowe came from a family with evangelical moderate antislavery credentials. Her story of slave life reflected these roots and touched the hearts of her readers. Demand was so great that over a million copies had been published by the following year. Stowe's triumph was followed in 1853 by the publication of a slave narrative which eerily echoed parts of her novel. Set in the same Red River Valley of Louisiana, it was a "strange history," as Frederick Douglass wrote, and "its truth [was] far greater than fiction." *Twelve Years A Slave* was the story of the kidnapping, enslavement, and eventual release from slavery of Solomon Northup. The letter Northup smuggled to his wife had reached her, but she had no idea how or where to look for him until twelve years later.[91]

Northup had nearly managed to communicate with her a few years before, but after waiting for nine years for an opportunity to possess a piece of paper and laboriously making ink with which to write on it, he had been betrayed and had to destroy the letter he had written. A few years later, in 1852, Northup carefully cultivated an acquaintance with Samuel Bass, a carpenter working on the plantation. Bass was a widely traveled Canadian, tolerated as a kind eccentric with locally unpopular opinions, particularly on the issue of slavery. When Northup finally warily confided his real identity, Bass miraculously took it as his mission to help Northup regain his freedom. Bass wrote letters to people Northup had known in Saratoga; Anne Northup was informed, affidavits were sworn, the governor of New York, a senator from Louisiana, and a Supreme Court justice were enlisted. Finally in January 1853, officials from New York and Louisiana confronted Northup's owner, and Northup was freed to return to his family. Northup's story caused a sensation. When he published his narrative that year, dedicating it to Harriet Beecher Stowe, it sold 8,000 copies within a month. Douglass clearly identified with Northup's tale. "Think of it!" Douglass wrote in his review. "For thirty years *a man*, with all a man's hopes, fears, and aspirations . . . then for twelve years *a thing*, a chattel personal, classed with mules and horses . . . torn from his home and family."[92]

Slave narratives like Douglass's and Northup's were powerful tools in the abolitionists' effort to enlist people in the fight against slavery. Called by Ralph Waldo Emerson the first truly American literary genre, over fifty such narratives were published between 1815 and 1865. *Uncle Tom's Cabin*, the personal tales of former slaves both in print and in person, antislavery conventions, rescues and attempted rescues of fugitive slaves all contributed to northern empathy with the slaves and a growing antislavery sentiment.[93]

Captures of fugitives continued, and many slaves were taken back to the South, but there were also a number of successful rescues, in small communities as well as large cities. Slaveholders observing these events believed that abolitionism had captured the North; this perception further weakened southern faith in the federal government's ability to protect their right to human property. A few especially dramatic incidents had reinforced southerners' skepticism. In 1851, on a farm in Christiana, Pennsylvania in Lancaster County, a local vigilance group headed by a former slave and farmhand, William Parker, had killed a Maryland slaveholder and badly wounded his son when they attempted to recover a fugitive. Although thirty-one blacks and five whites were arrested and charged with treason, murder, and riot, none had been convicted.[94] In 1854, Missouri fugitive Joshua Glover was arrested in Racine, Wisconsin but was freed when 100 men arrived by steamboat from Milwaukee and broke into the jail where he was being held. As in many other cases, the fugitive escaped to Canada and the rescuers were never punished. The only exception in this case was Sherman Booth who paid a fine and spent ten months in jail.[95]

Although there were abolitionist triumphs, their forces also suffered some disappointing defeats. In the same year as Glover's arrest, Anthony Burns, an escaped slave from Virginia, was seized in Boston. Burns's arrest triggered massive organization, mass protest, and an attack on the court-house that left one federal marshal dead, but Burns was returned to slavery. En route to the ship that would take him south, Burns walked through Boston streets lined with people, between buildings displaying American flags hung upside-down, and shop windows draped in black, passing under a large coffin labeled "Liberty." A regiment of infantry troops with orders to fire into the crowd if necessary guarded every inter-section, and another contingent of troops guarded Burns himself. Yet this was not a complete victory for the fugitive slave law. Already shifting opinion took on new antislavery militancy after Burns's return. Douglass posed the question, "Is It Right and Wise to Kill a Kidnapper?" and answered by saying that the federal officer slain defending slavery against abolitionist forces had "forfeited his right to live" when he took on the "revolting business of kidnapping." Douglass expressed the sentiments of more and more community members when he declared that every "slave-hunter who meets a bloody death in his infernal business is an argument in favor of the manhood of our race."[96] Even Charles Lenox Remond, though still a Garrisonian, was candidly proud to see so many black men take an assertive and manly stance, arming themselves and risking death for the freedom of a fugitive.

Although much obvious proslavery sentiment remained, black aboli-tionists in the East were also encouraged by the apparent change in northern opinion reflected in actions against the fugitive slave law by racially integrated groups. During the decade of the 1850s, although the vast majority of captured fugitive slaves were returned to slavery, each of the over eighty well-publicized fugitive slave rescues and attempted res-cues seemed to increase the strength of northern antislavery sentiment.[97]

In the West abolition was not only integrated, but it was increasingly armed and on the offensive. By the early 1850s, thousands of whites and hundreds of blacks had flocked to the West, seeking their fortunes in the goldfields of California and looking for opportunity and adventure.[98] Increased settlement encouraged plans for a transcontinental railroad linking eastern cities and the western frontier, plans which reopened the question of slavery in the western territories. Early in 1854, Senator Stephen A. Douglas of Illinois introduced the Kansas-Nebraska Act, cal-culated to open the lands west of Iowa to development and to ensure that Chicago would become the eastern end of a northern railway route across the West. Believing in a democratic solution to the problem of slavery, and also perhaps to gain southern support for a potential bid for the presidency, Douglas provided for popular sovereignty on the slavery issue, a measure that would effectively cancel the Missouri Compromise of 1820 prohibiting slavery above the northern border of Missouri, by allowing settlers themselves to decide whether or not to allow slaveholding.

The Kansas-Nebraska bill passed Congress in the spring, and it quickly sparked the organization of abolitionist societies for the settlement of the western territory and a reorganization of the political landscape. A broad coalition of groups opposed to slavery's extension met in July 1854 to form the Republican Party. This party brought together Conscience Whigs,[99] northern Democrats, who bristled at overriding the Missouri Compromise, political abolitionists from the virtually defunct Liberty Party, many antislavery Freesoilers, and an assortment of reformers including the anti-immigrant, anti-Catholic Know-Nothings. In the halls of Congress, the political debates over slavery became more bellicose. In May 1856, South Carolina Congressman Preston S. Brooks attacked and beat Massachusetts Senator Charles Sumner on the floor of the Senate chamber in retaliation for Sumner's "Crime Against Kansas" speech which condemned "slave power" in general and South Carolina Senator Andrew P. Butler (Brooks's relative) in particular.[100]

African Americans, with few practical political alternatives, cautiously supported the Republican Party. In 1856, a meeting of black Bostonians, Garrisonians among them, resolved to support John C. Fremont, Republican candidate for president, but their position was clear. "We do not pledge ourselves to go further with the Republicans," they declared, "than the Republicans will go with us."[101] Delegates to conventions held in New York and Ohio encouraged African Americans to support the Republicans on the grounds that a Democratic victory would be a disaster for all black people. It was clearly a practical choice. As one delegate from New York put it, "we do not for a single moment endorse all the political tenets of that party."[102]

In the West proslavery and antislavery groups used military force in clashes for the control of the territory of Kansas. Abolitionist John Brown, one of his sons, and his son-in-law entered the territory in the fall of 1854, and for the next two years Brown led battles against proslavery Missourians who crossed into Kansas. In letters to Frederick Douglass, he expressed optimism that antislavery would carry the day. Brown was called Captain of the Liberty Guards and "Old Ossawatomie," after a losing battle that his troops fought against a superior force in August of 1856. Despite misgivings over his execution of five slavery supporters at Pottawatomie Creek in the spring of 1856, he was a heroic figure in some antislavery circles.[103]

Willingness to consider violent antislavery strategies greatly increased after the Supreme Court dealt abolition a stunning blow with its ruling in 1857 in the case of Dred Scott. Scott, born a slave in Virginia, claimed his freedom after living for years outside the South with his master, a military man stationed in Illinois and in Wisconsin Territory where slavery was prohibited. The case passed through state and local courts and finally reached the Supreme Court where Chief Justice Roger B. Taney issued a ruling that greatly distressed African Americans and their allies. Taney concluded that Scott remained a slave and added that Congress had no right to legislate against slavery in the western territories, effectively declaring the Missouri Compromise of 1820 unconstitutional. Even more disturbing, Taney declared that blacks had no citizenship rights under the Constitution. Despite their service in the Revolution that won America's freedom and in the War of 1812 that reinforced and defended it, no matter that they voted in New England and with qualifications elsewhere, and regardless of the fact that many blacks held American passports, Taney proclaimed that black people had never been, were not, and could never be citizens of the United States. They had "no rights which the white man was bound to respect."[104]

The decision and Taney's opinion infuriated African Americans. They had faced increasing attacks on their rights for the entire decade and were then told by the highest court in the land that they had no rights. Standing before a Philadelphia protest meeting in the spring of 1857, just one month after the decision, Charles Lenox Remond expressed the rage that so many felt. "We owe no allegiance to a country which grinds us under its iron heel and treats us like dogs. The time has gone by for colored people to talk of patriotism."[105] At a New York meeting chaired by Garrison, Douglass continued to contend that the Constitution was a document that could be used to attack slavery. "As a man, an American, a citizen, a colored man of both Anglo-Saxon and African descent," Douglass argued, "I denounce the representation as a most scandalous and devilish perversion of the Constitution, and a brazen mis-statement of the facts of history."[106] Robert Purvis disagreed, "I assert that the Constitution is fitting and befitting those who made it—slaveholders and their abettors." Furthermore, he proclaimed that the federal government "in its formation and essential structure as well as its practice, is one of the basest, meanest, most atrocious despotisms that ever saw the face of the sun." Praising the antislavery society leading a new revolution against this despotism, Purvis continued, "I rejoice . . . that there is a prospect of this atrocious government being overthrown and a better one built up in its place."[107] In the aftermath of the Dred Scott decision, some blacks left the United States for Canada, but others redoubled their determination to stay and fight for the rights that the court had refused to recognize.

The intensified federal reaction to another rescue indicated that the government took the abolitionists' threats seriously. In the fall of 1858, John Price, a fugitive from Kentucky living in notoriously antislavery Oberlin, Ohio, was captured and taken to Wellington to await a train for the South. A large group of college students and townspeople from Oberlin followed them. According to one observer, "it seemed as though every male in Oberlin, white and black was racing to Wellington . . . intent on saving John Price."[108] They overtook the party at the Wadsworth Hotel in Wellington, surrounded the building, and demanded Price's return. The captors brought Price out on a balcony to address the crowd, to convince them that he was a slave being returned lawfully, but the group was intent on the rescue regardless of whether or not Price was a slave. John Copeland, a black Oberlin student, pointed a gun at one of the Kentuckians and told Price to jump from the balcony, but before he could fire, the fugitive was moved inside the hotel. Charles Langston attempted without success to negotiate with the police, and finally the crowd rushed the hotel, confronted the captors, and took Price back to Oberlin and eventually on to Canada. Abolitionists considered this a victory over the fugitive slave law and the administration of Democratic President James Buchanan who had been elected in 1856, but the affair did not end there. Unlike many previous cases, thirty-seven people, "from snowy white to sooty," were indicted for their roles in the rescue. Twelve were black— three fugitive slaves; six, including Charles Langston, former slaves; three, including carpenter and former Oberlin student John Copeland, freeborn. At least twenty spent time in jail, two were convicted and fined, and it was almost a year before legal negotiations freed all the rescuers from jail. Yet the intense popular reaction and widespread resistance made it clear that the federal success was only partial. At his trial, Langston's impassioned speech denouncing the unjust law brought cheers from those in the courtroom. The convictions of two of the Wellington rescuers occasioned mass meetings in Cleveland and other northern cities. Martyrs to the cause of antislavery, their heroes' welcome in Oberlin on their release from jail included a parade and a ceremony with speeches and songs that lasted well into the night.[109]

The proslavery federal attack on African-American rights also revived black interest in African emigration. The idea had never completely disappeared, and, despite strong and widespread opposition to the American Colonization Society, small numbers of black settlers had been transported to Liberia throughout the antebellum period. Liberia had become an independent nation in July 1847, and this made it more attractive. Although most blacks had chosen to remain in America demanding full citizenship, many were growing impatient.[110] The political and legal setbacks of the 1850s had an especially profound impact on black attitudes. Southern free blacks were apparently leaving the South in numbers large enough to worry state and local officials, prompting actions to discourage their emigration. In 1856 the Savannah City Council levied a $200 tax on each free black who emigrated and used the money raised, according to the mayor, "to prevent any further shipments of Negroes from this port to Liberia."[111] To further discourage emigration, any evidence of hardship in the Liberian colony received wide circulation in the southern press, and any black speaker who could relate firsthand stories of such hardships was supported and encouraged.[112]

Still, southern free blacks and a growing number of northern blacks remained interested in West Africa, especially in the region of the Niger Valley. Although letters from emigrants told of hardships, hard work, and even warfare with native Africans, many ended as did Seaborn Evans's from Greenville, Sinoe County, Liberia in 1856: "So I must say on the hole [sic], that I am much pleased with my new home. This is the place for a free black man to bring up his children."[113] New emigrants were attracted by the lectures and writings of Thomas Jefferson Bowen, a Baptist missionary who had lived in that region, which stressed the positive aspects of emigration and the advantages that awaited those adventurous enough to make the trip.[114]

One prominent leader who changed his position on emigration in response to the events of the 1850s was Henry Highland Garnet. During the previous decade, Garnet had announced that although he hated America's sins, particularly slavery, "America is my home, my country and I have no other." In the summer of 1858, Garnet launched the emigrationist African Civilization Society.[115] At a meeting in Philadelphia, he engaged Douglass in public debate on the wisdom of emigration and dispatched agents to explore West and Central Africa looking for settlement possibilities. Very different from the American Colonization Society, the African Civilization Society was organized and operated by blacks whose interest in emigration was based on a militant indictment of the American society that tolerated and protected slaveholding.

Martin R. Delany, like Garnet, also made the conversion from his earlier anti-emigration stand and by the late 1850s was a strong black nationalist. Under the auspices of emigrants in the Chatham settlement in Canada, Delany organized a competing African expedition to the Niger Valley.[116] Yet, even in the 1850s, Garnet, Delany, and their followers were not simply racial separatists. Like most African Americans, they were searching for the liberty that was the philosophical foundation of America. As emigrationists, however, they had given up the hope that America's promise would be fulfilled for people of color. Garnet and Delany accepted financial support from whites, but both were concerned with black self-determination and insisted on black control of policymaking within the society.[117] Garnet and many other emigrationist leaders were ministers, and they approached African settlement with a missionary zeal, hoping to bring Christianity and western civilization to Africans as they provided opportunities for settlers from America.[118]

These aims did not meet with universal acclaim; indeed, opposition was strong and often vehement. When in 1860 Boston minister John Sella Martin and Garnet addressed a black gathering in New York's Zion Church, arguing that American blacks might speed the modernization of Africa, disagreements resulted in a fist fight, and Garnet was forced to hold "controlled" meetings thereafter.[119] In addition to disagreements over the advisability of African emigration, there were some philosophical differences as well. A few exceptional individuals with personal knowledge were less likely to take such a paternalistic approach. William Craft, the abolitionist and fugitive slave who lived in Dahomey in West Africa for a number of years, believed that those who planned for African-American settlement in Africa did so without appreciating the culture and society of native Africans. It was ignorance, he believed, that led black and white Americans to assume that Africans were uncivilized; Christianity was doomed in Africa until Christians understood African culture and respected African traditions.[120] The new emphasis on African emigration also had a commercial component reminiscent of that which inspired Paul Cuffe two generations earlier. The dream was to expand trade between West Africa, Europe, and America by producing cotton grown with free labor in Africa to replace slave-grown American cotton. It was hoped this would generate revenue for the colony and drive American slavery out of business.[121]

As it had in earlier decades, emigrationist attention turned to other areas besides Africa. Small groups of blacks had continued to move to Canada and by the 1850s towns like Chatham, St. Catharines and Hamilton in Ontario and cities like Toronto and Montreal had sizable black populations. There were even growing black communities on Canada's Pacific coast. Some of Canada's most prominent black immigrants from America encouraged others to follow. In the pages of her newspaper *Provincial Freeman*, black editor Mary Ann Shadd Cary urged African Americans to find a new home in Canada. "Your national ship is rotten and sinking," she contended, "Why not leave it?"[122] Mary Ann Shadd had come north from Philadelphia in 1851, opened a school for blacks in Windsor, published a guide to Canada for fugitives, and become one of Canada's best-known abolitionist speakers. In 1856 she married black Toronto businessman Thomas J. Cary, and by then was a committed Canadian emigrationist. Most blacks were aware that Canada was no black utopia. Discrimination was omnipresent, and although small black communities might be tolerated, any assertion of black political, social, or economic power met with familiar hostility.

By the end of the 1850s, Haiti, not Canada, stood as the central alternative to Africa as a haven for African Americans. In 1858 the Haitian government renewed the offer of settlement to black American emigrants made decades before, and in 1859 a revolution brought in a new Haitian government with an even stronger invitation. Some African Americans were attracted by the Haytian Bureau of Emigration, especially after British abolitionist James Redpath opened its Boston office the following year with a $20,000 grant from the Haitian government. Even Douglass, who continued to oppose emigration, was forced to admit that "things in Hayti certainly do look at the present moment rather inviting to a certain class of our colored friends," although he was uncertain how long they would remain so.[123] Haiti was attractive to Douglass much as it was to other blacks partly because it was close to the United States, "where we are still within hearing distance of the wails of our brothers and sisters in bonds."[124] But emigrating to Haiti was not running away from the problems of slavery and race in America. Haiti continued to be the symbol of the possibility for black power in the hemisphere, a strong argument for racial equality, and a potential force for antislavery.

Emigration movements expressed the anger and discouragement of many African Americans, yet black opposition to emigration remained strong throughout the antebellum period. A convention of New England blacks in 1859 resolved that

> we deem it fit and proper to express our well-considered and full determined opposition to any concerted effort looking to the migration of the colored people to Africa, or any where else, from their native land: whether under the auspices of the American Colonization Society, the African Civilization Society, or any of their colonizing auxiliaries.[125]

The most common response among African Americans to the federal assaults of the 1850s was an even greater commitment to liberty and equality. The passage of the Fugitive Slave Law of 1850 and the intense reaction to the Dred Scott decision encouraged a black military association movement with its call for military preparedness. In 1855 Boston blacks petitioned the Massachusetts legislature to charter a black military company, and when their petition was rejected, they formed the Massasoit Guard without state sanction.[126] In November 1857, after the Dred Scott decision was announced, the Guard, armed and in full uniform, paraded through the streets of Boston.[127] At a state meeting of Massachusetts blacks in 1858, Boston's Robert Morris called for blacks to stand together against federal proslavery attack, saying, "If any man comes here to New Bedford and they try to take [any fugitive] away, you telegraph us in Boston, and we'll come down 300 strong, and stay with you; and we won't go until he's safe."[128]

In Cincinnati, African Americans formed the Attucks Guards, and Ohio blacks demanded that racial restrictions be removed from the state militia so they might take up arms in readiness for the fight they were sure was coming between the forces of freedom and the supporters of slavery. The Ohio convention of 1857 resolved that independent military companies should be established where blacks were denied their places in the state militia.[129] In New York, African Americans also called one of their units the Attucks Guards. In the large cities and smaller towns of the North, blacks readied themselves for self-defense and anticipated war. "Captain" J. J. Simmons of the New York unit prophesied that the time would soon come when northern black military units would be called to march through the South with "a bible in one hand and a gun in the other."[130]

Slavery had become the nation's central political issue. When Abraham Lincoln, railroad lawyer and moderate Republican, challenged Stephen A. Douglas for his Senate seat in 1858, their positions on slavery and on the Dred Scott ruling were the critical factors. Douglas accepted Taney's decision, while Lincoln argued that the ruling was a misreading of the intent of the framers of the Declaration of Independence. While acknowledging that the founders did not mean to "declare all men equal in all respects," Lincoln did believe they recognized the right of all men to basic liberty. He argued that they placed it in the Declaration, not because it was practical for their time, "but, for future use." Douglas and the Democrats referred derisively to the Republicans as "black Republicans," charging them with seeking to promote black equality. Republicans argued that keeping the West free of slavery would preserve it for free white labor and condemned the Dred Scott decision, calling it part of the "Slave Power Conspiracy" to subvert the federal government and extend slavery into all parts of the West.[131] Lincoln walked a fine line, condemning slavery and arguing for black rights without seeming to support race mixing. "Now I protest against the counterfeit logic," he declared, "which concludes that, because I do not want a black woman for a slave I must necessary want her for a wife."[132] Seven debates took the candidates thousands of miles crisscrossing the state of Illinois. Lincoln discussed the immorality of slavery, while Douglas focused only on the politics of the institution.[133]

Blacks could not vote in Illinois, and so could do little to prevent Lincoln's defeat, but in New York propertied blacks could vote, and they faced a difficult choice. In the gubernatorial contest, they could either support the Republican, Edwin D. Morgan, or support Gerrit Smith who was running on the Radical Abolitionist ticket. At a meeting in Troy, black New Yorkers debated their options—voting their hearts by supporting Smith and his party, though he had no real chance of success, or casting more practical and perhaps critical votes for the Republicans. A resolution advocating support for the Republicans was hotly debated and finally passed, although many like Garnet asked that "their name [not be] identified with it." Despite their differences, New York blacks helped elect the Republican to the governor's chair.[134]

Although Republican gains in 1858 changed the political prospects for abolition, it was direct and violent action that moved America toward the national conflict which so many blacks expected. By early 1858, John Brown had left the Kansas territory, was boarding with Frederick Douglass in Rochester, and was working on a constitution for a state in exile he planned to establish in Canada. Brown envisioned this as a preliminary step to striking against slavery on its home ground and establishing a province of freed slaves. A few years before he had managed to secure the secret financial backing of a small group of prominent New England and New York white abolitionists—Samuel Gridley Howe, George L. Stearns, Theodore Parker, Franklin Sanborn, Thomas Wentworth Higginson, and Gerrit Smith. Brown also enlisted the aid of many black reformers who sometimes doubted the wisdom of his plans but supported him nonetheless. He stayed with Douglass, black businessman and Chicago activist John Jones, Brooklyn minister James Gloucester, Philadelphia lumber dealer Stephen Smith, and other black reformers as he traveled across the North raising money and enlisting black support. In a secret meeting in Chatham, Ontario attended by thirty-five black men and twelve white men on May 8, 1858, blacks expressed their support for Brown's plans. Among those at this meeting was Martin Delany, who had moved his family to Chatham a few years before.[135]

In the fall of 1859, John Brown put his plans into action. He sent his son to Rochester to make arrangements with Douglass. Douglass and Shields Green, a fugitive working as his servant, were to go to Chambersburg, Pennsylvania by way of New York City and Philadelphia. There they would meet barber Henry Watson, who had arranged for Douglass to give a lecture, and then join Brown's group. Douglass had second thoughts about the undertaking, particularly since Brown's plans had changed from guerrilla action to a full-scale attack and decided not to accompany Brown; Shields Green decided he would go along.[136] John Brown and his band of thirteen white abolitionists and five blacks attacked the federal arsenal at Harper's Ferry, Virginia in mid-October 1859. One of his fighters, Dangerfield Newby, had personal reasons for accompanying Brown. A fugitive himself, Newby was surely interested in freeing his wife and children who were being held in Virginia near Harper's Ferry. Recent letters from his wife, Harriet, begged him to come for her and the children. "If I thought I should never see you this earth would have no charms for me," she wrote, "com [sic] this fall without fail."[137] African Americans John Copeland and Lewis Sheridan Leary had both participated in the rescue in Wellington, Ohio; Osborn Anderson had been at the organizing meeting in Chatham the year before.

Brown's plan was to use the weapons captured at the arsenal to arm slaves in the area and then to lead them in a revolt against slavery in the region. Although the party seized the armory, the plan failed—Brown's men were trapped and ten were killed or mortally wounded, including Newby and Leary. Brown, and four men, including Copeland and Green, were captured by federal troops under the command of Colonel Robert E. Lee. The captured men were convicted of treason and sentenced to be hanged, while authorities sought other conspirators. In Philadelphia, Frederick Douglass was warned by the telegraph operator just three hours before he delivered the order for Douglass's arrest to the sheriff. Douglass made his way cautiously to Canada and sailed for England near the end of November. Howe, Parker, and Sanborn also escaped to Canada, and Gerrit Smith spent two months in a mental institution.[138]

The Harpers Ferry raid shocked southerners and confirmed their belief that abolitionists were planning a war on the South that would incite slave revolts. Many African Americans also believed that a war over slavery was at hand. "Sooner or later, the clashing of arms will be heard in this country," predicted John Rock in 1858. "The black man's service will be needed . . . to strike a genuine blow for freedom . . . [with a] power which white men 'will be bound to respect.'"[139] By the time the Democrats and Republicans met to select their candidates for the 1860 presidential election, the entire Congress was said to be armed. One congressman had been killed and two had fought each other with guns and knives. Unable to agree on a candidate, the Democratic convention split into separate meetings. Some southerners selected a strong proslavery candidate, James G. Breckenridge of Kentucky, as their standard bearer, while the northern Democrats chose Stephen A. Douglas. Other southerners, hoping to maintain the union, formed the Constitutional Union Party and ran John Bell of Tennessee. Republicans met in Chicago in the spring and nominated Abraham Lincoln as their presidential candidate and Hannibal Hamlin of Bangor, Maine as his running mate.

African Americans followed these political events closely. They watched as Republicans rushed to denounce and disassociate themselves from John Brown's raid. Massachusetts blacks were furious when their Republican governor, Nathaniel P. Banks, vetoed legislation that would have allowed blacks to enlist in the state militia. New York blacks whose votes had helped elect Governor Morgan were disappointed when he failed "to utter an anti-slavery sentence" during his annual message. Most distressing, a Republican-introduced bill to repeal the Fugitive Slave Law failed when twelve Republicans voted against it and forty-three Republicans abstained. The Republicans' efforts to combat the "black Republican" label by declaring themselves "a white man's party," continually reminded blacks that they were essentially the lesser of potential political evils.[140] Some argued that the Republicans were in fact more dangerous to African-American rights than the Democrats, confusing blacks by seeming to be friends, when in reality, as John Rock believed, the Republican Party "aims to place white men and white labor against black men and black labor."[141] Others saw the antislavery professed by Lincoln and his wing of the Republicans and the old antislavery endorsed by the Whigs of the 1840s as virtually the same, and no antislavery at all. Despite the misgivings and doubts expressed by Douglass and other black leaders, in New York, Brooklyn, Boston, and several other northern cities blacks formed Republican clubs, and those who could vote voted for the victorious Lincoln in overwhelming numbers.[142]

Radical proslavery leaders in the South refused to accept the election's outcome, and before Lincoln could take office, South Carolina led a movement for secession. Lincoln assured the country that the federal government would not move against slavery and promised to support a constitutional amendment protecting slavery in the states where it existed, but many southerners were convinced that a "black Republican" in the White House portended the end of slavery, in their view, the very basis of their society. Secession moved quickly, with the formation of the Confederacy at the beginning of 1861 and a Confederate attack on the United States at Fort Sumter in the spring. African Americans generally greeted the news of southern secession with joy. Shortly after Lincoln's election, H. Ford Douglas, a former Virginia slave, expressed the feelings of most northern blacks. "Stand not upon the order of your going," he bid the South, "but go at once . . . there is no union of ideas and interests in the country, and there can be no union between freedom and slavery."[143] From the standpoint of free blacks, the removal of federal protection from the slave South was the first step to abolition. Despite Lincoln's contentions that the war was not about slavery, and that he was simply concerned with the preservation of the Union, northern free blacks believed from the beginning that the conflict would bring freedom for their four million friends and kin in bondage. Many had worked, waited, and prayed for an opportunity to strike slavery's death blow. As the United States went to war to preserve its union, and the South went to war to preserve slavery, African Americans again offered their service and risked their lives in hope of liberty.

Historian David W. Blight has observed that Frederick Douglass came to believe that freedom for the slaves and racial equality would come only through "national conflict and direct federal action" in a "Second American Revolution." African Americans, wrenched from their homelands and bound in forced labor for the enrichment of their captors, had taken the first American Revolution very seriously. The words of the Declaration of Independence and the preamble to the Constitution resonated most clearly for those who faced an even greater oppression than the framers of those documents denounced—their chains secured by the hands of those who proclaimed their love of liberty to the world. From the first settlement of the colonies in North America, Africans and African Americans contributed the folkways, values, and beliefs of their cultures to the unfolding multifaceted American culture. For the first century of the nation's history, blacks shared and helped form the national experience while continually calling on America to be true to its principles. Free blacks forged ties that created networks of family and community and, often allied with Indians and progressive white reformers, demanded freedom and opportunity for all people. Blacks in America constantly struggled against discouragement and despair. During the twelve generations before the Civil War, some gave up hope and seized opportunities to seek their freedom in other lands. Most could not leave; many refused to leave. Some remained as a commitment to the slaves, others were determined to stay in the place that was their home. For virtually all, being an African American was an ambivalent identity, incorporating all of the contradictions and conflicts of America itself. As race came to define social status, political rights, and human worth in America, African Americans became more determined to raise the voice of conscience in a society seemingly deaf to its own ideals. Strengthened by their faith in God and believing in the ultimate justice of the universe, they resolved never to surrender their own humanity.

In the end, most African Americans determined that the only real choice was to work for the abolition of slavery, which bound not only black Americans but America itself. Samuel Ringgold Ward expressed the views of many that the national question was not simply "whether the black man's slavery shall be perpetuated, but whether the freedom of any Americans can be permanent."[144] Frederick Douglass voiced the same recognition. "The Republic has put one end of the chain upon the ankle of the bondsman, and the other end about its own neck." To redeem the slave was to redeem the nation from self destruction. Many blacks embraced the war as the fulfillment of their long struggle. "The world has not seen," Douglass said, "a nobler and grander war than that which the loyal people of this country are now waging."[145] For those whose African ancestors and African-American forebears cried out for fidelity, this was the offer of a new "future with hope in it." After many raised hopes and dashed desires, African Americans once again dedicated themselves to the struggle that gave black people and the nation hope for a future with enduring liberty.[146]

Epilogue

The United States did not readily accept black military assistance. Although African Americans volunteered at Lincoln's first call for troops in April 1861, their service was refused. When Cincinnati blacks met to discuss the role they should play in the war, the chief of police broke up the meeting, telling them bluntly, "it was white men's fight, with which niggers had nothing to do."[1] Within a year, however, the bloody cost of the war had pressured the government to consider measures against slavery and had softened opposition to black military participation. At a lecture before the Emancipation League at Boston's Tremont Temple, Douglass asserted that blacks in both the North and the South were ready and eager to serve, noting sarcastically, "colored men were good enough to fight under Washington. They are not good enough to fight under McClellan."[2]

By the spring of 1862, Congress had followed the example of the personal liberty laws enacted by some northern states in the 1840s and 1850s and forbade United States officers from aiding in the capture or return of fugitive slaves. Indeed, from the war's inception, many federal officers had refused to participate in these actions. Lincoln also instituted moderate antislavery measures, recommending that Congress provide compensated emancipation for slaves in those slave states which had remained loyal to the United States and that it abolish slavery in the District of Columbia. In May General David Hunter organized an official regiment of former slaves into the First South Carolina Volunteers, the first black Civil War regiment. Congress finally authorized Lincoln to accept African Americans into military service on July 17, 1862.[3]

The war was going badly for the United States, and European nations dependent on southern cotton threatened to recognize and provide assistance to the Confederate States of America. Lincoln's answer was to reinterpret the purpose of the war. In September, using victory at Antietam as the context, the president issued a preliminary Emancipation Proclamation, to become official on January 1, 1863. It proclaimed the freedom of all slaves being held as of that date by those in rebellion against the United States of America.[4] "We shout for joy that we live to record this righteous decree," wrote Douglass. He reminded blacks that there was no assurance of freedom until the stroke of the new year, adding with strange prescience, "should Abraham Lincoln be then alive and President of the United States."[5]

For three months African Americans waited anxiously as they continued raising funds for the relief of the thousands of slaves who rushed to the protection of advancing federal troops and training for military service. On New Year's Eve in cities and towns throughout the North and in the border states, they gathered to await freedom's arrival. The more than three thousand people who packed Tremont Temple in Boston by eight that evening heard speeches by the ex-slave pastor of the church John Sella Martin, William Wells Brown, Frederick Douglass, and women's rights advocate and abolitionist Anna M. Dickinson. When the word came, the sanctuary exploded with the cheers and song. "Blow ye trumpet, blow," they sang, "Jehovah hath triumphed, his people are free." Then they poured into the street and made their way to the Twelfth Baptist Church, popularly known as the fugitive slave church, where the Reverend Leonard Grimes led them in a prayer of thanksgiving. The meetings and celebrations went on for days all over the North. In Philadelphia they gathered at Mother Bethel and at the Colored Presbyterian Church where the minister, Jonathan Gibbs, told the congregation, "The morning dawns! The long night of sorrow and gloom is past. . . . The Proclamation has gone forth, and . . . Man must be free."[6] Although the Emancipation Proclamation left the fate of slaves held in loyal states uncertain, and it would take two more years and the loss of hundreds of thousands of lives before emancipation would be written into the Constitution, this day vindicated the courage of generations of African-American men and women who had fought and persevered in the hope of liberty.

Black troops served with unequal pay and in the most dangerous circumstances, but black recruiters, Douglass, Delany, Garnet, Mary Ann Shadd Cary, and the others, urged black men to join the fight that had officially become one for freedom. Though most African Americans had hoped that liberty would be established through the force of rational and moral persuasion, they were prepared to bring it about through the force of arms, and in the process to force the government to provide blacks the protection of the Constitution. Most whites questioned whether black troops could be effective, but blacks remembered the Revolution and the War of 1812 and continued to hope that even their most skeptical critics would be convinced once the black man had "an eagle on his button, a musket on his shoulder, and the star-spangled banner over his head."[7]

Notes

Introduction

1. Culture includes people's customs, beliefs and values, worldview and philosophies, as well as their food, music, language, and dress. It is dynamic, changing over time as people adapt to changed circumstances, technological innovations, and influences from other groups. The development of a general African-American culture with local and regional variations, and the interplay of African-American culture and American culture are dealt with throughout this book and in particular detail in Chapter 7.

2. See *Freedom's Journal*, August 8, August 29, September 5 and 12, and October 3, 1828.

3. The most extensive biographical account of Horton is by Richard Walser, *The Black Poet: The Story of George Moses Horton, A North Carolina Slave* (New York: Philosophical Library, 1966); see also Blyden Jackson, *A History of Afro-American Literature*, I (Baton Rouge: Louisiana State University Press, 1980), 84–95, and M. A. Richmond, *Bid the Vassal Soar* (Washington, D. C.: Howard University Press, 1974), 81–209.

4. For an extended discussion of the many definitions of community and of types of community theories, see Roland L. Warren and Larry Lyon, eds., *New Perspectives on the American Community* (Chicago: The Dorsey Press, 1988). On the diversity of African-American communities, see James Oliver Horton, *Free People of Color: Inside the African-American Community* (Washington, D. C.: Smithsonian Institution Press, 1993).

5. *The Anglo-African Magazine* (January 1859 reprint, New York: Arno Press, 1968), 4.

Chapter 1

1. Nancy Prince, *A Narrative of the Life and Travels of Mrs. Nancy Prince* (Boston: Nancy Prince, 1853), 6.

2. James A. Rawley, *Transatlantic Slave Trade* (New York: W. W. Norton, 1981), 336–37.

3. Rawley, *Transatlantic Slave Trade*, 339–340.

4. Edward Pearson, "From Stono to Vesey: Slavery, Resistance, and Ideology in South Carolina, 1739–1822" (Ph. D. diss., University of Wisconsin, 1991). Pearson provides a detailed account of slavery in South Carolina, the transition from timber producing and herding to rice agriculture, and the importance of African gender conventions for work roles.

5. Lorenzo J. Greene, *The Negro in Colonial New England* (1942; reprint, New York: Atheneum Press, 1968), 103. For one of the best analyses of regional differences on the lives of slaves in the colonial period, see Ira Berlin, "Time, Space, and the Evolution of Afro-American Society on British Mainland North America," *American Historical Review* 85 (February 1980): 44–78, reprinted in Thomas R. Frazier, ed., *The Underside of American History*, 4th ed., vol. 1 (New York: Harcourt Brace Jovanovich, 1982), 35–72.

6. David Brion Davis, *The Problem of Slavery in Western Culture* (Ithaca, N. Y.: Cornell University Press, 1966); Jean R. Soderlund, *Quakers and Slavery* (Princeton, N. J.: Princeton University Press, 1985), 34.

7. Edward Raymond Turner, *The Negro in Pennsylvania: Slavery—Servitude—Freedom, 1639–1861* (Washington, D. C., 1911, reprint, New York: Negro Universities Press, 1969), 22; A. Leon Higginbotham, *In the Matter of Color: Race and the American Legal Process* (New York: Oxford University Press, 1978), 267–281, quote on 280; Gary Nash, *Forging Freedom: The Formation of Philadelphia's Black Community, 1720–1840* (Cambridge, Mass.: Harvard University Press, 1988).

8. The figure for the slave population in mid-eighteenth century Philadelphia is taken from the work of Gary Nash who computed these numbers from city death records, tax records, and slaveholders' wills. There were 590 slaveholders in Philadelphia's total population of 18,600 in 1767. See Nash, *Forging Freedom*, 33.

9. Davis, *Problem of Slavery*, 330; Soderlund, *Quakers and Slavery*.

10. Higginbotham, *In the Matter of Color*, 100–116; Joyce D. Goodfriend, *Before the Melting Pot: Society and Culture in Colonial New York City, 1664–1730* (Princeton, N. J.: Princeton University Press, 1992).

11. Berlin, "Time, Space, and the Evolution of Afro-American Society"; Goodfriend, *Before the Melting Pot*; Jim Potter, "Demographic Development and Family Structure," in Jack P. Greene and J. R. Pole, eds., *Colonial British America*, (Baltimore: The Johns Hopkins University Press, 1984), 123–156.

12. Donald R. Wright, *African Americans in the Colonial Era* (Arlington Heights, Ill.: Harlan Davidson, 1990).

13. Shane White, *Somewhat More Independent: The End of Slavery in New York City, 1770–1810* (Athens: University of Georgia Press, 1991), 3.

14. Clement Alexander Price, ed., *Freedom Not Far Distant: A Documentary History of Afro-Americans in New Jersey*, (Newark: New Jersey Historical Society, 1980), 5.

15. Peter Kalm, *Travels in North America* (1937, reprint, New York: Dover Publications, 1966); Philip D. Morgan, "British Encounters with Africans and African-Americans circa 1600–1780," in Bernard Bailyn and Philip D. Morgan, eds., *Strangers Within the Realm* (Chapel Hill: University of North Carolina Press, 1991), 157–219.

16. Price, ed., *Freedom Not Far Distant*, 3.

17. Greene, *Negro in Colonial New England*.

18. Greene, *Negro in Colonial New England*.

19. Greene, *Negro in Colonial New England*; see also William D. Piersen, *Black Yankees: The Development of an Afro-American Sub-Culture in New England* (Amherst: University of Massachusetts Press, 1988).

20. Greene, *Negro in Colonial New England*; Gary B. Nash, *The Urban Crucible: Social Change, Political Consciousness, and the Origins of the American Revolution* (Cambridge, Mass.: Harvard University Press, 1979), 13; Robert C. Twombly and Robert M. Moore, "Black Puritan: The Negro in Seventeenth Century Massachusetts," *William and Mary Quarterly*, 3d ser., 24 (April 1967): 224–242.

21. Greene, *Negro in Colonial New England*; Piersen, *Black Yankees*.

22. Arthur Zilversmit, *The First Emancipation* (Chicago: University of Chicago Press, 1967), quote 33–34; James A. Henretta, "Economic Development and Social Structure in Colonial Boston," *William and Mary Quarterly* 22 (1965): 75–92; Greene, *Negro in Colonial New England*, 84; Nash, *Urban Crucible*, 421.

23. Josiah Quincy, Jr., *Reports of Cases Argued and Adjudged in the Superior Court of Judicature of the Provence of Massachusetts Bay between 1761 and 1772* (Boston: Little, Brown, 1865), 31n, quoted in Edgar J. McManus, *Black Bondage in the North* (Syracuse, N. Y.: University of Syracuse Press, 1973), 63.

24. Even in the South, a slave might be able to negotiate an agreement whereby he or she could do work for someone other than the master ("hire out") and be allowed to keep all or part of the wages received. Hiring out was sometimes used by slaveowners to keep slaves, especially skilled workers, occupied during slack periods, or the work might be performed by slaves during their free time. Being hired out to someone in an urban area generally gave a slave slightly more independence, and occasionally slaves were able to buy their own freedom with the proceeds of such labor.

25. McManus, *Black Bondage*, 62–63; Nathan Dane, *A General Abridgement and Digest of American Law with Occasional Notes and Comments*, vol. 2, (Boston: Cummings, Hilliard, 1823–29), 313.

26. Piersen, *Black Yankees*; Robert J. Cottrol, *The Afro-Yankees: Providence's Black Community in the Ante-bellum Era* (Westport, Conn.: Greenwood Press, 1982), 125–126.

27. Quoted in Goodfriend, *Before the Melting Pot*, 114.

28. Berlin, "Time, Space, and the Evolution of Afro-American Society," 52. For the quote, see Jane De Forest Shelton, "The New England Negro: A Remnant," *Harper's New Monthly Magazine* (March 1894): 533–538, 534.

29. Rawley, *Transatlantic Slave Trade*, 332–334; Wright, *African Americans*. Until recently, historians agreed that most North American slaves were subjected to a West Indian seasoning or breaking-in period before being transported North. Theoretically, seasoning was a period during which discipline was imposed and Africans were initiated into the ways of their European captors. Seasoned slaves, scholars argued, brought a higher price. The time spent in the West Indies also allowed those who survived the horrors of the "middle passage," the six- to eight-week voyage from Africa, to partially recover from the ordeal, perhaps increasing their salability. See, for example, John Hope Franklin, *From Slavery to Freedom: A History of Negro Americans* (New York: Knopf, 1980), 69–70.

30. Darold Wax, "Preferences for Slaves in Colonial America," *The Journal of Negro History* 58 (1973): 375–376.

31. Wax, "Preferences for Slaves," 378.

32. Goodfriend, *Before the Melting Pot*.

33. Wax, "Preferences for Slaves."

34. Gary B. Nash, "Slaves and Slaveowners in Colonial Philadelphia," *William and Mary Quarterly* 3 (1973): 223–256, 229; see also Nash, *Forging Freedom*, 10–11.

35. Nash, "Slaves and Slaveowners"; Darold D. Wax, "The Negro Slave Trade in Colonial Pennsylvania" (Ph. D. diss., University of Washington, 1962), 284–287; Rawley, *Transatlantic Slave Trade*, 396–399.

36. Nash, "Slaves and Slaveowners," 226.

37. James G. Lydon, "New York and the Slave Trade, 1700–1774," *William and Mary Quarterly* 35 (1978): 385; Price, *Freedom Not Far Distant*, 26; Edgar J. McManus, *A History of Negro Slavery in New York* (Syracuse, N. Y.: Syracuse University Press, 1966), 28–30. New York City also received a number of slaves smuggled in from Long Island. See Goodfriend, *Before the Melting Pot*.

38. Nash's analysis of Philadelphia tax records for 1767 reveals that only 5 percent of the city's slaveholders came from the lower half of the tax rolls, while almost two-thirds were in the top quarter, and one-third were in the top tenth of taxpayers. See Nash, "Slaves and Slaveowners," 247–248.

39. Henretta, "Economic Development and Social Structure," 85; For data on New York City, see White, *Somewhat More Independent*, 11.

40. Nash, "Slaves and Slaveowners," 248, 250–251; *The American Weekly Mercury*, October 26, 1821; *Pennsylvania Gazette*, January 29, 1839; *Boston Weekly News Letter*, March 21, 1834.

41. *The Boston Evening Post*, October 24, 1743. Figures compiled from data found in Nash, "Slaves and Slaveowners" and in White, *Somewhat More Independent*.

42. Nash, "Slaves and Slaveowners," 249; White, *Somewhat More Independent*, 8; Wittington B. Johnson, "Negro Laboring Classes in Early America, 1750–1820" (Ph. D. diss., University of Georgia, 1970).

43. Sidney Kaplan, *The Black Presence in the Era of the American Revolution, 1770–1800* (Greenwich, Conn.: New York Graphics Society, 1973), 147.

44. Many historians of the colonial period ignored the presence of black skilled workers in the colonial North altogether. See, for example, Alfred Young, "The Mechanics and the Jeffersonians: New York, 1789–1801," *Labor History* 5 (1964): 247–276. Others dismissed the importance of the slave artisan in colonial cities. See, for example, Sean Wilentz, *Chants Democratic: New York City and the Rise of the American Working Class, 1788–1850* (New York: Oxford University Press, 1984). More recent research like Foner's in *History of Black Americans*, vol. 1, Nash's in *Forging Freedom*, and White's in *Somewhat More Independent* has supported Greene's earlier work in *Negro in Colonial New England*, Leonard P. Stavisky's in "Negro Craftsmen in Early America," *American Historical Review* 54, no. 2 (1949): 315–325, and Carl Bridenbaugh's in *The Colonial Craftsman* (1950; reprint, Chicago: University of Chicago Press, 1961) and has broadened our knowledge of the critical role slaves played in the skilled work of the period.

45. *Pennsylvania Journal*, May 27, 1762; *Pennsylvania Gazette*, May 6, 1762. On the importance of African ethnicity to southern planters, see Daniel C. Littlefield, *Rice and Slaves: Ethnicity and the Slave Trade in Colonial South Carolina* (Urbana: University of Illinois Press, 1991).

46. Wax, "Preferences for Slaves," 401.

47. Piersen uses the term "family slavery" in *Black Yankees*.

48. Jane G. Austin, *Dr. LaBaron and His Daughters* (Boston: Houghton, Mifflin & Co., The Riverside Press, Cambridge, 1892), 55.

49. Austin, *Dr. LeBaron.*

50. C. Wilson Larison, *Silvia Dubois (Now 116 Years Old.) A Biography of the Slave Who Whipped Her Mistress and Gained Her Freedom* (Ringoes: New Jersey, 1883), in Bert James Loewenberg and Ruth Bogin, eds., *Black Women in Nineteenth-Century American Life* (University Park: Pennsylvania State University Press, 1976), 39–47. Even at one hundred sixteen years of age in 1883 Larison found Silvia Dubois an imposing figure.

51. *Boston Weekly News Letter,* April 25-May 2, 1728.

52. John Van Horne, "Impediments to the Christianization and Education of Blacks in Colonial America: The Case of the Associates of Dr. Bray," *Historical Magazine of the Protestant Episcopal Church* 50 (1981): 258–260.

53. Walter M. Brasch, *Black English and the Mass Media* (Amherst: University of Massachusetts Press, 1981), 3–6.

54. Billy G. Smith and Richard Wojtowicz, *Blacks Who Stole Themselves* (Philadelphia: University of Pennsylvania Press, 1989), 20, 32; *New York Gazette,* November 11, 1760; *The Pennsylvania Gazette,* August 8, 1755.

55. *Pennsylvania Gazette,* September 24, 1741, June 6, 1746, July 31, 1740, July 4, 1745, September 20, 1764; *New York Gazette,* July 31, 1766.

56. Walter M. Brasch speculates that Tituba actually said, "Ah no hotem," which was "a distinct West African Pidgin-English phrase." Brasch, *Black English*, 3. For analysis and other examples, see Peter Wood, *Black Majority* (New York: Knopf, 1974).

57. Piersen, *Black Yankees*, 41.

58. Edward Amasa Park, *Memoir of the Life and Character of Samuel Hopkins* (Boston: 1854), 131 and 366. It is likely that African Americans in southern port cities maintained their multilingual skills far longer than most northern blacks because of the infusion of West Indian blacks and the significant presence of Africans among them through the late eighteenth and early nineteenth centuries.

59. Carleton Mabee, *Black Education in New York State from Colonial to Modern Times* (Syracuse, N. Y.: Syracuse University Press, 1979), 1–13.

60. Mabee, *Black Education.*

61. Greene, *Negro in Colonial New England,* 237–238.

62. Greene, *Negro in Colonial New England.*

63. Van Horne, "Impediments to Christianization," 246.

64. Van Horne, "Impediments to Christianization," 243–269.

65. Mabee, *Black Education,* 12–13.

66. Nancy Slocum Hornick, "Anthony Benezet: Eighteenth-Century School Critic, Educator, and Abolitionist" (Ph. D. diss., University of Maryland, 1974); Roger Bruns, "Anthony Benezet's Assertion of Negro Equality," *Journal of Negro History* 56 (1971): 230–238; Leonard Labaree and William Wilcox, eds., *The Papers of Benjamin Franklin,* 25 Vols. (New Haven: Yale University Press, 1959-); Nash, *Forging Freedom*; Vincent P. Franklin, *The Education of Black Philadelphia* (Philadelphia: University of Pennsylvania Press, 1979), 29.

67. *New York Gazette,* December 5, 1765.

68. De Forest Shelton, "New England Negro," 533–538, 536. William Piersen, in *Black Yankees* interprets the "fire and fall off" as black satire of a Euro-American military drill. He is undoubtedly correct, and it can be added that "fire and fall off," African-American style, required far greater horsemanship and agility.

69. Joseph P. Reidy, "Negro Election Day and Black Community Life in New

England, 1750–1860," *Marxist Perspectives* 1 (Fall 1978): 102–117; Sterling Stuckey, *Slave Culture: Nationalist Theory and the Formations of Black America* (New York: Oxford University Press, 1987); Piersen, *Black Yankees*, 117–128. Also see Piersen, "Afro-American Culture in Eighteenth Century New England: A Comparative Examination" (Ph. D.diss., Indiana University, 1975).

70. Piersen rightly saw these celebrations as striking evidence of the interaction of European and African cultural traditions.

71. Cottrol, *Afro-Yankees*, 23–24, 34.

72. Frances M. Caulkins, *History of Norwich, Connecticut* (New London, Conn.: H. D. Utbeg, 1895), 185.

73. Caulkins, *History of Norwich*, 185.

74. De Forest Shelton, "New England Negro," 535. Barbara Jeanne Fields describes a very similar situation in Maryland in the ninteenth century. Fields, *Slavery and Freedom on the Middle Ground: Maryland During the Nineteenth Century*, (New Haven, Conn.: Yale University Press, 1985).

75. Andrew D. Mellick, Jr., *Lesser Crossroads*, ed. Hubert G. Schmidt from Andrew D. Mellick, Jr., *The Story of an Old Farm* (1889 reprint, New Brunswick, N. J.: Rutgers University Press, 1948), 368–81.

76. Greene, *Negro in Colonial New England*, 196; Revolutionary War Pension Records, no. W. 751, Primus Hall, Records of the Veterans' Administration, Record Group #15, National Archives and Record Service, Washington, D. C. (hereafter RWPR, cited by applicant's name and application number.); Debra L. Newman, *Black History: A Guide to Civilian Records in the National Archives* (Washington, DC: National Archives Trust Fund Board, GSA, 1984); Rita Jean Roberts, "In Quest of Autonomy: Northern Black Activism between the Revolution and Civil War" (Ph. D. diss., University of California at Berkeley, 1988).

77. Abner Cheney Goodell, Jr., "The Trial and Execution, for Petit Treason, of Mark and Phyllis, Slaves of Capt. John Codman, Who Murdered their Master at Charlestown, Mass., in 1755; for which the Man was Hanged and Gibbeted, and the Woman was Burned to Death. Including, also, Some Account of other Punishments by Burning in Massachusetts" (Cambridge: John Wilson and Son, University Press, 1883), in Paul Finkelman, ed., *Slavery, Race and the American Legal System 1700–1872*, (New York: Garland Publishing, 1988), 1–39.

78. White, *Somewhat More Independent*, 107.

79. *Connecticut Courant*, February 23, 1773, quoted in Piersen, *Black Yankees*, 19.

80. Quoted in Ira Berlin, "Time, Space, and the Evolution of Afro-American Society," 41.

81. Piersen saw the fear of sale as one important factor discouraging slave women from getting pregnant. See also Clarence W. Bowen, *The History of Woodstock, Connecticut* (Norwood, Mass.: private printing by the Plimpton Press, 1926), 202; Greene, *Negro in Colonial New England*, 212–213.

82. Mellick, *Lesser Crossroads*, 368–381.

83. McManus, *Negro Slavery in New York*. See also McManus, *Black Bondage in the North*; RWPR, Primus Hall.

84. Twombly and Moore, "Black Puritan," 224–242.

85. *American Weekly Mercury*, March 20–27, 1735, 4; Twombly and Moore, "Black Puritan."

86. McManus, *Black Bondage in the North*; Roi Ottley and William J. Weatherby, eds., *The Negro in New York* (New York: New York Public Library, 1967), 22–30.

87. R. S. Rattray, *Ashanti Law and Constitution* (Oxford: Clarendon Press, 1929); W. J. Argyle, *The Fon of Dahomey* (Oxford: Clarendon Press, 1966); Cottrol, *Afro-Yankees.*

88. Peter Kolchin, *American Slavery, 1619–1877* (New York: Hill and Wang, 1993).

Chapter 2

1. John Van Horne, "Impediments to the Christianization and Education of Blacks in Colonial America," *Historical Magazine of the Protestant Episcopal Church* 50 (1981): 260.

2. Eugene Genovese, *Roll Jordan Roll: The World the Slaves Made* (New York: Pantheon Press, 1974).

3. Elizabeth L. Gebhard, *The Parsonage Between Two Manors: Annals of Clover Reach* (Hudson, N.Y.: Bryan Printing Co., 1909), 224–25, quoted in David Steven Cohen, "In Search of Carolus Africanus Rex: Afro-Dutch Folklore in New York and New Jersey," *Journal of the Afro-American Historical and Genealogical Society* 5, (Fall & Winter 1984): 147–162; Alexander Coventry, Diary, July 1783-August 1789, New York State Library Mss., 211, cited in Cohen, "In Search of Carolus Africanus Rex."

4. Marian Gouverneur, *As I Remember: Recollections of American Society During the Nineteenth Century* (New York: D. Appleton, 1911), 3.

5. Coventry, Diary.

6. Quotes from Alice Morse Earle, *Colonial Days in Old New York* (New York: Empire Book Company, 1926), 196–200. One of the earliest and best descriptions of the celebration comes from an account published in the *New York Evening Post*, June 29, 1803. Also see Shane White, *Somewhat More Independent* (Athens: University of Georgia Press, 1991).

7. James Fenimore Cooper, *Satanstoe* (1845, reprint, New York: G.P. Putnam's Sons, n.d.), 66–67. Folklorist David Steven Cohen suggests the similarity between this dance of Pinkster and the Vodun dances performed at New Orleans's Congo Square until the late nineteenth century.

8. See A. J. Williams-Myers, "Pinkster Carnival: Africanisms in the Hudson River Valley," *Afro-Americans in New York Life and History* 9 (1985): 7–17; Sterling Stuckey, *Slave Culture* (New York: Oxford University Press, 1987).

9. Joseph P. Reidy, "Negro Election Day and Black Community Life in New England, 1750–1860," *Marxist Perspectives* 1 (Fall 1978): 107–108; Ira Berlin, "Time, Space, and the Evolution of Afro-American Society on British Mainland North America," *American Historical Review* 85 (1980), 53.

10. Stuckey, *Slave Culture*, 73 and 80.

11. Interestingly, musical parades with such spectacles eventually became part of the general American political culture. Melvin Wade, "'Shining in Borrowed Plumage': Affirmation of Community in the Black Coronation Festivals of New England (c. 1750–c. 1850)," *Western Folklore* 40 (1941): 218; Stuckey, *Slave Culture.* Stuckey argues persuasively that these festivals helped to create African-American culture. See Sterling Stuckey, *Going Through the Storm: The Influence of African American Art in History* (New York: Oxford University Press, 1994).

12. Robert Farris Thompson, *Flash of the Spirit* (New York: Random House, 1983), 104.

13. Stuckey, *Slave Culture.*

14. Paul Boyer and Stephen Nissenbaum, *Salem Possessed: The Social Origins of Witchcraft* (Cambridge, Mass.: Harvard University Press, 1974).

15. John Putnam Demos, *Entertaining Satan: Witchcraft and the Culture of Early New England* (New York: Oxford University Press, 1982).

16. Demos, *Entertaining Satan*, 22; Thompson, *Flash of the Spirit*. Many of the practices derived from these African beliefs persist in the Americas today.

17. Roger D. Abrahams, ed., *After Africa* (New Haven, Conn.: Yale University Press, 1983), 27–28.

18. Joseph M. Murphy, "Ritual Systems in Cuban Sateria" (Ph.D. diss., Temple University, 1980), 193–194.

19. Cohen, "In Search of Carolus Africanus Rex," 154.

20. Wade, "'Shining in Borrowed Plumage,'" 226.

21. Samuel E. Morrison, "A Poem on Election Day in Massachusetts about 1760," *Proceedings of the Colonial Society of Massachusetts* 18 (February 1915): 54–61.

22. Absalom Aimwell, *Pinkster Ode* (Albany: Absalom Aimwell, Esq., 1803), quoted in Cohen, "In Search of Carolus Africanus Rex," 154.

23. Daniel K. Richter, *The Ordeal of the Long House: The People of the Iroquois League in the Era of European Colonization* (Chapel Hill: University of North Carolina Press, 1992).

24. Several examples of such complaints are quoted in William D. Piersen, *Black Yankees* (Amherst: University of Massachusetts Press, 1988), 88–89. Also see Daniel Williams, "The Gratification of That Corrupt and Lawless Passion: Character Types and Themes in Early New England Rape Narratives," in Frank Shuffelton, *A Mixed Race: Ethnicity on Early America* (New York: Oxford University Press, 1993), 194–221. There were similar complaints about the "immoral behavior" of white servants. See David Hackett Fischer, *Albion's Seed: Four British Folkways in America* (New York: Oxford University Press, 1989); James Axtell, *After Columbus* (New York: Oxford University Press, 1988), 111.

25. Samuel Sewall, "The Selling of Joseph, A Memorial," in *Proceedings of the Massachusetts Historical Society, 1863–64*, 7 (1864): 162; Josiah Quincy, Jr., *Reports of Cases Argued and Adjudged in the Superior Court of Judicature of the Province of Massachusetts Bay, Between 1761 and 1772*, (Boston: Little, Brown & Company, 1865), 30.

26. Williams, "Gratification of That Corrupt and Lawless Passion," 199–200.

27. Neal Salisbury, *Manitou and Providence* (New York: Oxford University Press, 1982), 221–222.

28. J. Leitch Wright, Jr., *The Only Land They Knew* (New York: Free Press, 1981), 129.

29. Although Robin Eldridge was probably African, Robin was a common name among slaves of Indian ancestry. See Jack D. Forbes, *Black Africans and Native Americans* (New York: Basil Blackwell, 1988).

30. Bert James Loewenberg and Ruth Bogin, eds., *Black Women in Nineteenth Century American Life: Their Words, Their Thoughts, Their Feelings* (University Park: Pennsylvania State University Press, 1976), 78–81.

31. Forbes, *Black Africans and Native Americans*.

32. Lamont D. Thomas, *Rise To Be a People* (Urbana: University of Illinois Press, 1986).

33. Williams, "Gratification of That Corrupt and Lawless Passion."

34. Carter G. Woodson, "The Relations of Negroes and Indians in Massachusetts," *Journal of Negro History* 5 (January 1920): 45–57; Forbes, *Black Africans and Native Americans*.

35. Roi Ottley and William J. Weatherby, eds., *The Negro in New York: An Informal Social History, 1626–1940* (New York: New York Public Library, 1967).

36. Debra L. Newman, "Black Women in the Era of the American Revolution in Pennsylvania," *Journal of Negro History* 61 (July 1976): 276–289; Peter Wood, *Black Majority* (New York: Alfred A. Knopf, 1974).

37. For an explanation of the colonial social hierarchy, see Gordon S. Wood, *The Radicalism of the American Revolution* (New York: Alfred A. Knopf, 1992). John Saffin, *A Brief and Candid Answer to a Late Printed Sheet . . .* (Boston, 1700), quoted in Gary Nash, *The Urban Crucible: Social Change, Political Consciousness, and the Origins of the American Revolution* (Cambridge, Mass.: Harvard University Press, 1979), 7.

38. Wood, *Radicalism of the American Revolution*, 38.

39. Wood, *Radicalism of the American Revolution*.

40. Nash, *Urban Crucible*, 7–8. See also Jean R. Soderlund, *Quakers and Slavery: A Divided Spirit* (Princeton, N.J.: Princeton University Press, 1985).

41. Nash, *Urban Crucible*, 20.

42. Bernard Bailyn and Barbara DeWolfe, *Voyagers to the West: A Passage in the Peopling of America on the Eve of the Revolution* (New York: Alfred A. Knopf, 1986), 166.

43. Bailyn and DeWolfe, *Voyagers to the West*, 324, 346.

44. David Galenson, *White Servitude in Colonial America: An Economic Analysis* (Cambridge: Cambridge University Press, 1981), 3–4; *New York Gazette Weekly Mercury*, July 23, 1770. Appreciation is expressed to Claudia Kidwell and Shelly Foote of the Division of Costume, National Museum of American History, Smithsonian Institution, for making their collection of runaway ads available for this study.

45. Bailyn and DeWolfe, *Voyagers to the West*, 324. Although it may be true, as Gordon Wood argued in *The Radicalism of the American Revolution*, that class consciousness based on occupation and wealth as we might define it today did not exist in eighteenth century colonial America, there was a sense of shared disadvantage among those at the bottom of American society. Likewise, there was a shared feeling of advantage among those at the top.

46. A. C. Goodell et al., eds., *Acts and Resolves, Public and Private, of the Province of Massachusetts Bay* vols. 1–4 (Boston: 1869–1922), 3:664, 647–648.

47. *Boston Gazette*, August 18, 1765.

48. Leonard W. Labaree, "The Conservative Attitude Toward the Great Awakening," *William and Mary Quarterly* 1 (1944): 339 and 336; David S. Lovejoy, "Samuel Hopkins: Religion, Slavery, and the Revolution," *The New England Quarterly* 40 (1967): 227–243.

49. Abbot Smith in Howard Zinn, *A People's History of the United States* (New York: Harper & Row, 1980), 46 and 53; see Kenneth Lockridge's description of the wandering poor in *A New England Town: The First Hundred Years* (New York: W.W. Norton, 1970).

50. Berlin, "Time, Space, and the Evolution of Afro-American Society," 44–78; Zinn, *People's History*; Robert J. Cottrol, *The Afro-Yankees: Providence's Black Community in the Antebellum Era* (Westport, Conn.: Greenwood Press, 1982); Nash, *Urban Crucible*; Edmund S. Morgan, *American Slavery and American Freedom: The Ordeal of Colonial Virginia* (New York: W.W. Norton, 1975), 327.

51. *Pennsylvania Gazette*, October 8, 1747; *Journal and Baltimore Advisor*, October 10, 1779; *The New York Gazette*, August 11, 1760.

52. Cottrol, *Afro-Yankees*, 19; *New York Weekly Journal*, August 9, 1742, quotation in Edgar J. McManus, *A History of Negro Slavery in New York* (Syracuse, N.Y.: Syracuse University Press, 1966), 87.

53. Daniel Horsmanden, *The New York Conspiracy*, ed. Thomas J. Davis (Boston:

Beacon Press, 1971). Davis has also provided an important account of the 1741 conspiracy in his *Rumor of Revolt: The Great Negro Plot in Colonial New York* (New York: Free Press, 1985).

54. Horsmanden, *New York Conspiracy.*

55. Sarah Kimball Knight, *The Journal of Madame Knight,* ed. George Parker Winship (1938, reprint, New York: Garrett Press, 1970), 38; Timothy Cooley, *Sketches of the Life and Character of Lemuel Haynes* (New York: John S. Taylor, 1839), 18–35; Zinn, *People's History,* 57–58.

56. For a description of the process of the concentration of colonial wealth and political power, see James A. Henretta, *The Evolution of American Society, 1700–1815: An Interdisciplinary Analysis* (Lexington, Mass.: D.C. Heath, 1973). Gary Nash has analyzed the tax records for Boston, New York, and Philadelphia from the late seventeenth to the late eighteenth century and found that in all three cities the rich increased their share of the community's wealth. See Gary Nash, "Social Change and the Growth of Prerevolutionary Urban Radicalism," in Gary Nash, ed., *Race, Class and Politics: Essays on American Colonial and Revolutionary Society* (Urbana: University of Illinois Press, 1986), 211–42.

57. Quincy, Jr., *Reports of Cases Argued and Adjudged,* 237–238; Nash, *Urban Crucible,* 8.

58. Gary Nash, "Up From the Bottom in Franklin's Philadelphia," *Past and Present* 77 (1977): 57–83; Eric Foner, *Tom Paine and Revolutionary America* (New York: Oxford University Press, 1976), 48.

59. Cottrol, *Afro-Yankees,* 19; *Pennsylvania Gazette,* June 26, 1740, September 14, 1749.

60. Nash, *Urban Crucible,* 36.

61. Jesse Lemisch, "Jack Tar in the Streets: Merchant Seaman in the Politics of Revolutionary America," *William and Mary Quarterly* 25 (1968): 371–407; 379; Kenneth Scott, "The Slave Insurrection in New York in 1712," *New York Historical Society Quarterly* 45 (1961): 43–74.

62. Nash, *Urban Crucible,* 109; W. E. B. Du Bois, *The Suppression of the African Slave Trade* (1896, reprint, Baton Rouge: Louisiana State University Press, 1965), 22.

63. Zinn, *People's History,* 51; Nash, *Urban Crucible,* 134–136; Benjamin Colman to - Mr. Samuel Holden, Boston, May 8, 1737, Colman Papers, vol. 2, Massachusetts Historical Society.

64. Lemisch, "Jack Tar in the Streets"; Zinn, *People's History,* 51; Nash, *Urban Crucible,* 221–223.

65. Lemisch, "Jack Tar in the Streets," 379; Nash, *Urban Crucible,* 108.

66. Philip D. Morgan, "British Encounters with Africans and African-Americans, circa 1600–1780," in Bernard Bailyn and Philip D. Morgan, eds., *Strangers Within the Realm* (Chapel Hill: University of North Carolina Press, 1991), 157–219; quote from J. Stewart, *View of the Past and Present State of the Island of Jamaica* (Edinburgh, Scotland: Oliver and Boyd, 1823), 178.

67. Winthrop Jordan, *White Over Black: American Attitudes Toward the Negro, 1550–1812* (Chapel Hill: University of North Carolina Press, 1968).

68. Anne Grant, *Memoirs of an American Lady* vol. 1 (New York: Dodd, Mead and Company, 1901), 85; Edgar J. McManus, *Black Bondage in the North* (Syracuse, New York: University of Syracuse Press, 1973), 63–64.

69. All quotes in Philip D. Morgan, "British Encounters with Africans and African Americans," 166–67.

70. Jordan, *White Over Black*; Lorenzo Greene, *The Negro in Colonial New England, 1620–1776* (1942, reprint, New York: Atheneum Press, 1968).

71. Gary Nash, *Red, White, and Black: The Peoples of Early America* (Englewood Cliffs, N.J.: Prentice-Hall, 1974), 285.

72. Goodell et al., eds., *Acts and Resolves,* 1: 535–536 and 4:462.

73. Nash, *Urban Crucible*, 13. Also see Gordon Wood, *Radicalism of the American Revolution* for the details of this argument which views colonial America as a society with a vertically organized social structure.

74. Wood, *Radicalism of the American Revolution*, 170.

75. Morgan, *American Slavery and American Freedom.*

76. Peter N. Caroll and David W. Noble, *The Free and the Unfree: A New History of the United States* (New York: Penguin Books, 1977), 93–124.

77. Ottley and Weatherby, eds., *Negro in New York*, 36–37.

78. William C. Nell, "Crispus Attucks Once a Slave in Massachusetts," *Liberator*, August 5, 1859, 124. See the *Boston Gazette and Weekly Journal*, October 2, November 13, and November 20, 1750 for the runaway ad for Attucks.

79. Cited in George Washington Williams, *History of the Negro Race in America, 1619–1880* (New York: G.P. Putnam's Sons, 1883, reprint, New York: Arno Press, 1968), 332.

80. Williams, *History of the Negro Race*, 332.

81. John Adams, quoted in Zinn, *People's History*, 67. See the *Boston Gazette*, March 12, 1770 for an eyewitness account of this event.

82. Benjamin Thatcher, *Traits of the Tea Party Being a Memoir of George R. T. Hewes* (New York: Harper & Bros., 1835), 103–104. See also William Cooper Nell, *The Colored Patriots of the American Revolution* (Boston: Robert F. Wallcut, 1855).

83. Thatcher, *Traits of the Tea Party*, 123–124.

84. Jack P. Greene, ed., *Reinterpretation of the American Revolution* (New York: Harper & Row, 1968), 169.

85. Scholars, writing about the period from the mid- to the late-1600s on Virginia's Eastern Shore, have argued that there was interracial coexistence on the basis of relative equality. Our argument for the North from the eighteenth century through the Revolution is a variation on this perspective, in that we find interracial cooperation within the lower ranks of American society. See T. H. Breen and Stephen Innes, *Myne Owne Ground* (New York: Oxford University Press, 1980).

Chapter 3

1. Letter "in behalf of our fellow slaves in this Province and by order of their committee," April 20, 1773, New York Historical Society.

2. Sidney Kaplan, *The Black Presence in the Era of the American Revolution, 1770–1800* (Greenwich, Conn.: New York Graphic Society, 1973), 11–13.

3. Kaplan, *Black Presence.*

4. Abigail Adams to John Adams, September 22, 1774, in Lyman H. Butterfield, ed., *Adams Family Correspondence*, vol. 1 (Cambridge, Mass.: Harvard University Press, 1963), 162, 13–14.

5. James Otis, *The Rights of British Colonies Asserted and Proved* (Boston: Edes & Gill, 1764), 37.

6. Nathaniel Appleton, *Considerations on Slavery* (Boston: Edes & Gill, 1767), 19–20; Benjamin Rush, *An Address to the Inhabitants of the British Settlements in*

America, Upon Slave-Keeping (1773; reprint New York: arno Press, 1969), quoted in Philip S. Foner, *History of Black Americans*, vol. 1 (Westport, Conn.: Greenwood Press, 1975), 301; Gary B. Nash, *Race and Revolution* (Madison, Wisc.: Madison House, 1990), 32.

7. Arthur Zilversmit, *The First Emancipation: The Abolition of Slavery in the North* (Chicago: University of Chicago Press, 1967), 61–83.

8. David Brion Davis, *The Problem of Slavery in Western Culture* (Ithaca, N. Y.: Cornell University Press, 1966). Some historians argue that the role of the Quakers in the early antislavery campaigns has been overemphasized, and that they were far less effective than has been assumed. For this view, see Donald L. Robinson, *Slavery in the Structure of American Politics, 1765–1820* (New York: Harcourt Brace Jovanovich, 1970).

9. Gary B. Nash, *Forging Freedom* (Cambridge, Mass.: Harvard University Press, 1988), 43. See also Davis, *Problem of Slavery*.

10. David Grimsted, "Anglo-American Racism and Phillis Wheatley's 'Sable Veil,' 'Length'ned Chain,' and 'Knitted Heart,'" in Ronald Hoffman and Peter J. Albert, eds., *Women in the Age of the American Revolution* (Charlottesville: University Press of Virginia, for the United States Capitol Historical Society, 1989), 374.

11. Grimsted, "Anglo-American Racism."

12. Samuel Hopkins, *A Dialogue Concerning the Slavery of the Africans; Shewing it to be the Duty and Interest of the American Colonies to emancipate all their African Slaves . . .* (Norwich, Conn.: 1776), in Gary B. Nash, *Race and Revolution* (Madison, Wisc.: Madison House, 1990), 100–111, 101.

13. Grimsted, "Anglo-American Racism."

14. Ellen Gibson Wilson, *The Loyal Blacks* (New York: Capricorn Books, 1976), 2–3.

15. Zilversmit, *First Emancipation*, 118.

16. Benjamin Quarles, *The Negro in the American Revolution* (1940, reprint, Chapel Hill: University of North Carolina Press, 1961).

17. Quarles, *Negro in the American Revolution*, 13–14.

18. Quarles, *Negro in the American Revolution*, 14.

19. John Hope Franklin, *From Slavery to Freedom*, 6th ed. (New York: McGraw-Hill, 1988), 68; William C. Nell, *Colored Patriots of the American Revolution* (Boston: Robert F. Wallcut, 1855), 21.

20. In this way Dunmore's offer was very much like Lincoln's offer of emancipation to slaves of the Confederacy almost one hundred years later, also a war measure of limited application. Wilson, *Loyal Blacks*, 25 & 22.

21. Wilson, *Loyal Blacks*, 21; Franklin, *From Slavery to Freedom*, 70.

22. Wilson, *Loyal Blacks*.

23. Wilson, *Loyal Blacks*; Howard Zinn, *A People's History of the United States* (New York: Harper & Row, 1980), 81.

24. See, for example, Herbert Aptheker, *American Negro Slave Revolts* (New York: International Publishers, 1943), 87–89, 200–201, 204–206.

25. *Pennsylvania Gazette*, June 12, 1780; Franklin, *From Slavery to Freedom*, 92. For information about the banditti, see Rachel N. Klein, *Unification of a Slave State: The Rise of the Planter Class in the South Carolina Backcountry, 1760–1808* (Chapel Hill: University of North Carolina Press, 1990), 95–99, quote from the *South-Car-*

olina Gazette June 12, 1784, in Klein, *Unification of a Slave State*, 99.

26. Paul Finkelman, *Slavery in the Courtroom: An Annotated Bibliography of American Cases* (Washington, D. C.: Library of Congress, 1985).

27. Foner, *History of Black Americans*, 1:296–297.

28. Wilson, *Loyal Blacks*, 27.

29. Wilson, *Loyal Blacks*. Leaders of the Southern Confederacy leveled a similar charge against the Emancipation Proclamation in 1863.

30. Wilson, *Loyal Blacks*, 28.

31. Wilson, *Loyal Blacks*, 42.

32. Roi Ottley and William J. Weatherby, eds., *The Negro in New York: An Informal Social History, 1626–1940* (New York: New York Public Library, 1967), 40.

33. Wilson, *Loyal Blacks*, 70–80.

34. Wilson, *Loyal Blacks*, 92–3, 113.

35. Wilson, *Loyal Blacks*, 42. Also see Robin W. Winks, *The Blacks in Canada: A History* (New Haven: Yale University Press, 1971).

36. Revolutionary War Pension Records, Jack Anthony, Records of the Veteran's Administration, Record Group #15, National Archives and Record Service, Washington, D. C. (hereafter RWPR cited by applicant's name).

37. RWPR, London Hazard.

38. RWPR, William Wanton.

39. RWPR, Henry Tabor, Dan Mallory, and Caesar Shelton.

40. William C. Nell, *Colored Patriots of the American Revolution* (Boston: Robert F. Wallcut, 1855, reprint, New York: Arno Press and the New York Times, 1968), 198.

41. James A. Henretta, *The Evolution of American Society, 1700–1815* (Lexington, Mass.: D. C. Heath, 1973), 158–161; John C. Miller, *The Wolf by the Ears: Thomas Jefferson and Slavery* (New York: Free Press, 1977), 24.

42. Miller, *Wolf by the Ears*; Quarles, *Negro in the American Revolution*, 60–67.

43. Matthew T. Mellon, *Early Views on Negro Slavery, from the Letters and Papers of the Founders of the Republic* (New York: Bergman Publishers, 1969) 57.

44. Lorenzo Greene, "Some Observations on the Black Regiment of Rhode Island in the American Revolution," *Journal of Negro History* 37 (January 1952): 142–172, 144.

45. Quarles, *Negro in the American Revolution*, 72.

46. RWPR, Barzilai Lew, Primus Hall, Titus Coburn, Obed Coffin, and James Cooper.

47. George Livermore, *An Historical Research Respecting the Opinions of the Founders of the Republic on Negroes as Slaves, as Citizens and as Soldiers, Annals of Congress, Sixteenth Congress, Second Session* (Boston: 1862), 154.

48. RWPR, Mingo Rodman and Richard Rhodes.

49. RWPR, Primus Coburn and Prince Hazeltine.

50. RWPR, Cato Cuff, Samuel Coombs, Prince Whipple, Oliver Cromwell, and Prince Bent.

51. RWPR, Windsor (or Winsor) Fry.

52. RWPR, Joseph Green.

53. RWPR, Thomas Hall.

54. RWPR, Primus Hall.

55. The ceremonial banner is in the collection of the Massachusetts Historical

Society, Boston, Massachusetts. For an account of Middleton's later life in Boston, see James Oliver Horton and Lois E. Horton, *Black Bostonians: Family Life and Community Struggle in the Antebellum North* (New York: Holmes & Meier, 1979).

56. Nash, *Race and Revolution*, 63–64.

57. Nell, *Colored Patriots*, 166–169.

58. Michael Cohn and Michael K. H. Platzer, *Black Men of the Sea* (New York: Dodd, Mead, 1978).

59. Roger Bruns, ed., *Am I Not a Man And Brother: The Antislavery Crusade of Revolutionary America, 1688–1788* (New York: Chelsea House, 1977), 452–6.

60. Foner, *History of Black Americans*, 1:347. At this time, Vermont was an independent state joined with 12 others under the Articles of Confederation.

61. Wilson, *Loyal Blacks*, 4; Leon Litwack, *North of Slavery* (Chicago: University of Chicago Press, 1961), 10.

62. Quarles, *Negro in the American Revolution*; Nell, *Colored Patriots*, 150–163.

63. Foner, *History of Black Americans*, 1:347.

64. Foner, *History of Black Americans*, 1:348; Zilversmit, *First Emancipation*, 116–117.

65. Robert J. Cottrol, *The Afro-Yankees: Providence's Black Community in the Antebellum Era* (Westport, Conn.: Greenwood Press, 1982), 31–32.

66. Nash, *Forging Freedom*, 34–35.

67. Pliny LeRoi Harwood, *History of Eastern Connecticut* (New Haven: Pioneer Publishing Company, 1932), 285.

68. Foner, *History of Black Americans*, 1:360–361; Debra L. Newman, "Black Women in the Era of the American Revolution in Pennsylvania," *Journal of Negro History* 61 (July 1976), 286. For a detailed picture of gradual emancipation in the North, see Zilversmit, *First Emancipation*, 110–138.

69. See *New Jersey Gazette*, September 20, 1780, October 4, 1780, or November 8, 1780; *New Jersey Journal*, November 29, 1780, December 27, 1780, or January 17, 1781.

70. Charles H. Wesley, "The Negroes of New York in the Emancipation Movement," *Journal of Negro History* 24 (January, 1939), 67; Zilversmit, *First Emancipation*, 147–148.

71. Zilversmit, *First Emancipation*, 222; Leonard P. Curry, *The Free Black in Urban America, 1800–1850* (Chicago: University of Chicago Press, 1981), 244–257.

72. Nash, *Race and Revolution*, 30.

73. J. R. Pole, *The Pursuit of Equality in American History* (Berkeley: University of California Press, 1978), ix.

74. Nash, *Race and Revolution*, 6, 30.

75. Grimsted, "Anglo-American Racism," 439.

76. Grimsted, "Anglo-American Racism," 443.

Chapter 4

1. Revolutionary War Pension Records, Records of the Veteran's Administration, Record Group #15, National Archives and Record Service, Washington, D. C. (hereafter RWPR); James Deetz, *In Small Things Forgotten: The Archeology of Early American Life* (Garden City, N. Y.: Anchor Doubleday, 1977).

2. John Vlach, research notes on Parting Ways. Our grateful thanks to Professor Vlach for generously sharing the field notes and research findings from his

work at the Parting Ways settlement.

3. Deetz, *Small Things Forgotten*, 148; Vlach, research notes.

4. Vlach, research notes; Karen Martin, "'Parting Ways' Links Africa with America's Hometown," *The Massachusetts Teacher* (May/June 1981): 20–22; Robert Farris Thompson, *Flash of the Spirit* (New York: Random House, 1983), 134.

5. Vlach, research notes; Jane G. Austin, *Dr. LeBaron and His Daughters* (1890; reprint, Boston: Houghton, Mifflin & Co., 1892).

6. Mary Beth Norton, *Liberty's Daughters* (Boston: Little, Brown, 1980); John Vlach, research notes.

7. RWPR, Cato Howe.

8. RWPR, Cato Fisk, various records dated from 1818–1853.

9. RWPR, Cato Fisk.

10. Paul Finkelman, *An Imperfect Union* (Chapel Hill: University of North Carolina Press, 1981), 80.

11. "Removal To the South, 1818," quoted in Clement Alexander Price, *Freedom Not Far Distant* (Newark: New Jersey Historical Society, 1980), 85–86.

12. Robert Fogel and Stanley L. Engerman, "Philanthropy at Bargain Prices: Notes in the Economics of Gradual Emancipation," *Journal of Legal Studies* 3 (1974): 393. Some historians, including Fogel and Engerman, contend that this helps to explain the relative shortage of black men in the urban North in the early nineteenth century. For a different view, see Gary B. Nash, "Forging Freedom: The Emancipation Experience in the Northern Seaport Cities, 1775–1820," in Ira Berlin and Ronald Hoffman, eds., *Slavery and Freedom in the Age of the American Revolution*, (Charlottesville: University Press of Virginia, for the United States Capitol Historical Society, 1983), 3–48.

13. Olive Gilbert, *Narrative of Sojourner Truth* (Battle Creek, Mich.:, 1878), quoted in Dorothy Sterling, ed., *Speak Out in Thunder Tones: Letters and Other Writings by Black Northerners, 1787–1865* (Garden City, N. Y.: Doubleday, 1973), 128.

14. Bert James Loewenberg and Ruth Bogin, eds., *Black Women in Nineteenth-Century American Life* (University Park: Pennsylvania State University Press, 1976), 234–242.

15. For quotes, see Jacqueline Bernard, *Journey Toward Freedom: The Story of Sojourner Truth* (New York: The Feminist Press at The City University of New York, 1990), 71. Also see, Harriet Beecher Stowe, "Sojourner Truth, The Libyan Sibyl," *Atlantic Monthly* 2 (April 1863): 473–481.

16. Bernard, *Journey Toward Freedom*.

17. *The Trial of Amos Broad and his Wife* (1809), reprint in Paul Finkelman, ed., *Free Blacks, Slaves, and Slaveowners in Civil and Criminal Courts*, 6th Ser., vol. 1 (New York: Garland Publishing, 1988), 179–209.

18. Ira Berlin, "The Structure of the Free Negro Caste," *Journal of Social History* 9 (Spring 1976): 297–318, 300.

19. Nash, "Forging Freedom," 5&7; Shane White, *Somewhat More Independent* (Athens: University of Georgia Press, 1991).

20. Nash, "Forging Freedom," 32–33.

21. White, *Somewhat More Independent*.

22. See James Oliver Horton, *Free People of Color* (Washington, D. C.: Smithsonian Institution Press, 1993), 122–144. The issue of color is both sensitive and long-standing among African Americans. For a discussion of stereotyping, see

John G. Mencke, *Mulattoes and Race Mixture: American Attitudes and Image, 1865–1918* (Ann Arbor: University of Michigan Research Press, 1976). For a general history see Joel Williamson, *New People* (New York: Free Press, 1980).

23. Joanna C. Colcord, ed., *Roll and Go, Songs of American Sailormen*, (Indianapolis, Ind.: The Bobbs-Merrill Co., 1924), 17, 32. For a novel in which the characterization of a mulatto woman fits this stereotype, see William Wells Brown, *Clotel; or The President's Daughter: A Narrative of Slave Life in the United States*, (London: Patridge & Oakey, 1853).

24. Frances Trollope, *Domestic Manners of the Americans*, ed., Donald Smalley (1832: reprint, New York: Alfred A. Knopf, 1949), 13.

25. Horton, *Free People of Color*, 137.

26. Nash, "Forging Freedom," 35.

27. Nash, "Forging Freedom," 35.

28. This couple-headed family pattern held for the large commercial cities of Cincinnati, Louisville, and Pittsburgh and for the small towns of Steubenville, Wheeling, Marietta, and Portsmouth. See Paul Lammermeier, "The Urban Black Family of the Nineteenth Century: A Study of Black Family Structure in the Ohio Valley, 1850–1880," *Journal of Marriage and Family* 35 (August 1973): 440–455.

29. Theodore Hershberg, "Free Blacks in Antebellum Philadelphia: A Study of Ex-Slave, Freeborn, and Socio-Economic Decline," *Journal of Social History* 5 (Winter 1971–72): 183–209.

30. We analyze the census data for 1850 and 1860 for Boston, Buffalo, Cincinnati, Chicago, Detroit, and Philadelphia; for 1850 for Russia Township, Ohio and Pittsburgh, and for 1860 for Oberlin and San Francisco. This historical context is important for the modern debate on single-parent black families that some have viewed as an indication of pathology. See, for example, Andrew Billingsley, *Black Families in White America* (Englewood Cliffs, N. J.: Prentice-Hall, 1968); Daniel Patrick Moynihan, *The Negro Family* (Washington, D. C.: U. S. Department of Labor, 1965); Reynolds Farley and Walter R. Allen, *The Color Line and the Quality of Life in America* (New York: Russell Sage Foundation, 1987); Carol Stack, *All Our Kin* (New York: Harper & Row, 1974); William Julius Wilson and Kathryn M. Neckerman, "Poverty and Family Structure: The Widening Gap Between Evidence and Public Policy Issues," in Sheldon H. Danziger and Daniel H. Weinberg, eds., *Fighting Poverty* (Cambridge, Mass.: Harvard University Press, 1986).

31. Nash, "Forging Freedom," 35.

32. Ranging from well over 50 percent in Cincinnati, 60 percent in Boston in 1850, and over 70 percent in the six smaller communities in 1860. Lammermeier found roughly three-quarters of the children in the postwar Ohio Valley living with two parents. See Lammermeier, "Urban Black Family" 451. In Detroit, about two-thirds of the children lived in two-parent families; over 80 percent of those under six, lived with both parents. In Chicago, 64 percent of the children under fifteen, but 80 percent of those under six, lived with two parents.

33. For similar findings, see Spencer Crew, *Black Life in Secondary Cities: A Comparative Analysis of the Black Communities of Camden and Elizabeth, New Jersey, 1860–1920* (New York: Garland Publishing, 1993); Lillian S. Williams, "The Development of a Black Community" (Ph. D. diss., SUNY Buffalo, 1979); Frances LaJune Johnson Powell, "A Study of the Structure of the Free Black Family in Washington, D. C., 1850–1880," (D. A. diss., Catholic University of America,

1980); Elizabeth Pleck, "The Two Parent Household: Black Family Structure in Late Nineteenth-Century Boston," *Journal of Social History* 6 (Fall 1973): 3–31; Elizabeth Hafkin Pleck, *Black Migration and Poverty* (New York: Academic Press, 1979).

34. Additionally, the number of single-parent families may be exaggerated, since men's work often kept them away from home for extended periods, and they may not have been recorded in the census with their families.

35. E. Franklin Frazier, *The Free Negro Family* (Nashville: Fisk University Press, 1932); Moynihan, *The Negro Family.*

36. Orville Vernon Burton, *In My Father's House Are Many Mansions* (Chapel Hill: University of North Carolina Press, 1985). Except in Boston, where they were about the same average age and were not overrepresented among female family heads.

37. Age seems to be the only valid predictor of female family headedness. The 1855 New York State census for Buffalo listed the length of time in the city for individual residents, but there was no correlation between length of residence and female headedness.

38. Cincinnati had the highest proportion of southern-born blacks and the highest proportion of single-parent households in any of the cities we studied. Southern-born tend to be older than northern-born. In Cincinnati in 1860, for example, 46 percent of northerners were eighteen to twenty-five years old, compared with 23 percent of southerners, whereas 41 percent of northerners and 50 percent of southerners were twenty-six to forty years old. Buffalo, Boston, and Chicago followed the same pattern. In Boston, 29 percent of northerners and 20 percent of southerners were eighteen to twenty-five, and 46 percent of northerners and 44 percent of southerners were 26 to 40.

39. Pleck, "Two Parent Household."

40. Hershberg, "Free Blacks in Antebellum Philadelphia." Lammermeier's interpretation of his data on the Ohio Valley communities parallels these findings. Lammermeier, "Urban Black Family."

41. Single-parent families were 2 percent of all families in 1850 and 4 percent in 1860. The increase was not statistically meaningful, involving an actual increase of only two female-headed families and was brought about largely by a general decline in the black population, to 630 in 1860. Melody Victoria Boyd, "Black Population of North Hempstead, 1830–1880" (Ph. D.diss., SUNY Stony Brook, 1981), 106, 131.

42. Burton, *In My Father's House.* See also Orville Vernon Burton, "The Rise and Fall of Afro-American Town Life," in Orville Vernon Burton and Robert C. McMath, Jr., eds., *Towards a New South?* (Westport, Conn.: Greenwood Press, 1982), 152–192.

43. Jacqueline Jones, *Labor of Love, Labor of Sorrow: Black Women, Work and the Family from Slavery to the Present* (New York: Basic Books, 1985), 35.

44. Zilpha Elaw, *Memoirs of the Life, Religious Experience, Ministerial Travels and Labours of Mrs. Zilpha Elaw* (London: 1846), in William L. Andrews, ed., *Sisters of the Spirit: Three Black Women's Autobiographies of the Nineteenth Century* (Bloomington: University of Indiana Press, 1986), 54. The high rate of black mortality was noted by several eighteenth-century observers. Poor urban dwellers were far more vulnerable to disease than those living in the country, and free blacks were

likely to be the poorest of poor urbanites. See J. P. Brissot de Warville, *New Travels in the United States of America, 1788*, ed., Durand Echeverria (Cambridge, Mass.: Harvard University Press, 1964).

45. Gary B. Nash and Jean R. Sonderlund, *Freedom By Degrees* (New York: Oxford University Press, 1991), 24; Billy G. Smith, *The "Lower Sort"* (Ithaca: Cornell University Press, 1990), 47; Leonard W. Johnson, Jr., "History of the Education of Negro Physicians," *Journal of Medical Education* 42 (May 1967): 439–446.

46. Howard P. Chudacoff and Judith Smith, *The Evolution of American Urban Society*, 3rd ed. (Englewood Cliffs, N. J.: Prentice Hall, 1988); Charles N. Glaab and A. Theodore Brown, *A History of Urban America*, 2nd ed. (New York: Macmillan, 1976); Elizabeth Blackmar, *Manhattan for Rent, 1785–1850* (Ithaca: Cornell University Press, 1989), 84–85. Different authorities give different years for urban epidemics, pointing up the difficulty perhaps of determining when an outbreak of disease reaches epidemic proportions. Blackmar, for example, lists the years 1792, 1796, 1799, 1803, and 1805 as epidemic years for yellow fever in New York City.

47. George Washington Williams, *History of the Negro Race in America* (1883, reprint, New York: Arno Press and *The New York Times*, 1968); J. H. Powell, *Bring Out Your Dead* (Philadelphia: University of Pennsylvania Press, 1949); Glaab and Brown, *History of Urban America*; Gary B. Nash, *Forging Freedom* (Cambridge, Mass.: Harvard University Press, 1988), 122.

48. Smith, *"Lower Sort"*; Blackmar, *Manhattan for Rent*; Leonard P. Curry, *Free Black in Urban America, 1800–1850* (Chicago: University of Chicago Press, 1981), 137–139.

49. Quoted in Curry, *Free Black in Urban America*, 137; John H. Griscom, *The Sanitary Conditions of the Laboring Population of New York, With Suggestions for Its Improvement* (New York: 1845), 18, cited in Curry, *Free Black in Urban America*, 53.

50. Sam Bass Warner, Jr., *The Private City: Philadelphia in Three Periods of Its Growth* (Philadelphia: University of Pennsylvania Press, 1968), 126–127.

51. Josiah Curtis, *Report of the Joint Special Committee on the Census of Boston, May 1855* (Boston: 1856); James Oliver Horton and Lois E. Horton, *Black Bostonians* (New York: Holmes & Meier, 1979), 3.

52. Nash and Sonderlund, *Freedom By Degrees*, 25. For the 1820 see Gary Nash, "Forging Freedom," 3–48, 38. The ratio of children to adult women is based on the number of children under the age of fourteen years divided by the number of women between twenty-six years and forty-four years. Horton and Horton, *Black Bostonians*, 3.

53. Nancy Prince, *A Narrative of the Life and Travels of Mrs. Nancy Prince*, 2nd ed. (Boston: Nancy Prince, 1853).

54. Since the 1850 census did not provide information about the relationship of family members to the family head, last name is the best indicator of such relationships.

55. See Horton and Horton, *Black Bostonians*, for data on informal adoption and expanded households in antebellum Boston. Also see Robert B. Hill, *Informal Adoption among Black Families* (Washington, D. C.: National Urban League, 1977).

56. Several important works focus on the nexus of African-American and African family arrangements and traditions. One of the most concise is Niara Sudarkasa, "Interpreting the African Heritage in Afro-American Family Organization," in Harriette Pipes McAdoo, ed., *Black Families* (Beverly Hills: Sage Publications, 1981), 37–53.

57. Sudarkasa argued this point effectively. See Sudarkasa, "Interpreting the African Heritage."

58. John S. Mbiti, *African Religions and Philosophies* (Garden City, New York: Doubleday, 1970); Kenneth Onwuka Dike, *Trade and Politics in the Niger Delta* (Oxford: Clarendon Press, 1956).

59. Herbert Gutman, *The Black Family in Slavery and Freedom* (New York: Pantheon Press, 1976), 448; Horton, *Free People of Color*.

60. The story of Robert Johnson was compiled from the U. S. Census for 1850 and 1860; the *Boston City Directory* 1848–49, 1850, 1855, and 1858; and from *the Records of the Boston Assessor* 1848, 1855, 1859, and 1860.

61. Over 70 percent.

62. The Will of Reuben Hawkins, 1837/1838; Cincinnati City Directory, 1836–37, 1841, and 1850; the U. S. Census for 1850 and 1860.

63. Horton and Horton, *Black Bostonians*, 16.

64. This influx increased the percentage of northern-born lodgers from 26 percent in 1850 to 30 percent by 1860.

65. Adult children were categorized as boarders. Since the census did not indicate relationships before 1880, it was safer to count all adults not in their own households as boarders. Though relatives had different relationships than unrelated persons, familial-type bonds often formed even between those who were not kin, making the line between actual kin and fictive kin indistinct.

66. Between 1850 and 1860 the average age of female boarders dropped from thirty-five years to just over thirty-two years, where as the average age for all of Cincinnati's black adult women (over the age of seventeen) rose from thirty-three to thirty-five years.

67. The Will of John Liverpool, 1863/1866, Cincinnati, Ohio; the Will of Mary Liverpool, 1877/1882, Cincinnati, Ohio; the U. S. Census for 1850 and 1860; various issues of the Cincinnati City Directory.

68. Willard B. Gatewood, Jr., ed., *Free Man of Color: The Autobiography of Willis Augustus Hodges* (Knoxville: University of Tennessee Press, 1982), xxiv.

69. Julia A. J. Foote, *A Brand Plucked From the Fire: An Autobiographical Sketch* (Cleveland: 1879), reprint in William L. Andrews, ed., *Sisters of the Spirit: Three Black Women's Autobiographies of the Nineteenth Century* (Bloomington: Indiana University Press, 1986), 168.

70. Percentages computed from the Philadelphia Quaker Census, 1847, provided to the Afro-American Communities Project at the National Museum of American History of the Smithsonian Institution by the Philadelphia Social History Project at the University of Pennsylvania.

Chapter 5

1. Arthur Zilversmit, *The First Emancipation: The Abolition of Slavery in the North* (Chicago: University of Chicago Press, 1967), 222.

2. George W. Williams, *History of the Negro Race in America*, vol. 2 (1882, reprint, New York: Arno Press and *The New York Times*, 1968), 127–130.

3. Williams, *History of the Negro Race*, 222–224.

4. Lee Calligaro, "The Negro's Legal Status in Pre-Civil War New Jersey," *New Jersey History* 85 (Fall & Winter 1967): 167–180; Marion T. Wright, "New Jersey Laws and the Negro," *Journal of Negro History* 38 (April 1943): 156–199.

5. Paul Finkelman, "Prelude to the Fourteenth Amendment: Black Legal Rights in the Antebellum North," *Rutgers Law Journal* 17 (Spring & Summer 1986): 415–482.

6. Carter G. Woodson, "The Negroes of Cincinnati Prior to the Civil War," *Journal of Negro History* 1 (January, 1916): 1–22; Paul Finkelman, *An Imperfect Union: Slavery, Federalism, and Comity* (Chapel Hill: University of North Carolina Press, 1981).

7. Henry J. Cadbury, "Negro Membership in the Society of Friends," *Journal of Negro History* 21 (April 1936): 151–213.

8. Frank U. Quillen, *The Color Line in Ohio: History of Race Prejudice in a Typical Northern State* (Ann Arbor, Mich.: G. Wahr, 1913); Robert A. Folk, "Black Man's Burden in Ohio, 1849–1863" (Ph. D. diss., University of Toledo, 1972).

9. Henry W. Farnam, *Chapters in the History of Social Legislation in the United States to 1860* (Washington, D. C.: Carnegie Institution of Washington, 1938). Richard Wade, "The Negro in Cincinnati, 1800–1830," *Journal of Negro History* 39 (January 1954): 43–57.

10. Wade, "Negro in Cincinnati." Leonard Curry suspects that the claims of substantial migration of Cincinnati blacks to Canada after the race riot of 1829 are greatly exaggerated. See Leonard P. Curry, *The Free Black in Urban America, 1800–1850: The Shadow of the Dream* (Chicago: University of Chicago Press, 1981), 305 n. 22.

11. E. Franklin Frazier, *The Free Negro Family* (1932; reprint, New York: Arno Press and *The New York Times*, 1968); William Cheek and Aimee Lee Cheek, *John Mercer Langston and the Fight for Black Freedom 1829–1865* (Urbana: University of Illinois Press, 1989).

12. Cheek and Cheek, *John Mercer Langston.*

13. Cheek and Cheek, *John Mercer Langston.* For a recent study of such unconventional stable relationships and families, see Adele Logan Alexander, *Ambiguous Lives: Free Women of Color in Rural Georgia, 1789–1879* (Fayetteville: University of Arkansas Press, 1992).

14. Cheek and Cheek, *John Mercer Langston*, 35.

15. W. Sherman Savage, *Blacks in the West* (Westport, Conn.: Greenwood Press, 1976).

16. William Francis Cheek III, "Forgotten Prophet: The Life of John Mercer Langston" (Ph. D. diss., University of Virginia, 1961); Kenneth Kusmer, *A Ghetto Takes Shape* (Urbana: University of Illinois Press, 1976). For excellent treatments of racial attitudes in the West and Midwest, see V. Jacque Voegeli, *Free But Not Equal: The Midwest and the Negro during the Civil War* (Chicago: University of Chicago Press, 1967), and Eugene H. Berwanger, *The Frontier Against Slavery: Western Anti-Negro Prejudice and the Slavery Expansion Controversy* (Urbana: University of Illinois, 1967). The first African American to hold elective office in the United States was Alexander Lucius Twilight who probably graduated from Middlebury College in 1823 and was elected to the Vermont legislature in 1836. See "The First Black American College Graduate," *Middlebury College Newsletter* (Spring 1974); Lerone Bennett, Jr., *Before the Mayflower*, 5th ed., (New York: Penguin Books, 1984).

17. William C. Gregg, "Reminiscences of Calvin Township, Cass County, Michigan" (undated typescript, Michigan Historical Collection); Booker T. Washington, *The Story of the Negro: The Rise of the Race From Slavery*, vol. 1 (New York:

Doubleday, Page and Co., 1909); William H. Pease and Jane H. Pease, *Black Utopia: Negro Communal Experiments in America* (Madison: The State Historical Society of Wisconsin, 1963).

18. Charles Wesley, "Negro Suffrage in the Period of Constitution-Making, 1787–1865," *Journal of Negro History* 32 (April 1947): 143–168; Leo H. Hirsch, "The Free Negro In New York," in "The Negro In New York, 1783–1865," *Journal of Negro History* 16 (October 1931): 415–453.

19. G. S. Rowe, "Black Offenders, Criminal Courts, and Philadelphia Society in the Late Eighteenth-Century," *Journal of Social History* 22 (Summer 1989): 685–712, 688. Rowe found that 44 percent were runaways during that period.

20. Billy G. Smith, *The "Lower Sort"* (Ithaca: Cornell University Press, 1990), 165; G. S. Rowe, "Black Offenders," 696. Crimes against the public order accounted for fewer than one-half of 1 percent of black males' crimes but nearly one-quarter of white males' crimes between 1780 and 1800 according to Rowe.

21. Curry reports that there were more than four times the number of blacks in Boston's house of correction as might be expected if all groups were evenly represented. Curry, *Free Black in Urban America*, 113.

22. Noel Ignatiev, "Black, White and Green: Relations Among Irish-American and African American Workers in the Early Nineteenth Century" (paper presented at the American Studies Association convention, New Orleans, November, 1990). Also see Noel Ignatieve, *How the Irish Became White* (New York: Routledge, 1995). During this period blacks were approximately 10 percent of Philadelphia's population.

23. Shane White, *Somewhat More Independent* (Athens: The University of Georgia Press, 1991), 31.

24. The federal government was located in Philadelphia at that time.

25. Pennsylvania Abolition Society records indicate that between 1787 and 1810, 508 French slaves were freed in the state. Forty-five of these were granted their immediate freedom, two purchased their own freedom, and the vast majority were indentured. Gary B. Nash and Jean R. Sonderlund, *Freedom By Degrees* (New York: Oxford University Press, 1991), 181.

26. White, *Somewhat More Independent*; Albert J. Raboteau, *Slave Religion* (New York: Oxford University Press, 1978).

27. Paul A. Gilje, *The Road to Mobocracy* (Chapel Hill: University of North Carolina Press, 1987), 149.

28. Melvin George Herndon, *William Tatham and the Culture of Tobacco* (Coral Gables, Fl.: University of Miami Press, 1969), 88–89.

29. Records of the Suffolk County Probate Court, estate #40544, 1856 inventory of James Gardner.

30. Whittington B. Johnson, "Negro Laboring Classes in Early America, 1750–1820", (Ph. D. diss., University of Georgia, 1970), 140–141.

31. Constance McLaughlin Green, *American Cities* (New York: Harper & Row, 1957); "Anthony D. Allen to Doctor Dougal," Honolulu, Hawaii, 1822 (copy on file at the Hawaiian Historical Society) published with introduction by Marc Scruggs in "Anthony D. Allen: A Prosperous American of African Descent in Early 19th Century Hawaii," *The Hawaiian Journal of History* 26 (1992): 55–93.

32. Lamont D. Thomas, *Rise To Be A People* (Urbana: University of Illinois Press, 1986). The name Kofi was a common one indicating he was born on Friday.

33. Thomas, *Rise To Be A People*.

34. Dorothy Sterling, ed., *We Are Your Sisters: Black Women in the Nineteenth Century* (New York: W. W. Norton, 1984).

35. Sterling, ed., *We Are Your Sisters*. Most of Paul Cuffe's and Michael Wainer's crew members were family members, including both sons and sons-in-law. Paul and Alice Cuffe had five daughters and two sons, and Michael and Mary Wainer had six daughters and six sons.

36. Lorin Lee Cary and Francine C. Cary, "Absalom F. Boston, His Family and Nantucket's Black Community." *Historic Nantucket Quarterly*, 25 (Summer 1977): 15–23.

37. Jeffrey Bolster, "African-American Sailors, 1700–1885" (Ph. D. diss., Johns Hopkins University, 1991). Bolster's work is the most complete study to date of black seamen in the Atlantic maritime world.

38. Quote from Thomas Hamilton, *Men and Manners in America*, vol. 1 (Edinburgh: 1834), 104. Unless otherwise indicated, all city statistical data is derived from the U. S. manuscript census.

39. See Daniel E. Sutherland, "Americans and Their Servants, 1800–1920" (Ph. D. diss., Wayne State University, 1976). Sutherland has produced an exhaustive and fine study of domestic workers in the nineteenth and early twentieth century.

40. Only 14 percent of total live-in domestics in 1860.

41. Eliza Leslie, *Miss Leslie's Behavior Book* (1859; reprint, New York: Arno Press, 1972), 97.

42. Sutherland, "Americans and Their Servants," 92–93.

43. Leslie, *Miss Leslie's Behavior Book*, 296.

44. Henry Watson, Jr. to Sophia Watson, August 17 and 20, 1860, Henry Watson, Jr. Papers, Perkings Library, Duke University, quoted in Sutherland, "Americans and Their Servants," 54–55.

45. In 1855, for example, more than one-third of all the housing African Americans owned in Buffalo was held by six barbers, three carpenters, and a painter. New York State Census for Buffalo, 1855.

46. Simeon F. Moss, "The Persistence of Slavery and Involuntary Servitude in a Free State (1685–1866)," *Journal of Negro History* 35, 3 (July 1950): 289–314.

47. Moss, "Persistence of Slavery."

48. See, for example, Martin R. Delany, *The Condition, Elevation, Emigration, and Destiny of the Colored People of the United States* (1852; reprint, New York: Arno Press, 1968); George Washington Williams, *A History of the Negro Race in America from 1619 to 1880* (New York: G. P. Putnam & Sons, 1882); W. Sherman Savage, *Blacks in the West* (Westport, Conn.: Greenwood Press 1976), 131; Williams Wells Brown, *The Black Man: His Antecedents, His Genius and His Achievements* (1863; New York: Arno Press, 1969); William Cooper Nell, *The Colored Patriots of the American Revolution* (Boston: R. F. Walcut 1855).

49. Sterling, ed., *We Are Your Sisters*, 100–101, 103, 217; *Weekly Anglo-African*, January 1, 1862.

50. The Female Trading Association: Colored American, June 7, 1841; Sterling, ed., *We Are Your Sisters*.

51. Elizabeth Keckley, *Behind the Scenes; or Thirty Years a Slave and Four Years in the White House*, (1868; New York: Oxford University Press, 1988).

52. *Weekly Anglo-African*, October 9, 1861.

53. Frederick Law Olmsted, *The Cotton Kingdom*, ed. Arthur M. Schlesinger (New York: Alfred A. Knopf, 1970), 233.

54. Willard B. Gatewood, Jr., ed., *Free Man of Color: The Autobiography of Willis Augustus Hodges*, (Knoxville: University of Tennessee Press, 1982), 39.

55. Benjamin C. Bacon, *Statistics of the Colored People of Philadelphia* (Philadelphia: T. E. Chapman, 1856), 15; Edward Abdy, *Journal of a Residence and Tour in the United States of North America, from April, 1833 to October, 1834* (London: J. Murray, 1835), 121–122. Curry found a similar situation in Baltimore where during the 1840s and 1850s black caulkers met open hostility from white craftsmen who forced many blacks out of the profession. He found the situation much better for blacks in cities farther south. Curry, *Free Black in Urban America*, 20–21.

56. Leonard Curry found only ten blacks listed as carters in the New York City directories for the 1840s, and that only 1 percent of all employed blacks pursued that trade during the 1850s. See Curry, *Free Black in Urban America*, 18.

57. Frederick Douglass, "My Escape to Freedom," *Century Magazine* 23 (November, 1881), 125–131, cited in Philip S. Foner and Ronald L. Lewis, eds., *The Black Worker*, vol. 1 (Philadelphia: Temple University Press, 1978), 135–137.

58. Philip Foner, *History of Black Americans*, vol. 2 (Westport, Conn.: Greenwood Press, 1983); Ohio Anti-Slavery Society, *Proceedings of the Ohio Antislavery Convention Held at Putnam on the Twenty-Second, Twenty-Third, and Twenty-Fourth of April, 1835* (n.d.), 19.

59. *Philanthropist*, November 10, 1841, December 21 and 28, 1842.

60. "Learn Trades or Starve," *Frederick Douglass' Paper*, March 4, 1853.

61. Esther Douty, *Forten the Sailmaker: Pioneer Champion of Negro Rights* (Chicago: Rand McNally, 1968).

62. Folk, "Black Man's Burden in Ohio"; Delany, *Condition, Elevation, Emigration*.

63. Folk, "Black Man's Burden in Ohio."

64. James Oliver Horton and Lois E. Horton, *Black Bostonians* (New York: Holmes & Meier, 1979).

65. Julie Winch, *Philadelphia's Black Elite: Activism, Accommodation, and the Struggle for Autonomy, 1787–1848*, (Philadelphia: Temple University Press, 1988). Professionals among these elites between 1787 and 1848 were 3 dentists, 12 ministers, 2 physicians, and 12 teachers.

66. The small community of blacks in Oberlin, home of Oberlin College—the first institution of higher learning to admit blacks and white women on an equal basis with white males—had a relatively high 5 percent of black workers who were professionals (7 individuals) and nearly one-third who were skilled workers or business owners. James Oliver Horton, "Black Education at Oberlin College: A Controversial Commitment," *Journal of Negro Education* 54 (Fall 1985): 477–499.

67. Leonard W. Johnson, Jr., "History of the Education of Negro Physicians," *Journal of Medical Education* 42 (May 1967): 439–446.

68. *Weekly Anglo-African*, July 23, 1859.

69. Johnson, "History of the Education of Negro Physicians," 440; Papers Relating to Negroes at Harvard" (unpublished); "Medical Faculty Minutes," November 4, 1850, December 26, 1850, and November 16, 1853.

70. Delany, *Condition, Elevation, Emigration*; Richard Bardolph, "Social Origins of Negroes, 1770–1865," *Journal of Negro History*, 40 (July 1955): 244–248.

71. Bardolph, "Social Origins."
72. Cheek, "Forgotten Prophet," 14–15, 38–39, 45–47.
73. Horton and Horton, *Black Bostonians*.
74. Revolutionary War veteran Lemuel Haynes was probably the first black minister to regularly serve a white congregation. He served a number of predominantly white congregations in Connecticut, New York State and Vermont before his death in 1833. W. H. Morse, "Lemuel Haynes," *Journal of Negro History* 41 (January 1919): 22–32; Timothy Mather Cooley, *Sketches of the Life and Character of the Rev. Lemuel Haynes* (New York: Harper & Brothers, 1837). The role of black ministers is discussed in Chapter 6.
75. Horton and Horton, *Black Bostonians*, 70–74. The first black college graduate in the nation was Edward Jones (Amherst College, August 23, 1826, two weeks before Russwurm). Foner, *History of Black Americans*.
76. Jim Bearden and Linda Jean Butler, *Shadd: The Life and Times of Mary Ann Shadd Cary* (Toronto: NC Press, 1977); Carla L. Peterson, *Doers of the Word: African American Women Speakers and Writers in the North (1830–1880)*, (New York: Oxford University Press, 1995).
77. In San Francisco the proportion of mulattoes and darker blacks was about even in the lower occupational levels, but mulattoes constituted more than two-thirds of those at the higher levels. In every city except San Francisco, well over half were married, compared with only about one-third of lower-level workers. San Francisco had a much higher proportion of single men, but the pattern was the same—less than 40 percent of upper-level workers and less than 20 percent of lower-level workers were married. In most cities upper-level workers were a year or two older than other workers, but in Boston and Cincinnati they were actually younger.
78. The will of Catherine Dorham, Hamilton County, Ohio (1866).
79. Will of Charlotte Browning, County of Hamilton, Ohio (1850/1852).
80. Delany, *Condition, Elevation, Emigration*; Folk, "Black Man's Burden in Ohio; Carter G. Woodson "The Negroes of Cincinnati Prior to the Civil War," *Journal of Negro History*, 1 (January 1916): 21–22; Linda Krane Ellwein, "The Negroes in Cincinnati: The Black Experience, 1870–1880," (master's thesis, University of Cincinnati, 1970); Will of Robert Gordon, County of Hamilton, Ohio (1883–84).
81. Carol Buchalter Stapp, *Afro-Americans in Antebellum Boston: An Analysis of Probate Records* (New York: Garland Publishing, 1993), 164.
82. Marilyn Richardson, ed., *Maria W. Stewart* (Bloomington: Indiana University Press, 1987).
83. *Liberator*, March 12, 1858, reprint in Thomas R. Frazier, ed., *Afro-American History: Primary Sources*, shorter ed., (New York: Harcourt Brace Jovanovich, 1971), 75.

Chapter 6

1. Alexis de Tocqueville, *Democracy in America*, ed., Phillips Bradley, vol. 2 (New York: Alfred A. Knopf, 1976), 106.
2. Gary B. Nash, "Forging Freedom: The Emancipation Experience in the Northern Seaport Cities, 1775–1820," in Ira Berlin and Ronald Hoffman eds., *Slavery and Freedom in the Age of the American Revolution* (Charlottesville: University Press of Virginia, 1983), 3–48, 46.

3. Leonard P. Curry, *The Free Black in Urban America, 1800–1850* (Chicago: University of Chicago Press, 1981); Loretta J. Williams, *Black Freemasonry and Middle-Class Realities* (Columbia: University of Missouri Press, 1980), 14, 69. The Baltimore lodge was the southern-most group established in these early years.

4. Williams, *Black Freemasonry*; William H. Grimshaw, *Official History of Freemasonry among the Colored People of North America* (New York: Broadway Publishing Company, 1903); Philip S. Foner, *History of Black Americans* , vol. 1 (Westport, Conn.: Greenwood Press, 1975), 560. Harry Reed correctly points out that this was the earliest attempt to establish a national black organization. See Harry Reed, *Platform for Change: The Foundation of the Northern Free Black Community, 1775–1865* (East Lansing: Michigan State University Press, 1994), 63.

5. Williams, *Black Freemasonry*. Ironically, despite the significance of Egyptian mythology in Masonic practices, scholars persist in depicting black Masons as simply adopting a European institution and in this way attempting to become part of a strictly European culture.

6. Gary B. Nash, *Forging Freedom* (Cambridge: Harvard University Press, 1988), 98.

7. James B. Browning, "The Beginnings of Insurance Enterprise Among Negroes," *Journal of Negro History* 22 (October 1937): 417–432.

8. See, for example, Melville J. Herskovits, *The Myth of the Negro Past* (New York: Harper & Bros., 1941); Sidney W. Mintz and Richard Price, "An Anthropological Approach to the Afro-American Past: A Caribbean Perspective," ISHI Occasional Paper, 2 (Philadelphia, 1976); Robert L. Harris, Jr., "Early Black Benevolent Societies, 1780–1830," *The Massachusetts Review* 20 (Autumn 1979): 603–625, 613.

9. Revolutionary War Pension Records (RWPR), Primus Jacobs, Records of the Veteran's Administration, Record Group #15, National Archives and Record Service, Washington, D. C.

10. Browning, "Beginnings of Insurance Enterprise."

11. Dorothy Sterling, ed., *We Are Your Sisters* (New York: W. W. Norton, 1984), 107–108.

12. Richard D. Brown, "The Emergence of Voluntary Associations in Massachusetts, 1760–1830," *Journal of Voluntary Action Research* 2 (April, 1973), 64–73.

13. See James Oliver Horton and Lois E. Horton, *Black Bostonians* (New York: Holmes & Meier, 1979), 31–32; James Oliver Horton, *Free People of Color* (Washington, D. C.: Smithsonian Institution Press, 1993), 98–121; Shirley J. Yee, *Black Women Abolitionists: A Study in Activism, 1828–1860* (Knoxville: University of Tennessee Press, 1992), 75–85.

14. Browning, "Beginnings of Insurance Enterprise," 419; Daniel Perlman, "Organizations of the Free Negro in New York City, 1800–1860," *Journal of Negro History* 56 (July 1971): 181–197.

15. Sterling, ed., *We Are Your Sisters*, 105; Browning, "Beginnings of Insurance Enterprise": 419.

16. Minutes of the Union Benevolent Sons of Bethel African Methodist Episcopal Church, 1826–1844, The Holdings of the Mother Bethel African Methodist Episcopal Church Historical Museum (Microfilm Collection, Bethel AME Church, Philadelphia). Selected rolls of the microfilmed records are on file at the Afro-American Communities Project at the National Museum of American History, Smithsonian Institution, Washington, D. C.

17. James Oliver Horton and Lois E. Horton, "Black Theology and Historical Necessity," in Miles L. Bradbury and James B. Gilbert, eds., *Transforming Faith: The Sacred and Secular in Modern America* (Westport, Conn.: Greenwood Press, 1989).

18. Allen D. Austin, *African Muslims in Antebellum America: A Sourcebook* (New York: Garland Publishing, 1984), 15–21. The story of Bilali and his descendants is the basis of William S. McFeely's *Sapelo's People* (New York: W. W. Norton, 1994).

19. Austin, *African Muslims*, 22.

20. Sir Hans Sloane, *A Voyage to the Islands of Madera, Barbados, Nieves, St. Christophers, and Jamaica* . . . , vol. 1 (London: printed by B. M. For the author, 1707), xl, and Charles Leslie, *A New and Exact Account of Jamaica* (Edinburgh: 1739), in Roger D. Abrahams and John F. Szwed, eds., *After Africa* (New Haven: Yale University Press, 1983), 163–164.

21. Sterling Stuckey, *Slave Culture: Nationalist Theory and the Foundations of Black America* (New York: Oxford University Press, 1987); William D. Piersen, *Black Yankees: The Development of an Afro-American Subculture in Eighteenth-Century New England* (Amherst: The University of Massachusetts Press, 1988).

22. Charles Joyner, *Down by the Riverside: A South Carolina Slave Community* (Urbana: University of Illinois Press, 1984), 141.

23. Such cults were descendants of the snake god worship popular among the Ewe, Bantu, Dahomey, and Ouidah nations of coastal West Africa.

24. See for example, Increase Mather, "Remarkable Providences," and Cotton Mather, "Wonders," in Richard M. Dorson, ed., *America Begins: Early American Writings* (Greenwich, Conn.: Fawcett, 1950), 348–349, 362–366.

25. Elizabeth H. Pleck, *Black Migration and Poverty, Boston, 1865–1900* (New York: Academic Press, 1979).

26. See Nathan O. Hatch, *The Democratization of American Christianity* (New Haven: Yale University Press, 1989) or Mechal Sobel, *Trabelin' On: The Slave Journey to an Afro-Baptist Faith* (Princeton, N. J.: Princeton University Press, 1988).

27. Albert J. Raboteau, *Slave Religion* (New York: Oxford University Press, 1978), 128.

28. Sobel, *Trabelin' On*, 65.

29. Hatch, *Democratization of American Christianity*, 9, 11.

30. Lorenzo Dow, quoted in Hatch, *Democratization of American Christianity*, 20. See also Sobel, *Trabelin' On*.

31. Important information on the rise of the independent black Methodist church and its preachers can be found in Graham Russell Hodges, ed., *Black Itinerants of the Gospel: The Narratives of John Jea and George White* (Madison, Wisc.: Madison House, 1993).

32. Daniel A. Payne, *Recollections of 70 Years* (1888; reprint, New York: Arno Press, 1969), 250–254; Portia K. Maultsby, "Music of Northern Independent Black Churches During the Ante-Bellum Period," *Ethnomusicology* (September 1975): 416.

33. Hatch, *Democratization of American Christianity*; Olly Wilson, "The Association of Movement and Music as a Manifestation of a Black Conceptual Approach to Music-Making," in Irene V. Jackson, ed., *More Than Dancing: Essays on Afro-American Music and Musicians* (Westport, Conn.: Greenwood Press, 1985), 9–23. Most historians acknowledge the appeal of evangelical religion for blacks, but few appreciate the extent to which those practices were actually shaped by traditional African religious practices. See, for example, Reed, *Platform for Change*, 19–20.

34. "Budget Flahaven Cary to Matthew Cary," August 5, 1806, Historical Soci-

ety of Pennsylvania, AA #789, Budget F. Cary.

35. Sobel, *Trabelin' On.*

36. Maultsby, "Music of Northern Independent Black Churches," 405.

37. William L. Andrews, ed., *Sisters of the Spirit* (Bloomington: Indiana University Press, 1986), 71.

38. Andrews, ed., *Sisters of the Spirit.*

39. Hatch, *Democratization of American Christianity*, 102. See also Sobel, *Trabelin' On*; Stuckey, *Slave Culture*; Andrews, ed., *Sisters of the Spirit*; Milton H. Sernett, *Black Religion and Afro-American Evangelicalism, 1787–1865* (Metchen, N.J.: Scarecrow Press, 1975).

40. Nathaniel Paul, "An Address Delivered on the Celebration of the Abolition of Slavery in the State of New York, July 5, 1827," in Carter G. Woodson, ed. *Negro Orators and Their Orations* (New York: Russell and Russell, 1969), 69.

41. James H. Cone, "Black Theology in American Religion," *Journal of the American Academy of Religion* 53 (December 1985): 755–771, 757.

42. George Levesque has argued that Baptist doctrine acted as a conservative force, curbing the reform action of the black Baptist, churches of antebellum Boston. We believe that this is a misreading of the evidence. First, one is hard pressed to identify what he calls "Baptist Orthodoxy," and second, the black Baptist church, like most black churches, was an active center of reform activity in Boston and elsewhere. See George A. Levesque, "Inherent Reformers-Inherited Orthodoxy: Black Baptists in Boston, 1800–1873," *Journal of Negro History* 60, 4 (October, 1975): 491–525.

43. Richard Allen, *The Life Experience and Gospel Labor of the Right Reverend Richard Allen* (1887; reprint, New York: Abingdon Press, 1960), 25–26. For a biographical treatment of Allen, see Carol V. R. George, *Segregated Sabbath: Richard Allen and the Emergence of Independent Black Churches, 1760–1840* (New York: Oxford University Press, 1973).

44. Allen, *Life Experience*, 10–11; George, *Segregated Sabbath*, 28–31.

45. Nash, *Forging Freedom*, 111; Allen, *Life Experience*; George, *Segregated Sabbath*; William J. Simmons, *Men of Mark* (Cleveland: George M. Rewell, 1887, reprint, New York: Arno Press, 1968).

46. Nash, *Forging Freedom*, 111–114.

47. Allen, *Life Experience*, 18, 14; George, *Segregated Sabbath.*

48. George, *Segregated Sabbath.*

49. Allen, *Life Experience*, 29.

50. Nash, *Forging Freedom*, 127.

51. Nash, *Forging Freedom*, 195.

52. William Douglass, *Annals of the First African Church in the United States of America, Now Styled the African Episcopal Church of St. Thomas* (Philadelphia: King and Baird, 1862), 94, quoted in Nash, *Forging Freedom*, 131.

53. Allen, *Life Experience*, 29–30.

54. Quoted in Eileen Southern *The Music of Black Americans: A History*, 2nd ed. (New York: W. W. Norton, 1983), 75–79.

55. Southern, *Music of Black Americans*, 79.

56. Quoted in Southern, *Music of Black Americans*, 75–79.

57. Rosalind Cobb Wiggins, ed., "Paul Cuffe, Quaker: His Logs and Letters" (unpublished manuscript, n.d.). See Rosalind Wiggins, ed., *Captain Paul Cuffe's Logs and Letters, 1808–1817* (Washington, D. C.: Howard University Press, 1996).

58. There are several good accounts of such tent meetings. See for example, Andrews, ed., *Sisters of the Spirit*, 64–67, and Sobel, *Trabelin On*, 139–149. Although the style of services often suited blacks, the practice of segregated seating or standing only for blacks encouraged the development of black-sponsored tent meetings after 1820. These meetings seated whites among the predominantly black participants.

59. Sobel, *Trabelin' On*, 143; Southern, *Music of Black Americans*.

60. Nash, *Forging Freedom*, 198; Hatch, *Democratization of American Christianity*.

61. For an excellent account of the events leading to the formation of St. Thomas Church, see Douglass, *Annals of the First African Church*.

62. Daniel A. Payne, *History of the African Methodist Episcopal Church* (Nashville, Tenn.: Publishing House of the A. M. E. Sunday-School Union, 1891).

63. Payne, *History of the AME Church*; Daniel Alexander Payne, *Recollections of Seventy Years* (Nashville Tenn.: Publishing House of the A. M. E. Sunday School Union, 1888), 100–101; Sernett, *Black Religion*, 122–123. For a discussion of the significance of skin color among antebellum blacks, see Horton, *Free People of Color*, 122–145.

64. Harry Reed presents a more heavy-handed "pugnacious" Allen who forced the AME council to reconsider its election of Coker, then pressured Coker to decline the bishop's position and refused to share power with him. See Reed, *Platform for Change*, 14, 32–33. Ironically, Coker later migrated to the Sierra Leone colony in West Africa, arguing that American blacks should follow his example. Allen, on the other hand, remained in the United States and, except for a few years before the early 1820s, was unwilling to support African colonization.

65. George, *Segregated Sabbath*, 121, 108.

66. Ira Berlin, *Slaves Without Masters: The Free Negro in the Antebellum South* (New York: Pantheon Books, 1974), 289–290; Raboteau, *Slave Religion*, 204–205; Payne, *History of the AME Church*, 58.

67. Sylvia R. Frey, *Water From the Rock* (Princeton, N. J.: Princeton University Press, 1991).

68. Douglass, *Annals of the First African Church*, 130. The conclusion that the Episcopalians were elite and Methodists less likely to be is supported by data collected by Leonard Curry. Also according to Curry, the Baptists appealed to the masses of blacks, and Presbyterians were closer to the Episcopalians. See Curry, *Free Black in Urban America*, 192. Julie Winch also found class differences between the AME and the Presbyterian churches. See Winch, *Philadelphia's Black Elite: Activism, Accommodation and the Struggle for Autonomy, 1787–1848* (Philadelphia: Temple University Press, 1988).

69. Paul had been one of the organizers of the congregation. He had come to Boston from New Hampshire when he was sixteen and had begun worshipping with the group the year they started meeting in Faneuil Hall. He was thirty-one years old at his installation. Horton and Horton, *Black Bostonians*, 39–40.

70. Horton and Horton, *Black Bostonians*, 40–41.

71. Horton and Horton, *Black Bostonians*; Robert J. Cottrol, *The Afro-Yankees: Providence's Black Community in the Antebellum Era* (Westport, Conn.: Greenwood Press, 1982), 57–60; Hatch, *Democratization of American Christianity*, 102.

72. Nash, *Forging Freedom*, 199–201.

73. C. Peter Ripley et al., eds., *The Black Abolitionist Papers: The United States, 1830–1846*, vol. 3 (Chapel Hill: University of North Carolina Press, 1991), 95–96.

Dorothy Sterling says that Cornish was born free in Baltimore. See Dorothy Sterling, ed., *Speak Out In Thunder Tones: Letters and Other Writings by Black Northerners, 1787–1865* (New York: Doubleday, 1973), 373.

74. Hatch, *Democratization of American Christianity*, 102.

75. John Thompson, *The Life of John Thompson, a Fugitive Slave: containing His History of Twenty-Five Years in Bondage, and His Providential Escape: Written by Himself* (Worcester, Mass.: by the author, 1856), 18–19, quoted in Hatch, *Democratization of American Christianity*, 104.

76. Thompson, *The Life of John Thompson*.

77. Sobel, *Trabelin' On*, 222.

78. Sobel, *Trabelin' On*, 81.

79. Quoted in Southern, *Music of Black Americans*, 131.

80. Wilson Jeremiah Moses, *Alexander Crummell: A Study of Civilization and Discontent* (New York: Oxford University Press, 1989), 8.

81. Sobel, *Trabelin' On*, 145.

82. Horton and Horton, *Black Bostonians*, 32–33; Southern, *Music of Black Americans*, 104–105. This interest in European classical music, seen by most whites and some blacks as respectable music, coincided with the rise of the nineteenth-century middle-class ideal. See Stuart M. Blumin, *The Emergence of the Middle Class: Social Experience in the American City, 1760–1900* (Cambridge : Cambridge University Press, 1991).

83. Andrews, ed., *Sisters of the Spirit*.

84. Horton and Horton, *Black Bostonians*; Andrews, ed., *Sisters of the Spirit*, 206.

85. Sobel, *Trabelin On'*, 143.

86. Southern, *Music of Black Americas*, 127–129.

87. Minutes and Trial Book, Bethel AME Church, 1822–1835, Philadelphia, August 19, 1823, The Holdings of Mother Bethel African Methodist Episcopal Church. A microfilm copy of these records is on file at the Afro-American Communities Project at the National Museum of American History of the Smithsonian Institution.

88. Minutes and Trial Book, September 16, 1823 and October 6, 1823.

89. Minutes and Trial Book, July 22, 1829.

90. Apparently Reed found that women served on some Bethel juries. If so, this violated the rules set forth by the church trustees. We found women serving on select investigative committees and reporting committees but not on church juries. See Reed, *Platform for Change*, 37.

91. Trenton Circuit Record Book, July 1828, Benjamin Tucker Tanner Papers, Carter G. Woodson Collection, Reel 4, Manuscript Division, Library of Congress.

92. Original Records of the Union Colored Baptist Church, Cincinnati, Ohio, 1834.

93. Trenton Circuit Record Book, May 19, 1837.

94. Vincent P. Franklin, *The Education of Black Philadelphia* (Philadelphia: University of Pennsylvania Press, 1979). The Reverend Absalom Jones attended the Quaker schools in Philadelphia during the 1770s.

95. Quoted in Franklin, *Education of Black Philadelphia*, 31.

96. Nash, *Forging Freedom*, 202–209.

97. "An Address delivered at Bethel Church, Philadelphia; on the 30th of September, 1818 ... by Prince Saunders" (Philadelphia: 1818), reprint in Herbert

Aptheker, ed., *Documentary History of the Negro People in the United States*, vol. 1 (New York: Citadel Press, 1951), 72–73.

98. See Franklin, *Education of Black Philadelphia*, 31–32; Harry C. Silcox, "Delay and Neglect: Negro Public Education in Antebellum Philadelphia," *Pennsylvania Magazine of History and Biography* 97 (1973): 75–98; Benjamin Bacon, *Statistics of the Colored People of Philadelphia* (Philadelphia: T. E. Chapman, 1856); Etta Williamson, "The History of the Separate Public Schools of Negroes in Pennsylvania" (master's thesis, Howard University, 1935).

99. Sterling, ed., *We Are Your Sisters*, 126–129.

100. John Russwurm graduated from Bowdoin College on September 6, 1826, three years after Alexander Lucius Twilight received a B. A. from Middlebury College in Vermont and three weeks after Edward A. Jones graduated from Amherst College in Massachusetts. Stanley K. Schultz, *The Culture Factory: Boston Public Schools, 1789–1860* (New York: Oxford University Press, 1973), 157–60; Horton and Horton, *Black Bostonians*, 70–71.

101. Horton and Horton, *Black Bostonians*, 70–71.

102. Nash, *Forging Freedom*, 206; Franklin, *Education of Black Philadelphia*, 29–33.

103. Carleton Mabee, *Black Education in New York State* (Syracuse: Syracuse University Press, 1979), 22.

104. Ivan D. Steen, "Education to What End? An Englishman Comments on the Plight of Blacks in the 'Free' States, 1830," *Afro-Americans in New York Life and History* 7 (January 1983): 55–60, Introduction to excerpt from Thomas Hamilton, *Men and Manners in America* (Edinburgh: W. Blackwood, 1833), 91–98; Roi Ottley and William J. Weatherby, *The Negro in New York* (New York: Praeger, 1967), 63–64.

105. Mabee, *Black Education*, 71.

106. *The Aristocratic Journey: Being the Outspoken Letters of Mrs. Basil Hall Written during a Fourteen Month's Sojourn in America, 1827–1828*, ed. and with a preface by Una Pope-Hennessy (New York: G. P. Putman's Sons, The Knickerbocker Press, 1931), 25–26.

107. Mabee, *Black Education*, 71.

108. Buffalo Superintendent of Common Schools, Seventh Annual Report, for 1843, 8, cited in Mabee, *Black Education*, 72.

109. Leon Litwack, *North of Slavery: The Negro in the Free States, 1790–1860* (Chicago: University of Chicago Press, 1961), 132–133.

110. V. Jacque Voegeli, *Free But Not Equal: The Midwest and the Negro During the Civil War* (Chicago: University of Chicago Press, 1967), 2.

111. The Gilmore school was established in 1844 and directed by Gilmore himself until 1848, when he turned the school over to one of the teachers to administer. See Carter G. Woodson, *The Education of the Negro Prior to 1861* (New York: G. P. Putnam, 1915), 124–129.

112. Curry, *Free Black in Urban America*, 150–151.

Chapter 7

1. Rush quoted in James A. Henretta, *The Evolution of American Society, 1700–1815* (Lexington, Mass.: D. C. Heath, 1973), 174.

2. George M. Fredrickson, *White Supremacy: A Comparative Study in American and South African History* (New York: Oxford University Press, 1981), 145.

3. We are using "multicultural" in the sense captured by the foregoing discussion, the creation of a multifaceted culture with many variations out of the foundation and influence of the many cultures that located and met in the Americas. This is more than culturally distinct groups coexisting in the same society or the recognition of America's diversity. It describes the shaping of a unique American cultural form and tradition.

4. Martin Delany, *Blake: or the Huts of America* (1859), in Eileen Southern, *The Music of Black Americans*, 2nd ed. (New York: W. W. Norton, 1983), 147.

5. Southern, *Music of Black Americans*.

6. Southern, *Music of Black Americans*; William L. Stone, *Reminiscences of Saratoga and Ballston* (New York: Virtue and Verston, 1875), in Roger Haydon, ed., *Upstate Travels: British Views of Nineteenth Century New York* (Syracuse: Syracuse University Press, 1982), 75.

7. Southern, *Music of Black Americans*.

8. Robert Walm, *The Hermit in America* (Philadelphia: 1819), in Southern, *Music of Black Americans*, 108.

9. Charles C. Jones, *Religious Instruction of the Negroes* (Savannah, GA: 1842), in Southern, *Music of Black Americans*, 146.

10. Paul A. Gilje and Howard B. Rock, eds., *Keepers of the Revolution: New Yorkers at Work in the Early Republic* (Ithaca, New York: Cornell University Press, 1992), 220.

11. Joanna C. Colcord, comp., *Roll and Go: Songs of American Sailormen* (Indianapolis: Bobbs-Merrill, 1924), 15.

12. Southern, *Music of Black Americans*, 91.

13. The Jim Crow character became the symbolic expression of the belief in black inferiority, and the term Jim Crow was used in the late nineteenth and twentieth centuries to denote the southern system of legal segregation. Southern, *Music of Black Americans*, 94–95.

14. Eric Lott, *Love and Theft: Black-face Minstrelsy and the American Working Class* (New York: Oxford University Press, 1993), 40.

15. George Odell, *Annals of the New York Stage*, 15 vols. (New York: Columbia University Press, 1927–49).

16. Frances Trollope, *Domestic Manners of the Americans*, ed. Donald Smalley (1832; reprint, New York: Alfred A. Knopf, 1949), 350.

17. Southern, *Music of Black Americans*, 118; Peter Neilson, *Recollections of a Six Years' Residence* (Glasgow: D. Robertson, 1830), 20; Trollope, *Domestic Manners of the Americans*, 350.

18. Southern, *Music of Black Americans*, 120; Odell, *Annals*, vol. 3, 70–71, 224, 228, 293; Gerald Bordman, *American Musical Theater* (New York: Oxford University Press, 1978), 7–11; "Biographical Index of the Principal Persons Mentioned in the Calendar," *Calendar of the Manuscripts in the Schomburg Collection*, Part 3, Schomburg Collection, New York Public Library.

19. George G. Foster, *New York by Gas-Light and Other Urban Sketches*, ed. Stuart M. Blumin (1850, Berkeley; reprint, University of California Press, 1991), 142–43.

20. Charles Hansford Adams, *"The Guardian of the Law" Authority and Identity in James Fenimore Cooper* (University Park: Pennsylvania State University Press, 1990), 5.

21. Paul A. Gilje, *The Road to Mobocracy: Popular Disorder in New York City, 1763–1834* (Chapel Hill: University of North Carolina Press, 1987).

22. Gilje, *Road to Mobocracy*.

23. Gilje, *Road to Mobocracy*; Howard Zinn, *A People's History of the United States* (New York: Harper & Row, 1980).

24. Prince Hall, "A Charge Delivered to the African Lodge, June 24, 1797, at Menotomy," in Thomas R. Frazier, ed., *Afro-American History: Primary Sources* (New York: Harcourt, Brace & World, 1970), 46–52.

25. William Otter, Sen., *History of My Own Time* (Emmitsburg, Md.: 1835), 114–117, in Richard B. Stott, ed., *History of My Own Time/William Otter* (Ithaca: Cornell University Press, 1995).

26. Otter, *History*. For several similar incidents in Boston, see James Oliver Horton and Lois E. Horton, *Black Bostonians* (New York: Holmes & Meier Publishers, 1979).

27. Barbara Meil Hobson, *Uneasy Virtue: The Politics of Prostitution and the American Reform Tradition* (New York: Basic Books, 1987).

28. Gilje, *Road to Mobocracy*. For an important analysis of the creation and political significance of whiteness during this period, see Noel Ignatiev, *How the Irish Became White* (New York: Routledge, 1995).

29. David Roediger, *The Wages of Whiteness: Race and the Making of the American Working Class* (New York: Verso, 1991), 103, 105. Shane White has described a shift during this period from black festivals to black parades as an assertion of black political rights. Shane White, "'It was Proud Day': African Americans, Festivals, and Parades in the North, 1741–1834," *Journal of American History* 81 (June 1994): 13–50.

30. For a description of these and other race riots of the period, see Gilje, *Road to Mobocracy*; Julie Winch *Philadelphia's Black Elite* (Philadelphia: Temple University Press, 1988); Leonard P. Curry, *The Free Black in Urban America, 1800–1850* (Chicago: University of Chicago Press, 1981).

31. Roediger, *Wages of Whiteness*, 13.

32. Anthony Rotundo, *American Manhood: Transformations in Masculinity from the Revolution to the Modern Era* (New York: Basic Books, 1993).

33. Linda K. Kerber, "The Paradox of Women's Citizenship in the Early Republic: The Case of Martin vs. Massachusetts, 1805," *American Historical Review* (April 1992): 349–378, 351.

34. Winthrop Jordan, *White Over Black: American Attitudes Towards the Negro, 1550–1812* (Chapel Hill: University of North Carolina Press, 1968), 437. We thank Joanne Pope Melish for alerting us to sources documenting early theories on race. See Charles White, *An Account of the Regular Gradation in Man, and in Different Animals and Vegetables; and from the Former to the Latter* (London: Printed for C. Dilly, 1799); John Augustine Smith, "A Lecture introductory to the Second Course of Anatomical Instruction in the College of Physcians and Surgeons for the State of New York," *New York Medical and Philosophical Journal and Review* 1 (1809): 84–96; Joanne Pope Melish, "The Embodiment of 'Race' in the Discourses of Emancipation and 'Science,' 1700–1830" (unpublished paper, Organization of American Historians, annual meeting, Chicago, 1996).

35. Gordon S. Wood, *The Radicalism of the American Revolution* (New York: Alfred A. Knopf, 1992); also see Henretta, *Evolution of American Society*.

36. Phyllis F. Field, *The Politics of Race in New York* (Ithaca: Cornell University Press, 1982); Curry, *Free Black in Urban America*; Paul Finkelman, "Prelude to the Fourteenth Amendment: Black Legal Rights in the Antebellum North," *Rutgers Law Journal* 17 (Spring and Summer 1986): 415–482.

37. Field, *Politics of Race*. Under New York's first constitution, the property requirements for voting were a $50 freehold to vote for a congressmen and a $250 freehold to vote for a senator or governor.

38. Historians generally associate populism with the grassroots farm-labor coalition of the late nineteenth century. We are using the term to describe a general political orientation and grassroots rhetoric characterized by an appeal to the common man of which this coalition would be one example. In the American context, the privileged and powerful have periodically used race to divide the popular constituency and to counter the common class interests of blacks and whites. Even Lincoln, one of the least overtly racist of those who ran populist campaigns, expressed this ideology during his presidential campaign of 1860.

39. For a discussion of the debate over women's status and property rights in the post-Revolutionary period, see Kerber, "The Paradox of Women's Citizenship."

40. Rotundo, *American Manhood*, 177.

41. Seamen's Protection Certificates, Bureau of Customs, Record Group 36, National Archives, Washington D. C. For a description and discussion of these records, see Ira Dye, "Seafarers of 1812—A Profile," *Prologue* (Spring 1973): 3–13. Black men could vote in Maine, Massachusetts, New Hampshire, and Vermont, and some could vote in New York and Pennsylvania (though they lost the vote in Pennsylvania in the 1840s). Mulatto men could vote in Ohio between 1842 and 1859, and black men could vote in school board elections in Michigan after 1855. Finkelman, "Prelude to the Fourteenth Amendment."

42. Richard R. John, *Spreading the News* (Cambridge, Mass.: Harvard University Press, 1995), 141; "Gideon Granger to Senator James Jackson," American State Papers: Documents, Legislative and Executive of the Congress of the United States, Part 7: Post Office (Washington, D. C.: 1834), cited in Bruce Levine, *Half Slave and Half Free* (New York: Hill and Wang, 1992).

43. *The North Star*, April 14, 1848.

44. *Frederick Douglass' Paper*, July, 28, 1854. Jennings later brought suit against the company and was awarded $225 by the court.

45. Undated clipping, Beman Papers, Beinecke Library, Yale University, quoted in Dorothy Sterling, ed., *Speak Out In Thunder Tones: Letters and Other Writings by Black Northerners, 1787–1865* (Garden City, New York: Doubleday, 1973), 99.

46. *Liberator*, August 11, 1832.

47. "Sarah Forten to Angelina Grimké," Philadelphia, April 15, 1837, Weld-Grimké Papers, quoted in Sterling, ed., *Thunder Tones*, 87.

48. Horton and Horton, *Black Bostonians*.

49. David Walker, *Appeal, in Four Articles* . . . , the complete text in Herbert Aptheker, ed., *One Continual Cry* (New York: Humanities Press, 1965), 61–147.

50. Walker, *Appeal* in Aptheker, 78.

51. Walker, *Appeal*, 79, 80, 94. Donald M. Jacobs, "David Walker and William Lloyd Garrison: Racial Cooperation and the Shaping of Boston Abolition," *Courage and Conscience* (Bloomington: Indiana University Press, 1993), 1–20.

52. Walker, *Appeal*, 89.

53. Marilyn Richardson, ed. *Maria W. Stewart, America's First Black Woman Political Writer* (Bloomington: Indiana University Press, 1987).

54. Richardson, *Maria W. Stewart*, 55.

55. Richardson, *Maria W. Stewart*, 46.

56. Richardson, *Maria W. Stewart*, 57.

57. Richardson, *Maria W. Stewart*, 58, 57, 59–60, 62; Shirley J. Yee, *Black Women Abolitionists* (Knoxville: University of Tennessee Press, 1992), 115.

58. Richardson, *Maria W. Stewart*, 68, 69.

59. Richardson, *Maria W. Stewart*, 37, 40; "Proceedings of the First Convention of the Colored Citizens of the State of Illinois, Convened in the City of Chicago . . . October 6–8, 1853," in Philip Foner and George Walker, eds., *Proceedings of the Black State Conventions, 1840–1865* (Philadelphia: Temple University Press, 1980), 62.

60. Mary P. Ryan, *Women In Public* (Baltimore: Johns Hopkins University Press, 1990), 173. Somewhat ironically, after she left Boston, Stewart did not continue a career as a public speaker. She was a teacher at a black school in New York City for many years and became the principal there in 1847. In the 1870s she moved to Washington, D. C. and became the matron of the Freedmen's Hospital and Asylum. She died in Washington in 1879.

61. Ralph Ellison, *Going to the Territory* (New York: Random House, 1986), 142.

Chapter 8

1. Lamont D. Thomas, *Rise to be a People: A Biography of Paul Cuffe*, (Urbana: University of Illinois Press, 1986).

2. Gary Nash, *Race and Revolution* (Madison, Wisc.: Madison House, 1990).

3. "Negro Petitions for Freedom," *Collections of the Massachusetts Historical Society*, 5th ser., vol. 3 (1877): 436–437, quoted in Floyd J. Miller, *The Search for a Black Nationality* (Urbana: University of Illinois Press, 1975), 5.

4. Our argument is that people who had a concrete intimate connection with Africa, either because they themselves were born there or because they identified with specific family members who were born there, generally a generation or two before, were likely to see themselves as Africans in America. For generations with many such people, Africa represented a remembered place as well as a concept and ideal.

5. Robert L. Harris, Jr., "Early Black Benevolent Societies, 1780–1830," *The Massachusetts Review* 20 (Autumn 1979): 603–625. For information on African Institutions formed in New York City, Philadelphia, Boston, and Baltimore, see Thomas, *Rise to be a People*. Also see James Oliver Horton, *Free People of Color* (Washington, D. C.: Smithsonian Press, 1993).

There were many other organizations during this period which included African in their titles. The Zion African Methodist Episcopal Church was founded in New York City in the fall of 1800, the African Meeting House was built in Boston to house the African Baptist Church and the African School in Boston in 1806, and the African Methodist Episcopal Church organized a national network of black churches in 1816. In 1827 the African Woolman Benevolent Society of Brooklyn, New York, undertook the construction of a black school, which, when completed, took the name African Public School Number One. The African Marine Fund of New York City, the New York African Society for Mutual Relief, Newport's African Benevolent Society, and Baltimore's Free African Civilization Society can also be added to the list.

6. Ellen Gibson Wilson, *The Loyal Blacks* (New York: G. P. Putnam's Sons, 1976).

7. For information on Thornton's background and plans, see Thomas, *Rise to Be a People*. For the letter quoted, see Dorothy Sterling, ed., *Speak Out in Thunder*

Tones: Letters and Other Writings by Black Northerners, 1787–1865 (Garden City: Doubleday, 1973), 6.

Gary Nash may have overstated the degree of enthusiasm Thornton found among blacks in Boston, but his depiction and analysis of the reaction of Philadelphia blacks to Thornton's plan are convincing. See Gary B. Nash, *Forging Freedom: The Formation of Philadelphia's Black Community, 1720–1840* (Cambridge, Mass.: Harvard University Press, 1988).

William Thornton never managed to free his slaves, much less settle them in Africa. When he died in 1828, his estate still contained the half of the sugar plantation on Tortola he had inherited and 120 slaves. Wilson, *Loyal Blacks.*

8. Nash is convincing on this point. See his *Forging Freedom.*

9. Wilson, *Loyal Blacks.*

10. Anthony Taylor, Newport, October 4, 1787, in Sterling, ed., *Speak Out in Thunder Tones*, 6; Miller, *Search for a Black Nationality.* It is not clear why Hopkins was unwilling to endorse the venture, but since he considered the project a religious mission and had been involved in arranging for a few black men to receive formal seminary training at Princeton, it is likely that he did not consider Olney, McKenzie, and Gardner suitable because they were not seminary trained.

11. Thomas, *Rise to Be a People.*

12. Thomas, *Rise to Be a People*, 51.

13. Thomas, *Rise to Be a People.*

14. Frank A. Cassell, "Slaves of the Chesapeake Bay Area and the War of 1812," *Journal of Negro History* 57 (April 1972): 144–155.

15. *New York Evening Post*, August 20, 1814, quoted in Shane White, *Somewhat More Independent* (Athens: University of Georgia Press), 150.

16. William C. Nell, *Colored Patriots of the American Revolution* (Boston: Robert F. Wallcut, 1855, reprint, New York: Arno Press, 1968).

17. Nell, *Colored Patriots.*

18. William Jeffery Bolster, "African American Seamen: Race, Seafaring Work and Atlantic Maritime Culture, 1750–1860" (Ph. D. diss. Johns Hopkins University, 1991).

19. For information about "Big Dick" see Bolster, "African American Seamen" and George Hugh Crichton, "Old Boston and Its Once Familiar Faces" (unpublished manuscript, 1881).

20. Bolster, "African American Seamen"; Nathaniel Pierce, "Journal of Nathaniel Pierce of Newburyport, Kept At Dartmoor Prison, 1814–15." in *The Essex Institute Historical Collection* 73 (January 1937): 24–59.

21. Bolster, "African American Seamen," 238.

22. James Roberts, *The Narrative of James Roberts: Soldier in the Revolutionary War and at the Battle of New Orleans* (1858; reprint, Hattiesburg, Miss.: The Book Farm, 1945); Robert C. McConnell, *Negro Troops of Antebellum Louisiana: A History of the Battalion of Free Men of Color* (Baton Rouge: Louisiana State University Press, 1968); Nell, *Colored Patriots*, 286.

23. Roberts, *Narrative of James Roberts*, 10.

24. Nell, *Colored Patriots*, 288; Roberts, *Narrative of James Roberts*, 32.

25. Thomas, *Rise to Be a People*; Rosalind Cobb Wiggins, ed., "Paul Cuffe, Quaker: His Logs and Letters," vol. 1 (unpublished manuscript). See Rosalind Wiggins, ed. *Captain Paul Cuffe's Logs and Letters, 1808–1817*(Washington, D. C.: Howard University Press, 1966).

26. Paul Cuffe to William Allen, Sierra Leone, April 1, 1816, in Wiggins, "Paul Cuffe, Quaker," 360–362.

27. Marie Tyler McGraw, "Richmond Free Blacks and African Colonization, 1816–1832," *Journal of American Studies* 21, no. 2 (1987): 207–224. David Rothman saw the rise of the American Colonization Society as coinciding with that of institutions like penitentiaries, almshouses, and other asylums. An African colony would be an asylum to which free blacks could be committed. Cuffe saw the need for African colonization quite differently. See David J. Rothman, *The Discovery of the Asylum: Social Order and Disorder in the New Republic* (Boston: Little Brown, 1971).

28. "Paul Cuffe to James Forten, Westport, January 8, 1817," quoted in Sterling, ed., *Speak Out in Thunder Tones*, 24–25; Thomas, *Rise to Be a People*.

29. James Forten to Paul Cuffe, Philadelphia, January 25, 1817, in Shelton H. Harris, *Paul Cuffe: Black America and the African Return* (New York: Simon and Schuster, 1972), 243–245.

30. *Boston Recorder*, March 25, 1817. This meeting is also described in Miller, *Search for a Black Nationality*, 50.

31. "Paul Cuffe to James Forten, Westport, March 1, 1817" in Sterling, ed., *Speak Out in Thunder Tones*, 27.

32. Miller, *Search for a Black Nationality*.

33. Tyler-McGraw, "Richmond Free Blacks and African Colonization."

34. William Wells Brown, *My Southern Home* (1880) included in William L. Andrews, ed., *From Fugitive Slave to Free Man* (New York: Mentor Book, 1993).

35. Terry Alford, *Prince Among Slaves: The True Story of an African Prince Sold into Slavery in the American South* (New York: Oxford University Press, 1977); Allan D. Austin, *African Muslims in Antebellum America: A Sourcebook* (New York: Garland Publishers, 1984), 124–263. Alford refers to him as Ibrahima, Austin gives his name as Abdul Rahahman and his father's name as Ibrahima Yoro Pate Sari; contemporary sources are inconsistent.

36. C. Peter Ripley reported that Rahahman and Isabella had "about thirteen" children, but he may be confusing some of the grandchildren with the children. See C. Peter Ripley et al., eds., *Black Abolitionist Papers: The United States, 1830–1846*, vol. 3 (Chapel Hill: University of North Carolina Press, 1991), 78. Terry Alford, in his biography of Rahahman says that he and Isabella had nine children, five sons and four daughters. He also had a wife and son in Africa whom he never saw again after his enslavement. See Alford, *Prince Among Slaves*, 55, appendix.

37. *New Bedford Mercury*, September 19, 1828.

38. Brother of Arthur and Lewis Tappan.

39. Austin, *African Muslims*, 124–167.

40. Austin, *African Muslims*, 180–182, 263.

41. *New Bedford Mercury*, November 13, 1829.

42. Alford, *Prince Among Slaves*, 182–187.

43. Wilson Jeremiah Moses, *Alexander Crummell: A Study of Civilization and Discontent* (New York: Oxford University Press, 1989).

44. Donald R. Hickey, "America's Response to the Slave Revolt in Haiti, 1791–1806," *Journal of the Early Republic* 2 (Winter 1982): 361–379; Julie Winch, *Philadelphia's Black Elite* (Philadelphia: Temple University Press, 1988).

45. During the early nineteenth century, planters in Jamaica and in the American

South also feared invasion by Haitian forces. C. L. R. James, *The Black Jacobins* (1938; reprint, New York: Vintage Books, 1963); Percy Waxman, *The Black Napoleon* (New York: Harcourt, Brace, 1931); Ralph Korngold, *Citizen Toussaint* (Boston: Little, Brown, 1944).

46. William Woodis Harvey, *Sketches of Hayti From the Expulsion of the French to the Death of Christophe* (1827, reprint, Westport, Conn.: Negro Universities Press, 1971).

47. Prince Saunders to Paul Cuffe, Boston, March 21, 1815, in Wiggins, "Paul Cuffe Quaker"; "Biographical Index of the Principal Persons Mentioned in the Calendar," *Calendar of the Manuscripts in the Schomburg Collection*; part 3, Schomburg Collection, New York Public Library. Winch, *Philadelphia's Black Elite*; Nash, *Forging Freedom*; Philip Foner, *History of Black Americans*, vol. 1 (Westport, Conn.: Greenwood Press, 1975).

Prince Saunders is referred to variously in historical sources as of pure African blood, a Haitian, and the Vermont-born son of immigrant slave parents. It is likely that he was the American-born son of Haitian immigrants which, along with his superior education, religious commitment, and sophistication, would have made him especially well-suited for the mission for which the British abolitionists selected him.

48. Prince Saunders settled in Haiti where he died in 1839. Foner, *History of Black Americans*, 539. See also James O'Dell Jackson III, "The Origins of Pan-African Nationalism: Afro-American and Haitian Relations, 1800–1863" (Ph. D. diss., Northwestern University, 1976).

49. *Niles' Weekly Register* June 26, 1824. Also quoted in Jackson, "Origins of Pan-African Nationalism," 70.

50. Winch, *Philadelphia's Black Elite*; Charles L. Coleman, "A History of the Negro Baptists in Boston" (master's thesis, Andover Newton Theological Seminary, 1956); Miller, *Search for a Black Nationality*; *Genius of Universal Emancipation* 4 (August 1825); *African Repository*, 5 (August 1829), 185; John Edward Baur, "Mulatto Machiavelli, Jean Pierre Boyer, and the Haiti of his Day," *Journal of Negro History* 32 (July 1947): 307–353, 326.

Thomas Paul had been interested in Haiti since independence and had applied to the Baptist Missionary Society to go there in 1808 and in 1823. His application approved in 1823, Paul was somewhat discouraged because he didn't know French, but found the people friendly and believed economic opportunities there to be promising. Sometime after 1829 when he retired from his church in Boston, Paul emigrated to Haiti; he died in 1831.

51. Winch, *Philadelphia's Black Elite*, 57. Jackson, "Origins of Pan-African Nationalism," 262; *United States Gazette*, April 18, 1825.

52. Jackson, "Origins of Pan-African Nationalism."

53. Alexis Beaubrun Ardouin, *Etudes Sur L'Histoire D'Haiti*, ed. Dr. Francois Dalencour (Port-au-Prince, Haiti: Chez L'Editeur, 1958), quoted in Jackson, "Origins of Pan-African Nationalism," 81.

54. David Walker's Appeal, edited with an introduction by Charles M. Wiltsen, 3rd ed. (June 1830; reprint, New York: Hill and Wang, 1965), 21; L. D. Reddick, "Une Immigration de Noirs Americains Sous Boyer," in Ruix Leon, *Pros d'Historire d'Haiti* (Port-au-Prince, Haiti: Imprimente de l'Etat, 1945), 203, quoted in Jackson, "Origins of Pan-African Nationalism," 74; Jean Pierre Boyer, *Niles' Weekly Register*, 26: 272, quoted in Baur, "Mulatto Machiavelli," 326.

55. *United States Gazette*, March 1, 1825; Harry Hoetink, "'Americans' in Samana," *Caribbean Studies* 2 (April 1962): 3–23. Also see Jackson, "Origins of Pan-African Nationalism."

56. Miller, *Search for a Black Nationality*, 81–82.

57. E. A. Park, *Memoir of the Life and Character of Samuel Hopkins* (Boston: 1854), in Sterling, ed., *Speak Out in Thunder Tones*, 28.

58. *Freedom's Journal*, March 16, 1827. Those in attendance included David Walker, John T. Hilton, William Brown and Rev. Thomas Paul.

59. Miller, *Search for a Black Nationality*, 84–85.

60. *Freedom's Journal*, June 29, 1827. See *Freedom's Journal*, August 24, 1827 for Cornish's reply.

61. *Freedom's Journal*, March 30, 1827.

62. James W. Alexander, *The Life of Archibald Alexander, D.D, L.L.D.* (Philadelphia: 1857), 395–397, quoted in David Swift, *Black Prophets of Justice* (Baton Rouge: Louisiana State University Press, 1989), 38.

63. *Freedom's Journal*, July 6, 1827, 66; July 27, 1827, 77–78; August 17, 1827, 91.

64. Alford, *Prince Among Slaves*.

65. Ripley et al., eds., *Black Abolitionist Papers*, 78.

66. John Russwurm to Gurley, July 24, 1829, American Colonization Society Papers, Library of Congress, quoted in Moses, *Alexander Crummell*, 13.

67. James Forten to William Lloyd Garrison, Philadelphia, May 6, 1832, American Anti-Slavery Collection, Boston Public Library. Also published in Ripley et al., eds., *Black Abolitionist Papers*, 86–87.

68. William Lloyd Garrison, *Thoughts on African Colonization*, part 2, (Boston: Garrison and Knapp, 1832), 26, 33.

69. Basil Davidson, *The Search for Africa: History, Culture, Politics* (New York: Random House, 1994), 232. There is currently a debate about the racial origins of the ancient Egyptians with some claiming that Egyptian culture was not an African culture, but one created by the ancient Greeks. This view is sometimes presented as a counter argument to Afrocentric historical interpretations. For a major reinterpretation of classical civilization, see Martin Bernal, *Black Athena*, vols. 1 and 2 (New Brunswick, N. J.: Rutgers University Press, 1987 & 1991).

70. Davidson, *Search for Africa*, 320; George M. Fredrickson, *The Black Image in the White Mind* (New York: Harper & Row, 1971).

71. *David Walker's Appeal*, 76.

72. Howard Holman Bell, ed., *Minutes of the Proceedings of the National Negro Conventions, 1830–1864* (New York: Arno Press and *The New York* Times, 1969), 4–5.

73. Peter Williams, *A discourse Delivered in St. Philip's Church, for the Benefit of the Coloured Community of Wilberforce in Upper Canada, on Fourth of July, 1830* (New York: 1830), quoted in Leonard I. Sweet, *Black Images of America, 1784–1870* (New York: W. W. Norton & Company, Inc., 1976), 55.

74. Martin E. Dann, ed., *The Black Press, 1827–1890* (New York: G. P. Putman's Sons, 1971); *Weekly Advocate*, February, 25 1837.

75. James Oliver Horton and Lois E. Horton, *Black Bostonians* (New York: Holmes & Meier, 1979), 91.

76. *Colored American*, March 4, 1837.

77. *Minutes of the Fifth Annual Convention for the Improvement of the Free People of Color . . . 1835*, in Bell, ed., *Minutes*, 15.

Chapter 9

1. This 1822 law provided for the imprisonment of black sailors while their vessels were anchored in South Carolina's harbors. There was, perhaps, some potential for argument in the interpretation of the Supreme Court's ruling since the particular case considered involved a British seaman.

2. William W. Freehling, *Prelude to Civil War: The Nullification Controversy in South Carolina, 1816–1836* (New York: Harper & Row, 1965), 114.

3. W. Jeffrey Bolster, "'To Feel like a Man': Black Seamen in the Northern States, 1800–1860," *The Journal of American History* 76, (March 1990):1173–1199.

4. Freehling, *Prelude to Civil War*, 111–118; Ira Berlin, *Slaves Without Masters: The Free Negro in the Antebellum South* (New York: Pantheon Books, 1974), 216; Carol Wilson, *Freedom At Risk: The Kidnapping of Free Blacks in America, 1780–1865* (Lexington: University of Kentucky Press, 1994), 58–63.

5. *The Liberator*, November, 30, 1838.

6. *Colored American*, October 17, 1840.

7. *The North Star*, May 25, 1849.

8. John Hope Franklin, *A Southern Odyssey: Travelers in the Antebellum North* (Baton Rouge: Louisiana State University Press, 1976), 148.

9. Brenda Stevenson, ed., *The Journals of Charlotte Forten Grimke* (New York: Oxford University Press, 1988), 139–40.

10. Quoted in John Chester Miller, *The Wolf by the Ears: Thomas Jefferson and Slavery* (New York: New American Library, 1977), ix.

11. Herbert Aptheker, *One Continual Cry: David Walker's Appeal to the Colored Citizens of the World, 1829–1830, Its Setting and Its Meaning* (New York: Humanities Press, 1965), 137 and 137n.

12. Louis Ruchames, ed., *Racial Thought in America* (Amherst: University of Massachusetts Press, 1969), 202–203, 205. This bold statement coming as early as it did contradicts contentions that Walker's militant call to arms was the first direct threat to white society. See Harry Reed, *Platform for Change: The Foundations of the Northern Free Black Community, 1775–1865* (East Lansing: Michigan State University Press, 1994), 27–28, 68–69, 172–173.

13. Olive Gilbert, *Narrative of Sojourner Truth* (Battle Creek, Mich.:, 1878), quoted in Dorothy Sterling, ed., *Speak Out in Thunder Tones: Letters and Other Writings by Black Northerners, 1787–1865* (Garden City, N. Y.: Doubleday, 1973), 128.

14. Aptheker, *One Continual Cry*, 77.

15. *Freedom's Journal*, March 16, 1827.

16. *African Repository* 4 (June 1828), 118, quoted in George M. Fredrickson, *The Black Image in the White Mind: The Debate on Afro-American Character and Destiny, 1817–1914* (New York: Harper & Row, 1971), 17.

17. Richard Brown, *Knowledge Is Power: The Diffusion of Information in Early America, 1700–1865* (New York: Oxford University Press, 1989), 8–9.

18. In Buffalo, Chicago, and Detroit, about 65 percent of black adults were listed as literate in the 1850 census. Almost 70 percent of Cincinnati's black adults were literate, and 80 percent in Philadelphia and 86 percent in Boston were literate.

19. Bell published the *Weekly Advocate* for one month during January 1837 until he was joined by Cornish, and the paper's name was changed to the *Colored American*.

20. Donald M. Jacobs, ed., *Antebellum Black Newspapers* (Westport, Conn.: Greenwood Press, 1976), 3–4, 161–162, 229–230.

21. Martin E. Dann, *The Black Press, 1827–1890: The Quest for National Identity* (New York: G. P. Putnam's Sons, 1971), 18–20. An article in the *Pennsylvania Freeman*, August 27, 1850 indicated that Ruggles had resumed publication at that time. C. Peter Ripley, Roy E. Finkenbine, Michael F. Hembree, and Donald Yacovone, eds., *Black Abolitionist Papers, 1830–1865* (New York: Microfilming Corporation of America, 1981–83), microfilm reel 6, frame 557.

22. C. Peter Ripley et al., eds., *Black Abolitionist Papers: The United States, 1830–1846*, 5 vols. (Chapel Hill: University of North Carolina Press, 1985–92), 3:175n.

23. James Oliver Horton and Lois E. Horton, *Black Bostonians* (New York: Holmes & Meier, 1979), 82–83.

24. Ripley et al., eds., *Black Abolitionist Papers*, 4:79n.

25. Dann, *Black Press*, 19–20; Philip S. Foner, *History of Black Americans*, vol. 2 (Westport, Conn.: Greenwood Press, 1983), 257.

26. *The Anglo-African Magazine* 1 (October, 1859). Grice migrated to Haiti in 1832 and was appointed the Director of Public Works in Port-au-Prince in 1843. Grice was interviewed in New York where he visited regularly. This article gives him a more prominent role in the call for a convention, but time and memory probably embellished his role and its importance.
Harry Reed uses black newspapers and the conventions as two major components of what he calls the "platform for change," the foundation on which black political action was based. See Reed, *Platform for Change*, 4–5.

27. Howard Holman Bell, ed., *Minutes of the Proceedings of the National Negro Conventions, 1830–1864* (New York: Arno Press and *The New York Times*, 1969).

28. Ronald T. Takaki, *Iron Cages: Race and Culture in 19th-Century America* (Seattle: University of Washington Press, 1979), 97–100.

29. "An Address to the Citizens of New York," January 1831, quoted in William Lloyd Garrison, *Thoughts of African Colonization*, part 2, "Sentiments of the Free People of Color" (Boston: Garrison and Knapp, 1831; reprint, New York: Arno Press, 1968), 16–17, also see pages 44–45.

30. Austin Steward, *Twenty-Two Years a Slave, and Forty Years a Freeman* (Wm. Alling, 1856, reprint, New York: Negro Universities Press, 1968), 167.

31. *Minutes of the Fifth Annual Convention for the Improvement of the Free People of Color . . . 1835*, in Bell, ed., *Minutes, 11*.

32. Bell, *Minutes*, 15–20.

33. Bell, *Minutes*, 10–11.

34. Ripley et al., eds., *Black Abolitionist Papers*, 2: 4–5.

35. Apparently Lewis was dishonest with both the company and with many of the blacks who settled in Wilberforce, so that some of the black settlers were not able to retain the land they thought they had purchased. See Steward, *Twenty-Two Years a Slave*, 190–192, 231–273.

36. Robin Winks, *The Blacks in Canada: A History* (New Haven: Yale University Press, 1971).

37. Steward, *Twenty-Two Years A Slave*. Minister Nathaniel Paul was the brother of Thomas Paul of Boston and was twenty years younger than Thomas. He and another brother, Benjamin, were both ministers at the Wilberforce colony. Nathaniel was charged with soliciting money for the colony from European sources, Lewis with collections in the United States. Ripley et al., eds., *Black Abolitionist Papers*, vol. 2; Horton and Horton, *Black Bostonians*.

38. Michael F. Hembree, "The Question of 'Begging' Fugitive Slave Relief in Canada," *Civil War History* 37 (December 1991): 314–327.

39. Wendell Phillips Garrison, *William Lloyd Garrison, 1805–1879: The Story of His Life Told By His Children*, vol. 1 (Boston: Houghton, Mifflin, 1885 & 1889), 140.

40. Watkins in particular became a life-long friend and supporter; Jacob Greener was the grandfather of Richard T. Greener, the first African American to graduate from Harvard College in 1870. Garrison, *Garrison*, 1:141.

41. Garrison, *Garrison*, 1:184.

42. Garrison, *Garrison*, 1:214–216.

43. Garrison, *Garrison*, 1:217.

44. Garrison, *Garrison*, 1:225.

45. David Walker to Thomas Lewis, Boston, December 8, 1829. We thank Peter Hinks for providing us with a copy of this letter.

46. Stephen B. Oats, *The Fires of Jubilee: Nat Turner's Fierce Rebellion* (New York: New American Library, 1975).

47. Thomas C. Holt, *The Problem of Freedom: Race, Labor, and Politics in Jamaica and Britain, 1832–1938* (Baltimore: Johns Hopkins University Press, 1992), 13–15.

48. Garrison, *Garrison*, 1:236–250.

49. Other white reformers present at the convention included S. S. Jocelyn, white minister of a black church in New Haven, Thomas Shipley and Charles Pierce, both of Philadelphia. Their active participation in the convention was encouraged. The convention resolved that these men "have permission to make any inquiries or communications, which they might deem proper." Minutes of the First Annual Convention for the Improvement of the Free People of Color . . . 1831, in Bell, ed., *Minutes*, 5. See also James Brewer Stewart, *William Lloyd Garrison and the Challenge of Emancipation* (Arlington Heights, Ill.: Harlan Davidson, 1992), 60.

50. Minutes of the Fifth Annual Convention for the Improvement of the Free People of Color . . . 1835, in Bell, ed., *Minutes*, 11.

51. Minutes of the First Annual Convention for the Improvement of the Free People of Color . . . 1831, in Bell, ed., *Minutes*, 6.

52. Sterling, ed., *Speak Out in Thunder Tones*, 91; Stewart, *Garrison*.

53. Minutes of the Second Annual Convention for the Improvement of the Free People of Color . . . 1832, in Bell, ed., *Minutes*, 34.

54. Robert H. Abzug, *Passionate Liberator: Theodore Dwight Weld and the Dilemma of Reform* (New York: Oxford University Press, 1980), 60–61.

55. The Lane Debates were led by Weld, Henry B. Stanton, John Alvord, Sereno W. Streeter, and Calvin Waterbury.

56. Stewart, *Garrison*, 58–59.

57. Abzug, *Passionate Liberator*, 78–95; John B. Shotwell, *A History of the Schools of Cincinnati* (Cincinnati: The School Life Company, 1902), 447–465; Ripley et al., eds., *Black Abolitionist Papers*, 3:140–141n; Nat Brandt, *The Town that Started the Civil War* (Syracuse: Syracuse University Press, 1990).

58. Carlton Mabee, *Black Education in New York State* (Syracuse: Syracuse University Press, 1979), 108–166; Ripley et al., eds., *Black Abolitionist Papers*, 3:337n.

59. Alexander Crummell, "Eulogium on Henry Highland Garnet, D. D.," May 4, 1882, reprint in Wilson Jeremiah Moses, ed., *Destiny and Race: Selected Writings, 1840–1898* (Amherst: University of Massachusetts Press, 1992), 55–60.

60. Alexander Crummell, *The Eulogy on Henry Highland Garnet, D.D. Presbyterian Minister, etc.* (Washington, D. C.: [n.p.], 1882), 13.

61. Brandt, *Town that Started the Civil War*; James Oliver Horton, "Black Education at Oberlin College: A Controversial Commitment," *The Journal of Negro Education* 54 (Fall 1985): 477–499; Abzug, *Passionate Liberator*, 123–125.

62. James McCune Smith, *A Memorial Discourse by Henry Highland Garnet*, (Philadelphia: Joseph M. Wilson, 1865), 21–23. Thomas Hamilton, *Men and Manners in America*, vol. 1(Edinburgh: W. Blackwood, 1833), 90–91. This story provides a context for Garnet's later militancy.

63. Crummell, *Eulogy on Henry Highland Garnet*, 25–26.

64. Horton and Horton, *Black Bostonians*, 33.

65. "Report of the Condition of the People of Color in the State of Ohio" (April 1835), reprinted in Herbert Aptheker, *Documentary History of Negro People in the United States* (New York: Citadel Press, 1951), 157–158.

66. James Oliver Horton, *Free People of Color* (Washington, D. C.: Smithsonian Institution Press, 1994), 41–53.

67. Dorothy Sterling, ed., *We Are Your Sisters: Black Women in the Nineteenth Century* (New York: W. W. Norton, 1984), 181–182.

68. Pliny LeRoi Harwood, *History of Eastern Connecticut* (New Haven: Pioneer Publishing Co., 1932), 284. Julia Williams, one of Crandall's students and "a good Christian and a scholar," according to her future husband H. H. Garnet, became an active abolitionist and chaired the Free Labor Bazaar at the London meeting of the World Peace Congress in 1851. Joel Schor, *Henry Highland Garnet: A Voice of Black Radicalism in the Nineteenth Century* (Westport, Conn.: Greenwood Press, 1977), 15, 124.

69. Minutes of the Fifth Annual Convention for the Improvement of the Free People of Color . . . 1835, in Bell, ed., *Minutes*, 17.

70. The American Baptist Free Missionary Society was an antislavery sect formed in May 1843 at the integrated Tremont Temple in Boston for the express purpose of having no connection, even through mission activities, with slaveholders. New York Central College Records, 1847–1866, Cortland Historical Society, Cortland, New York.

71. New York Central College Records; Seymour B. Dunn, "The Early Academies of Cortland County," *Cortland County Chronicles* 1 (Cortland, N. Y.: Cortland County Historical Society, 1957): 57–76.

72. A. T. Foss and E. Matthews, *Facts for Baptist Churches* (Utica, New York: American Baptist Free Mission Society, 1850), New York Central College Records.

73. The highest enrollment at New York Central was 230, with 46 in the collegiate department; in 1859 Oberlin had a total of 1,200 students. New York Central College Records; Brandt, *Town that Started the Civil War*, 38.

74. William G. Allen, *American Prejudice Against Color: An Authentic Narrative, Showing How Easy the Nation Got into an Uproar* (London: 1853) (BAP microfilm), reel 8, frame 1–28; R. J. M. Blackett, "William G. Allen: The Forgotten Professor," *Civil War History* 26 (March 1980): 39–52; Ripley et al., eds., *Black Abolitionist Papers*, 4:135–136n.

75. Gerrit Smith suggested they make it a black school. At least three black colleges, Avery near Pittsburgh, Lincoln in Pennsylvania and Wilberforce in Ohio, had been established by the 1850s. McCune Smith and Reason believed the school would need an endowment of at least $50,000. Smith proposed an integrated

college, including an integrated faculty, noting that his proposal for a black college had been soundly defeated at the 1853 Rochester convention, and he thought neither blacks nor whites would support it in 1859. James McCune Smith to Gerrit Smith, New York, January 29, 1859, Gerrit Smith Papers, George Arents Research Library, Syracuse University, Syracuse N. Y.; Mabee, *Black Education*, 169; Albert Hazen Wright, "Pre-Cornell and Early Cornell VIII," Studies in History No. 23 (Ithaca, New York: A Publication of New York State College of Agriculture, Cornell University, 1960, typescript).

76. Lorenzo de Zavala, *Journey to the United States of North America*, trans. by Wallace Woolsey (Austin, Tex.: Shoal Publishers, 1980), 109.

77. Frances Trollope, *Domestic Manners of the Americans* (1832, reprint, New York: Alfred A. Knopf, 1949), 14–15. For more information on Wright's socialist utopia of Nashoba, see William H. Pease and Jane H. Pease, *Black Utopia* (Madison: The State Historical Society of Wisconsin, 1963) and Rosabeth Moss Kanter, *Commitment and Community* (Cambridge, Mass.: Harvard University Press, 1972).

78. George A. Levesque, "Interpreting Early Black Ideology: A Reappraisal of Historical Consensus," *Journal of the Early Republic* (Fall 1981), 269–287.

79. Theodore Weld to Lewis Tappan, Utica, February 22, 1836, in Abzug, *Passionate Liberator*, 143.

80. Joseph Tracy, *Natural Equality: A Sermon before the Vermont Colonization Society of Pennsylvania, Delivered October 17, 1833* (Windsor, Vt.: Chronicle Press, 1833), 3–22, cited in Larry E. Tise, *Proslavery: A History of the Defense of Slavery in America, 1701–1840* (Athens: University of Georgia Press, 1987), 269–273.

81. Louis R. Mehlinger, "The Attitude of the Free Negro Toward African Colonization," *Journal of Negro History* 1 (July 1916): 276–301.

82. For information on Jay, see Merton L. Dillion, *The Abolitionists: The Growth of a Dissenting Minority* (De Kalb: Northern Illinois University Press, 1974), 53–54.

83. William S. McFeely, *Frederick Douglass* (New York: W. W. Norton, 1991), 94.

84. From the *National Reformer*, quoted in the *Emancipator*, March 12, 1840, cited in Benjamin Quarles, *Black Abolitionists* (New York: Oxford University Press, 1969), 92.

85. Christine Stansell, *City of Women* (New York: Alfred A. Knopf, 1982), 63–73; Barbara Meil Hobson, *Uneasy Virtue* (New York: Basic Books, 1987), 51–54.

86. "Address by William Whipper, Alfred Niger and Augustus Price," June 3, 1835 quoted in Ripley et al., eds., *Black Abolitionist Papers*, 3:147.

87. Minutes of the Fifth Annual Convention for the Improvement of the Free People of Color . . . 1835, in Bell, ed., *Minutes*, 8.

88. "Address by William Whipper, Alfred Niger and Augustus Price," June 3, 1835 quoted in Ripley et al., eds., *Black Abolitionist Papers*, 3:148.

89. Ruchames, ed., *Racial Thought In America*, 201.

90. This was not a call for the complete exclusion of whites but for an organization that would be controlled by blacks. Whites were present at many national meetings and on occasion they gave reports and participated in committee work.

91. Sparsely attended annual meetings of the American Moral Reform Society in Philadelphia essentially supplanted the national convention meetings and continued with dwindling attendance until a new national convention was called for in 1843.

92. *Colored American*, March 15, 1838.

93. It is worth noting that in 1837, and for the following few years, an economic

depression that took its toll on the financial standing of most Americans was especially difficult for northern free blacks. This may have contributed in some small measure to the low turnout by those who would have had to expend funds to travel a distance to attend the Philadelphia meeting.

94. *National Enquirer*, September 21, 1837, *Black Abolitionist Papers*, reel 2, frame 0192.

95. Frederick Cooper, "Elevation the Race: The Social Thought of Black Leaders, 1827–50," *American Quarterly* 24 (December 1972), 604–625. For a critical analysis of Cooper's argument, see Horton, *Free People of Color*, 7–8.

96. *Liberator*, April 4, 1851, cited in Quarles, *Black Abolitionists*, 92.

97. Minutes of the Fifth Annual Convention for the Improvement of the Free People of Color . . . 1835, in Bell, ed., *Minutes*, 29–30.

98 Minutes of the Fifth Annual Convention for the Improvement of the Free People of Color . . . 1835, in Bell, ed., *Minutes*, 4.

99. James McCune Smith to Gerrit Smith, New York, April 9, 1858, Gerrit Smith Papers, George Arents Research Library, Syracuse University, Syracuse, N. Y.

100. Theodore Weld to Lewis Tappan, Rochester, March 9, 1836, in Abzug, *Passionate Liberator*, 142.

101. Adam Dewey Simmons argued that there were two separate abolition movements, one black and one white. While we do not make the distinct separation that he made, we do agree that often, more so after 1840, blacks attempted to establish organizations that they controlled and often worked with white-controlled groups. See Simmons, "Ideologies and Programs of the Negro Antislavery Movement, 1830–1861" (Ph. D. diss., Northwestern University), 1983, 96–144.

102. Quarles, *Black Abolitionists*, 248; Merton L. Dillon, *The Abolitionists: The Growth of a Dissenting Minority* (De Kalb: Northern Illinois University Press, 1974), 58–59.

103. Patricia H. Gaffney, ed., *The Emily Howland Paper: A Guide to the Microfilm Publication* (Ithaca, N. Y.: Cornell University Libraries, 1975), 10.

104. Stewart, *Garrison*, 82.

105. Horton and Horton, *Black Bostonians*; Ripley et al., eds., *Black Abolitionist Papers*, 144n. AASS is the American Anti-Slavery Society.

106. Carolyn Luverne Williams, "Religion, Race, and Gender in Antebellum American Radicalism: The Philadelphia Female Anti-Slavery Society, 1833–1870," (Ph. D. diss., UCLA, 1991), 1152–156.

107. Abzug, *Passionate Liberator*, 150–152; Lois E. Horton, "Community Organization and Social Activism: Black Boston and the Antislavery Movement," *Sociological Inquiry* 55 (Spring 1985): 182–199.

108. Philip Foner, *History of Black Americans*, 2:407.
Abolitionists were not the only targets of mob violence, what Stewart has called an "extension of the political rally or the ballot box." In the increased violence of the mid-1830s, mob targets included abolitionists, Masonic lodges, banks, convents, black communities, and yellow fever hospitals. Stewart, *Garrison*, 81–82.

109. James D. Richardson, ed., *A Compilation of the Messages and Papers of the Presidents*, vol. 3 (Washington, D. C.: Government Printing Office, 1896), 175.

110. Dillon, *The Abolitionists*, 90. Several southern postmasters complained to Samuel L. Gouverneur, postmaster of New York City, about the volume of abolitionist material being mailed to the South. Gouverneur asked Kendall's advice and

was told that the president, the secretary of state, the secretary of war and the secretary of the navy agreed that steps should be taken to stop the distribution of this material, even though to do so was illegal. See Leonard L. Richards, *Gentlemen of Property and Standing: Anti-Abolition Mobs in Jacksonian America* (New York: Oxford University Press, 1970), 74.

111. Garrison was in England in 1833 to raise funds for the manual labor school but used the opportunity to lecture on his *Thoughts of African Colonization* and against slavery. Once Britain outlawed slavery in the British West Indies in 1834, British abolitionists turned their full attention to American slavery, joining forces with the American abolitionists. Stewart, *Garrison*, 65–66.

112. An errand boy and printer's devil in the *Liberator* office named James Burr, grandson of Plato Turner of the Parting Ways settlement, Plymouth, Massachusetts, was a witness to Garrison's capture. *The Boston Sunday Globe*, Sunday, December 8, 1895; Horton and Horton, *Black Bostonians*, 84; Stewart, *Garrison*, 85–86.

113. Dorothy Sterling, *Ahead of Her Time: Abby Kelly and the Politics of Antislavery* (New York: W. W. Norton, 1991), 65–66.

114. Abzug, *Passionate Liberator*, 150–151.

115. Horton and Horton, *Black Bostonians*, 61–62.

116. McFeely, *Frederick Douglass*.

117. Frederick Douglass, *My Bondage and My Freedom*, with an introduction by William L. Andrews (1855; reprint, Urbana: University of Illinois Press, 1987), 218–219; McFeely, *Frederick Douglass*, 82–92.

118. *Advocate of Freedom*, November 2, 1839, cited in Ripley et al., eds., *Black Abolitionist Papers*, 2:314–316.

119. Charles Lenox Remond to Isaac and Amy Post, September 27, 1843 in Ripley et al., eds., *Black Abolitionist Papers*, 3:416–420, 417.

120. *Liberator*, October 30, 1857.

121. Henry Bibb, *Narrative of the Life and Adventures of Henry Bibb an American Slave* (New York: Negro University Press, 1849).

122. *Prigg v. Pennsylvania*, 16 Peters (US) 539, 613 (1842).

123. The earliest vigilance committee had been formed in New York City in 1835. *New York Committee of Vigilance, First Annual Report* (New York: Piercy & Reed, printers, 1837).

124. Allan D. Austin, *African Muslims in Antebellum America* (New York: Garland Publishing, 1984), 636.

125. Horton and Horton, *Black Bostonians*, 99. By 1860 every New England state and the Middle Atlantic states north of Delaware had passed Personal Liberty laws. In the Midwest, Ohio, Michigan, and Wisconsin passed the strongest laws, with Indiana, Illinois, and Iowa providing weaker protections to fugitives. See Paul Finkelman, "Prelude to the Fourteenth Amendment," *Rutgers Law Journal* 17 (Spring and Summer 1986):415–482.

126. William Craft and Ellen Craft, *Running a Thousand Miles for Freedom* (1860; reprint, New York: Arno Press, 1969).

127. William Still to James Miller McKim, Philadelphia, August 8, 1850, in Ripley et al., eds., *Black Abolitionist Papers* 4:53–58.

128. Deborah Gray White, *Arn't I A Woman?: Female Slaves in the Plantation South* (New York: W. W. Norton, 1985), 70–72, quote, 72.

129. Paul Jefferson, ed., *The Travels of William Wells Brown* (New York: Markus Wienier Publishing, 1991), 1–3, 50.

130. Jefferson, *Travels of William Wells Brown*, 2, 53–55.

131. Jefferson, *Travels of William Wells Brown*, 61, 66–68.

132. Quoted in Horton, *Free People of Color*, 64.

133. William Still, *The Underground Railroad* (Philadelphia: Porter and Coates, 1872), 297.

134. Henrietta Buckmaster, *Let My People Go: The Story of the Underground Railroad and the Growth of the Abolition Movement* (1941, reprint, Columbia: University of South Carolina Press, 1992), 215.

135. "A Slave Until Gerrit Smith Brought Him North," unidentified and undated newspaper clipping, Box #152, Gerrit Smith Papers, Syracuse University Archives, Syracuse, New York.

136. Catherine M. Hanchett, "What Sort of People & Families . . . : The Edmonson Sisters," *Afro-Americans in New York Life and History* 6 (July 1982): 21–37.

137. Daniel Drayton, *Personal Memoir of Daniel Drayton for Four Years and Four Months a Prisoner in Washington Jail, Including a Narrative of the Voyage and Capture of the Schooner Pearl* (Boston: Bela Marsh, 1854); John H. Paynter, *Fugitives of the Pearl* (Washington, D. C.: Associated Publishers, 1930).

138. Saunders Colony typescript, undated, Michigan Historical Collections, Bentley Historical Library, University of Michigan, Ann Arbor, Michigan. For information on the settlement that Saunders established, see "The Calvin Negro Colony of Cass County, Michigan," Western Michigan Archives and Regional History Collection, Western Michigan University, Kalamazoo, Mich., undated typescript.

139. William E. Farrison, "William Wells Brown in Buffalo," *Journal of Negro History* 39 (October 1954): 298–314, 302.

140. Horton, *Free People of Color*, 69.

141. Clement Eaton, "A Dangerous Pamphlet in the Old South," *Journal of Southern History* 2 (August 1936): 326–329. See also William Jeffrey Bolster, "African-American Seamen: Race, Seafaring Work, and Atlantic Maritime Culture, 1750–1860" (Ph. D. diss., Johns Hopkins University, 1992).

Chapter 10

1. Solomon Northup, *Twelve Years a Slave*, ed., Sue Eakin and Joseph Logsdon (Buffalo: Derby, Orton, and Mulligan, 1853; reprint, Baton Rouge: Louisiana State University Press, 1968), 6.

2. Northup, *Twelve Years a Slave*, 8–11.

3. William Henry Harrison was the ninth president of the United States, elected in 1840. Only one month after he was elected he died of pneumonia. He was the first president to die in office.

4. Northup, *Twelve Years a Slave*, 252. Kidnapping was especially common after 1836 when Texas broke away from Mexico, which had outlawed slavery, to become an independent slaveholding republic. Abolitionist Benjamin Lundy also contended that kidnapping of free blacks grew more common after the opening of the Texas market increased the demand for and the value of slaves. See the *National Enquirer*, January 14, 1837. Lundy believed free blacks in New York, New Jersey, and Pennsylvania to be especially vulnerable.

For a book-length treatment of the kidnapping of free blacks, see Carol Wilson, *Freedom At Risk: The Kidnapping of Free Blacks in America, 1780–1865* (Lexington: University Press of Kentucky, 1994).

5. Robert's kidnappers had apparently been arrested, and he returned to his home. Northup, *Twelve Years a Slave*, 48–65.

6. The term "manhood rights" was used by blacks during the nineteenth century to connote the rights of citizenship exercised by men in American society. Although the term carried obvious gender implications, it was used to refer to rights that could protect the race and that could be directly or indirectly exercised by men or women. See James Oliver Horton, "The Manhood of the Race: Gender and the Language of Black Protest in the Antebellum North" (unpublished paper presented at the Sojourner Truth Conference, Scripps College, January 1994).

7. The *Colored American* serialized a major statement by William Whipper on moral reform, nonviolence and nonresistance in several issues. There were also articles which offered counter arguments. See the *Colored American*, September 9, 16, 23, and 30, 1837. Quotes are found in September 23rd issue.

8. *Colored American*, September 9, 1837.

9. *Colored American*, December 9, 1837.

10. James Brewer Stewart, *William Lloyd Garrison and the Challenge of Emancipation* (Arlington Heights, Ill.: Harlan Davidson Inc., 1992), 108.

11. James Oliver Horton and Lois E. Horton, "The Affirmation of Manhood: Black Garrisonians in Antebellum Boston," in Donald M. Jacobs, ed., *Courage and Conscience: Black and White Abolitionists in Boston* (Bloomington: Indiana University Press, 1993), 127–154.

12. Garrison's beliefs, about which there was varying opinion in the black community, included pacifism, a determination not to participate in a political system that included slavery and slaveholding (including not voting), and a repudiation of churches that accepted slaveholders as members. *The Liberator*, September, 22, 1837.

13. *Liberator*, October 6, 1837.

14. *Liberator*, October 6, 1837. Note that Cornish did not feel the need to describe "colored men" as abolitionists, indicating that their abolitionism was understood in a way that it was not for white men.

15. *Colored American*, October 14, 1837.

16. Shirley J. Yee, *Black Women Abolitionists: A Study in Activism, 1828–1860* (Knoxville: University of Tennessee Press, 1992), 101–103.

17. Jane H. Pease and William H. Pease, *They Who Would be Free: Blacks' Search for Freedom, 1830–1861* (New York: Atheneum, 1974), 79–81.

18. Kathryn Kish Sklar, "Women Who Speak for an Entire Nation: American and British Women Compared at the World Anti-Slavery Convention, London, 1840," *Pacific Historical Review* 59 (November 1990), 453–499.

19. Horton, "Manhood of the Race"; Elsa Barkely Brown makes an important argument on this point in her "To Catch the Vision of Freedom: Reconstructing Southern Black Women's Political History, 1865–1885" (unpublished paper, cited with permission).

20. *Pennsylvania Freeman*, December 16, 1847, in C. Peter Ripley, Roy E. Finkenbine, Michael F. Hembree, and Donald Yacovone, eds., *Black Abolitionist Papers, 1830–1865* (New York: Microfilming Corporation of America, 1981–83) microfilm reel 5, frame 537.

21. *Colored American*, April 18, 1840.

22. *Colored American*, August 29, 1840.

23. "The Poor Man's Party," Broadside, Peterboro, N.Y., October 17, 1846, Cornell University Archives, Ithaca, N.Y.

24. Catherine M. Hanchett, "Agitators for Black Equality and Emancipation: Cortland County, 1837–1855," (undated and unpublished paper, cited with permission), 91, on file at the Cortland Historical Society, Cortland, New York.

25. In October of 1845, blacks from western New York State held a meeting in Geneva, New York to protest racial restrictions on voting. They alerted the state's blacks to be ready to act if a convention was called to amend the state constitution. Among those attending were William Wells Brown and Samuel Ringold Ward. See *Ithaca Chronicle*, October 1, 1845.

26. "Gerrit Smith Esq., . . . Great Meeting of the Colored People in Troy" (undated newspaper clipping), Box 152; "Gift of Land and Money to Negroes" (undated names list), Box 145 "To Gerrit Smith Grantees" (small Broadside, October 4, 1854), Box 145, Gerrit Smith Papers, George Arents Research Library, Syracuse University, Syracuse, New York. See also C. Peter Ripley, Roy E. Finkenbine, Michael F. Hembree, and Donald Yacovone, eds., *The Black Abolitionist Papers*, vol. 3 (Chapel Hill: University of North Carolina Press, 1991), 482.

27. "History of John Brown," from Ed Cotter to the North Elba Historical Society, History Collection of the North Elba Historical Society, four-page typescript, undated. See also William S. McFeely, *Frederick Douglass*, (New York: W. W. Norton, 1991), 151.

28. Herbert Asbury, *The Gangs of New York: An Informal History of the Underground* (Garden City, N. Y.: Garden City Publishing Co., 1927), 40.

29. For information on the Dayton riot, see *Colored American*, February 13 and 27, 1841.

30. William Cheek and Aimee Lee Cheek, *John Mercer Langston and the Fight for Black Freedom, 1829–65*, (Urbana: University of Illinois Press, 1989), 62, 63–65; *Colored American*, September 11, 18, and 25, 1841.

31. Frederick Douglass, *Life and Times of Frederick Douglass* (1892; reprint, London: Collier-MacMillian, 1962), 143.

32. On the question of black manhood, see James Oliver Horton, *Free People of Color* (Washington, D. C.: Smithsonian Institution Press, 1993), 80–97, and Horton and Horton, "Affirmation of Manhood." For general information on manhood during the antebellum period, see J. A. Mangan and James Walvin, eds., *Manliness and Morality: Middle-Class Masculinity in Britain and America, 1800–1940*, (Ithaca, N. Y.: Cornell University Press, 1989), and David Leverenz, *Manhood and the American Renaissance* (Ithaca, N. Y.: Cornell University Press, 1989).

33. *Colored American*, September 18, 1841.

34. Carter G. Woodson, *The Mind of the Negro: As Reflected in Letters Written During the Crisis, 1800–1860*, (Washington, D. C.: The Association for the Study of Negro Life and History, 1926), 337.

35. *Emancipator*, March 25, 1841; see also Horatio T. Strother, *Underground Railroad in Connecticut* (Middleton, Conn.: Wesleyan University Press, 1962), 75–76.

36. *Colored American*, February 27, 1841.

37. Howard Jones, *Mutiny on the Amistad: The Saga of a Slave Revolt and Its Impact on American Abolition, Law and Diplomacy*, (New York: Oxford University Press. 1987), 205.

38. *The North Star*, May 11, 1849; Edward D. Jervey and C. Harold Huber, "The Creole Affair," *Journal of Negro History* 65 (Summer 1980): 196–211. In 1853 a joint U. S. and British commission awarded compensation to the slaveholders who had lost their slaves in the Creole affair.

39. Ripley et al., eds., *Black Abolitionist Papers*, 3:410.

40. *Colored American*, April 15, 1837.

41. *Liberator*, August 13, 1841. Minutes of the National Convention of Colored Citizens, Buffalo, 1843, in Howard H. Bell, ed., *Minutes of the Proceedings of the National Negro Conventions, 1830–1864* (New York: Arno Press and *The New York Times*, 1969), 10. For criticism of Philadelphia black leaders by other Pennsylvania blacks, see *Colored American*, July, 3, 1841.

42. *Liberator*, August 4, 1843. Although only the names of Douglass and Remond appear on the list of official delegates, William C. Nell and John T. Hilton also attended.

43. *The National Anti-Slavery Standard*, September, 7, 1843.

44. "Minutes of the National Convention of Colored Citizens, Held in Buffalo, 1843," in Bell, ed., *Minutes*, 15–16.

45. "Minutes of the National Convention of Colored Citizens, Held in Buffalo, 1843," in Bell, ed., *Minutes*, 7.

46. Henry Highland Garnet, *Walker's Appeal, With a Brief Sketch of his Life, And Also Garnet's Address to the Slaves of the United States of America* (New York: J. H. Tobitt, 1848), 90–96.

47. "Minutes of the National Convention of Colored Citizens, Held in Buffalo, 1843," in Bell, ed., *Minutes*, 23.

48. Jemain W. Loguen, *The Rev. J. W. Loguen, as a Slave and as a Freeman* (Syracuse, New York: J. G. K. Truair and Co., 1859), 379.

49. For information on the Broadway Tabernacle, see Carleton Mabee, *Black Education in New York State: From Colonial Times to Modern Times* (Syracuse, N. Y.: Syracuse University Press, 1979), 41, 59.

50. Ripley et al., eds., *Black Abolitionist Papers*, 3:409.

51. Philip S. Foner, *History of Black Americans*, vol. 2 (Westport, Conn.: Greenwood Press, 1983), 543.

52. *National Anti-Slavery Standard*, October 15, 1846, 77.

53. *The North Star*, March 17, 1848.

54. "Report of the Proceedings of the Colored National Convention," Cleveland, Ohio, 1847, in Bell, ed., *Minutes*, 17.

55. Adam Dewey Simmons speculates that the Philadelphia and the New York City blacks did not attend the convention in part because they were unable to control it and its agenda. See Simmons, "Ideologies and Programs of the Negro Antislavery Movement, 1830–1861" (Ph. D. diss., Northwestern University, 1983), 190–191.

56. "Report of the Proceedings of the Colored National Convention," Cleveland, Ohio, 1848, in Bell, ed., *Minutes*, 14, 16–17.

57. Quoted in James Oliver Horton and Lois E. Horton, *Black Bostonians* (New York: Holmes & Meier, 1979), 102.

58. "State Convention of Colored Citizens of Ohio, Columbus," in Philip S. Foner and George E. Walker, eds. *Proceedings of the Black State Convention*, vols. 1 and 2 (Philadelphia: Temple University Press, 1979), 229.

59. *North Star*, February, 9, 1849, quoted in Robert C. Dick, *Black Protest: Issues and Tactics* (Westport, Conn.: Greenwood Press, 1974), 138.

60. Foner, *History of Black Americans*, 2:549.

61. James McCune Smith to Gerrit Smith, Esq., New York, July 28, 1848, Gerrit Smith Papers.

62. Frederick Douglass, *My Bondage and My Freedom*, ed. William L. Andrews (1855; reprint, Urbana: University of Illinois Press, 1987), 220.

63. McFeely, *Frederick Douglass*, 99–122.

64. McFeely, *Frederick Douglass*.

65. For information on the Douglass-Garrison split, see McFeely, *Frederick Douglass*, 142–50; Benjamin Quarles, "The Breach Between Douglass and Garrison," *Journal of Negro History* 23 (April 1938), 144–54. For the masthead, see *North Star*, December 3, 1847.

66. Sarah M. Douglass et al., *North Star*, July 13, 1849, BAP microfilm reel 6, frame 44.

67. *National Anti-Slavery Standard*, May 16, 1844, 199.

68. *National Anti-Slavery Standard*, May 27, 1841, 203.

69. *National Anti-Slavery Standard*, May 11, 1843, 194.

70. *The North Star*, February 9, 1849. For an enlightening discussion of Douglass's turn to an antislavery interpretation of the Constitution, see David W. Blight, *Frederick Douglass' Civil War: Keeping Faith in Jubilee* (Baton Rouge: Louisiana State University Press, 1989), 26–59.

71. *Liberator*, May 23, 1851.

72. *Liberator*, May 23, 1851.

73. When Fillmore was a lawyer in Buffalo during the 1830s, he served without charge as defense counsel for a fugitive slave, according to William Wells Brown. William E. Farrison, "William Wells Brown in Buffalo," *Journal of Negro History* 39 (October 1954): 298–314.

74. Robert J. Rayback, *Millard Fillmore: Biography of a President* (Buffalo, N. Y.: Buffalo Historical Society, 1959).

75. Jane H. Pease and William H. Pease, *The Fugitive Slave Law and Anthony Burns: A Problem in Law Enforcement* (Philadelphia: J. B. Lippincott, 1975).

76. "Document 31: An act to amend, and supplementary to, the act entitled 'An act respecting fugitives from justice, and persons escaping from the service of their masters,' approved February twelfth, one thousand seven hundred and ninety-three," reprint in Albert P. Blaustein and Robert Zangrando, eds., *Civil Rights and the American Negro: A Documentary History* (Evanston, Ill.: Northwestern University Press, 1991), 127–133, quote 128.

77. C. C. Andrews, ed., *Official Opinions of the Attorneys General of the United States*, vol. 6 (Washington, D. C.: Robert Farnham. 1856), 272–274.

78. Pease and Pease, *Fugitive Slave Law*, 11–12.

79. *Pennsylvania Freedman*, October 31, 1850, quoted in Ripley et al. eds., *Black Abolitionist Papers*, vol 4:68.

80. *National Anti-Slavery Standard*, September 5, 1850, quoted in Dick, *Black Protest*, 142.

81. Olivia Mahoney, "Black Abolitionist," *Chicago History* 20 (1991): 22–37.

82. *Liberator*, November 1, 1850; "Read and Ponder the Fugitive Slave Law," Broadside, Cornell University Archives, Ithaca, N. Y. (n.d.).

83. "Slave-Hunters in Boston," *Liberator*, November 1, 1850.

84. For a more complete account of the Crafts in Boston, see William Craft, *Running a Thousand Miles for Freedom* (London: 1860), reprint in Arna Bontemps, ed., *Great Slave Narratives* (Boston: Beacon Press, 1969), 269–331.

85. Horton and Horton, *Black Bostonians*, 104–105.

86. Robert V. Remini, *Henry Clay: Statesman for the Union* (New York: W. W. Norton & Co., 1991), 768–769.

87. Pease and Pease, *Fugitive Slave Law*, 16–17; *Boston Slave Riot and Trial of Anthony Burns* (Boston: Fetridge and Co., 1854), 38.

88. Horton and Horton, *Black Bostonians*, 106–107; *Liberator*, April 11, 1851; Thomas Wentworth Higginson, *Cheerful Yesterdays* (Boston: Houghton Mifflin, 1898), 140.

89. Stanley W. Campbell, *The Slave Catchers: Enforcement of the Fugitive Slave Law, 1850–1860*, (Chapel Hill: University of North Carolina Press, 1968), 155–157; Wendell Phillips Garrison, *William Lloyd Garrison, 1805–1879*, vol. 3 (Boston: Houghton Mifflin, 1894), 336.

90. Campbell, *Slave Catchers*, 156–157.

91. *Liberator*, August 26, 1853. Harriet Beecher Stowe was Lyman Beecher's daughter, New York minister Henry Ward Beecher's sister, and the wife of Calvin Stowe.

92. *Liberator*, August 26, 1853; Northup, *Twelve Years a Slave*.

93. Pease and Pease, *They Who Would Be Free*; William L. Andrews, *To Tell a Free Story* (Urbana: University of Illinois Press, 1986).

94. Thomas P. Slaughter, *Bloody Dawn: The Christiana Riot and Racial Violence in the Antebellum North*, (New York: Oxford University Press, 1991).

95. *Liberator*, March 24, 1854.

96. Horton and Horton, *Black Bostonians*, 111–113.

97. Stewart, *William Lloyd Garrison*, 159; Campbell catalogues 156 fugitive slave cases involving 300 slaves during the 1850s. Of these, 18 were successfully rescued, 1 escaped, 11 were released, and 270 were returned to slavery. Campbell, *Slave Catchers*, 199–207.

98. By 1850 there were 1,000 blacks in California, a number which grew to 4,000 by 1860. In the northern gold rush areas Sacramento, Marysville, and Stockton were considered "Yankee Towns." See Doris Muscantine, *Old San Francisco* (New York: G. P. Putnam's Sons, 1975), 115; Kevin Starr, *Inventing the Dream: California Through the Progressive Era* (New York: Oxford University Press, 1985), 11.

99. They were called Conscience Whigs because they voted their antislavery consciences, as opposed to Whigs connected to textile manufacturing whose views were shaped by the demands of southern cotton production.

100. Bruce Levine, *Half Slave and Half Free: The Roots of Civil War* (New York: Hill and Wang, 1992).

101. *Liberator*, September 5, 1856.

102. *Liberator*, October 1, 1858.

103. Benjamin Quarles, *Allies for Freedom: Blacks and John Brown* (New York: Oxford University Press, 1974), 32–36.

104. *Dred Scott v. Sanford* (1857), 19 Howard, 393.

105. "Address by Charles L. Remond," April 3, 1857, in Herbert Aptheker, *Documentary History of Negro People in the United States* (New York: Citadel Press, 1951), 394.

106. "The Dred Scott Decision," a speech delivered before the American Anti-Slavery Society, New York, May 11, 1857, in Philip S. Foner, ed., *The Life and Writings of Frederick Douglass*, vol. 2 (New York: International Publishers, 1950), 421, 423.

107. *National Anti-Slavery Standard*, May 23, 1857, 1.

108. Nat Brandt, *The Town that Started the Civil War* (Syracuse, N. Y.: Syracuse University Press, 1990), 85.

109. Quarles, *Black Abolitionists* (New York: Oxford University Press, 1969), 213–214; Deputy Marshal Anson Dayton who captured Price was later harassed by Oberlin residents who exerted financial pressure on him and his family. He was

finally driven from Oberlin after shots were fired into his home and his house was invaded by a group of angry blacks. Brandt, *Town*, 116, 114, 129; Cheek and Cheek, *John Mercer Langston*.

110. *The North Star*, November 16, 1849.

111. Edward G. Wilson to William McLain, July 27, 1856, Letters Received, ser. 1, vol. 144, American Colonization Society Papers, Library of Congress, Manuscript Division, cited in Philip S. Foner, *History of Black Americans*, vol. 3 (Westport, Conn.: Greenwood Press, 1983), 168.

112. "Black Hope and Despair in Antebellum Georgia: The William Norn Correspondence," *Prologue* 8 (Fall 1976): 159–161, cited in Foner, *History of Black Americans*, 3:168.

113. "Seaborn Evans to Josiah Sibley" (Greenville, Sinoe County, Liberia, November 5, 1856), in Bell I. Wiley, *Slaves No More: Letters from Liberia, 1833–1869* (Lexington: University Press of Kentucky, 1980), 269–270.

114. T. J. Bowen, "Africa Opening to Civilization and Christianity," *African Repository*, 33 (April 1857): 97–114, cited in Foner, *History of Black Americans* 3:168.

115. Henry Highland Garnet, *The Past and the Present Condition, and the Destiny, of the Colored Race: A Discourse* (Washington, D. C.: Morland Foundation, 1848; reprint, Miami: Mnemosyne Publishing Co., 1969), 24.

116. M. R. Delany and Robert Campbell, *Search for a Place: Black Separatism and Africa, 1860*, with an introduction by Howard H. Bell (Ann Arbor: University of Michigan Press, 1969).

117. For an analysis of the meaning of self-determination as a significant issue among blacks during and beyond the antebellum period, see V. P. Franklin, *Black Self-Determination: A Cultural History of the Faith of the Fathers* (Westport, Conn.: Lawrence Hill, 1984).

118. This is not to ignore the strong emotional ties that Delany and others had toward Africa, but their motivation contained a very American ethnocentrism toward Africa and Africans that assumed their need for the "civilization" that African Americans could bring.

119. *Weekly Anglo-African*, April 5, 1860; David W. Blight, "They Knew What Time It Was: African-Americans and the Coming of the Civil War," in Gabor S. Boritt, ed., *Why the Civil War Came* (New York: Oxford University Press, 1995).

120. See R. J. M. Blackett, *Beating Against the Barriers: Biographical Essays in Nineteenth-Century Afro-American History*, (Baton Rouge: Louisiana State University Press, 1986), 107–121.

121. Benjamin Coates, *Suggestions on the Importance of the Cultivation of Cotton in Africa in Reference to the Abolition of Slavery in the United States through the Organization of an African Civilization Society* (Philadelphia: C. Sherman & Son,1858).

122. *Provincial Freeman*, April 18, 1857, quoted in Quarles, *Black Abolitionists*, 231. We thank David W. Blight for bringing this quote to our attention. See also Carla L. Peterson, *Doers of the Word: African American Women Speakers and Writers in the North (1830–1880)*, (New York: Oxford University Press, 1995).

123. *Douglass' Monthly*, May 1859, 449.

124. *Douglass' Monthly*, December 1860.

125. "New England Colored Citizens' Convention, August 1, 1859," in Foner and Walker, eds., *Proceedings*, 2:220.

126. *Douglass' Paper*, September 7. 1855.

127. *Liberator*, November 27, 1857.

128. *Liberator*, August 13, 1858.

129. Proceedings of the State Convention of Colored Men of the State of Ohio, Held in the City of Columbus, January 21st, 22d & 23d, 1857," in Foner and Walker, eds., *Proceedings*, 1:320.

130. Ripley et al., eds., *Black Abolitionist Papers*, 4:319.

131. "A Standard Maxim for Free Society," Springfield, Ill., June 26, 1857, in Mario M. Cuomo and Harold Holzer, eds., *Lincoln and Democracy* (New York: HarperCollins 1990), 90–91.

132. "Standard Maxim for Free Society," in Cuomo and Holzer, eds., 90.

133. David Zarefsky, *Lincoln, Douglas and Slavery: In the Crucible of Public Debate* (Chicago: University of Chicago Press, 1990).

134. "Gerrit Smith Esq., . . . Great Meeting of the Colored People in Troy" (undated newspaper clipping), Box 152, Gerrit Smith Papers; "Suffrage Convention of the Colored Citizens of New York, Troy, New York, September 14, 1858," in Foner and Walker, eds., *Proceedings*, 1:100–101.

135. Quarles, *Allies for Freedom*, 32–51; McFeely, *Frederick Douglass*, 190–192.

136. McFeely, *Frederick Douglass*, 196; Brandt, *Town*, 242.

137. Quarles, *Allies for Freedom*, 86–87.

138. McFeely, *Frederick Douglass*, 198–203; Quarles, *Allies for Freedom*.

139. *Liberator*, March 12, 1858.

140. Quoted in Foner, *History of Black Americans*, 3:270–271.

141. *Liberator*, January 27, 1860, quoted in James M. McPherson, *The Negro's Civil War: How American Negroes Felt and Acted During the War for the Union* (New York: Vintage Books, 1965), 5.

142. *Anglo-African*, February 4, 1860; *Liberator*, October 19, 1860. See also McPherson, *Negro's Civil War*, 10.

143. *Chicago Daily Times and Herald*, November 20, 1860.

144. Samuel Ringgold Ward, *Autobiography of a Fugitive Negro*, (London: John Snow, 1855), 77.

145. *New York Independent*, August 22, 1861, quoted in Blight, *Frederick Douglass' Civil War*, 112.

146. Douglass, *Life and Times of Frederick Douglass*, 351.

Epilogue

1. McPherson, *The Negro's Civil War* (New York: Vantage Books, 1965), 35.

2. "The Future of the Negro People of the Slave States" (Boston, February 12, 1862), in Philip S. Foner, ed., *The Life and Writings of Frederick Douglass, vol. 2 (New York: International Publishers, 1950)*, 213.

3. McPherson, *Negro's Civil War*, 164–165.

4. "Preliminary Emancipation Proclamation," in Mario Cuomo and Harold Holzer, eds., *Lincoln and Democracy* (New York: HarperCollins, 1990), 257–260.

5. Douglass' Monthly, October, 1862.

6. Foner, *History of Black Americans*, 3:347–349.

7. Frederick Douglass, *Life and Times of Frederick Douglass* (1892; reprint, London: Collier-MacMillian, 1962), 338. Cary was the only black woman officially commissioned as a recruiting agent, but several other women worked unofficially.

Index